LYNDON B. JOHNSON

::

Also by Robert Dallek

Democrat and Diplomat: The Life of William E. Dodd

Franklin D. Roosevelt and American Foreign Policy, 1932–1945

The American Style of Foreign Policy: Cultural Politics and Foreign Affairs

Ronald Reagan: The Politics of Symbolism

Lone Star Rising: Lyndon Johnson and His Times, 1908–1960

Hail to the Chief: The Making and Unmaking of American Presidents

Flawed Giant: Lyndon Johnson and His Times, 1961–1973

An Unfinished Life: John F. Kennedy, 1917–1963

LYNDON B. JOHNSON

::

PORTRAIT OF A PRESIDENT

Robert Dallek

OXFORD
UNIVERSITY PRESS

2004

OXFORD
UNIVERSITY PRESS

Oxford   New York
Auckland Bangkok Buenos Aires Cape Town Chennai
Dar es Salaam Delhi Hong Kong Istanbul Karachi Kolkata
Kuala Lumpur Madrid Melbourne Mexico City Mumbai Nairobi
São Paulo Shanghai Taipei Tokyo Toronto

Copyright © 2004 by Robert Dallek

Published by Oxford University Press, Inc.
198 Madison Avenue, New York, New York 10016

www.oup.com

Oxford is a registered trademark of Oxford University Press

Library of Congress Cataloging-in-Publication Data

Dallek, Robert.
Lyndon B. Johnson : portrait of a president / Robert Dallek.
p.   cm.
This work is a one volume abridgment of Dallek's 2-volume biography
of Lyndon B. Johnson v. 1. Lone star rising (1991); v. 2, Flawed giant (1998).
Includes bibliographical references (p.   ) and index.
ISBN: 978-0-19-515921-9
1. Johnson, Lyndon B. (Lyndon Baines), 1908–1973.
2. Presidents—United States—Biography.
United States—Politics and government—1963–1969.
I. Dallek, Robert. Lone star rising.
II. Dallek, Robert. Flawed giant. III. Title.
E847.D26   2003   973.923'092—dc21   2003011360

9 8 7 6 5 4 3 2 1
Printed in the United States of America
on acid-free paper

To Matthew and Rebecca Dallek, our children,
and Michael Bender, our son-in-law

:: Contents

Preface   ix

1   The Making of a Politician   1

2   The Congressman   36

3   The Senator   72

4   The Vice President   112

5   From JFK to LBJ   145

6   "Landslide Lyndon"   171

7   King of the Hill   190

8   Foreign Policy Dilemmas   208

9   Retreat from the Great Society   227

10   "Lyndon Johnson's War"   251

11   A Sea of Troubles   272

12   Stalemate   295

13   Last Hurrahs   318

14   Unfinished Business   343

15   After the Fall   362

Suggestions for Further Reading   379
Index   382

:: *Preface*

This relatively brief book is an abridgment of my two-volume life of Lyndon B. Johnson, published in 1991, *Lone Star Rising*, and in 1998, *Flawed Giant*. It is not a revision of those studies but an attempt to bring them within the reach of a wider audience, especially students, that has neither the time nor the inclination to read more than 1,200 pages on Johnson's life and times.

While preparing this condensed history, I had an opportunity to think anew about this extraordinary man and reconsider his impact on the national well-being. Controversies about Johnson's presidency, which remained relatively intense when I published the first volume twenty years after he had left office, have now, fifteen years later, subsided. Arguments over principal Great Society programs such as civil rights, Medicare-Medicaid, and federal aid to education have all but disappeared. Debate remains over how best to manage racial equality of treatment, to fund health insurance programs for the elderly and the poor, and to use federal monies to improve instruction and learning in the schools. But only a very small number of die-hard critics would suggest abolishing these social reforms.

Likewise, Johnson's great foreign policy failure, Vietnam, has become more an object of historical curiosity and an analog for what not to do in an overseas conflict than an ongoing source of angry debate. The defeat of Soviet communism and a search for foreign policies that can effectively meet the challenges of a post–Cold War world—above all the threat of Islamic terrorism since September 11, 2001—have eclipsed lingering resentments toward Johnson's unsuccessful fight to preserve South Vietnam from a Communist takeover.

The ebbing of the controversies might have pushed Johnson to the back of our historical consciousness. But to the contrary, he remains a larger-than-life figure whose political career continues to have current significance. His conscious effort to bring the South into the mainstream of the country's economic and political life by ending segregation and funneling federal largesse to the region has revitalized the area's role in national politics. The fact that four of our last five presidents—Jimmy Carter, Bill Clinton, and the two Bushes—have been from Georgia, Arkansas, and Texas speaks to the renewed political power of the South. The altered standards for migration to the United States, the existence of departments of transportation and housing and urban development, consumer safety rules, environmental protections, public radio and television, food stamps, Head Start for preschool children, and legal services are only a handful of the wide-ranging programs that have had an enduring impact on the nation. Johnson's continuing hold on the country's imagination is also the product of the more than nine thousand taped conversations he made in the White House. Periodic releases evoke memories of what an effective politician he was and provide an ongoing standard by which we can judge presidential leadership. It is no wonder that in a 1996 assessment of his presidency by thirty-two scholars, fifteen saw Johnson as a near-great president.

Johnson's legacy will continue to be a matter of historical debate. But whatever future biographers may say about him, I am confident that his impact on the country beginning in the 1930s and lasting until the end of the 1960s, when he left the national scene, will be remembered as considerable.

Although this book has no notes or bibliography, it is the product of fourteen years of research that underpinned my two volumes. Anyone wishing to learn the origins of what I assert in this shorter book should consult those studies.

Washington, D.C.   Robert Dallek
January 2003

LYNDON B. JOHNSON

::

1 :: THE MAKING OF A POLITICIAN

:: ORIGINS

From Andrew Jackson to Ronald Reagan, the image of the self-made man has effectively served occupants of the White House. All who could, made much of their rags to riches odyssey. "When I was young, poverty was so common we didn't know it had a name," Lyndon Johnson often said. A poor boy in a remote Texas town isolated from the mainstream of early twentieth-century American life, he grew up without indoor plumbing or electricity and sometimes made do on a bare subsistence diet. The rural small towns in which he received his elementary, secondary, and college schooling did little to broaden his horizons.

Yet Lyndon came to maturity believing he was special — a young man destined for exceptional things. And he was. Fueled by his early poverty, his ambition, like Lincoln's, "was a little engine that knew no rest." It helped carry him to the U.S. House of Representatives and Senate, the vice presidency and the White House. But ambition alone did not give him the wherewithal, the inner confidence, to imagine himself in the Congress or the Oval Office. His family history gave initial stirrings to such dreams. In one of the many paradoxes that would shape his life, Lyndon was not simply an impoverished farm boy who made good, but the offspring of prominent southern families. Although he suffered painful self-doubts throughout his life, his heritage was a constant source of belief in a birthright to govern and lead. Stories told by his parents and grandparents about famous, influential ancestors were a mainstay of his early years. From the first, he thought of himself not as a poor boy consigned to a life of hardship, but as an heir of Johnsons and Buntons, Baineses and Huffmans, men and women who commanded the respect of their contemporaries and shaped public affairs.

A Texas journalist remembers how Lyndon "reveled in stories of Johnsons and Baineses who'd fought marauding Indians, of old uncles who drove cattle up the famous trails, of a hardy pioneer spirit in his genes. 'Listen, goddammit,' he once said, 'my ancestors were teachers and lawyers and college presidents and governors when the Kennedys in this country were still tending bar.' "

Lyndon's father, Sam Ealy Johnson, Jr., the oldest of nine children, was born on a farm in the Texas Hill Country in 1877. A man of consuming ambition, which he passed on to his oldest son, Sam won election to the state House of Representatives in 1904 at the age of 27. Serving two terms until 1908, he was an "agrarian liberal" or populist who fought to put the power of government on the side of farmers and laborers with regulations controlling railroads and utilities.

Unlike most of the other legislators, Sam would not allow himself to be bought by lobbyists who dominated the proceedings. Providing "beefsteak, bourbon and blondes," paying legislators' living expenses, and buying votes outright, which they sometimes even cast for absent members of the House, lobbyists set much of the legislative agenda. Sam would have no part of it. Not because he was a strict moralist; on the contrary, according to numerous sources, he was as ready as the next fellow to indulge his passions, drinking and whoring in the orgies that were an accepted part of the capital's life. It was more a case of being his own man. He could not bend the knee to anyone; he could not be under someone else's control. He "will bear gentle reproof, but will kick like a mule at any attempted domination," the Texas House chaplain observed.

On August 20, 1907, Sam married Rebekah Baines, whom he had met in Austin the previous year. Like the Johnsons, her line of descent provided Lyndon with a sense of inherited superiority. The Baineses were particularly formidable folk: Baptist ministers who were known as "frontier saints." Rebekah herself, a graduate of Baylor University in Waco, Texas, was teaching elocution and writing for local newspapers when she had met Sam.

Sam, who was almost thirty, and Rebekah, twenty-six, set up house in Gillespie County between the tiny communities of Hye and Stonewall on the north bank of the Pedernales. Although Rebekah had grown up in the Hill country, nothing had prepared her for the hardships of life on the Pedernales as a member of the last American generation of pioneer women. She was a romantic, delicate young woman who dressed in crinolines and lace and wore "broad-brimmed, beribboned hats with long veils." She "made a ritual out of . . . serving tea in very thin cups" and meals on tablecloths, which needed washing and ironing, rather than on oilcloth which could be wiped clean and used at the next sitting. She read poetry—Browning and Tennyson—and biographies about Texas governors, American presidents or anyone, as long as they were about real people.

But life on Sam's Hill Country farm afforded her few of these pleasures. Daily life was sheer drudgery. With no indoor plumbing or electricity, washing, ironing, cooking, and heating—the chores modern housewives perform with a minimum of physical exertion—were labors that taxed the strength of even the most robust woman. Wood for the fireplace over which Rebekah cooked had to be carried into the house in countless loads from piles outside. Water in seemingly endless amounts had to be pumped from the well and the four-gallon, thirty-two-pound bucket lugged into the kitchen. Each person in the house usually needed ten buckets, forty gallons, of water a day. Clothes had to be boiled in huge vats, scrubbed by hand "in hours of kneeling over rough rub-boards," and pressed with heavy flatirons that were reheated repeatedly on the stove. Three full meals a day had to be prepared for Sam and his farmhands, and there were unceasing daily chores, sewing, feeding chickens, washing floors, canning fruits and vegetables. The work left most Hill Country women stooped and old before their time.

As much as the physical strain, the cultural poverty of pioneer living worked a painful hardship on Rebekah. Her sense of isolation, of having no one to discuss ideas with except Sam, was a source of constant frustration. Her neighbors and relatives were all uneducated and barely literate. The newspapers of the time and place, the *Gillespie County News* and the *Blanco News*, testify to the limited horizons of these people. Ads to sell horses, watches, ribbons, woolens, headstones, liquors, and cigars and to provide medical, dental, and barbering services filled the pages of these weeklies. Patent medicines, like "Dr. King's New Life Pills for sick and nervous headaches" and "Electric Bitters," a curative for rheumatism, liver, kidney, stomach and bowel troubles and a suicide preventive, were evidence of the primitive state of medical care.

In a place and time when families struggled to make ends meet, to survive, Rebekah and Sam, remembering their heritage, had some style and dreamed of better things. They never thought of themselves as ordinary Hill Country folks, and surviving relatives and neighbors have vivid memories of them sixty and seventy years later as a bit apart from the crowd—maybe even special: Rebekah was "a gentle, gentle woman," "a princess," "a lady," and Sam, "a swell dresser" and "proud steppin'" man.

:: CHILDHOOD

On August 27, 1908, a little over a year after she had been married, Rebekah gave birth. "The first year of her marriage was the worst year of her life," Lyndon later said. "Then I came along and suddenly everything was all right again. I could do all the things she never did."

"We welcomed you—Daddy and I with great hope," his mother wrote thirty years later. " . . . We felt that in you we would realize dear dreams, cherished ambitions and fond hopes."

Rebekah remembered Lyndon's birth as a momentous occasion: "It was daybreak. . . . Now the light came in from the east, bringing . . . a stillness so profound and so pervasive that it seemed as if the earth itself were listening." She viewed him as so special that she could never acknowledge his delivery by a midwife substituting for the local physician who only arrived several hours later. Sam was as enamored of the boy. When Otto Lindig, a neighbor, came by four hours after the birth to sell a span of horses, Sam ushered him into the house to show off his son, who he predicted would "be Governor of Texas some day." When Lindig replied, "He's certainly got his mother's head," it made Sam "mad."

During Lyndon's first year, Rebekah and Sam marveled at his every action. When he was nearly six months old, Rebekah penned a letter in his name to her sister-in-law: "I can sit alone now, and perform many amusing capers. My father says that I am quite an orator and translates my speech into political axioms. Mother thinks I have the studious look of a professor and is always wondering what problem I am struggling to solve." Shortly after, Sam brought home the first photo ever taken of Lyndon. Rebekah recalled how Sam "raised his hand holding the package as he saw me waiting on the porch and began to run. I ran to meet him and we met in the middle of the Benner pasture to exclaim rapturously over the photograph of our boy." Not long after, Rebekah took the baby to visit her mother in San Marcos, where Rebekah reported: "It would turn your head to hear the compliments showered on our boy. People just rave over him. . . . They think he is the sweetest baby in the whole world, as he really is of course."

Encouraged by the affection and praise and endowed with considerable intelligence, Lyndon showed himself to be a gifted child. He learned the alphabet from blocks before he was two; knew the Mother Goose rhymes and poems from Longfellow and Tennyson by the age of three; and could read and "spell almost anything that he could hear" by the time he was four. "I'll never forget how much my mother loved me when I recited those poems," Lyndon said later. "The minute I finished she'd take me in her arms and hug me so hard I sometimes thought I'd be strangled to death."

Yet all was not idyllic in Lyndon's first years. His primacy as the only child receiving his parents' undivided attention ended when he was two with the birth of his sister Rebekah and was further challenged in the next six years by the birth of three other siblings. Lyndon's tension at losing center stage in the household manifested itself at age four when he began running away from home and alarming his parents, who feared he might be lost or injured.

To escape the primitive conditions, isolation, and poor schooling their children would receive, Rebekah and Sam agreed to move the family fourteen miles east to Johnson City in September 1913, when Lyndon was five. But life there was only marginally better. An inland town of 323 people surrounded by "an ocean of land," Johnson City, as one member of the community recalled, "had nothing there." Consisting of ten, north-south, numbered streets and eight, east-west, lettered streets, the town had a bank capitalized at $23,000, a café with no set hours for serving meals, a corrugated-tin cotton gin, a two-story court house, a rickety hotel with no indoor plumbing, a "sanitarium" or four-bed hospital on the second floor of "Doc" Barnwell's home, a school building housing all the local students, and a few one-story, wood stores on H or Main Street. There was no electricity, no indoor toilets, only two houses with bathtubs and running water, no place you could buy a loaf of bread or fresh meat, and almost nothing to do or any place to go.

There were no railroads through the area until after 1917, and one resident of Johnson City remembers being taken as "a great big girl" some twenty-five miles north to Marble Falls to see a train. There were no paved roads leading in and out of Johnson City, and the fifty-mile trip east to Austin or the thirty-mile journey west to Fredericksburg could be an all-day affair or longer. One resident who moved to Johnson City from San Antonio in the spring of 1912 recalls that it took "parts of three days" for his family to travel the sixty miles between the two cities. Rains often made the roads impassable, and when they could be used, flat tires were a common occurrence that made travel along Hill Country highways a test of one's endurance. When a group of Johnson City students was taken to the teachers' college in San Marcos for a debate and housed in a dormitory for the night, they did not know how to turn off the electricity in their room. They pulled down the light globes suspended on cords, put them in a dresser, and closed the draw before going to bed. When Stella Gliddon, the editor of the local newspaper, came to Johnson City from Fredericksburg in 1919, she felt as if she "had come to the end of the world."

The greatest influence on the young Lyndon was not Johnson City but his father. His interest in political doings from an early age was palpable, especially after Sam returned to the legislature for six years in 1918, when Lyndon was almost ten. Lyndon watched and listened as people visited Sam at his home to ask political advice. Sometimes he was allowed to sit with the men on the front porch or around the fireplace in the evening while they discussed local and state affairs. And if he was excluded from one of these meetings, he would hide in the bedroom next to the porch, listening through an open window to what was being said.

Sam began taking him to the legislature, where Lyndon would "sit in the gallery for hours watching all the activity on the floor and then would wander around the halls trying to figure out what was going on." Often, he would come on the House floor and stand or sit next to his father. Though he was not an official page, he would run errands for Sam and other members of the House. One legislator remembered him as being "a very bright and alert boy with plenty of energy and personality." He "was friendly to everyone." Another recalled how much, as a teenager, he was like Sam: Six-feet tall, skinny, dark hair and eyes, with huge ears and a large nose, he "walked the same, had the same nervous mannerisms, and Lyndon clutched you like his daddy did when he talked to you. He was a little on the rough side, too."

The only thing Lyndon liked more than spending time in Austin with Sam was going with him on the campaign trail. "We drove in the Model T Ford from farm to farm, up and down the valley, stopping at every door. My father would do most of the talking. He would bring the neighbors up to date on local gossip, talk about the crops and about the bills he'd introduced in the legislature, and always he'd bring along an enormous crust of homemade bread and a large jar of homemade jam. When we got tired or hungry, we'd stop by the side of the road. He sliced the bread, smeared it with jam, and split the slices with me. I'd never seen him happier. Families all along the way opened up their homes to us. If it was hot outside, we were invited in for big servings of homemade ice cream. If it was cold, we were given hot tea. Christ, sometimes I wished it could go on forever."

He was proud to be Sam Johnson's boy. After his father won reelection in November 1918, Sam took him to San Antonio for a celebration. There, in the largest city Lyndon had ever been in, they bought tamales and chili con carne from Mexican street vendors and visited the Alamo, where Lyndon saw paintings of Jim Bowie and Davey Crockett and a photo of Sam, recording the part he had played in saving the Mission.

Lyndon's interest in his early education and religious training never matched his attention to politics and adolescent high jinx. At school he established a reputation as an indifferent student who treated everything as a joke and scored Bs chiefly because he was quicker than the other students and could fool his teachers. Despite his mother's strong ties to the Baptist Church, he defied her by joining the Christian Church. But it had more to do with a girl he fancied than with a genuine conversion. His childhood friends recall that he had no interest in religion as a boy and that he only went to Sunday School when his mother insisted.

From the time he was fifteen he was more interested in running with his friends, sometimes staying out until three and four in the morning. Despite Prohibition, they bought or stole booze, got drunk, and drove recklessly. Once, they burned down a barn, and occasionally they taunted a local deputy sheriff, who was always after them. Fearing that Lyndon was turning into "a hopelessly incorrigible delinquent," Sam stormed about the house shouting: "That boy of yours isn't worth a damn, Rebekah! He'll never amount to anything. He'll never amount to a Goddamned thing!" And Grandmother Baines, a strict Christian lady, began predicting, "That boy is going to end up in the penitentiary—just mark my words!"

Yet the family's concerns were overblown. Although he struggled with adolescent tensions, Lyndon was more in command of himself than his parents or grandmother believed. In May 1924, for example, he completed the eleventh and final grade of the Johnson City High School with more units than he needed to graduate. Not yet sixteen, he was the youngest member of the class and was believed to be the youngest graduate of the school. The class prophecy of the five other graduates was that he would one day become governor of Texas. However much the idea of being governor or making a great success of his life may have appealed to him, and however great the pressure from his parents and his peers at school, all of whom were going to college, he was not yet ready to embark on a fixed course toward some distant goal.

Instead, he ran away to California. But even this was less the act of an incorrigible delinquent than of a defiant but ambitious teenager trying to find an alternate path to success to the one prescribed by his parents. In the spring and summer of 1924 parental pressure on him to go to college was unrelenting. Pressing him to understand that without an education he would be doomed to a life of hard physical labor, they insisted that he

enroll in Southwest Texas State Teachers College at San Marcos. As best
one can piece the story together from sketchy evidence, in the early summer of 1924 Lyndon entered the subcollege at S.W.T.S.T.C., where students from unaccredited high schools, like the one in Johnson City, could
take the twelfth-grade courses needed for admission to the College. But it
was apparently too much for him, and, as he later said, he "got kicked out
of school."

And so he joined a group of four Johnson City friends heading west in
search of better things. Though Sam and Rebekah had refused to let him
go and Sam had warned that he would yank him out of the car by his
britches if he tried, Lyndon went anyway. Thoughts of adventure and an
escape from hard times in Johnson City helped him rationalize his defiance. The year 1924 was a terrible one for Hill Country farmers, and young
men looking for work could find no jobs. California meant the chance to
earn a living. "They thought they'd go out there and make a lot of easy
money," Lyndon said later. Otho Summy, one of the boys on the trip,
recalled: "They put out a report here that money was on trees out there and
you would only have to reach up and get it." More than fantasy fueled their
hopes: There was also the fact that Ben Crider and John Koeniger, two
Johnson City friends, were working in California and that Tom Martin, an
attorney, who was Lyndon's cousin, was practicing law in San Bernardino.

Although Lyndon later described his stay in California as a "vagabond
life" tramping up and down the coast doing menial labor and earning
barely enough to survive, the trip was a controlled experiment in adult
living—a fifteen- or sixteen-month absence from home in relatively comfortable circumstances with a fixed purpose approved by his parents.

Lyndon had gone to California not strictly to defy his parents but to fulfill their ambitions for him on his own terms. Although he had put geo-
graphical distance between himself and them, he remained strongly tied
to home. He returned there, however, with mixed feelings. Although he
had managed to stay away for over a year, he did not think of the trip as giving him the independence he craved. He came back "with empty hands
and empty pockets," he said later. Worse, his parents renewed their pressure on him to go to college. But he still would not do it. Instead, he lived
at home and relied on his father to get him a road construction job on the
highway being built between Johnson City and Austin. Dependent on his
parents for a place to live, earning only $2 or $3 a day in an exhausting job,
Lyndon was more frustrated than ever.

He gave vent to his tensions in a fresh outburst of rebelliousness. He
became part of a group of young men called the "wild bunch." They drank,

got into fights, held drag races in family cars they drove without permission, and defied the local sheriffs by stealing dynamite from the state Highway Department and setting it off in the middle of the night in town. At work, he was as defiant. One of the men he worked for complained that "he's the hard-headest thing I ever tried to work with. He could do better if he'd let you tell him something, but he won't listen." Once, he went to get some supplies for a tractor in Austin, where he apparently insulted the district highway engineer. The man showed up on the road the next day and "nearly fired everybody." Lyndon managed to stay on the job for over a year or until January 1927, when a new administration led by Dan Moody replaced "Ma" Ferguson as governor and notified all her appointees in the Highway Department, including Sam and Lyndon, that they would also be replaced.

In the winter of 1926–27, Lyndon was going nowhere. Nevertheless, he was still intensely ambitious and eager to be unique, special, someone people would notice and admire. He "always talked big . . . he had big ideas . . . and he wanted to do something big with his life," a co-worker on the road recalls. He also continued to call attention to himself by his dress and manner. He wore brightly colored silk shirts to evening dances and swaggered and strutted about the hall. But however much he might strut, at the age of eighteen and a half he was an uneducated and unskilled laborer who was about to lose his job. Moreover, on a Saturday night in February 1927, he met his "Waterloo," as his cousin Ava Johnson Cox says. He attended a dance in Fredericksburg, where his overbearing manner provoked a fight with a German farm boy who "had fists like a pile-driver" and beat him unmercifully until blood from his nose and mouth soaked his white silk crêpe de Chine shirt and Lyndon gave up. "But that was the making of it," Ava says. " . . . It made a believer out of him." It "made him realize that he wasn't cock of the walk." The next morning, after his mother cried and expressed bewilderment that "my eldest son would be satisfied with a life like this," Lyndon agreed to go to college.

:: STUDENT AND TEACHER

In deciding to go to college Lyndon took on a substantial challenge. Although tuition, books, room, and board at Southwest Texas State Teachers College at San Marcos, where he intended to go, cost only about $40 a month, he didn't have the money. But like other poor youngsters in south-central Texas, who were the principal students at San Marcos, Lyndon scraped together enough cash to attend.

But financing his education was just one of his problems. He also needed to satisfy the school's admission standards, and then discipline himself to do college-level work. Three years after graduation from high school, where he had never been diligent about his studies, he had reason to doubt himself. Yet his ambition to earn a college degree and make something special of his life outweighed his fears.

San Marcos, as most students called the college, was a small provincial school with little standing in the world of higher education. Opened in 1903 as a Normal School established to train public-school teachers, it only became an accredited four-year college in 1925. But even then, it barely met the standard. A library of 21,000 volumes and a single holder of a doctorate among its fifty-six faculty members, some of whom had no degree at all, gave it official standing in Texas as only a "third-class" college. Although it offered standard college subjects, such as biology, chemistry, economics, education, English, history, mathematics, modern languages, and physics, most of the college's twenty departments consisted of only one or two faculty members. Academic standards were lax and course requirements were closer to those of a high school than a college. Parochialism and a lack of diversity among students were other limitations. Almost all its 700 students, approximately 500 women and 200 men, were white Anglo-Saxon Protestants from south-central Texas. A handful of students with central and eastern European and Hispanic backgrounds attended, but the great majority were descendants of northern Europeans whose families lived on farms and in small towns within a hundred miles of San Marcos.

Nevertheless, to Lyndon and most of his fellow students, San Marcos had much to recommend it. Above all, it represented an opportunity to escape the rural poverty in which their parents lived. A degree promised the possibility of a better life through a career in education, business, dentistry, civil service, law, or medicine. As important, the schooling at San Marcos was inexpensive, costing generally no more than $400 for an academic year of nine months divided into three terms. Moreover, students could pay part of their way through the college by working in the school's administrative offices, bookstore, library, or construction and maintenance departments.

However limited its academic standing and however close to home, the college opened vistas many of the students had not glimpsed before. When Lyndon arrived in San Marcos in 1927, the campus itself, with its ten buildings, shops, laboratories, gymnasiums, and athletic fields, was an exhilarating beehive of activity. "Old Main," the principal campus structure on the highest hill in town, resembling a medieval castle with "spires, peaks and parapets," was the largest building many of the students had ever seen. A library with thousands of books, some teachers with degrees from universities as far away as New York, Chicago, and California, and visiting lecturers, theater, orchestral, and choral groups provided a measure of intellectual stimulation never before available to them. The social life and organized athletics at San Marcos had an even greater impact on boys and girls who had grown up in isolated communities. The chance to attend parties, dances, "Bobcat" basketball and football games or a movie theater showing the latest silent films, participate in an annual "Bathing Regatta" or parade on the San Marcos River, listen to groups of boys serenading coeds beneath dormitory windows, or dress like a fashionable twenties "flapper" were memorable events for San Marcos students. Southwest Texas State Teachers College was not the University of Texas, but to most of its students it was a new world in which they could grow and make a start on fulfilling what they thought of as "the promise of American life."

As with so many other college freshman, Lyndon's first regularly enrolled term in college was a trial by fire. He received a "D" in debate or argumentation, an English class in which he didn't do much preparation and the teacher found him hard to handle. He also did poorly in grammar, describing himself as "a tired homesick freshman . . . floundering in a sea of sentences in English 101." The rest of his work was passing or better, two Cs and a B.

He became so discouraged with the undistinguished school record he was making and, even more, with the constant financial pressures and deprivation he faced day to day that he laid plans to quit school.

Instead, to pay his way, he worked as a school janitor, messenger boy, hand delivering written memos from one campus office to another, and writing editorials for the school paper, which were exercises in stilted prose, conventional homilies, and boosterism. By the close of the spring term, Lyndon decided to earn a two-year teacher's certificate as quickly as possible. This meant attending school for six straight terms or until the end of the 1928 summer term.

During this time, Lyndon made an indelible impression on fellow students, instructors, and administrators. They recall a tall, lanky, "big, all bone, Western boy," six feet three and a half inches, with black, curly hair, and brown eyes. Described as "a slat," nicknamed "old rattle and bones," Lyndon had to "kind of unwind to get up" in class, where he usually sat with his legs crossed or curled under him. Though some remember him as handsome, he was self-conscious about his looks and took special pains with his appearance, usually dressing in a suit with a bow tie, which became one of his trademarks. Before a date he would spend considerable time studying himself in a mirror, "patting his hair to be sure the waves were right" and scrunching "his neck down into his collar to make his face seem fuller." Appeasing painful doubts, he would banter with his room-mate about their irresistibility to girls.

Fellow students remember his being in perpetual motion, "always in high gallop," never resting or letting up. He was "clamoring for recognition," one classmate says. "It pained him to loaf," another recalls. He was constantly rushing about the campus, walking "with long, loping strides, almost like a trot." "I can see him going up the side of that hill now," one of them recalls, "swinging them long arms, just walking like the seat of his britches was on fire. . . . And he always looked busy. He could look busy doing nothing." "He was aggressive . . . had a quick answer for everything," and left most everyone convinced that he "was going somewhere." A close campus friend describes him as "the only fellow I ever knew who could see around the corner."

His assertiveness, an affinity for exaggeration and distortion, and an obsequiousness toward campus authorities offended some of his San Marcos contemporaries. One of the boarders at the rooming house where he lived recalls how Lyndon wouldn't let other boys get a word in edgewise: "He'd just interrupt you—my God, his voice would just ride over you until you stopped. He monopolized the conversation from the time he came in to the time he left. I can still see him reaching and talking, reaching and talking." By contrast, he was unfailingly deferential and often even worshipful toward the faculty: "Words won't come to describe . . . how kowtowing he was, how suck-assing he was, how brown-nosing he was," another classmate says. Fellow students also remember how he would exaggerate his family's importance, his father's political influence, and his own successes with women, as a debater, a student, and a campus notable. "Lyndon would have you believe, if you'd listen to him, that there wasn't anybody in the Alamo except Johnsons and . . . Bainses," one college friend said.

Lyndon was overbearing, self-centered, and all too ready to ease his own self-doubts with overblown descriptions of his virtues. But he also had qualities that endeared him to most of the people he met. He was not only aggressive and ambitious but also extraordinarily personable and empathic or understanding of other people's interests and concerns. He spoke long and loud, but he also tried to amuse and please his listeners. At the boardinghouse he didn't simply take the floor, he entertained his tablemates with political stories and imitations of amusing characters.

At San Marcos, Lyndon was a paradox: driven, grating, self-serving, on one hand; warm, enjoyable, giving on the other. It was less contradictory than it seems. The two sides of Lyndon were comfortably linked: in return for the attention, influence, and power he craved and aggressively pursued, he gave concern, friendship, and benevolent support. "Some men," Lyndon said much later, "want power simply to strut around the world and to hear the tune of 'Hail to the Chief.' Others want it simply to build prestige, to collect antiques, and to buy pretty things. Well I wanted power to give things to people—all sorts of things to all sorts of people, especially the poor and the blacks."

The ethos of the 1920s in America generally and in rural Texas in particular reinforced Lyndon's impulses to advance himself and serve the less fortunate. Lyndon's views on ambition, duty, work, sacrifice, and service were the accepted pieties of his place and time. During most of his college years, Calvin Coolidge, who "suggested the rugged honesty of the New England hills, rural virtues, clean living, religious faith, public probity," served in the White House. As the historian William E. Leuchtenburg writes, "In years when American society was changing at a frightening pace and Americans sought security by incanting their continued allegiance to older virtues at the same time that they were abandoning them, Coolidge was the most usable national symbol the country could have hoped to find." "It is not through selfishness or wastefulness or arrogance, but through self-denial, conservation, and service, that we shall build up the American spirit," Coolidge said. Such attitudes were particularly alive in "small-town Texas where," as Doris Kearns observes, "success was a reward for virtuous effort, ambition was an admired good, and there was little room for cynicism." In his eagerness to succeed and simultaneously benefit others, Lyndon was not only satisfying some inner need but also conforming to the social norms of his day.

His attitudes and actions found ready acceptance from the San Marcos faculty and administrators. They viewed him as an exceptional young man, but not because of his academic performance. Although he later boasted that he got almost all As in college—in thirty-five out of forty or thirty-eight out of forty-five courses—his school work was generally undistinguished. He told biographer Ronnie Dugger that he had about a B- average, which is borne out by his transcript: The record shows a total of 51 academic courses with 11 As, 22 Bs, 14 Cs, 4 Ds, and 1 F in Physical Education, a subject in which he "displayed supreme disinterest" and one for which President Evans apparently allowed him to substitute special written assignments.

His high standing with the staff rested partly on Lyndon's conscious efforts to ingratiate himself with the men and women who were judging him. He took special pains to flatter his instructors, invariably agreeing with them and often "sitting at the professor's feet." In informal bull sessions on the campus, "he would just drink up what they were saying, sit at their knees and drink it up, and they would pour out their hearts to him," one student remembers. Lyndon also made a point of lauding them in his editorials. One he wrote about President Evans in the summer of 1928 is typical: "Great as an educator and as an executive, Dr. Evans is greatest as a man. . . . With depth of human sympathy rarely surpassed, unfailing cheerfulness, geniality, kind firmness, and friendly interest in the youth of the state, Dr. Evans has exerted a great influence for good upon the students of S.W.T.S.T.C. He finds great happiness in serving others."

Deference was only one element in Lyndon's appeal to the staff at San Marcos. His uniqueness among a student body of seven hundred was even more important. His friend and fellow student Wilton Woods recalls that Lyndon "was seeking information from any and all professors and he talked to them at length after hours about everything, but of course anything political. And there were so few [like him]. Apparently of the seven hundred at San Marcos, he was probably the only one doing that. The rest of them were interested in playing poker and a hundred other things, but not interested in politics or how people got elected. But Lyndon was." During 1928, an election year in which a President, a U.S. Senator from Texas, and a host of other national and state candidates were to be chosen, Lyndon besieged his friends with "marathon talk about political personalities and how he would run a campaign if he were a candidate." "He was a fighter," one of Lyndon's teachers recollects. "The college faculty was not accustomed to a student with such initiative."

Lyndon's activities during the 1927–28 school year extended not only to establishing himself as an exceptional young man in the eyes of faculty and administrators but also to participation in a number of campus clubs: the Harris-Blair Literary Society, the Schoolmaster's Club for future teachers, and the journalism society. He was also one of six students selected as a member of the debate team.

His failure, however, to become a Black Star, the most influential student group on campus, put a pall over his other achievements. A secret organization made up exclusively of athletes, the Black Stars initially devoted themselves to campus high jinks, breaking College rules by stealing chickens for barbecues or going to a speakeasy for a few drinks. By the mid-twenties, however, five years after it began, it had become an exclusive group enjoying special privileges and political power. As athletes, Black Star members went to the head of the cafeteria and registration lines, received the best housing assignments, and missed chapel without punishment, something other students could not do. The Black Stars also chose class officers and members of the Student Council, which selected the editors of the *College Star* and the *Pedagog*, the campus annual, and allocated student activity fees, assuring that the bulk of this money would be spent on athletics rather than debates, guest lecturers, or music and drama programs. In addition, the Black Stars associated with coeds belonging to the Shakespeare Literary Society, the leading campus social club made up chiefly of the prettiest girls.

Boody Johnson, the head of the Black Stars, was Lyndon's closest college friend. They were seen together so often that people took to calling them "Johnson and Johnson." Boody tried as hard as he could to make Lyndon a Black Star. First, he urged Lyndon to go out for the baseball team, but when nothing came of that, he proposed him for membership anyway, arguing that Lyndon was close to Prexy and "could help us out if we needed it." When this didn't win Lyndon an invitation, Boody told them that Lyndon had read their secret constitution, which Boody had left lying about their apartment, and that they should admit him as a way to keep their rules secret. Both Boody and Lyndon later claimed that a single blackball, by a boy Lyndon had crossed, barred Lyndon's admission.

But others contend that the opposition was more widespread. Lyndon wasn't an athlete, and "there wasn't a chance in the world for him to get in there," one of them said. Other Black Stars remember that they "laughed" in Lyndon's face, and told him, "You're too scrawny and skinny, and we want real men." In the 1928 *Pedagog*, the "Cat's Claw" or humor section of the annual included a picture of a jackass with the caption: "Lyndon Johnson—As he looks to us on the campus every day."

Whatever the cause of Lyndon's exclusion from the Black Stars, it hurt him and stirred his competitive urges to outdo the people rejecting him. But an effort to square accounts had to wait another full year, until 1929–30. Continuing financial problems forced him to leave college in the fall of 1928. He arranged for a $125-a-month job beginning in September 1928 at a Mexican-American grade school in Cotulla, Texas, a town southwest of San Antonio and sixty miles north of the Mexican border near the Nueces River. At a time when the average annual salary for male teachers in Texas was $93.50 a month, Lyndon was to be unusually well paid. When he came to Cotulla, he learned why.

It was "a little dried-up . . . dying" place that Lyndon remembered as "one of the crummiest little towns in Texas." The surrounding area was a flat, treeless, wilderness called the South Texas brush country, where temperatures of 110 degrees baked the summer landscape, and infrequent torrential rains turned dirt roads into muddy streams.

When Lyndon arrived there in September 1928, the town had added certain creature comforts like running water, electricity, and fifteen paved streets in the business district. But three-quarters of the town's inhabitants were Mexicans living in hovels or dilapidated shanties without indoor plumbing or electricity on the east side of the Missouri-Pacific railroad tracks. Treated "just worse than you'd treat a dog," Lyndon later said, the Mexicans worked at the nearby ranches and farms for slave wages. Many of the Anglos to the west of the tracks were not much better off, living in small wooden houses built on stilts to protect them from termite infestation.

Despite the depressing prospect of spending the better part of the next nine months in such impoverished surroundings, Lyndon was determined to make a favorable impression that would recommend him to other school boards as an outstanding teacher. A local farmer remembers that on his first day in town he trudged through a muddy field dressed in a suit and tie to introduce himself as Lyndon Johnson from Johnson City, the new teacher for the fifth, sixth, and seventh grades in Welhausen Elementary School. Named after a county judge, the segregated Mexican school on the east side of the railroad tracks was housed in a relatively comfortable two-year-old red brick building. There was little else about the surroundings, however, that was attractive or calculated to encourage learning. Rows of dilapidated hovels on nearby streets, a debris-littered vacant lot in front, and a dirt-covered playground with no equipment to the rear provided the school's setting.

The children themselves contributed to the feeling of deadening poverty. The twenty-eight boys and girls in Lyndon's combined class left an indelible impression on him. He remembered youngsters "mired in the slums . . . lashed by prejudice . . . [and] buried half alive in illiteracy." The wretched condition of his students struck a sympathetic chord in Lyndon. Where the other five teachers in the school, all local women from influential families in the town, kept their distance from the children, doing the minimum required in their jobs, Lyndon threw himself into the work with unbounded energy. He would arrive before everyone else in the morning and be the last to leave in the evening.

Lyndon gave the children a sense of importance most of them had never known before. He distributed packages of toothpaste his mother sent him and organized extracurricular activities — debate, declamation, spelling bees, band, baseball, track — and a parents-teachers association to help with after-school functions. Moreover, he encouraged all of the children to believe that they could do something better with their lives — become a teacher, a doctor, even President of the United States. Although Lyndon's version of the American dream had little relation to their reality and although he showed little regard for their own heritage when lecturing them on the virtues of speaking English and the justification for a Texas independent of Mexico and American annexations in the Mexican War, he nevertheless left them and his fellow teachers believing that he had "helped" them "tremendously."

In May 1929, Lyndon returned to San Marcos, where he re-established contacts with friends and threw himself into a variety of activities. He attended the summer quarter, in which he took a six- instead of a normal five-course load. In the year between September 1929 and August 1930, when Lyndon received his B.S. degree in education and history, he worked at a feverish pace. "I never worked so hard in all my life," he said later. He squeezed twenty-three courses into four terms, including three terms of student teaching in civics and government.

In July, during his last term at the college, Lyndon involved himself in a state Senate campaign that would later open the way to his first job in Washington, D.C. Although successful, Lyndon's work as a campaign manager did not translate into any other immediate return. But Lyndon hadn't assumed it would. In the spring, he had asked Uncle George Johnson, his father's brother, to help him get a teaching job in Houston. A successful high school history teacher in Port Arthur and Beaumont, Uncle George had become the chairman of the history department at the Sam Houston High School. Using his considerable influence with E. E. Oberholtzer, Houston's school superintendent, Uncle George got Lyndon an appointment in his school as a public speaking and business arithmetic teacher at $1,600 a year.

Houston and its central high school with nearly 1,700 students and seventy teachers provided Lyndon with larger opportunities. Located fifty miles above the Gulf of Mexico with a population of almost 300,000, the largest of any Texas city, Houston was a haven for people on the make. To be sure, in the fall of 1930, the unemployed and hungry haunted the downtown streets, leaning against walls, sitting on window ledges, standing in bread lines, and waiting to eat at soup kitchens. But some Houstonites, despite the depression, continued to prosper in the City's cotton, lumber, and oil businesses or from the millions of dollars spent by the Federal government on the construction of a shipping channel from the Gulf to make Houston a major world port.

In the fall of 1930, when Lyndon arrived at the Sam Houston High School, his mind was focused on being the best speech and debate instructor, and maybe even the best teacher, the school had ever seen. In almost no time at all, he impressed himself on his colleagues and students as "a steam engine in pants." He worked "as if his life depended on it," a fellow teacher said.

Lyndon's career as a high school teacher, however, was brief. In November 1931 he accepted appointment as secretary to a new U.S. congressman from the Fourteenth District in Texas. Early in the month, after Harry M. Wurzbach, the incumbent, died, Richard Kleberg, a member of the wealthy King Ranch family in south Texas, became one of eight candidates running in a special election to finish Wurzbach's term. Seeking every possible advantage in a very competitive contest, Kleberg's campaign manager, Roy Miller, a former mayor of Corpus Christi and a lobbyist for Texas Gulf Sulphur, followed a suggestion that he enlist Sam Johnson's support in Blanco and surrounding counties. Sam was "very helpful," and Lyndon apparently did a small amount of work in the brief twelve-day campaign. The day Kleberg won he invited Lyndon to come to Corpus Christi for an interview. Making a strong impression at the interview as a "likable type of fellow" who was "agreeable" and eager "to be of personal service," Kleberg offered him the job.

A few days later, after arranging a leave of absence from his teaching job, Lyndon boarded a train in Houston with Congressman Kleberg for Washington, D.C. He remembered feeling "excited, nervous, and sad. I was about to leave home to meet the adventure of my future. I remembered the many nights I had stood in the doorway listening to my father's political talk. Now all that was behind me." And an extraordinary political career in the nation's capital was about to begin.

:: KLEBERG'S SECRETARY

From the moment they began their journey to the nation's capital on December 2, 1931, Kleberg introduced Lyndon to material comforts and men of influence he had never known before. Sharing a stateroom with his "chief" and taking meals in the dining car, Lyndon had his first taste of Pullman travel aboard the *Bluebonnet*, a sleek streamliner operating between Houston and Washington, D.C. In the capital they stayed at the

Mayflower on Connecticut Avenue in a carpeted $13-a-day room with twin beds. Their stay at "Washington's finest hotel," drinking early morning coffee delivered by room service, and riding cabs from the hotel to the House Office Building cost Kleberg over three times Lyndon's weekly salary at the Sam Houston High School.

During their first few days in town, Lyndon met several Texas political celebrities, including Congressman John Nance Garner, a dominant Washington figure who was about to become Speaker of the House, and Senator Morris Sheppard. Lyndon and Kleberg spent over an hour with Garner, a self-contained man with "cold blue eyes and tight small mouth" who some predicted would become a Texas Coolidge. Lyndon "just listened — something hard for me to do — but quite proper for secretaries." They met Sheppard at the Occidental, "an exclusive Washington eating place," which advertised, "Where Statesmen Dine."

Lyndon's taste of the good life, however, was soon over. After four days at the Mayflower, he began looking for a place to live. Robert M. Jackson, an aide to another Texas congressman, remembered how "this long, tall young man came in and sat about two seats behind me and started introducing himself to everybody there. . . . He reached over a whole row of seats and shook hands with me and when I told him who I was, he wanted to know . . . where I was living and everything else. . . . I was so countrified myself, and to have someone booming out there, asking me questions . . . embarrassed me." When Jackson told him that he had a room in the Dodge Hotel, where a number of congressional aides lived, Lyndon, said, "I'll move there."

Although his starting salary was $3,900 a year, more than double what he had been paid in Houston and a substantial income for a single man in the Depression, Lyndon, who sent much of his salary to his struggling parents, had a limited budget. To make ends meet, he and other congressional aides took most of their meals in cheap nearby eateries: the drugstore around the corner from his hotel, where they left nickel tips on the fountain; the All States Cafeteria on Massachusetts Avenue which served a "Fo' bitter," a filling meal for fifty cents; Child's Restaurant across from Union Station, where they got by for twenty-five cents each; or "a chili joint" behind Child's which served spicy dishes that Lyndon liked more than the other boys. Once a month, on a Sunday, they splurged and ate a one-dollar dinner at the Dodge Hotel restaurant, where a steward with a brass warming tray around his neck served them rum buns using tongs.

Lyndon's hardships, however, were modest compared with those of most Americans in the winter of 1931–32, the second year of the Depression.

Employed and able to help support his family in Texas, Lyndon had what millions of others in the country lacked. In December 1931, ten million Americans were unemployed, over 20 percent of the workforce, with more people losing their jobs all the time. Many who continued to work labored at miserably low wages, with industrial workers receiving 7.5 cents an hour and less. In Tennessee mills, women earned $2.39 for a 50-hour week; Connecticut sweatshops paid young girls one to two cents an hour, between 60 cents and $1.10 for a 55-hour week. Some American families forced on to relief rolls received less than $2.50 a week.

In the midst of the worst economic crisis in American history, the Federal government in Washington became the focus of attention and hope. By the end of 1931, however, after three years of Hoover's presidency, few Americans had much faith that the administration could devise ways to overcome the crisis. What faith existed in the capacity of the national government to make things better fixed on the Congress, and in particular on the Democratic and progressive Republican opponents of the administration. In the 1930 congressional elections, Republican majorities in the House and the Senate largely disappeared. The 17-seat advantage held by Senate Republicans in the first two years of Hoover's term became a one-seat margin in 1931. Moreover, when the House organized itself in December 1930, the Democrats, who had numbered a hundred fewer representatives than the Republicans, had a two-seat majority. Kleberg's election to replace Wurzbach, the only Republican congressman from Texas, had made a significant difference. Before Kleberg's victory, the count in the House had stood at 217 Democrats, 215 Republicans, one Farmer-Laborite, who seemed likely to vote with the Republicans, and two vacancies. Had the two vacant seats gone Republican, the GOP would have kept its hold on the House. But Kleberg's success ruled this out. It also expanded the power of Texas Democrats, who won control of the Speakership and five major House committees.

Although Kleberg helped give the Democrats a slim majority in the House, he contributed little else to the political give and take in a government desperately seeking ways out of the collapse. A super-rich, self-indulged man, Kleberg had little taste for work of any kind. The son of Robert and Alice King Kleberg, Richard had grown up on the King Ranch founded by his maternal grandfather, a vast estate in south Texas stretching nearly a hundred miles north of the Rio Grande along the Gulf of Mexico. Consisting of 1.28 million acres, twice the size of Rhode Island, on which nearly a million cattle grazed, the Ranch, the largest in the world, made the Kings and Klebergs multimillionaires and gave "Mr. Dick," as

Ranch employees and congressional aides called him, the wherewithal to be a playboy.

Kleberg left the entire work of his office to Lyndon, a raw twenty-three-year-old who, for all his intelligence and energy, hadn't a clue about how to manage a congressman's business. He didn't know how to discriminate among the mass of requests for help pouring in from Kleberg's Fourteenth District or deal with the Federal bureaucracy which might answer those demands. During his first few days on the job, Lyndon relied for guidance on an experienced stenographer who had worked for several prominent congressmen. But she offered him little more than a "mechanical" approach to the mail.

During his second week in the office, Lyndon initiated a systematic effort to do better. His first night at the Dodge he took four showers in the communal bathroom so that he could meet some of the other congressional aides living on the "B" floor. The next morning, to meet the rest, he washed his face and brushed his teeth five times at ten-minute intervals. At the end of the week he had identified five young men whose intelligence and experience he put in the service of his education. At the same time, he made a point of seeking out congressmen and other staff members outside of the Dodge circle who might give him a short course on how to do his job.

Lyndon required no instruction to know that Kleberg's success depended on satisfying the needs of his 500,000 constituents, twice as many as in most Texas districts. Many of them were veterans who stayed in the area after serving at Fort Sam Houston, the largest army post in the United States, or at one of several military air fields. In addition, cotton farmers, small truck farmers producing fruits and vegetables, cattle ranchers, and business interests in San Antonio, Corpus Christi, and Port Aransas, the district's major cities, were principal elements in the life of the area. Serving the district meant answering within twenty-four hours thousands of requests asking increased pensions, disability benefits, early payments on bonuses promised World War vets, guaranteed crop prices, appointments to government jobs, or help in refinancing farm mortgages or in getting some kind of government loan.

Lyndon's formula for making the office function effectively was unstinting effort: twelve hours or more a day, seven days a week, week after week. "His energy—it is almost impossible to exaggerate," Robert Jackson says. "He was just a bundle of nervous energy—he was moving, going all the time. He would never rest." To make the office as productive as possible, Lyndon hired Gene Latimer and Luther E. Jones, former Houston High students.

Between December 1932 and July 1935, when Latimer and Jones worked for Lyndon, they found it difficult to think about the future or anything except the day's labor. They worked phenomenally hard—fourteen-, sixteen-, often eighteen-hour days. At times, Latimer and Jones found it nearly impossible to keep working for Lyndon. He was so demanding and occasionally so overbearing and abusive that they periodically wanted to quit. Receiving a personal phone call or taking a work break to drink coffee or smoke a cigarette was forbidden. Even going to the bathroom was frowned upon. "If he caught you reading a letter from your mother, or if you were taking a crap, he'd say, 'Son, can't you please try a little harder to do that on your own time?'"

Although Kleberg was nearly twice his age, Lyndon also dominated him. Kleberg allowed him not only to run the office but also manage some of his personal and business affairs. Inattentive to family and financial matters, Kleberg left it to Lyndon to write letters to his mother and a son at the Virginia Military Institute and pay his bills. Kleberg was a free spender who lived at the Shoreham, Washington's most expensive hotel, employed chauffeurs, sent his four children to private schools, and purchased almost everything on credit. While he was exceptionally rich, much of his money was tied up in property and he didn't have "a lot of cash." Consequently, "Lyndon had to parcel out the income to keep everybody happy with a part payment. . . . Lyndon would sit him down and tell him, 'Look, I got to have so much money to pay this bill, and so much for that bill.'" Kleberg was so reluctant to bother with money matters that he even had Lyndon sign his name on personal checks.

Lyndon also played a large part in shaping Kleberg's political actions. Nothing during his years in Kleberg's office more fully captured his attention than politics. As one of the office staff remembered, "he lived and breathed it." And Lyndon began to develop convictions about good policy and good politics. Hoover's unresponsiveness to the nation's suffering troubled him. To Lyndon, Hoover stood for "do-nothing government" that was content to let corn burn for lack of a market and cotton sell for a nickel, wheat for two bits, and calves for three cents. Hoover thought that "'constitutional government' gave every man, woman, and child the right to starve," Lyndon said later.

The timid response of Congress to the Depression also bothered Lyndon. Divided between a Republican Senate and a Democratic House, in which the Democrats were more interested in preventing Hoover's reelection than in constructing an effective program, the Congress passed little significant legislation to help the needy or revive the economy.

Consequently, Franklin Roosevelt's New Deal won Johnson's enthusiastic support. Lyndon delighted in the election of New York's progressive governor to the White House and Democratic control over both houses of Congress. He later recalled attending Roosevelt's inauguration in March 1933 when people "believed that their nation had come to a dead end." But they took heart when they saw "that great man march up and hold on to that podium and say, 'The only thing we have to fear is fear itself.'"

Lyndon justifiably felt that he had a small part in the creation of the New Deal. However limited Kleberg's day-to-day involvement in his duties, he had general notions about the role of government which ran counter to most everything Roosevelt and other New Dealers favored. The sort of tampering with market forces embodied in the Agriculture Adjustment Act, the National Industrial Recovery Act, the Tennessee Valley Authority, the Securities Exchange Act, and the relief and welfare measures incorporated in the Federal Emergency Relief Act and the Social Security Act impressed Kleberg as being "socialistic." Despite his identity as a Democrat and the general appeal of Roosevelt's program, Kleberg wanted to vote against all these New Deal measures. But Lyndon and Roy Miller, a lobbyist, who was as conservative as Kleberg, convinced him that it was poor politics and a meaningless gesture to boot. When Kleberg, who served on the Agriculture Committee, told them that he intended to vote against the AAA, Lyndon pointed out that mail from the district supported it by thirty to one. When Kleberg insisted on sticking to his principles, Lyndon and Miller advised him that the bill was going to pass anyway and Lyndon threatened to quit. Although Kleberg asserted himself by voting against the FERA and TVA, he gave in on the AAA and all the other major reform bills, including Social Security. When that bill was before the House in 1935, Lyndon pressed him to vote "Yes." Kleberg "genuinely believed that it [Social Security] would destroy this country. And I pled with him: 'Please, please, please go and support that measure'; and he finally did."

Yet like so many Americans in the early thirties, Lyndon had no well-developed set of ideas about economic and social questions. He was not someone with a considered philosophy, but a young man with his eye on the main chance and an affinity for practical politics. Above all, he was interested in being effective — in learning how to win elections, use government for practical ends, and carve out a niche for himself in the world of politics.

When it came to winning elections, he learned by doing. In June 1932 he had returned to Texas to run Kleberg's primary campaign against three other Democrats. Since the Democratic nomination was tantamount to election to a full two-year term, Lyndon had spared no effort in Kleberg's behalf. Believing it essential for Kleberg to visit all of the district's eleven counties before the July primary, Lyndon laid the groundwork by criss-crossing the district and making necessary advance contacts. Lyndon's hard work paid off when Kleberg won the primary by more than 8,500 votes out of some 50,000 cast, capturing ten of the eleven counties in the Fourteenth District.

The election taught Lyndon not only the value of careful grassroots' work but also how little a liberal or conservative ideology meant in such a campaign. Kleberg was more conservative than his opponents and when one of them had attacked his support of a regressive sales tax and tax exemptions for Texas Gulf Sulfur, he permitted his supporters to describe the man as a "communist." Yet despite his conservatism and smear tactics, the Citizens' League in San Antonio, a reform organization opposed to the corrupt City-County machine, backed Kleberg.

Lyndon was learning his trade and establishing a reputation among his fellow Texans as something of a political *Wunderkind*, but politics wasn't the only thing on his mind in 1934. The first week in September he met Claudia Alta (Lady Bird) Taylor during a visit to Austin on business for Kle-berg. The attraction between them was immediate, mutual, and enduring, as a ten-week whirlwind romance and more than thirty-eight years of mar-riage would demonstrate.

Born on December 22, 1912, in Karnack, a small town in east Texas named after the temples of Egypt by a poor speller, Claudia Taylor was the daughter of an emotionally troubled mother, Minnie Lee Patillo, and a highly successful merchant and farmer, Thomas Jefferson Taylor. As a schoolgirl and teenager, she was shy and unworldly. But during four years at the University of Texas, she matured into a self-confident attractive young woman. She considered becoming a journalist, but such a career for a proper young woman from a well-to-do family was out of the ordinary in 1934. In August 1934, during the year after her graduation, while she was busy remodeling her father's home, a friend in Austin introduced her to Lyndon. Lady Bird remembered him as "very, very good-looking, lots of hair, quite black and wavy, and the most outspoken, straightforward, deter-mined young man I'd ever met." She found him "a little bit scary—so dynamic and so insistent. He came on very strong, and my instinct was to withdraw." Only twenty-four hours after they had met, he asked her to marry him. She "thought it was some kind of joke."

But it wasn't. Lyndon was dead serious. He felt at once that she was per-fectly suited to him. She impressed him as having great common sense, reasonableness, and dependability. And to boot, like him, she was ambitious to go places, or more precisely to find a man with large dreams in which she could share. Lady Bird instantly understood that he would be a perfect compliment to her own desires, and so within three months of meeting, they married.

The principal question for Lyndon at the end of 1934 was how to get on with a career. After three years, the attractions of being a congressional secretary were few. He wanted to be a congressman. Now past twenty-six, more than a year beyond the qualifying age for election to the Lower House, and having essentially been the congressman from the Fourteenth District in all but name, he wished to hold an office he felt supremely qualified to fill. "I'm not the assistant type," he told a friend at about this time. "I'm the executive type." Moreover, when one of Lyndon's assistants addressed a letter over his signature to Secretary of the Treasury Henry Morgenthau, Jr., "Dear Henry," Lyndon objected. "Look, I can't call him Henry. There's going to come a day when I will, but it's not now."

Lyndon now considered earning a law degree as a way to advance himself. He knew that many, if not most, congressmen were lawyers and that a law degree might make it easier for him to become one when the moment for him to run arrived. But a brief stint at Georgetown University's evening law program in September 1934 convinced him that he lacked the patience to do the required work. The training impressed him as too historical and impractical. When the instructor had used some Latin phrases in explaining the background of English legal concepts, Lyndon had complained, "Why don't they stick to the plain English." When the teacher had covered ground he knew from watching Congress enact a law, he had muttered, "He's not telling me anything I don't know."

Instead, Lyndon temporarily fixed his attention on becoming the president of Texas A&I University in Kingsville, an institution partly founded with Kleberg money and dominated by the Kleberg family. According to Luther Jones, somebody connected with the University approached Lyndon, and he began discussing plans for how he would get "better professors," do "things in agriculture that had never been done before," and turn the school into "one of the top universities in the world." Probably because he was too young and too little qualified to hold the post, it was never offered to him. Shortly after, Horatio H. Adams, the chief Washington lobbyist for the General Electric Corporation, invited Lyndon to work for him. Carrying a salary of $10,000 a year, more than two and a half times what he was earning, the job sorely tempted Lyndon. When Roy Miller explained, however, that becoming a corporate lobbyist might shorten his chances of winning a Texas election, he hesitated to accept the position. "Why don't you take it, man? You'll never get a job like that," Malcolm Bardwell, Maury Maverick's secretary, told him. "He said, 'No. No. It's not in keeping with what I want to do. Money doesn't mean everything.'"

But Kleberg was forcing his hand. Knowing that Lyndon was ambitious for his seat and fearing that he might run against him, Kleberg decided to push Lyndon out.

Lyndon, in fact, had been building a political power base for himself in Texas. He had arranged patronage jobs for friends, advertised his part in helping district constituents, and ingratiated himself with Texas businessmen and lobbyists by arranging hotel accommodations and appointments with government officials. Yet he recognized that he could not go after Kleberg's seat unless the congressman retired or took another job. Since Kleberg enjoyed Washington's social life and the amenities of being a congressman, the first alternative seemed unlikely. The second was a greater possibility, and beginning in 1933 Lyndon had encouraged talk that Kleberg would become Ambassador to Mexico or some other Latin American country. It was soon clear, however, that Kleberg had too little standing with the Administration to receive a significant appointment of any kind. In 1935, Kleberg's Fourteenth District seat was beyond Lyndon's reach.

An opportunity for a high-level appointment in the National Youth Administration answered Lyndon's hopes for a significant job. On June 26, 1935, Franklin Roosevelt issued an Executive Order establishing the NYA. Its aim was to help young people between the ages of sixteen and twenty-five stay in school or get job training. When someone told Lyndon that Aubrey Williams, the head of the new agency, needed a Texas state director, Lyndon said, "I'd like that job." He then asked the administrative aides to Senators Connally and Sheppard to press the case for him with their bosses.

At the same time, Lyndon enlisted House Speaker Sam Rayburn's help. As with some of the faculty at San Marcos, Lyndon had begun establishing a father-son relationship with Mister Sam, as Lyndon called him. Rayburn, who had been briefly married and had no children, was drawn to the young man. Also having made his own way in politics by cultivating powerful older sponsors, Rayburn was happy to take on a protege. In addition he had warm memories of Sam Ealy Johnson, with whom he had served in the Texas legislature. By 1935, Rayburn had grown so fond of Lyndon that when the young man was hospitalized with pneumonia, he took up a vigil at his bedside and told him, "Now Lyndon don't you worry. Take it easy. If you need money or anything, you just call on me." When the NYA job appeared, Lyndon did, and Rayburn spoke to Senator Tom Connally. "One day Sam Rayburn, who had never been friendly toward me, came to see me," Connally recalled. "He wanted me to ask President Roosevelt to appoint Lyndon Johnson to run the Texas NYA, and he said he knew this fell in my patronage basket. Sam was agitated and wouldn't leave until I agreed to do this."

Lyndon also asked Texas Congressman Maury Maverick's help, and he promised to talk to the President and Aubrey Williams. Roosevelt was reluctant to appoint someone so young, but he agreed with Maverick that Lyndon would be in a better position than someone older to understand the problems of the people he would be helping. Williams, who had already announced an appointee and then withdrew it at the advice of University of Texas Professor Robert Montgomery, was receptive to the suggestion, especially when it was reinforced by conservative Congressman Martin Dies. In a letter to Maverick eighteen years later, Williams remembered "that the first time I ever heard of [Lyndon Johnson] . . . was one night when . . . you laid his name in my lap and said he was a good guy. Then, as I recall it he got Martin Dies to call me. The first and only time that bastard ever did me the honor. And I concluded that if Maury Maverick and Martin Dies both recommended a guy that he must be a safe bet. I have no recollection that Sam Rayburn was guilty of starting that tumble bug on his way. It was you and your buddy Martin Dies." FDR remained reluctant to appoint someone who at the age of twenty-seven would be the youngest of the state directors, but with both Texas senators amenable, leading Texas congressmen enthusiastic, and Williams recommending it, Roosevelt gave him the job.

:: THE N.Y.A.

The National Youth Administration expressed the concern of Roosevelt's New Deal to save a generation of young people from ignorance, unemployment, and enduring hardship. When FDR took office in 1933, between a quarter and a third of America's thirteen million unemployed were sixteen to twenty-five years old. During the next two years the Civilian Conservation Corps and the Federal Emergency Relief Administration made special efforts to employ young people or help them stay in school long enough to develop marketable skills. But these were limited efforts with small impact. By the spring of 1935, 20 percent of the nations twenty-two million youngsters remained out of school and either on relief or wandering the country looking for work.

Some people in the Roosevelt administration urged a special effort to help the young. But the President himself was reluctant to single out young Americans for special help. Early in 1935 he told his wife, Eleanor, that the problem of the young could not be separated from the difficulties of all the people. Appealing to the "practical politician" in her husband, Eleanor pointed out that the young would be voters one day. "There is a good deal to what you say," Franklin replied. "I have determined that we shall do something for the Nation's unemployed youth because we can ill afford to lose the skill and energy of these young men and women," he said when announcing the birth of the NYA.

If FDR partly aimed to create a generation of Democratic voters by establishing the youth agency, Lyndon also saw political advantages in becoming head of the Texas NYA. He could build local and state-wide contacts for future campaigns. After being appointed, he told a friend, "When I come back to Washington, I'm coming back as a Congressman."

Like FDR, however, Lyndon's first concern was to help needy youngsters. Throughout his life, nothing in politics appealed more to him than marrying his ambition to help for the poor. Seeing the NYA as principally opening avenues of opportunity to youngsters who might otherwise never realize their potential, Lyndon was thrilled to help administer the program.

But making the NYA work wasn't easy. At the start of the program no one had a clear idea of how to proceed. In August 1935, nearly two months after the NYA was born, Harry Hopkins, the head of the Works Progress Administration (WPA), said, "I have nothing on my mind to offer as a solution to our problems, and I know of no one else who has . . . a satisfactory program for young people. I want to assure you that the government is looking for ideas."

Lyndon quickly recognized that Texas had its own special difficulties. In 1935, nearly 125,000 Texans between the ages of sixteen and twenty-five were on relief, and represented approximately 5 percent of youngsters in the forty-eight states needing help. Even more daunting was the variety of conditions in Texas that had to be considered in trying to devise and administer state-wide programs: Nearly one-ninth the area of the continental United States and divided into 254 counties, Texas seemed too big and varied for any single program to work effectively across the state. Moreover, Lyndon had only half a million dollars to spend in the first year, less than 2 percent of the annual NYA budget of $27 million.

He approached the job with ferocious energy. When Williams appointed Lyndon on July 25, he asked him not to hire anyone or make any commitments until the Washington office had a clearer idea of what it wanted done. But Lyndon thought that helping thousands of high school and college students resume classes in the fall term meant getting started at once. Consequently, he began publicizing the program, enlisting the help of state and local officials, recruiting a staff, and developing plans to keep young people in school during his first week in office.

Lyndon's pace was too fast for NYA headquarters in Washington, which asked him to hold off appointing deputies. But Lyndon, who thought it a mistake to wait, recruited his principal assistants and opened an office immediately. He convinced two college classmates, Willliam Deason and Jesse Kellam and a childhood chum, Sherman Birdwell, to give up other jobs to join his staff. He was "just a great salesman," Deason said of his decision to accept Lyndon's offer.

Shortly after, Lyndon traveled to Washington for a state directors' meeting and a ceremonial visit to the White House, where the President gave them marching orders. At the meeting, Lyndon's first face-to-face encounter with FDR, the President pointed out that past groups had come "to talk about education, child welfare and various things like that. They had very interesting discussions and they passed very nice resolutions. . . . Everybody went home; and little, if anything, resulted from their efforts. Our procedure is different. We have asked you here to start something. . . . It is the first time the Federal Government has attempted a great national project of this kind. It is an experiment, but we are going to get something more than mere resolutions out of it. We are going to get action." FDR, who wanted to meet the program's youngest state director, asked Lyndon to stay after the others had left. Lyndon recalled that the President "kinda petted me."

Lyndon needed no encouragement to produce concrete results. When he returned to Austin, he began a routine that tested his endurance and that of his most devoted co-workers. Sixteen-, eighteen-hour days, seven days a week, week in and week out became the norm. Starting usually at seven in the morning, Lyndon often worked until after midnight. He ate lunch at his desk and dinner at home with associates discussing the day's problems. At about eight, he habitually returned with them to the office for another few hours, where they had to work by antiquated gaslight and walk down six flights of stairs in the dark because the building superintendent turned off the electricity at 10:30.

Lyndon inspired his staff with a sense that they were making history— that they were reaching out to desperate young people whose lives would be profoundly affected by what the NYA did. Everyone in the office knew the story of the hostile San Antonio businessman at a club luncheon who told Lyndon, "All these kids need to do is get out and hustle." Having seen Mexican-American children rummaging through a garbage can behind a cafeteria from which they took grapefruit rinds to gnaw on, he answered: "Right. Last week over here I saw a couple of your local kids hustling—a boy and a girl, nine or ten. They were hustling through a garbage can in an alley." "Put them to work; get them into school!" he urged his staff. "Put them to work! Get them out of the boxcars!" he pleaded.

By almost any standard the NYA nationally, and in Texas particularly, was a great success. By early 1937, after only eighteen months, it had some 428,000 students at all levels enrolled in its programs and another 190,000 employed on work projects. Texas accounted for approximately 5 percent of the totals with nearly 29,000 young people—over 20,000 students and more than 8,000 project workers—on NYA payrolls. In Johnson's later estimate, "if the Roosevelt Administration had never done another thing, it would have been justified by the work of this great institution for salvaging youth." The NYA, he said in 1939, "relieved the pressure upon our over-taxed labor market like a great dam, storing flood waters to be released in times of thirst and drought. It . . . kept thousands of boys and girls in high school and college, where they belonged. It . . . eased the emergency and insured youth the training twentieth-century life demands as a requisite for success."

High officials in the Roosevelt administration believed that much of the credit for what happened in Texas belonged to Lyndon Johnson. By the spring and summer of 1936, NYA officials were singing his praises. Russell Ellzey, a field representative, told Dick Kleberg that "you have the best Youth Director in the Nation in Lyndon Johnson, and he has the finest organization in Texas of any I have seen." Lyndon, who made a special effort to help black youngsters, also won the appreciation of black officials in Washington, who said that "the Texas Director is doing what many of us are talking." Small wonder, then, that Aubrey Williams publicly described the Texas operation as a "first-class job," and privately called it a standing "example to other states' youth administrations."

Also hearing about the good work being done by Johnson, Eleanor Roosevelt wrote him in January 1936 to applaud his efforts to find "employment for young people." She visited Texas later in the year "to find out why the Texas NYA director was doing such an effective job." She conferred with Lyndon and accompanied him to a vocational training center for girls on East Sixth Street in Austin and to college campuses running NYA programs. In June, when the President came to Texas to open a Centennial Exposition, Lyndon had the satisfaction of watching the President throw back his head and laugh as his motorcade drove by 155 NYA boys saluting him with shovels at present arms. When Jesse Kellam succeeded Lyndon as director in 1937, Williams called him to Washington and said, "Kellam, you haven't got but one way to go and that's down. This man Johnson was operating the best NYA program in all of the states. . . . You can't do a better job than he was doing. I hope you can do as well."

:: THE MAKING OF A CONGRESSMAN

The opportunity to run for Congress had decided Lyndon to resign. When Congressman James B. "Buck" Buchanan of the Tenth District died on February 22, 1937, Lyndon seized the chance to run for his House seat. As Buchanan's career demonstrated, once someone won election to the U.S. House of Representatives from Texas, he was likely to stay in office for over twenty years.

Despite his eagerness to enter the special election, a winner-take-all contest requiring only a plurality of the votes for victory, Lyndon understood that he was not well known in the district and had only an outside chance of winning. On February 23, when the *Austin Statesman* discussed possible successors to Buchanan, Lyndon wasn't even mentioned. "You boys are talking about Lyndon Johnson," Sam Fore, a leading Texas Democrat, remembered Mayor Tom Miller of Austin telling him. "Nobody knows him." "Who the hell is Lyndon Johnson?" Claude Wild, the manager of Governor Jimmy Allred's successful campaign in 1934, said when asked to run Lyndon's campaign. But those who knew Lyndon well did not worry about his public obscurity at the start of the campaign.

Among the small group of Texans who believed in Lyndon's ability to succeed, none was more important than Alvin J. Wirtz, a former state senator and then Austin attorney. Through their contacts in Washington when Lyndon had worked for Kleberg and in Austin when they had worked together for the NYA, Wirtz, who was twenty years Lyndon's senior, had come to admire Lyndon's intelligence and capacity for hard work and to have an affection for him a father reserves for a son. Mary Rather, Wirtz's secretary, remembered one day in 1934 when she first saw Lyndon in Wirtz's Austin office. "He didn't stay long, but he turned the place upside down. He was very fast and quick and busy." He made Rather think of Josephine's first impression of Napoleon as "a tornado."

In almost every respect, Lyndon Johnson was an ideal candidate for Wirtz to back for his district's congressional seat. A highly intelligent and deferential young man with a working knowledge of congressional politics and the Federal bureaucracy, Lyndon seemed likely to be a highly effective representative for both the Tenth District and Wirtz's interests in Washington. In 1937, these included support for FDR and New Deal programs in general and additional allocations of Federal money for continued work on Lower Colorado River dams in particular. As counsel to the Lower Colorado River Authority, Wirtz believed that the dams not only would spare central Texas from destructive floods and open the way to cheaper electric power but also add to his wealth and influence in Texas and Washington.

However valuable, Wirtz's backing did not eliminate several other obstacles to Lyndon's candidacy. Eight other candidates entered the race. Five of them seemed likely to win more votes than Lyndon. The youngest candidate, from Blanco, the smallest county in the district, Lyndon seemed an able and energetic young man whose ambitions outran his political reach.

Lyndon worked to perfect a campaign strategy that would allow him to overcome his opponents. A decision at the start of the race to trumpet Lyndon's identification with FDR and all his programs, including Court-packing, was central to this effort. Hoping to capitalize on Roosevelt's popularity in the district, which he had carried by a nine-to-one margin in 1936, Wirtz urged Lyndon to be "a total Roosevelt man. . . . Of course, there will be those who will be bitter at you," Wirtz advised, "but to hell with them. They're in the minority. The people like Roosevelt." Wirtz understood that Roosevelt symbolized not only a way out of the Depression for Tenth District folks but a new day in the history of Texas and the South. The federal government was being put in the service of southern economic needs and was moving the region toward a more prosperous future.

Lyndon was enthusiastic about the strategy. He admired FDR and believed his programs essential to the national and regional well-being. But he also knew that a strong identification with Roosevelt in general and his controversial Court-packing plan in particular was excellent politics. During the campaign, straw polls showed that as many as seven out of eight Tenth District voters were sympathetic to FDR's plans for Court reform.

As everyone involved in the Johnson campaign understood, identifying with FDR was an obvious strategy that other candidates would adopt as well. Lyndon's aim, therefore, was to outdo his opponents in tying himself to FDR and to make it seem that he was the only one genuinely behind the President. His campaign became a celebration of FDR and an appeal to the idea that Lyndon Johnson was the single candidate in the race who would give the President unqualified support. Journalists amused by Johnson's reverential attitude toward the President in his self-aggrandizing campaign suggested the slogan: "Franklin D., Lyndon B. and Jesus C."

Weak campaigns run by Lyndon's opponents added to the advantage he gained by his identification with FDR. None of the other candidates came close to matching the time and energy expended by Johnson and his supporters. Where Lyndon began campaigning on March 2, the day after he announced his candidacy, the others did not get out on the hustings until days and weeks later. "Young Johnson worked harder to win than any one of the many candidates," one local paper recorded after the election. He "spoke first, last and the loudest."

Johnson even managed to turn his youth, the principal issue on which his opponents were able to score points against him, to his advantage. Concerned that voters might be reluctant to send someone only twenty-eight years old to Congress, he usually described himself as "almost thirty." "This Johnson is a young, young man," an opponent declared. "It's bad enough when you get too old a man in the Congress. But it's worse to take off the baby robe and put on the toga."

The spirit of Johnson's campaign was a never-say-die effort in every corner of the district. It was a formidable job. The district stretched some 175 miles from east to west and some 100 miles from north to south. Its approximately 50,000 registered voters in a population of 264,000 were scattered across an area of almost 8,000 square miles. Though 88,000 of its citizens were concentrated in Austin, the rest of the district's population lived in small towns and on farms, to which any candidate had to travel if he hoped to win a plurality in a nine-man race. "Don't ever let me be in the house where there's daylight and keep the screen locked until dark," Lyndon told Lady Bird when he began the campaign.

She never had to take him up on his injunction. He drove himself night and day giving over two hundred speeches in forty-two days and traveling to every town in the district. At the edge of a town, he would get out of his car and walk its length, shaking hands with everyone he met and stopping in stores. Meanwhile, campaign workers using a loudspeaker mounted on his car would play martial music and appeal to folks to come hear Lyndon Johnson talk. The speech, usually a rousing enunciation of his eagerness to serve the district by helping Roosevelt, lasted no more than five minutes. To meet as many voters in person as possible, he would stop at every filling station on the road between towns, where he would buy a gallon of gas, talk to everyone who would listen, and leave a campaign poster in a prominent spot. Every time he saw a farmer at work, he would stop his car, vault a fence, and slog through the field to shake hands and appeal for the man's vote.

He was at his best in a face-to-face meeting and informal talks. Grasping a man's arm with one hand and holding his hand with the other, he would get him talking about himself, his family, his work, his shared concerns with Lyndon Johnson. By contrast, when he gave formal speeches, which he usually did at set rallies, his delivery was strained and awkward.

Despite the hard work and significant gains during the first five weeks of the campaign, the outcome remained in doubt. Problems with the weather and getting people interested enough to come meet him dogged his efforts. The uneven response to Lyndon's campaign persuaded Claude Wild, the principal campaign manager, that they were going to have to "throw a little dirt." The Johnsons were initially reluctant. Lady Bird complained to Wild that she had helped finance this race and she "wasn't going to have her husband slinging mud. She wanted him to be a gentleman." Wild responded: "Well, do you want him to be a gentleman or a Congressman?" Lyndon also objected, saying, "No, no, if I have to do that I don't want the office." But when Wild threatened to quit the campaign and emphasized again the importance of attacking his opponents, Lyndon gave in.

Subsequently his opponents charged that Johnson carried his determination to win beyond the limits of legality. Johnson campaign workers persuaded Federal officials to let Lyndon hand out parity checks to farmers, which, as Emmett Shelton, another candidate said, "was of course illegal." Moreover, Shelton believed that the Johnson campaign paid Elliott Roosevelt, FDR's son, $5,000 to endorse Lyndon.

Yet if Johnson's campaign was far from a model of civic virtue, it was not much different from those of his opponents. They also used a no-holds-barred approach to the election. And the candidates were so distrustful of one another that when Lyndon had his appendix removed two days before the election, two of his opponents charged that it was a faked illness to win a last-minute sympathy vote. Because Lyndon feared that he would be accused of a political trick, he tried to hold off having the surgery. And when he became too ill to wait, he insisted that another candidate's brother, who was a physician, assist in the operation to counter any suggestion that it was a "put up job."

Lyndon's aggressive identification with Roosevelt, the stumbling campaigns of his opponents, his unrelenting efforts to become known in every corner of the district through personal appearances, newspaper ads, mailings, and radio talks gave him a surprisingly large victory margin on election day. Although he received only a shade less than 28 percent of the vote—8,280 out of 29,943 cast—he got almost 3,200 votes more than his closest opponent. The third place finisher had nearly 3,900 votes fewer than Lyndon. A breakdown of the vote by counties showed that Lyndon finished third in two, second in two, and first in six, including Travis, where he got nearly 3,000 of the 10,300 votes. Unlike his opponents, who made strong showings in only one or two counties, Johnson ran well across the whole district.

A photograph of him in a hospital bed the day after the election shows him flanked by two nurses, and covered by—indeed up to his chin in— congratulatory telegrams. Though his thin unshaven face, uncombed hair, and the dark circles under his sunken eyes show the effects of his grueling six-week campaign and his recent surgery, a warm smile reflects the satisfaction of a man who had fulfilled a longstanding hope. Capturing Lyndon in an uncharacteristic moment of enforced repose, the photo is unique in the remarkable political career that unfolded over the next thirty-two years.

2 :: THE CONGRESSMAN

Shortly after his election, Lyndon was told by a friend that "some country folks near Taylor when asked who they would vote for said, 'I tank Yonson must be a pretty good Swede—I'll vote for him.'" Johnson knew that chance and peculiar circumstance would always play a part in Texas and even national politics. But from the moment he set his sights on electoral office, he operated on the assumption that political success depended primarily on planning and hard work, actions that left as little to happenstance as possible. He believed that if he were to hold his congressional seat and ultimately win a higher office, he needed to become an influential figure in Washington and effectively serve the interests of his district, state, and region.

After leaving the hospital on April 24, Lyndon stayed in Texas until May 11 to meet with the President. On April 20, after FDR had decided to combine a political junket with a fishing holiday in the Gulf of Mexico, an aide proposed that when they got to Texas, the President see the Congressman-elect. Acting as the intermediary, Governor Jimmy Allred advised Johnson that he would be invited to join the President's party at Galveston.

On May 11, Johnson joined Roosevelt on his special train from Galveston to College Station, where the President spoke to 3,000 ROTC cadets at Texas A&M. Afterward, Johnson traveled by train with the presidential party to Fort Worth. During that day-long journey, two of America's premier twentieth-century politicians sized each other up and struck an unspoken agreement to serve their mutual interests. Roosevelt, whose worries about foreign affairs, and German, Italian, and Japanese aggression in particular, were growing, wanted to strengthen his hold over defense planning.

He especially wanted to expand American naval power, which, among other things, meant having a pliable House Naval Affairs Committee. He "wanted somebody from Texas that would vote for a strong Navy," the President told Lyndon.

The young man "came on like a freight train," FDR later told an aide. Lyndon boldly asked for assignment to the Appropriations Committee, one of the two most important committees in the House and the one on which his predecessor Buck Buchanan had served as chairman. When Roosevelt said that would have to wait, Lyndon described a long-standing interest in the U.S. Navy, and raised the possibility of establishing a naval air base at Corpus Christi.

If Lyndon was a bit obvious in his attempt to ingratiate himself, Roosevelt saw more in the young man than just another freshman congressman on the make. As Lyndon was about to leave, Roosevelt gave him Thomas G. Corcoran's telephone number in Washington and told him to call "Tommy the Cork," as his White House assistant was known, to discuss the Naval Committee assignment and any other matter on which they could be of help. Before Johnson called, the President himself telephoned Corcoran: "I've just met the most remarkable young man. Now I like this boy, and you're going to help him with anything you can." Roosevelt also told Harold Ickes, his Secretary of the Interior, and Harry Hopkins, his director of relief efforts, that meeting Lyndon Johnson had caused him some frustration: "If he hadn't gone to Harvard, that's the kind of uninhibited young pro he'd like to be—that in the next generation the balance of power would shift south and west, and this boy could well be the first Southern President."

The meeting immediately marked Lyndon as a strong Roosevelt man and gave him access to administration officials who could help his congressional career. Roosevelt had already made this possible by talking to Corcoran, Ickes, and Hopkins. And they, in turn, talked to others about Johnson, especially Corcoran, who commanded extraordinary influence. Ickes also talked up Lyndon. At lunch one day, he told Eliot Janeway, the business editor of *Time*, that he ought to meet this "new kid Lyndon Johnson." When Janeway returned to New York that evening from Washington, he had a call from Edwin Weisl, a Wall Street lawyer and personal counsel to Harry Hopkins, who wanted to know if Janeway had "ever heard of some kid called Lydie Johnson." Together, Corcoran recalls, the New Dealers created an "atmosphere, a consensus about the new boy and his immediate future in the House."

Lyndon also made special efforts to win the approval of House leaders. And he quickly convinced them that he was an effective legislator and reliable Democrat. "He made a very profound impression from the outset upon his colleagues," John W. McCormack of Massachusetts, the later Majority Leader and Speaker of the House, recalled. " . . . His interest in committee work on the floor of the House clearly marked him out as one who was destined for greater responsibilities and higher honors." McCormack believed that Roosevelt's regard for Johnson was "certainly . . . helpful" to him, but "Johnson earned his position and his prestige and his standing as a result of his own contributions in committee and in the House."

No one in the House was more important to Lyndon, however, than Sam Rayburn. At the age of fifty-five, after twenty-four years in the House, Rayburn had become Majority Leader in January 1937. A bachelor with few interests outside of the House of Representatives, which he once described as "my life and my love," Rayburn was a lonely man. Lyndon and Lady Bird became his surrogate family.

The warmth of their relations extended to doings on the Hill. At the close of business every day, Rayburn invited a favored few to join him at the "Board of Education," his hideaway office directly under the House Speaker's formal office. There, they socialized and, as John Nance Garner, who originated the phrase, said, struck "a blow for liberty" with some bourbon and branch water. "Only two House members had keys and didn't have to gain admittance," Rayburn said. "I had one key; Lyndon Johnson had the other."

Like so many others who entered government service in the thirties, Lyndon's sense of participation in something larger than himself helped make him a committed New Dealer. The fact that he represented a strong pro-Roosevelt district also played a part. But his whole life experience was at the core of his identity as a southern New Dealer or liberal nationalist who aimed to integrate the South into the mainstream of American economic life. The plight of the children at Cotulla and his sense of exhilaration at being able to help them, the feelings of accomplishment when answering the cries for aid from people in Kleburg's district, the suffering caused by the Depression and the humane response of FDR's government, all made Lyndon a strong believer in using Federal power for the good of needy Americans everywhere, but especially in the South.

By 1938–39 some Administration leaders thought of Lyndon Johnson as the "best New Dealer from Texas." He was viewed as someone who not only backed the Roosevelt administration but also did all he could to obtain Federal benefits for his constituents, including the most needy. No group in Johnson's district benefited more from his actions than impoverished Hill Country farmers. Money was in such short supply in the early thirties that the area functioned as a barter economy. Moreover, with the land so unproductive—only 35,000 acres or 10 percent of Blanco County was under cultivation in 1933—New Deal programs, which paid farmers for reducing their crops, could provide little cash to the Hill Country. But Johnson found ways to help. In 1938–41, when hundreds of farmers couldn't qualify for Farm Security Administration loans because they had no collateral, Johnson persuaded the FSA to waive the requirement and give each of 400 families a $50 loan. In addition, he facilitated the implementation of a "Range Conservation" program in the Hill Country that cleared thousands of acres of soil-depleting brush and increased the amount of land under cultivation by 400 percent in three and a half years. At the same time, he helped provide federal funds for paved farm-to-market roads which facilitated the shipment of increased produce to market before it spoiled. He also obtained millions of dollars in WPA grants for building projects. And then there was the conservation and public power through dam building on the Lower Colorado River, which brought cheap power to the region and rural electrification that transformed people's lives. In this, Lyndon joined a group of self-serving altruists who used the dams simultaneously to acquire wealth and influence.

No one used the dam-building more to their advantage than Brown & Root, a construction company in Austin controlled by George and Herman Brown. With Lyndon's help they won government contracts that turned a small road-building firm into a multimillion dollar business. Their success gave Lyndon a financial angel that could help secure his political future.

As a reward for his good work, in July 1939, Roosevelt asked Johnson to become the administrator of the Rural Electrification Administration (REA). But unwilling to give up a secure seat in Congress for an administrative job he might lose after a few years, Johnson declined. His decision neither surprised nor upset anyone in the Administration. In fact, Ickes and Corcoran had counseled against taking the job, and Corcoran had told him that FDR preferred to have him in Congress. The offer was largely a symbolic expression of regard for the man Ickes now described as "the only real liberal in Congress" from Texas. "He got more projects, and more money for his district, than anybody else," Corcoran said later. "He was the best Congressman for a district that *ever* was."

Corcoran may have been right. But he can hardly be described as an objective commentator on Johnson's congressional work. For like Lyndon, Alvin Wirtz, Lyndon's first mentor, and the Brown brothers, Corcoran's public service carried a self-serving price tag. His efforts to help Johnson with dam-building and electrification were a prelude to business ties with

Brown & Root and other Texas corporations which paid his Washington, D.C., law firm handsome fees beginning in the 1940s.

The Brown brothers, whose construction firm largely built the dams, were even more selfish than Corcoran. PWA records are studded with complaints about their requests for "change orders," cost overruns, and labor practices that violated the spirit and the letter of the law and lined their pockets with undeserved profits. Government contracts made the Browns what some facetiously called "socialized millionaires." Though they gained substantially from the New Deal, the Browns denounced it as welfare programs for people too lazy to work.

For Johnson, the Colorado River projects involved much more than selfish gain, however. He also took genuine satisfaction from raising living standards in south-central Texas. For him, politics meant not simply the accumulation of influence but overcoming the poverty that afflicted the lives of so many Texans. Johnson was a self-serving opportunist who used his connections to advance himself; but he was also a new breed southerner who saw the federal government as a vehicle for advancing the interests of his state and region. He was not only a shrewd operator with his eyes on the main chance but also a man of vision who worked effectively for a larger good.

:: HARDBALL POLITICS

By the fall of 1939, despite having established an almost unbreakable hold on his district, Lyndon wanted to move on to the Senate.

He tied his hopes for a Senate seat to Roosevelt's continuing hold on power. It was a gamble. For FDR to remain a political force he had to run for an unprecedented third term. During the first half of 1939, no one knew if he would run again, and if he did, whether he could overcome resistance to the two-term limit. Moreover, even without the third-term question, an erosion of his popularity and influence by the seventh year of his presidency made another successful national campaign doubtful. In 1938, when he tried to defeat conservative Democrats in local and state primaries, he had suffered "a humiliating drubbing." "President Roosevelt could not run for a third term even if he so desired," one astute Washington journalist said after the 1938 elections. In Texas, the defeat by conservative opponents of Maury Maverick and W. D. McFarlane, the two most outspoken New Deal congressmen in the state, signaled the decline of Roosevelt's influence.

At the same time, however, Johnson understood that his close identification with the President was doing him more good than harm, that Roosevelt probably would run again, and that even if he did not, he maintained sufficient influence to keep the Democratic party in liberal hands. The outbreak of the Second World War in September 1939 decided Roosevelt to seek another term. His problem, then, in the words of FDR biographer James MacGregor Burns, was "to be nominated in so striking a manner that it would amount to an emphatic and irresistible call to duty. This party call would be the prelude to a call from the whole country at election time."

Lyndon's special part in the 1940 campaign was as congressional campaign manager for the House. After Rayburn warned that losing Congress "would tear him to pieces just like it did President Wilson after 1918," Roosevelt called Johnson to the White House. There is no record of their conversation, and Lyndon came away from the meeting with no formal title for his assignment. But it is clear that Roosevelt wanted him to proceed without any special title or public fanfare that could identify him as working for the President. Lyndon was described as simply assisting the Congressional Campaign Committee. In fact, he now began to play a significant part in national political affairs.

Three hours after he saw Roosevelt, Lyndon rented a one-room office in downtown Washington on the third floor of the old, narrow Munsey Building at 1329 E Street, NW. Furnishing it with a desk and swivel chair, three other chairs, a divan, a telephone, and a typewriter, Johnson, helped by John Connally, his new aide from Texas, began working fifteen- to eighteen-hour days.

His first concern was *how* to help House Democrats threatened with defeat. Everyone agreed that a good many Democrats were going to get beat unless they got money for aggressive campaigns. Lyndon, however, had not conceived of his job as "raising and expending funds." And House Democratic leaders believed that the Democratic National Committee (DNC) would give House candidates the money. After the DNC gave the Congressional Campaign Committee a check for only $10,000, a tenth of what Rayburn had asked, hopes were dampened.

Fund-raising now became Lyndon's highest goal. Most incumbents in 1940 could run an effective campaign for under $5,000. In large cities like New York, the cost was more than double that amount, but in many places around the country it was no more than $2,000. Yet finding the $2,000 to $5,000 was not easy for most House Democrats. Traditionally, the party had depended on a limited number of big donors to supply congressional and presidential campaign funds. But the introduction of progressive income, gift, and inheritance taxes in the thirties reduced the number of contributors willing to make five-and six-figure donations. The passage of the Hatch Act in 1940 also limited party funds by restricting annual individual contributions to $5,000. The Republicans had managed to overcome the problem by hiring a professional fund-raiser who had systematically built up a large war chest for the 1940 campaign. By contrast, informality and confusion characterized Democratic fund-raising: A handful of individuals operated independently of the party's National Committee, which had little say over how the money would be spent.

During his first days in the job, Johnson, helped by Rayburn, devoted himself exclusively to raising cash. Having been encouraged by George Brown not to show "any timidity" in asking a return on the favors done for Brown & Root, Johnson now drew on this account. He asked the Browns to make a significant contribution to a congressional campaign fund. At the same time, Rayburn urged Clint W. Murchison and Sid Richardson, both independent Texas oil men, to provide some support. The response exceeded all expectations. Although Federal law prohibited corporations from contributing to political campaigns, and individuals from giving more than $5,000, the Browns arranged for Lyndon to receive $30,000 in Brown & Root money by mid-October. Johnson collected an additional $15,000 from Rayburn's sources. Lyndon then told Swager Sherley at the National Committee: "We have sent them [congressional candidates] more money in the last 3 days than Congressmen have received from any committee in the last 8 years."

But it was not enough to do the job. There were 101 House Democrats "in trouble," Johnson believed, 29 in the Midwest, 26 elsewhere who had won by only a few hundred votes in 1938, 21 whose margin had been only a few thousand votes, and 25 who were in "real danger." Lyndon believed that saving these congressmen from defeat required more than $45,000. He wired Rayburn, who was in Texas, that a careful check showed 105 Democrats needed money, but that the "Barrel has been scraped." He now asked the Garment and the United Mine Workers unions, Wall Street investment bankers, and Charles Marsh to help. At the same time, he urged Rayburn to press on "our friends down there" the importance of being helpful.

All of these contributors, north and south, added thousands of dollars to the party's war chest. Though some of them, like the UMW and independent oil producers Rayburn went to see in Dallas and Fort Worth, had little use for Roosevelt, they had selfish reasons for wanting a Democratic Congress. The Mine Workers wished to preserve New Deal gains made by unions, while the Democrats had arranged special tax advantages for the oil men. "Bring in a Republican Congress, with a new Speaker and new committee chairmen," Rayburn told them, "and they'll tear your depletion allowance and intangible-drilling write-offs to pieces."

Yet however great the flood of money, it was not enough to finance more than a hundred congressional races. To Lyndon, the objective was not simply to give money indiscriminately to Democratic candidates, but to support those with a good chance to win. To this end, he consulted with party leaders across the United States.

The money, generally in amounts between $200 and $500, was what the candidates needed most. Some, like two Ohio congressmen, said they wanted nothing else. But most asked for other things as well: a visit to their home area by the President or other prominent public figures, endorsements from Democratic leaders who had wide name recognition among their constituents, or help with getting public works projects for their districts approved before election day. Lyndon worked hard to satisfy these requests.

The result in the congressional races was better than even Lyndon dared hope. He bet White House insider Jim Rowe that the Democrats would lose fewer than thirty House seats. Rowe, reflecting the White House view, thought it would be thirty or more. But Lyndon, like other close observers at the time, anticipated a close contest, even for the President, who accurately foresaw that this was going to be his toughest race.

About midnight on election day, after Roosevelt had learned that he would receive a third term, he called Johnson and Rowe, who were together at a party in Georgetown, where Lyndon had been getting reports on the House races. Although Roosevelt beat Willkie by five million votes, it was only half the margin he had won by in 1936 and the smallest plurality of any winner since 1916. Also recalling party losses in 1938, Roosevelt feared a further reduction in Democratic majorities. The President asked Lyndon "how many seats are we going to lose." Johnson replied: "We're not going to lose. We're going to gain.'" "It *was* impressive," Jim Rowe said. ". . . And it impressed the hell out of Roosevelt." The fact that the Democrats gained six House seats, especially while they were losing three Senate seats, impressed a lot of other people as well, including particularly the candidates Johnson had helped. They sent him warm expressions of gratitude for his part in saving them from defeat.

:: SENATE RACE

Roosevelt's pay-off to Johnson for his loyalty to the administration came in the spring and early summer of 1941 when he ran for a Senate seat. On

April 9, Morris Sheppard, the senior senator from Texas, died after a brief illness. A special election to complete Sheppard's term meant that Lyndon could run without giving up his House seat.

Although Lyndon had doubts about winning, he never hesitated about running. On April 11, Wirtz, Charles Marsh, and Harold Young, a Texas attorney on Vice President Henry Wallace's staff, laid plans for Lyndon's campaign. They discussed getting Texas Governor W. Lee O'Daniel to make him interim senator until the special election on June 28, when and how FDR should endorse him, and the themes Lyndon would sound in the race.

By April 17, Lyndon had begun raising campaign funds. He had arranged with the Brown brothers to make the first of many hidden contributions. Convinced that Lyndon would have more influence on defense spending as a senator than he would as a congressman, the Browns were eager to support a campaign that promised to serve their long-term interests. They also saw a means of making it serve their immediate ones as well. On the 17th, a check for $6,000 was given to D. G. Young, the secretary of Brown & Root. It was listed in the corporation's records as a bonus authorized on December 27, 1940, and as an expense deduction in Brown & Root's tax returns. In fact, on the same day Young received the check, he gave $5,270 in cash to Lyndon's campaign.

Though operating outside the law, Lyndon and the Brown brothers believed that if their campaign stayed within the $25,000 limit allowed by Federal law, it would mean certain defeat. Since a state-wide radio talk cost $1,300, a highway billboard ad $200–$300, a small newspaper ad $25–$50, it was an unspoken assumption of the campaign that anyone making a serious bid for the office would exceed the $25,000 limit many times over.

Lyndon's first concern in the two weeks after Sheppard died was not campaign financing but Roosevelt's public blessing. The defeat of congressional candidates FDR had endorsed in the 1938 primaries made him reluctant to take a stand in the Texas Senate race. But Rowe assured him that Johnson would avoid "the mistakes of the 1930 'purge,'" and advised him that the alternatives to Johnson were "too frightful for contemplation." Roosevelt, who had thoughts of getting Johnson on the Senate Military Affairs Committee, agreed.

Johnson met privately with Texas Governor "Pappy" O'Daniel, who assured him that he had no intention of running for Sheppard's seat. Having resisted suggestions that he resign the governorship and let Lieutenant Governor Coke Stevenson appoint him interim senator while he campaigned for a six-year term, O'Daniel seemed to be operating in good faith.

Later that day, when he appointed eighty-six-year-old Andrew Jackson Houston, Sam Houston's son, O'Daniel eliminated the advantage of incumbency from the campaign. Houston, who would die on June 26, two days before the election, was too frail to think of running for a regular term. Houston's appointment also left open the possibility that O'Daniel would later join the race. The fact that O'Daniel had coupled his appointment of Houston with an appeal to Texans for "advice, prayers, and suggestions" on whether he should seek the job convinced many observers that he would run. Lyndon mistakenly took him at his word.

In backing Johnson, Roosevelt was betting on a long shot. A statewide poll published on April 21 showed Lyndon with only 5 percent of the vote. O'Daniel commanded support of 33 percent of the state's voters, while Gerald C. Mann, the Texas attorney general, had 26 percent and Martin Dies, the east Texas congressman from Orange, had 9 percent. Twenty-seven candidates entered what some national magazines would call the "Screwball Election in Texas" or the "Screwy Texas Race."

At the beginning of May, O'Daniel seemed certain to become a candidate and the odds-on favorite. A superb actor and salesman, O'Daniel had established himself as the most successful vote-getter in Texas political history. In 1927, at the age of thirty-seven, he had come from Kansas to Fort Worth, where he became the sales manager for a flour manufacturer. He increased sales by advertising the company's Light Crust Flour on a local radio station. A country and western band played and sang sentimental and religious tunes he had composed. Calling himself "Pappy," O'Daniel was introduced at the start of each show by a woman asking him to "Please pass the biscuits, Pappy." By 1938, Pappy had organized a band consisting of his two sons and a daughter that made personal appearances with him around the state. His radio show had begun reaching millions of Texans on a statewide network. "At twelve-thirty sharp each day," a national magazine reported, "a fifteen-minute silence reigned in the state of Texas, broken only by mountain music, and the dulcet voice of W. Lee O'Daniel." That year, he had asked listeners if he should run for governor, and when more than 50,000 wrote to say, "yes," he had declared himself a candidate. He had won the governorship and been reelected in 1940 despite a failure to deliver on any campaign promises. He seemed certain to win the Senate race.

Johnson and Wirtz mapped a campaign to overcome the advantages of O'Daniel, Mann, and Dies. Their first goal was to raise a large campaign fund which would allow them to finance a better traveling circus than O'Daniel's and to blitz the state with campaign material that would make Johnson a household name. In addition, they planned to emphasize Johnson's ties to FDR, cultivate black and Mexican voters, and publicize the weaknesses of the three frontrunners.

Raising large sums of money proved to be easier than Johnson and Wirtz had thought possible. No candidate outdid Lyndon in attracting financial support. The campaign "was Brown & Root funded," Lyndon said later. The Browns gave nearly $300,000. Bonuses of $150,800 listed in fraudulent minutes of December 27, 1940, were paid to key corporate officers in the spring of 1941 and then transferred in checks and cash to Johnson's campaign. According to a 1944 Internal Revenue Service report, another $19,600 in phony attorneys' fees, some of them from Victoria Gravel Company, a Brown & Root subsidiary, ran "from the taxpayer to the Johnson Campaign Fund." A $100,000 bonus paid by the W. S. Bellows Construction Company, another Brown & Root subsidiary, also found its way into Johnson's Senate race. A petty cash account or "slush fund" at Brown & Root was tapped as well for campaign money. There was more: Perhaps another $200,000 came in from northern labor unions and businessmen, independent Texas oil men, and Charles Marsh.

The Johnson campaign used some of its money for a traveling road show that outdid O'Daniel's. As soon as O'Daniel entered the race, the Johnson managers looked for ways to turn their rallies into something more than set speeches by the candidate. At first they tried a "Band Concert and Rally" that featured a speech by Lyndon identifying him with Roosevelt's "defense of democracy against aggression." They next tried a mix of songs, poems, and local speakers in a "Program" emphasizing America's, Roosevelt's, and Johnson's virtues in this time of crisis. Things only came together, however, when they turned to Harfield Weedin, a Houston radio personality and advertising executive. Agreeing to pay him $1,000 a week, put airplanes at his disposal, and use his ad agency, the Johnson people accurately foresaw that Weedin could make their rallies exciting enough to attract large crowds and put votes in Lyndon's column.

Crowd reactions and statewide polls demonstrated the effectiveness of Johnson's campaign. In early June, when Supreme Court Justice William O. Douglas, who was motoring crosscountry with his family, pulled into Big Spring in west Texas, a town of 10,000 people, Lyndon was "pouring it on" to an audience of 3,000. "Every time he mentioned your name," Douglas wrote FDR, "the crowd cheered. Every time he mentioned [Charles] Lindbergh the crowd booed. It was an enthusiastic Roosevelt crowd." A voter survey published on June 8 showed that Lyndon still trailed his three principal rivals, but his share of the vote had risen to 19.4 percent; he was only 7.6 percent behind Gerald Mann, who led O'Daniel by about one percent and Dies by almost 3.5 percent. By June 21, however, Johnson was in a virtual deadlock with O'Daniel and Mann for the lead.

Twenty-four hours after the polls closed on Saturday June 28, with 96 percent of the vote counted, Lyndon led O'Daniel by 5,150 votes. The next day the Texas Election Bureau and newspapers around the state declared Johnson the unofficial winner. Johnson campaign workers were jubilant, parading around the Stephen F. Austin Hotel with Lyndon on their shoulders. Lyndon was so confident of victory that he "practically hired a staff."

But Johnson and Wirtz underestimated the resourcefulness of a coalition of political forces determined to put O'Daniel in the Senate, or more precisely, to get him out of the governor's chair. Two days before the election, Mayor Tom Miller of Austin told Charles Marsh that Lyndon had a lead in the race, but "gambling, horse racing and whiskey-beer combination will throw behind O'Daniel to get him out of state. [Coke] Stevenson [the lieutenant governor] may become Governor and stop prohibition drive which O'Daniel started last week."

Their confidence rested on knowing how many votes they needed to win and how to get them after the polls were closed. On Sunday, the 29th, with some 18,000 rural east Texas votes still to be counted, the anti-O'Daniel beer and liquor interests conspired with fifteen state senators to put enough of these ballots in O'Daniel's column to give him the election. In these east Texas counties, where initial results had shown a plurality for Dies, O'Daniel suddenly became the leading vote-getter. By Monday night, June 30, Lyndon's lead had fallen to 77 votes and by Tuesday evening O'Daniel held a 1,095-vote advantage.

Lyndon put the best possible face on his defeat. Lady Bird remembered how he looked when he walked off to catch a plane for Washington, "very jaunty, and putting extra verve into his step. His head was high, and he was stepping along real spryly. I know how much nerve and effort were now required for him to keep up that courageous appearance." In fact, he was "in a very black mood," and even Roosevelt could not cheer him up. The President "kidded the hell out of him": "'Lyndon, up in New York the first thing they taught us was to sit on the ballot boxes.'" What partly kept him going was the thought of another go round: "Did you ever see a shooting gallery with its circular, rotating discs with lots of pipes and rabbits on the circuit?" he asked Tommy Corcoran. "Well, when you miss one the first time, you get a second chance. And the sonofabitch who trimmed you will always come up again. And then you can get him."

The elections of 1940 and 1941 had reminded Lyndon that Texas and national politics were not for the fainthearted. The violations of campaign finance laws and ballot box manipulations were hardly revelations to him. But the 1940 House victories and the 1941 Senate defeat had convinced him as never before that politics was a dirty business in which a willingness to be more unprincipled than your opponents was a requirement for success. It was a lesson which would have echoes throughout the rest of his political career. Likewise, the fact that his identification with FDR as a new South politician had gone far to give him an edge over O'Daniel strongly impressed itself on him. The popularity of Roosevelt's domestic and defense programs in Texas was something he filed away for use in a future state-wide race.

:: NAVY SERVICE

Lyndon described the months after his defeat as "the most miserable in his life. I felt terribly rejected, and I began to think about leaving politics and going home to make money." In the end, he "couldn't bear to leave Washington," where he saw important work in response to the European war. Moreover, the Japanese attack on Pearl Harbor on December 7 and American involvement in the fighting decisively shifted Johnson's focus from politics to winning the war.

Lyndon had already prepared to serve the country by obtaining an appointment as a U.S. Naval Reserve officer. In the spring of 1940, when Nazi victories in Europe made it seem that the United States might eventually be drawn into the war, he applied for a commission. Although he "had not trained a day to qualify for it," as he told a friend and had several physical problems — chronic tonsilitis and sinusitis, a kidney ailment, and skin rashes brought on by nervous tension — he received his naval appointment as a lieutenant commander.

Lyndon asked the President to assign him "immediately to active duty with the Fleet." Although he became one of the first members of Congress to enter the armed services, he had no preparation for combat and the navy refused to assign him to a warship.

Lyndon did not appeal the navy's decision but chose instead "to work on production and manpower problems" that were slowing the output of ships and planes. He was assigned to the Navy Under Secretary's office, where he took responsibility for war production in Texas and on the West Coast. It was an assignment for which he was well qualified. Bottlenecks in the production of warships, troop transports, and merchantmen was jeopardizing the war effort. During the second half of 1941, despite plans for expansion, fewer navy and cargo ships were produced than in the first half of the year. In January, 1942, Roosevelt stressed the need to strain every existing arms-producing facility to the maximum, asking, for example, that merchant ships increase nearly sixfold from 1.1 million tons in 1941 to 6 million tons in 1942 and to 10 million tons in 1943. A lack of transports that would inhibit major troop movements for the next two years informed the President's goals. Similarly, shortages of skilled labor and the inefficient use of available manpower created production tie ups that plagued the country throughout the nearly four years of fighting.

Characteristically, Johnson threw himself into his war work with unbridled energy. For four months beginning at the end of December he spent most of his time traveling in Texas, California, and the state of Washington, trying to assess the labor needs of war production plants and to suggest answers to their problems. Everywhere he went he found a variety of administrative and technical difficulties that reflected what he saw as a deeper problem, namely, that Americans weren't yet sure what the war was about. In particular, Johnson complained of a division of authority that immobilized attempts to get the most from available resources. "The word 'conference' is coming to mean lost man hours," he said in a memo. It is time to quit 'conferring' and to go to work."

Despite some success in advancing war production, Lyndon quickly found himself frustrated by bureaucratic problems. He wanted a larger arena for his talents, which could serve his political interests as well as the war effort. He believed that a future successful bid for higher office would partly depend on a record of significant war service. As one friend told him, "Get your ass out of this country at once where there is danger, and then get back as soon as you can to real work. If you can't sell the Navy on ordering you out, you are not as good as I think you are."

Lyndon lived up to his friend's expectations. The President gave him an assignment to his liking. At a White House meeting, Roosevelt told him: "Will send you to Southwest Pacific on job for me re our men there. We may need to take additional steps for their health and happiness. You won't need to stay at Pearl Harbor but a couple of days then you can go to Australia New Zealand etc."

It is difficult to know what Roosevelt intended in sending Johnson to the Southwest Pacific. It simply may have been his way of accommodating Lyndon's wishes. But he also could have wanted a firsthand report from a loyal subordinate on the state of morale among America's fighting men in the area. When they talked in late April, Allied fortunes against the Japanese were at a low ebb. Guam and Wake Island, Burma, the Philippines, the Malay Peninsula, including Singapore, the Dutch East Indies, and some of New Guinea and the Solomon Islands had fallen, or were about to fall to Japanese arms. The victories opened Australia, New Zealand, and India to invasion and put Japan on the verge of what Roosevelt called "a dominating position from which it would prove most difficult to eject her." Despite promises of help to General Douglas MacArthur, first in the Philippines and then in Australia, where he had taken command of all Allied forces in the Southwest Pacific in March, Roosevelt had found it impossible to send men and matériel in the numbers MacArthur had requested. By sending Lyndon Johnson, Roosevelt may have been offering MacArthur and his staff a small gesture of concern to help sustain morale until desperately needed aid could begin to arrive in the region.

Whatever Roosevelt intended, Lyndon aimed to get firsthand information on America's fighting men in the Pacific and a taste of combat that tested his courage and gave him something to advertise in future political campaigns. Bryce Harlow, who was on General George C. Marshall's staff in 1942, remembered that Lyndon was one of four congressmen in the service for whom he arranged "a special escort through a combat area. . . . It was really, of course, a political charade." But it was more than that. Although the political gain from getting close to the action was a central consideration with Lyndon, he also hoped to advance the war effort by assessing conditions on the front line.

Leaving Washington, D.C., on May 2, it took him six days to reach Honolulu. He stayed there for five days waiting to fly to Auckland, New Zealand. After three days in Auckland, he flew to Melbourne, where he met MacArthur on May 25. Johnson convinced MacArthur and his staff to let him participate in a combat mission as a way to "see personally for the President just what conditions were like."

Johnson's insistence on observing an air raid was reckless. The attacks by American B-25 and B-26 medium bombers against Japanese bases in Rabaul on New Britain Island and Lae on New Guinea had cost American air forces heavy casualties in men and planes. Lacking effective fighter cover for the bombers and unable to match the quality of the Japanese Zero fighters and the skill of the Japanese pilots at this early stage of the war, American raiders sometimes lost a quarter of their planes and crews on a mission. The raid including Johnson on June 9 against Lae consisted of three B-17 heavy bombers attacking from 30,000 feet, followed by twelve B-25s that were to draw off the Zeros at 18,000 feet while twelve B-26s were to drop their bombs from only 10,000 feet.

During the one-hour flight to the target Johnson was all over the plane seeing everything he could. As they approached Lae, two dozen Zeros broke off their engagement with the B-25s to attack the B-26s before they made their bombing run. The "Wabash Cannonball" was quickly hit by cannon fire and crashed into the ocean killing the entire crew. Meanwhile, Lyndon's plane, the "Heckling Hare," had lost power in one engine and couldn't make the final approach to the target. Instead, Walter Greer, the pilot, had to drop out of formation, jettison his bombs, and turn for home. Eight Zeros came after the crippled plane. Going into a weaving, skidding dive to escape the pursuers, Greer managed to keep from being shot down. But not without absorbing hits on the wings and fuselage from the attacking Zeros. "I sure am glad to be back on this ground," Johnson exclaimed after they landed. "It's been very interesting," he told the crew as he left. He was "as cool as ice," one of them remembered.

On June 18, Johnson had another meeting with MacArthur. After listening to an hour-long report, MacArthur concluded the meeting by announcing that Johnson would receive a Silver Star. The crew members who died on the "Wabash Cannonball" received only Purple Hearts, while Johnson was the only one on the "Heckling Hare" who got a medal for the June 9 mission.

It is difficult not to suspect political back scratching. Lyndon went home with a "war record" and a medal and MacArthur had a new vocal advocate in Washington with some access to the President and more to Congress and the press. Indeed, even before Johnson left Melbourne, American newspapers carried stories about his participation in the raid on Lae and how he "got a good first-hand idea of the troubles and problems confronting our airmen."

:: PERSONAL GAIN

After coming home, Lyndon was eager to leave the navy and return to Congress, where he saw important war work. But his hopes of exercising greater influence in the House were undermined when the Republicans gained forty-four seats in the 1942 elections, cutting the Democrats' advantage in the House to thirteen. Lyndon was particularly worried that the Republicans might run the House with the help of some conservative Democrats and that while Democrats would chair committees, the Republicans might actually control them.

Lyndon's discouragement partly related to concern that an Internal Revenue Service investigation of Brown & Root might lead to criminal indictments against the Browns for income tax evasion and mean the destruction of his political career. In the fall of 1941 two deputy IRS collectors advised intelligence agents in Washington that Brown & Root "had unlawfully evaded a large part of its income taxes for the year 1940 and was expected to use the same method in evading larger tax liability for the year 1941." An audit of B & R in June 1942 aroused further suspicions and led to inquiries about the "business expenses," "attorneys' fees," and "bonuses" that had in fact gone into Johnson's Senate campaign. In September, the IRS concluded that a "full investigation" was necessary and agents were assigned to the case.

In the fall of 1942 the possibility that the investigation would lead to his political demise moved Lyndon to consider an alternative career and means of support. Yet even if he remained in Congress, he wanted to cash in on the booming war economy, as many others in Texas and around the country were, to build a nest egg for his family.

Lyndon was also eager to find an outlet for Lady Bird's considerable talents. Like him, she had strong ambitions. And until the fall of 1942 she had largely channeled them into Lyndon's career. To meet their mutual desire for larger earnings and Lady Bird's gainful employment, they considered buying a newspaper, a prospect that especially appealed to Bird, whose interest in journalism dated from her college years. But instead, Lyndon and Lady Bird decided to go after KTBC, a failing radio station in Austin. Although Lyndon didn't "know anything about running a radio station," he quickly recognized that favorable rulings from the Federal Communications Commission (FCC) could turn the station into a profitable business. He had good reason to believe that the FCC would be responsive to his requests.

Lyndon privately acknowledged that political considerations were involved. When Elliott Roosevelt, FDR's son, who was in the radio business in Texas, heard that the Johnsons had bought KTBC, he sent word through John Connally that they were going to take business away from his stations by keeping KTBC alive and that he intended to retaliate in any way he could. The Johnsons replied that their acquisition of KTBC prevented its purchase by "enemies of the Congressman, enemies of Elliott and enemies of the President. It was purely and simply a question of having a friend or a foe operating the other station. It was not a question of the station going out of existence at all."

Lyndon's involvement in a business that largely depended on the actions of a Federal agency for its success created a clear conflict between his private interests and public position. Although he later insisted that he had never lobbied the FCC in behalf of KTBC and that he had never cast a congressional vote on a controversial radio or television issue, he was less than candid. His close identification with the Roosevelt administration and ties to FCC commissioners played a part in the uniform and rapid consent Lady Bird won for all her requests serving KTBC. Moreover, the fact that Lyndon was a well-connected congressman could hardly have been lost on the various businessmen he or, in most cases, his agents pressed for commitments to KTBC.

In acquiring and turning the station into a profitable enterprise, Lyndon was walking a thin ethical line. But he never saw it that way. To him, the chance to acquire KTBC was essentially a reward for public service well done. In his eyes he was doing no more than seizing an opportunity in a free enterprise system to make a lot of money by hard work and aggressive business practices. Initially, however, it meant even more to him — the possibility for an alternative livelihood should his political career come to a sudden end. And during 1943, as the IRS investigation of Brown & Root went forward, this remained a serious concern. In the ten months after the inquiry resumed in January, the IRS had concluded that fraud had been committed and that Brown & Root owed back taxes of approximately $1,161,000, including about $300,000 in fraud penalties. In addition, criminal charges for alleged fraud and perjury by B & R officers and employees made it possibile that some people would go to jail. But Johnson and Alvin Wirtz persuaded the President to kill the investigation. Under pressure from the White House, the IRS assessed B & R only $372,000 in back taxes.

:: FAITHFUL NEW DEALER

At the same time the IRS investigation posed a threat to Lyndon's congressional career, a shift to the right in Texas and nationally also made him doubt his political future. Despite the shift in mood, he continued to speak out for New Deal liberalism. In May 1943, for example, he made a state-wide appeal in Texas for postwar internationalism that closely reflected administration thinking. At the same time, when a conservative coalition in Congress of southern Democrats and Republicans began an assault on the "social gains of the last ten years" by liquidating the NYA and the National Resources Planning Board, cutting the budget of the Farm Security Administration, and threatening to weaken the Securities and Exchange Commission and the Holding Company Act, Lyndon was one of a handful of congressmen asked by administration leaders to hold the line and win support for tax and other legislation it wished to steer through Congress.

Shortly after, Roosevelt, in the most radical speech he ever gave, declared the need for a strong program of economic stabilization and an economic bill of rights. He called for a tax on all unreasonable profits, and "a useful and remunerative job" for all Americans. In February, when the Congress passed a tax bill that raised $2.3 billion in new revenues instead of the $10.5 billion FDR asked, Lyndon voted against the substitute measure. Moreover, when FDR vetoed the bill as providing relief "not for the needy but for the greedy," Lyndon was one of only ninety-five House members voting to sustain the President's veto.

By 1944, both Rayburn and Lyndon felt that they were fighting for their political lives. Targeted by Texas reactionaries as principal advocates of Roosevelt's drive to replace free enterprise and political liberty with socialism and dictatorship, Rayburn and Johnson were subjected to the strongest attacks they had yet experienced in their public careers. In a campaign costing nearly $200,000—which Rayburn said was more than had been spent on an election in the Fourth District "in the past 30 years combined"— Rayburn's opponent, a Texas state senator, saturated the district with charges that the Speaker favored "creeping socialism" and the Fair Employment Practices Commission (FEPC), a "Negro controlled" federal agency. Pointing to the extraordinary gains his north Texas constituents had made during his sixteen terms in the House and especially under the New Deal, Rayburn won, but only by 6,000 votes out of the 43,000 cast.

Although the challenge to Johnson proved to be less substantial, Lyndon had to take it seriously. His opponents mounted shrill attacks that did Lyndon more good than harm. By appealing to racial antagonisms with assertions that Johnson favored the destruction of the "white primary," calling him a "millionaire," and describing him as friendly to labor racketeers and hostile to war veterans, they aroused indignation in Johnson's favor. Carrying nine of the ten counties in his district, Lyndon won by a margin of almost two and a half to one.

Lyndon entered 1945 in an upbeat mood. He was particularly pleased at the birth of his and Lady Bird's first child. After nearly ten years of marriage, during which three miscarriages had deprived them of children and caused them much sadness, Lady Bird gave birth to a healthy girl in March 1944. At the same time, he took great satisfaction from the progress of his political and business fortunes. The settlement of the Brown & Root tax case coupled with his and FDR's reelections in 1944 rekindled his hopes for a higher elected or appointed office.

In 1945, Lyndon's political fortunes remained closely tied to FDR's presence in the White House. Despite some differences with the administration in the war years, Johnson continued to be seen, especially in Texas, as an unqualified pro-Roosevelt man. Although Lyndon had never been a true White House insider, he was nevertheless an ally with meaningful ties to the President that would echo through the rest of his political career. But on April 12, 1945, Johnson's reliance on FDR's political support ended when the President died suddenly of a brain hemorrhage.

Like so many other Americans, Johnson was devastated. He had a profound sense of loss. As he told a reporter later that day, "'I was just looking up at a cartoon on the wall [of Rayburn's office]—a cartoon showing the President with that cigarette holder and his jaw stuck out like it always was. He had his head cocked back, you know. And then I thought of all the little folks, and what they had lost. He was just like a daddy to me always; he always talked to me just that way. . . . I don't know that I'd ever have come to Congress if it hadn't been for him. But I do know I got my first great desire for public office because of him—and so did thousands of other young men all over the country.'" A secretary remembered that Lyndon's "grief was just unreal. He just literally wasn't taking phone calls and he just literally shut himself up. His grief was vast and deep and he was crying tears. Manly tears, but he actually felt . . . that it was just like losing his father." The day of Roosevelt's funeral he was so upset he went to bed. And his grief lasted for weeks and months.

Roosevelt's passing engendered a profound sense of loss in millions of Americans, but it did not mean the end of the ideas and programs launched in the preceding twelve years. Johnson, like others in and out of the government, was a bearer of the New Deal legacy. Although he would tack back and forth between liberalism and conservatism in the next fifteen years, positioning himself to run for the Senate and the presidency, he never forgot the lessons learned from the Roosevelt era: A sound economy, social justice, and national security depended in large measure on a wise use of Federal power by the White House and the Congress. The states, localities, and private enterprise all had a significant role to play in assuring the national well-being, but Federal action was a requirement of change and progress. This was especially true for the South, which Johnson believed had the most to gain from Federal economic and racial policies. And though he cautiously felt his way on these matters from 1945 to 1960, often letting expediency guide him into actions that angered progressive Democrats, he was a liberal nationalist biding his time until circumstances favored a new round of activism that would carry the country beyond where it had been when FDR passed from the scene.

:: POSTWAR POLITICS

Roosevelt's death and the end of the war in 1945 opened up a period of uncertainty in Johnson's life. He remained eager to get to the Senate, but with FDR gone and a more conservative mood settling over the country, he saw the need for a sea change in his political identity. He was not about to abandon the New Deal faith; indeed, whenever possible he continued to vote for liberal measures that seemed unlikely to get much attention in Texas.

Publicly, however, he presented a different picture of himself. Republican control of the House and Senate after the 1946 elections strengthened his belief that his political future depended on a turn to the right. Consequently, in 1947–48, he established a conservative track record on labor, civil rights, and off-shore or tideland oil rights—all highly visible and emotional issues in Texas that would make or break a candidate for statewide office.

With organized labor alienating voters across the country by a series of unpopular strikes, the Congress tried to rein in unions with the Taft-Hartley bill, which prohibited the closed shop or the right of labor organizations to keep jobs from non-union workers. In June, 1947, Lyndon joined 102 Democrats and 217 Republicans in approving the bill. Later in the month, he voted with 105 Democrats and 225 Republicans to override Truman's veto. When the issue generated the greatest volume of mail ever received by Johnson's office, most of it favoring his support of Taft-Hartley, he answered that his vote served the interests of all the people and that he shared the widespread desire to control "irresponsible, racketeering, self-inflated labor leaders."

On civil rights as well he unequivocally went along with the opposition of most Texas voters. During his congressional career he had kept a low profile over the issue of black rights, shunning all controversy. Conditions in 1946–48, however, changed this. Anti-black violence in the South coupled with defections of black voters to the Republican party in 1946 moved Truman to appoint a civil rights committee that would propose Federal means of defending the rights of all Americans. In October 1947, the committee's book-length report, *To Secure These Rights*, provided detailed recommendations for stronger legal machinery to protect civil rights and broaden equality of opportunity. On February 2, 1948, Truman sent a "Special Message to the Congress on Civil Rights," an unprecedented act for an American President. He asked for anti-lynching and anti-poll tax laws, a permanent Fair Employment Practices Commission, a permanent Commission on Civil Rights, and a Joint Congressional Committee on Civil

Rights to consider the need for other legislation. The President's message touched off an explosion of southern opposition that made civil rights questions a litmus test for office seekers throughout the South. "I am certain that I express the attitude of Texas when I state that I am unequivocally opposed to this fantastic federal idea of Negro-white social equality," one Austin citizen wired Johnson.

In private Johnson was ready to acknowledge that "there is much that can be said for their [the black, pro-civil rights] viewpoint." He also described himself as horrified by lynching and opposed to a poll tax. "I have no racial or religious prejudices," Johnson wrote in a form letter he sent to all advocates of the President's civil rights program. "I have always defended, and shall continue to defend, the right of every citizen, regardless of race, color, or creed, to all the liberties guaranteed by our Constitution." But that same Constitution, he argued, inhibited the federal government from appropriating the rights of the states to legislate against lynching and other crimes and on the qualifications of voters. Nor did the federal government have the constitutional power to say whom an individual had to hire, no more than it had the right to say for whom an individual had to work. Opponents of the President's program who wrote Johnson received no lecture on constitutional principles; only assurances that he had "voted against all anti-poll tax, anti-lynching, and all FEPC legislation since I came to Congress and expect to continue to do so."

The growing influence of the oil industry in Texas, state revenues produced by offshore oil fields, and a resurgent concern with states' rights made the tidelands oil question another matter on which a state-wide candidate had to take a stand. In September 1945, Truman issued a proclamation claiming federal jurisdiction and control over offshore oil. Led by the South and California, the Congress passed a joint resolution in the summer of 1946 nullifying the proclamation and asserting state control. The President vetoed the resolution, saying the Supreme Court should decide the question, and the House narrowly sustained his veto. Away in Texas, Johnson conveniently took no position on the issue. In April 1948, after the Supreme Court had decided that the Federal government had paramount rights to the tidelands, the House overturned the Court's ruling by affirming the states' title to submerged lands and natural resources three miles off their shores. Lyndon voted with the 93 Democrats and 163 Republicans approving the bill. Although it died in the Senate, his vote insulated him from potential political attacks.

If there was substantial expediency in Johnson's conservative labor, civil rights, and tidelands votes, he was genuinely in tune with patriotic and

nationalistic impulses in postwar Texas that favored greater federal spending for national defense. Between the end of the war in 1945 and the spring
of 1948, Johnson had remained vitally interested in national security affairs,
serving on the Naval Affairs Committee, the Armed Services Committee,
which replaced the Naval and the Military Affairs committees in 1947, and
the Joint Committee on Atomic Energy. His contributions to their work
gave him great satisfaction and allowed him to strike a resonant chord with
most Texans.

Lyndon was not shy about advertising his national defense work. In the
spring of 1946, he arranged to have Assistant Secretary of War for Air Stuart Symington, with whom he had established a warm friendship, visit
Texas, where there were the largest number of air bases in any state.
Symington's inspection of air fields and luncheon and dinner talks, which
Lyndon hosted, served the congressman's political standing in his home
district and throughout the state.

The same applied at the end of 1946, when he openly protested the efforts
of Standard Oil of California to amend its contract with the Navy Department for the development and operation of the Elk Hills Naval Petroleum
Reserve. Johnson publicly objected that the contract changes "are unrelated
to the conservation of oil in the Elk Hills Reserve and would be detrimen-
tal to the financial interest of the United States." Putting his case in a statement to the Naval Affairs Committee and in letters to President Truman and
Secretary Forrestal, Johnson won praise from some citizens. "The Congressman was from a state that had a very big stake in oil," Lyndon's friend,
the attorney Donald Cook later said, "and yet when he had the choice to
make—namely between an oil company orientation and being a true patriot
in every sense of the word—he made what I regarded . . . as the right
choice."

But Lyndon wasn't quite as heroic on the Elk Hills dispute as Cook
believed. If his outspokeness pitted him against Standard Oil of California,
it had no direct impact on Texas oil companies. It also sat well with most
Texas voters, who shared Johnson's genuine concern to put the national
security of the United States above the interests of any single corporation,
oil or otherwise.

As tensions with the Soviet Union mounted in Europe and the Near
East in 1947, Johnson became more attentive to foreign affairs. On one
hand, he was genuinely concerned about a Communist threat to national
security, and on the other, he was sensitive to what would serve him best
in a 1948 Senate campaign. He satisfied both purposes by supporting Truman's Doctrine in March 1947 aiding Greece and Turkey and Marshall's

Plan in June to rebuild Western Europe's economy. European tensions in March 1948 allowed him further to emphasize his service to the nation and Texas in behalf of national defense. During the month, a Soviet-sponsored coup brought Czechoslovakia firmly into the Communist camp, and Soviet-American tensions mounted over plans to create an independent West German state aligned with the West. After the West European nations signed a collective defense agreement in Brussels, President Truman asked a joint session of Congress to restore the draft, pass a Universal Military Training law, and fund the Marshall Plan. Lyndon sent Truman an approving letter, and urged him to suspend the "sale at sacrifice prices [of] various plants and housing projects constructed during the last war . . . because . . . [they] may be urgently required in a matter of days." Releasing his letter to the press and radio, it "received wide use," and encouraged one of Lyndon's aides to suggest that he hold a press conference: "it would be a good opportunity to get some wide play in Texas at this time."

On no defense issue, however, did Johnson push harder in the spring of 1948 than a 70-group air force of 12,441 planes. Johnson became the chief House advocate of the program. In private letters, public speeches, the press, before the Armed Services Committee, and on the floor of the House, he urged a rapid and sustained buildup of air power that would assure America's safety from air attack and secure the peace. "What was the Seventy Group Air Force?" Bryce Harlow, a professional staff member of the House Armed Services Committee in 1947, later said. "Nobody knew. . . . It could be as big or as little as 'group' meant. It was a slogan superbly drawn up by the air force and merchandised beautifully by Symington."

Seventy groups meant federal money serving the Texas economy: "The House passed a 70-group Air Force appropriation just the other day, and I have hopes that it will be successful in passing the Senate," Johnson wrote the manager of the Brownwood, Texas, Chamber of Commerce. "Once this 70-group program becomes a law, then we can anticipate an expansion in the Air Program in the State of Texas."

Although much of what Johnson did in 1947 and early 1948 was calculated to help him in a Senate race, he was not sure that he would run. Unlike 1941, a Senate bid now meant giving up his House seat and a possible end to his political career. Such an outcome, however, did not put him off entirely. In 1947 Lady Bird had given birth to Lucy Baines Johnson, their second child, and the thought of managing their lucrative radio business, acquiring a television station, and spending more time with his family were alternatives with which Lyndon believed he could live. Yet politics remained his vocational passion, and he could not easily accommodate himself to the thought of giving up his House seat.

Lyndon's caution was well advised. There was much to suggest that he would not win. In the spring of 1947, Joe Belden, the Texas pollster, took initial soundings on the 1948 Senate race. In a contest between Johnson and Pappy O'Daniel, Johnson was projected as a clear winner: 64 percent of the sample said they would vote for Johnson. The poll demonstrated what Texas political observers already knew—namely, that O'Daniel's performance in the Senate, particularly appeals for isolation from world affairs and bitter attacks on unions and Federal officials as setting up a Communist dictatorship, had alienated Democratic colleagues and limited his ability to represent Texas. Further, revelations of highly profitable business dealings shattered his reputation as a man of the people and assured that he would not win a second term. O'Daniel's political vulnerability, however, was small comfort to Lyndon. Former Governor Coke Stevenson and incumbent Governor Beauford Jester, two other potential candidates, defeated O'Daniel by three-to-one margins and seemed likely to beat Johnson in a Senate race.

Johnson genuinely feared losing and had substantial reservations about making the physical and emotional sacrifices tied to a Senate race. Yet, as he later told Doris Kearns, feeling that "something was missing from [his] life" and wanting, as one friend remembered, "to be Senator more than anything else in the world," he quietly planned a campaign in the spring of 1948. He announced his candidacy at an afternoon press conference in the Driskill Hotel in Austin on May 12.

Although he viewed his decision as possibly marking the end of his political career, he exuded confidence to the assembled journalists and friends. He deserved to be a Senator, he said. He had actually won the seat in 1941 against O'Daniel but his opponents had altered the tally to deprive him of the victory. "I was urged to contest that result, but I tried to be a good sport. Lots of people said they'd support me next time, but the war intervened. . . . I know the fair-minded people of Texas will help me win that promotion to which I came so close before." He emphasized that his long service in the Congress, his youthfulness and energy compared with that of his opponents, his accomplishments in helping raise the living standard of all his constituents, his experience on the Armed Services and Atomic Energy committees, where he had schooled himself in the great issues of war and peace, all made him the best candidate for the office and demonstrated that he would be a highly effective senator. His announcement began a political struggle that would echo through the rest of his public career.

:: "LANDSLIDE LYNDON"

Johnson's decision to run for the Senate triggered an explosion of activity. With less than eleven weeks to go before the July 24 election, Lyndon faced a formidable challenge. Winning over a majority of the more than 1.2 million Democrats who would vote in the party primary seemed too much to achieve in so short a time. If he could hold Coke Stevenson under 50 percent, while he ran a close second, he could force a one-on-one run-off that would give him another month to overcome Stevenson's lead. The campaign was a decisive moment in his career: He would either become a U.S. Senator or lose his House seat and the eleven years of seniority and influence that went with it. Johnson launched the most energetic, all-consuming drive for office he had ever made.

To get his name and message before the electorate and overcome Stevenson's lead in the polls, Johnson and John Connally hit on the idea of using a helicopter. An uncommon aircraft in 1948, it seemed certain to draw a crowd wherever Johnson went. In addition, it promised to give Johnson greater capacity to speak in more towns in a shorter period of time than if he traveled on commercial airlines between major cities and drove from one town to another. To avoid having the daily $250 rental cost charged to his primary campaign, which was limited by law to $10,000 in direct spending, Johnson invented the fiction that the Dallas Veterans for Johnson committee rented the craft. Naming his machine the Johnson City Windmill, Lyndon announced a plan on June 12 to go to every town in northeast Texas, and see folks who rarely met a candidate for state-wide office."

On June 15, Johnson launched his helicopter blitz of Texas that carried him to 118 cities and towns in the next seventeen days. Crisscrossing northern and central Texas, from Lubbock in the western panhandle to Texarkana on the Arkansas border and Austin in the south, Johnson reached over 175,000 people. On Sunday the 14th—after ordering that a loudspeaker be fastened to one of the landing gear struts and that his name be painted in large white letters on the sides—Johnson and "a retinue of about 14 people" had the first of what would become weekly strategy sessions on how to proceed during the next seven days. They agreed to have campaign workers reach each town before Lyndon and attend to the details of a successful visit. "I don't think we consciously realized we were starting a brand new era of advance men," one of Johnson's aides later said. But it occurred because Johnson wanted everything to go just right at each of his stops.

Lyndon quickly established a routine with the helicopter that effectively served his campaign. It not only allowed him to reach a larger audience, it also gave him an unprecedented means of capturing voter attention and fixing his name in their minds. Flying a few hundred feet above the ground, Johnson had the pilot hover over communities not on their itinerary, where he would shout over a loudspeaker, "Hello, down there. This is Lyndon Johnson; your candidate for the U.S. Senate." While he added a little spiel appealing for their votes, aides showered startled folks below with campaign leaflets. To make it easier to throw them out and reduce the temperature inside the craft, Johnson had the doors removed. Occasionally, Johnson had the pilot make unscheduled landings, where he would greet amazed onlookers personally. Aides also compiled lists of people in small towns between stops who at one time or another had written the congressman. As they flew over them, Johnson said: "Hello, there, Mr. Jones. This is your friend, Lyndon Johnson. I'm sorry we can't land today, but I want you to know that I'm up here thinking of you and appreciate your kind letter and comments. I just want you to be sure and tell your friends to vote for me at election time." The business of talking over the loudspeaker to folks between towns became so routine that Johnson had one of his aides or the pilot do it while he rested. Handing the microphone to one of them, Johnson would say, "Tell them about me."

During his time on the road, Johnson usually worked a twenty-hour day. He arose at five in the morning to make a local radio broadcast to farmers at six or 6:15. He then campaigned until noon when he took a three-hour break to clean up, eat lunch, and rest. Dirty and sweaty from the dust flying in the open doors of the helicopter and the summer heat, he showered, ate lunch in his pajamas, and took a brief nap before picking up his afternoon schedule. Often, though, the nap lost out to pressing phone calls, or meetings with staff and local people. The evening offered no pause from the hectic pace. Banquets and receptions followed by meetings to review the day's activities, especially the unexpected foul-ups, and the next day's schedule lasted most nights until two or three in the morning.

Johnson barely held up under the strain. By the end of the third week on the road Johnson could "hardly stand." At a reception in Lubbock he "was literally propped against the wall . . . with somebody on each side of him, because he was just at the point of total exhaustion." Too tired to speak, he greeted folks lined up to meet him by extending "his left hand with the little life that was still in it." Flying between towns during the day, he often fell asleep with his body stretched out and wrapped around the controls of the helicopter.

Underwriting Johnson's whole enterprise was a lot of money. Although Texas forbid spending more than $10,000 in a primary, the law had a huge loophole. The limit applied only to the candidate himself or the organization directly under his control. Campaign committees that "voluntarily" sprang up in support of a candidate could also spend money in his behalf. The Dallas Veterans for Johnson committee, which supposedly contributed the helicopter to the campaign, was only one case in point. Claude Wild, Johnson's campaign manager in 1941, and "Chairman of the Johnson-for-Senate committees" in 1948 was another. John Connally was the "campaign manager" and Wild headed up a group of so-called independent committees that spent a lot of money.

Convinced that certain defeat awaited anyone who tried to stay within the campaign spending limits, Johnson and Stevenson spent hundreds of thousands of dollars in their fight for the nomination. Stevenson later complained that Johnson "spent more than a million dollars." Johnson spent $30,000 in phone bills alone, someone inside the campaign later revealed. Johnson's spending on radio broadcasts must have exceeded that figure. During just 23 days in July, there were talks on local rural stations, regular 15-minute broadcasts every morning in Dallas, Wichita Falls, San Antonio, Houston, and Austin and seven state-wide night broadcasts. If it cost $1,500 for one state-wide radio speech, what did it cost the Johnson campaign for all the radio time it consumed? Stevenson didn't lag far behind in his spending. Why should he follow the $10,000 legal limitation while Stevenson ignored it with impunity? Johnson asked during the campaign.

Who financed Johnson's campaign? There were numerous backers: George and Herman Brown, Sid Richardson and Wesley West, independent oil producers; Amon Carter, the Fort Worth newspaper publisher and oilman; Houston Harte, the publisher of a dozen Texas newspapers; Maco Stewart, a Galveston insurance millionaire; Gus Wortham, the head of American General Insurance Companies in Houston; Hobart Taylor, Sr., a black Houston businessman and civic leader; the aircraft industry generally, and Hughes Aircraft in particular; and synthetic rubber producers. Attorney General Tom Clark, Washington lawyers Abe Fortas and Paul Porter, and Wall Street attorney Ed Weisl arranged contributions from wealthy New York attorneys and movie people like George Skouras of Twentieth Century-Fox and Howard Hughes of RKO. The exact cost of Johnson's campaign is unknown. It is clear, however, that he received large contributions, especially from Sid Richardson and the Browns. Richardson's support was in return for valuable help Johnson gave him in his business dealings with the Federal government and out of fondness for Johnson, whom he would fly to his privately owned island in the coastal Gulf for weekend socializing.

As in 1941, the Brown brothers were the biggest contributors. Did you help Johnson in the 1941 campaign? an interviewer asked George Brown in 1969. "'I did everything I could to help him get elected,'" Brown replied. "'. . . You were raising money for him?'" the interviewer asked. "'I didn't raise any money for him. I spent money of my own. . . .' Then in the future campaigns, did you also help Lyndon Johnson again?' 'Yes, in '48,'" Brown answered. "'In much the same way?'" the interviewer asked. "'In the same way.'" The Browns had more reason than ever to help in 1948. They were indebted to him not only for wartime ship-building contracts but also for two postwar deals that opened new opportunities for growth and profit. In 1946, when Johnson was a member of a House subcommittee on U.S. governance of former Japanese-controlled islands, the Browns won part of a $21 million Defense Department contract to build navy and air force bases on Guam.

The Browns profited even more from the acquisition of oil and natural gas pipelines built during World War II, which Johnson helped them buy from the government. They joined with Charles I. Francis, a Houston oil and gas attorney, and twenty-four others to form the Texas Eastern Transmission Company. It bought the Big Inch and Little Big Inch pipelines in February 1947 for $143 million, $12 or $13 million over what a competing group represented by Tommy Corcoran offered. Nine months later the twenty-eight original investors turned a $150,000 investment into a paper profit of $9,825,000, a 6,550 percent return. The pipelines carried crude oil and natural gas from east Texas to the northeastern United States and played a central part in helping Texas Eastern multiply its worth tenfold to $1.4 billion in the next twenty years.

Johnson needed the money to keep up with Stevenson, who was very popular. "Coke Stevenson was just like the Coca-Cola," a state legislator said. "He was a state-known product. . . . And the *Dallas News* had built up his image as 'our cowboy governor.'" Born in a log cabin in Kimble County in west-central Texas in 1888, Stevenson was a self-made man. Studying law while he worked in a bank as a janitor and a cashier, he built a successful law practice, became a county judge, entered the Texas House in 1928, and became its Speaker in 1933. His election as lieutenant governor in 1938 and 1940 made him governor when Pappy O'Daniel won the 1941 special election for senator. His five and a half years in the state house was a time of general prosperity, allowing him to turn a $30 million state deficit into a $35 million surplus. His personal characteristics joined with his successful management of state affairs to make him the most appealing Texas politician of his time.

Yet Stevenson was not as benign as his popular image made him appear. Sam Rayburn called him a "mountebank politician," and liberals viewed him as a reactionary who partly built a budget surplus by slashing state services. He reduced funds for river authorities, starved schoolteachers, and abolished the Old Age Assistance Special Fund, which supported the aged, the blind, and dependent children. The Texas writer and liberal J. Frank Dobie said, "Coke stands for dollars and he does not stand for civilized life as it is furthered by schools, hospitals, and other institutions that must be promoted at public expense." Stevenson was also a racist who denounced the Supreme Court's 1944 decision on black voting rights in Texas as a "monstrous threat to our peace and security." He refused to take any action against a wartime lynching in Texarkana, saying in private that "certain members of the Negro race from time to time furnish the setting for mob violence by the outrageous crimes which they commit." Stevenson was also an isolationist. In 1947 he opposed the Marshall Plan and said that some of the European nations were "beggars" and ought to do more for themselves. Dobie believed that Stevenson knew "as much about foreign affairs as a hog knows about Sunday."

Stevenson and his closest advisers hoped that they would win a majority of the vote on July 24 and avoid a run-off. In his 1942 and 1944 primary campaigns for Governor, Stevenson had won by record-setting margins and avoided run-offs. But his campaign against Johnson was a different matter. Running as an isolationist for a Senate seat was not the same as running for governor. Polls of June 20 and July 3 showed Stevenson with 46.6 and 46.5 percent of the vote. Johnson was a strong second in both polls, 36.8 percent in the first and 38.2 percent in the second. To reach 50 percent, the Stevenson forces encouraged the idea that George Peddy, who received only a 12 percent share in the June poll and 11 percent in July, had no chance to win or even come in second and that his supporters, who preferred Stevenson to Johnson, should vote for Stevenson now and save themselves the trouble of voting for him later in a run-off. But Peddy, who refused to concede, stepped up his campaign in the closing days of the race and raised his share of the vote to 14.5 percent in a poll published on July 21. The survey showed Johnson trailing Stevenson by only 4.4 percent, 38.8 to 43.2 percent.

The election on July 24 frustrated all three of the front runners. Stevenson, who won 477,077 of the 1.202 million votes or 40 percent, was forced into more campaigning in a five-week run-off. Peddy, who received 237,195 votes or a surprising 20 percent, was knocked out of the race. And Johnson, who won 405,617 votes or 34 percent, faced an almost insurmountable challenge. He trailed by over 71,000 votes, had won only 72 counties to Stevenson's 168 and had placed third behind Stevenson in all of the 14 Peddy counties. Lyndon needed to capture 200,000, or nearly two out of three, of the 320,000 votes cast for Peddy and the eight other minor candidates. "We thought we were going to come out of it winning or be real close to the top," Lady Bird said, "and we were overwhelmingly, vastly, horribly behind. . . . It looked hopeless."

However strong the momentary letdown, Johnson had no intention of quitting. If we work hard enough, we can win, he told his friends, and they all immediately resumed the campaign.

Unrelenting effort over the next five weeks pulled Johnson even with Stevenson. One opinion poll saw the election as too close to call. The initial returns on election day, Saturday, August 28, favored Stevenson. According to the Texas Election Bureau, an unofficial agency run by Texas newspapers, Stevenson led at midnight by 2,119 votes out of 939,468 counted. But Stevenson's lead evaporated the next day. By 9 p.m. Sunday Lyndon held a 693-vote edge out of 979,877, with an estimated 11,000 votes yet to be counted. By Monday evening, Stevenson had swung back into the lead by 119 votes with 400 ballots still uncounted. The following day, the 31st, the lead increased to 349 votes. When the Bureau gave its final unofficial return on September 2, Stevenson's lead stood at 362 votes.

During the five days after the election, both sides had jockeyed to ensure a favorable outcome. Recognizing that the greatest possible vigilance was essential in so close a contest, the Johnson and Stevenson camps monitored each other's actions. Remembering how early reporting of pro-Johnson counties in 1941 had told O'Daniel's men how many votes they needed to win and how a failure to watch east Texas counties closely had turned Lyndon's victory into a defeat, Johnson backers now withheld final official tallies in several of his counties for as long as possible and kept close watch on ballot boxes all over the state.

Both sides were well advised to watch the other. But in the last-minute manipulation of votes, the Stevenson campaign was no match for Johnson's. Bob Murphey, Stevenson's nephew and driver during the campaign, later told an interviewer: "We've got 254 counties in this state, and if you didn't change but 10 votes per county, you're talking about over 2,500 votes. And this was the strategy of the Johnson forces. We knew that. We had information, and it's kind of like fighting a war there."

The Johnson camp, seeing itself as "fighting fire with fire," put Johnson in the lead when the official returns came in to the state Democratic Executive Committee in Austin on September 3 and 4. The "corrected" returns on September 3 reduced Stevenson's total by 205 votes and increased Johnson's by 174, giving him a 17-vote lead. The biggest single shift had come from the town of Alice in Jim Wells County in south Texas, where Johnson received an additional 202 votes and Stevenson one. Other "corrections" from around the state the next day increased Johnson's lead to 162.

The altered results generated charges of fraud. On September 3, Stevenson complained that "it is becoming increasingly obvious that a concentrated effort is being made to count me out of this Senate race." Stevenson, convinced that he had won the actual election and that Johnson's victory rested on the superior ability of his campaign to manipulate final returns, tried to discredit the results in south Texas, an area notorious for boss rule, bloc voting, and doctored ballots. Like every close observer of Texas politics, Stevenson knew that south Texas counties had managed elections and that George Parr, the "Duke" of Duval County, was famous for arranging landslides for his chosen candidates. The heir to a political dynasty or political machine his father, Archer, had established early in the century, George was the patron of the county's Mexican-Americans, who outnumbered Anglos by two to one. In three of his state-wide races Stevenson had been the beneficiary of Parr's largesse, receiving majorities in Duval County of 3,643 to 141; 2,936 to 77; and 3,310 to 17. Committed to no ideology, except the survival of his machine, Parr favored and opposed politicians according to his needs.

The Stevenson people viewed the results in Duval and Jim Wells counties in south Texas as particularly open to suspicion. Returns from Duval on election day showed Johnson ahead, 4,197 to 40. The following day—during which Johnson turned an over-all 2,119-vote deficit into a 693-vote lead—Duval added 425 ballots to his total. The additional 203 votes from Box 13 in Alice in Jim Wells County, where Parr had a close alliance with Ed Lloyd, the local boss, seemed even more suspicious. In the corrected result given on September 3, six days after the election, the Alice officials had increased the total vote by nearly 25 percent, from 825 to 1,028. Since the local official had been given only about 600 ballots for Box 13 and only 499 votes had been cast for gubernatorial candidates and 501 for U.S. Senate contestants in the first primary, it was an astonishing total vote.

Stevenson tried to enlist the aid of state and Federal officials in challenging the results in south Texas. But almost no one was willing to help. Johnson discouraged an investigation by making clear that it would force Texas and Federal officials to confront publicly the widespread manipulation of ballots in a Texas election. Gathering a file on thirty "possible election irregularities which benefited Coke Stevenson," Johnson used a radio address on September 6 to mention some of these and put other political leaders on notice that a challenge to his election would embarrass them as well. Good-naturedly describing himself as "Landslide Lyndon," Johnson reminded listeners that he had not protested the questionable outcome in 1941.

Stevenson believed he had nothing to lose and everything to gain from pressing a challenge. But he had little hope that an Alice judge, who was a Parr ally, would allow a recanvass of the vote. Instead, they focused their attention on the State Democratic Executive Committee meeting on September 13 and the party's state convention on September 14 in Fort Worth. Under party rules the Committee was responsible for counting statewide primary returns from the counties and certifying the nominees for the fall elections. At a jam-packed meeting of the Executive committee on the 14th, it reported an 87-vote victory for Johnson.

But Stevenson wouldn't give up his fight and took his case to federal court. T. Whitfield Davidson, federal district judge for North Texas, a conservative anti-New Dealer and a Stevenson friend, agreed to a hearing on September 21.

In response, Johnson's attorneys unsuccessfully appealed to the state Supreme Court. Johnson's nine attorneys, led by Abe Fortas, then mapped strategy to overcome Stevenson's challenge. Their first line of defense was to argue that the federal court had no jurisdiction in the matter, and they drew up a motion citing twenty-two reasons why Davidson should throw out Stevenson's petition. Since they were unable to persuade Davidson, they appealed to Associate Supreme Court Justice Hugo Black, an FDR appointee, who was responsible for the Fifth Circuit.

A Court order from Black saved Johnson from a trial in Davidson's courtroom and his likely replacement on the ballot by Stevenson. Johnson had the law on his side in halting Stevenson's appeal to a federal court. "With all respect to Coke Stevenson and his lawyers," Abe Fortas said, "there really was no question about the merits of the case. The injunction was improvidently entered; that is, the federal judge enjoining the state election under these circumstances was just plain wrong." Black saw it that way. Stevenson should have brought his suit in a state court, and if there wasn't time to get a ruling before the election, as he asserted, he could have presented his case to the U.S. Senate, which has the right to determine its own membership.

Did someone in the administration or close to Truman intercede with Black to help Johnson? Truman himself, Sam Rayburn, and Abe Fortas were all later described as having done so. But no one ever produced evidence to support these assertions. Attorney General Tom Clark, who was strong for Lyndon and was shunning any investigation of the primary at this time, might have taken on the job. He later said, "I knew that they had filed a petition . . . that they had asked Justice Black . . . to pass on it, and I being a student of the Supreme Court, of course I had kept up with it pretty carefully; and being a friend of Mr. Johnson I was naturally interested in it." Hardly an admission that he had lobbied Black, but given the fact that Clark was indebted to Lyndon for helping him become Attorney General and that Lyndon's political future was hanging by a thread, something of the kind might have occurred. A detailed record of the controversy over the run-off primary Clark compiled as it developed and a later expression of appreciation from Lyndon to Clark for all he did in helping him get back to Washington add to the possibility that Clark interceded with Black. Later observers of the Johnson presidency who wondered over his selection of Ramsey Clark, Tom's son, as Attorney General might find part of the answer in Tom's help to Lyndon in 1948.

Joe Rauh, one of Lyndon's attorneys, "always thought that Tom Corcoran had spoken with Black before the hearing." In 1970, perhaps emboldened by his success in 1948, Corcoran, according to the *New York Times*, "visited [Supreme Court] justices, all old friends, on behalf of El Paso Natural Gas Company, a client desperate to secure a reversal of an adverse court ruling." On that occasion, all "the justices showed 'Tommy the Cork' the door." But it is reasonable to assume that Black, a political friend of Johnson's, would have listened to Clark's and Corcoran's private pleas. Twenty years later, when the U.S. Senate debated Abe Fortas's confirmation as chief justice of the Supreme Court, Black, now a strong opponent of Fortas's, secretly persuaded Alabama Senator Lister Hill to vote no. Black was not above committing an impropriety. Justice William O. Douglas believed that political considerations influenced Black's thinking in Johnson's 1948 appeal.

Now that he was securely on the ballot, Lyndon fixed his attention on the November election. Normally, a Republican had no chance for a Texas Senate seat. There had never been a Republican senator from Texas, and Johnson's people expected the tradition to hold in 1948. Yet the long drawn-out primary contest had convinced the public that there was fraud and raised the possibility of a Democratic defeat on November 2. A Stevenson decision to support Jack Porter, the Republican nominee, compounded the problem. Nevertheless, most observers thought Johnson would win, but that he would face future problems: Because half of his party's voters opposed him, he would be a one-term senator. To counter these difficulties, Johnson publicly emphasized that he was going to be the next senator, that he "was an innocent victim of circumstance about vote fraud," and that *next time* he will win by a lop-sided majority all over the state."

Yet Stevenson and Porter made it difficult for him to leave the vote fraud issue behind. On October 18, Stevenson made a radio speech in which he reviewed recent events and challenged Johnson's right to be on the ballot. Porter took advantage of the dispute by distributing flyers citing evidence in Davidson's court showing fraud in Johnson's primary campaign. Johnson felt compelled to refute the charges: On October 19, he asked Jimmy Allred to make a speech answering Stevenson, and on the 28th, he gave his own reply in a state-wide radio address. Declaring himself the victim of "malice and hate" heaped upon him by "poor losers," he described the allegations against him as "mis-statements and half-truths" by "parrots of special privi-lege" intent on electing a Republican senator. When Lynn Landrum, a columnist for the conservative *Dallas Morning News*, repeatedly accused Johnson of fraud in six articles in October and urged him to save his honor by forgoing the nomination, Lyndon replied in an emotional letter on October 31. He decried "the biased and polluted columns of the *Dallas News*," which catered to "Johnson haters" with grossly distorted accounts of the facts, and refused to step aside and let an "oilcrat, Republican" take the Senate seat.

Despite the sharp exchanges in the closing days of the campaign, John-son was confident that he would win. While he fought Porter and Steven-son, he took time from his campaign to help raise some badly needed money for Truman's election. In early October, he persuaded Wright Mor-row, a Houston oilman and party official, to contribute $10,000 of the $39,000 needed for a Truman radio talk. In the middle of the month, he carried an administration request to five Texans, including the Brown brothers, for funds that he was to deliver to Louis Johnson at the Demo-cratic National Committee in New York. The money helped Truman score an upset victory over Dewey in the election and restore Democratic con-trol over both houses of Congress. Lyndon won election by two to one, 702,985 to 349,665. But alongside of Truman, who received 750,000 votes in Texas, and Democratic Governor Beauford Jester, who won 320,000 more votes than Johnson, it was a disappointing showing and raised con-cerns about Lyndon's chances for reelection in six years.

Tainted means had played a significant part in giving Lyndon his vic-tory. Had they simply been his secret, he might have taken pleasure from having outsmarted the competition. But the ballot manipulation was there for all to see, calling into question his legitimate claim on his seat, and driv-ing him to justify his presence in the Senate. Had he entered the Senate without suspicions of vote fraud, he still would have challenged himself to be the best senator Texas ever had. His ambition would have required nothing less. But the cloud which hung over his election intensified his determination to make a mark that would equal and, if possible, eclipse what the most distinguished members of the Senate had accomplished in the preceding one hundred and sixty years. At the end of his term, he wished to be remembered as one of the greatest members of the upper house in U.S. history.

3 :: THE SENATOR

Forty years of age when he entered the U.S. Senate in January 1949, Johnson was a well-known figure among Washington insiders. He had lived in the capital for fifteen of the last seventeen years and was more at home in Washington than in Texas. Moreover, his election to the Senate gave him an ideal locus for his interests and talents. Prominent Federal officials, past and present, who knew Johnson well, expected his presence in the "Club," as many called the 96-member upper house, to benefit both Texas and the nation. Yet opinion about Johnson at the start of his Senate term was not uniformly enthusiastic. As was the case throughout his life, Johnson appealed greatly to some people and offended others. All agreed on one thing, however: He was a memorable character. At six feet three and a half inches, with long arms, big ears, a prominent nose, and outsized personality to match, Johnson left a lasting impression on everyone he met. Interviews about him done twenty, thirty, and even forty years after 1949 are fresh and vivid, as if people were describing yesterday's events. Bryce Harlow, a counsel to the House Armed Services Committee and a Special Assistant to President Dwight Eisenhower, remembers encounters with Lyndon as memorable: "They were searing; they were big; they were tough; they were exciting; they were out of the ordinary, because he was bigger than life."

Part of the legend Johnson created for himself revolved around his work habits. Work was a huge part of his life: It was as essential to him as breathing; he was a workaholic, an addict who needed a regular fix. And like everything he did, he tried to be the best at it and use it to impress people with his uniqueness. "My husband was always a taut, driving perfectionist who lived with constant tension," Mrs. Johnson said. Hubert Humphrey, liberal senator from Minnesota who entered the upper house with Johnson in 1949, remembered his total absorption with politics. "He knew all the little things that people did. I used to say he had his own private FBI. If you ever knew anybody, if you'd been out on a date, or if you'd had a drink, or if you'd attended a meeting, or you danced with a gal at a nightclub, he knew it! It was just incredible! I don't know how he was able to get all that information, but he lived and breathed and walked and talked politics."

Johnson was also a highly intelligent man. "The Johnson IQ took a back seat to very few others — perhaps even to none," his aide George Reedy contends. "His mind was magnificent — fast, penetrating, resourceful." Harry McPherson, another Johnson aide, believes that when he dealt with sophisticated men, he was their equal, and that this goes far to explain why he enjoyed the support of so many prominent Washington attorneys and officials over the years. Abe Fortas said he "had one of the brightest, ablest minds I have ever encountered. . . . He had a great power to retain information," which he could retrieve "accurately and effortlessly."

From the start of his term, Johnson made conscious efforts to learn about and establish himself in the good graces of Senate leaders. "I want to know who's the power over there, how you get things done, the best committees, the works," he told Senate Secretary Bobby Baker. "He solicited opinions of, and thumbnail sketches of, senators little known to him; he peppered me with keen questions for a solid two hours. I was impressed," Baker recalls. "No senator had ever approached me with such a display of determination to learn, to achieve, to attain, to belong, to get ahead. He was coming into the Senate with his neck bowed, running full tilt, impatient to reach some distant goal I then could not even imagine." But then neither could Johnson. Typically trying to master the new surroundings in which he found himself, ensure his success, and, in some undefined way, make himself a dominant, outstanding figure in the upper house, Johnson threw himself into his Senate work with unrestrained energy.

Like Sam Rayburn in the House, Johnson cultivated Richard Russell from Georgia, arguably the most powerful senator. There was much about Russell that Johnson genuinely admired. He was a man of uncommon talent who had been the youngest governor in Georgia's history and had served in the Senate since 1932. His knowledge of American history and politics was legendary. Johnson and Russell also shared an affinity for many New Deal social programs, an antagonism to labor "bosses," a military able to defend American global interests, and Federal spending that boosted their state and regional economies. Although Russell was much more southern and committed to racial segregation than Johnson, they both opposed Federal activism in behalf of civil rights in the early fifties. More important, they both worked for the fuller integration of the South and the West into the nation's economic and political life. They wanted both regions to gain a larger share of the national wealth and power than they had controlled during the first half of the century.

Russell had many supplicants for his attention and support. But none succeeded as well as Johnson in gaining his affection and backing. The two men were very different in temperament and personality. Quiet, courtly, aloof, and introspective, Russell "dressed like a small-town banker and worked in an austere office devoid of any token of power or wealth." Johnson was flamboyant, earthy, and intimate, with a taste for plush surroundings and an inclination to self-promotion that Russell shunned. In his first Senate years, Johnson toned down his behavior to court Russell. Whereas he called other senators by their first names and aggressively barged into their offices without even a "how d'ya do," he always referred to Russell as "Senator Russell" and made polite overtures before entering his office. He impressed Russell as being "quiet and gentle" and doing "everything . . . with great deliberation and care." As important, Lyndon was "thoughtful and attentive" toward Russell, who was a lonely bachelor. Johnson "took pains . . . to make his family Dick Russell's family," often having lunch with him at the Senate on Saturdays and inviting him home for weekend meals.

The result was that in 1950, after a 12-seat Democratic majority had shrunk to two, Johnson's cultivation of other senators, but especially Russell, had catapulted him into running for party Whip. Circumstances had come together to make Johnson a leading candidate for the job. A conservative-liberal split among Democratic senators made a moderate with a foot in each camp a way to hold the party together. Johnson had established himself as a party centrist. An anti–civil rights stand and militant anticommunism gave him credibility with conservatives, while support of domestic social programs redeemed him with liberals. And Johnson was eager to take the job. Though liberal senators made some bows in the direction of Alabama's John Sparkman, on January 2, 1951, by acclamation, Johnson became the youngest Whip in party history. Although the Whip's job carried no real power, "it lifted him out of the rut of freshman senator," and allowed Johnson to "be noticed." Most important, it enlarged his reputation in Texas, where newspapers carried stories about his "remarkable recognition" after only two years in the Senate as "one of the most powerful men in the Capital." State pride in his accomplishment made his reelection likely, while pro oil, anti–civil rights, and hard line anticommunism over the next three years made it all but certain.

:: BUILDING A FAMILY FORTUNE

At the same time he established a secure hold on his Senate seat, Johnson devoted himself to his family's financial future. By 1951–52, the Johnsons were already well off. The radio station, KTBC, which in 1947 Lady Bird had signed over to a company she called the Texas Broadcasting Corporation, had increased in value to $488,000. Moreover, in the spring of 1952, the Johnsons looked forward to the possibility of significant financial gains from the acquisition of an FCC license to construct the only Very High Frequency (VHF) television station in Austin. Between 1945 and 1948 the FCC had allocated only 106 television stations for the entire country. In 1948, as pressure built for new allocations, the FCC had declared a moratorium on issuing new licenses and launched a four-year study of where and how many new stations should be constructed across the United States.

As early as the spring of 1948, Lyndon and Lady Bird had considered entering the television business—both as a broadcaster and a distributor in the Austin area for the Dumont network and TV manufacturer. But they were hesitant. The cost of setting up a station was considerable and the long-term prospects for the industry were uncertain. The existing stations in Texas were losing money, and Lyndon believed it might take ten years before a new station could turn a profit. By July 1952, however, when the FCC lifted its freeze and began allocating 1,945 new television stations, it was reasonably certain that acquisition of a VHF station promised a large return.

Given how lucrative a VHF station seemed likely to be, it is surprising that Lady Bird's Texas Broadcasting Company had no competition for the one VHF channel allocated to Austin. As one of the applicants for a less desirable Ultra High Frequency (UHF) station in Austin in 1952 explained it: "Lyndon was in a favorable position to get that station even if somebody contested it. Politics is politics." Yet Johnson and many of his associates emphatically denied that politics played a part and not surprisingly few traces of Johnson's actions at the FCC showed up in the Commission's files.

Yet Johnson knew that he could count on a friendly reception for Lady Bird's requests from certain commissioners, but his efforts to influence the Commission did not stop there. In September 1945, for example, when the movie star Gene Autry asked him "to put in a plug" for a radio license in Tucson, Arizona, Lyndon replied: "There is not much I can do on the matter you mentioned but you can count on me putting in a good word for you." He was not so coy with Tommy Corcoran, who in November 1945 asked him on the telephone to help block an application for a New York radio station. Johnson said he understood. In February 1946, when Lyndon wanted to know if NBC was planning to go into Austin, Corcoran, who had close contact with Charles Denny, who was about to become FCC chairman, assured Lyndon that he knew "how to do that" and promised to "find that out for you." Lyndon, of course, had his own contacts at the FCC, one of whom in 1946 let him read the application from the "Texas Regulars" for a competing radio station in Austin. He also had a well-developed knowledge of how to make things happen at the FCC.

Johnson's influence at the Commission extended to assuring that KTBC-TV would enjoy a "'monopoly' on television broadcasting in Austin" throughout the fifties. Where the Dallas–Fort Worth area received five VHF stations, Houston four, and San Antonio four, Austin got only one. The FCC contended that technical considerations about signal interference and population were the determining factors in these allocations. Yet in 1952, Corpus Christi, with a population of 108,000 compared with Austin's 132,000, got two stations and a license for a third in 1959, which could not be used to start broadcasting for five years because of signal interference. The two existing stations in Corpus Christi had objected that their city could not support a third station and suggested that it be put in Austin. The FCC rejected their proposal. Moreover, Amarillo, a city with a population only 60 percent the size of Austin's in the late fifties, had three stations compared with Austin's one. By the early sixties, there were 107 single-channel communities in the United States. Unlike Austin, however, most of them were "located in 'overlap' areas where advertisers can reach the set owners via other nearby stations." KTBC's monopoly allowed it to charge higher advertising rates. One "overlap" community, Rochester, Minnesota, a city of comparable size to Austin, received $325 an hour for network programming in 1964. The rate for Austin was $575 an hour.

Johnson aggressively managed the radio and television stations. "No one in recent years has had any dealings with KTBC without being aware that the driving force behind the operation was Lyndon Baines Johnson," *Life* magazine said in 1964. Johnson's attentiveness to his radio and television interests paid large dividends. By the end of February 1953, the Texas Broadcasting Company had assets of $734,220, with excellent prospects for more growth as additional homes in the greater Austin community acquired television sets.

During the next four years, Johnson's Texas Broadcasting made additional direct and indirect acquisitions and gains. In 1955–56 the FCC granted KTBC-TV an increase in power to 316 kilowatts, allowed Texas Broadcasting to change its name to the LBJ Company and to acquire part of KRGV-TV and radio in the Rio Grande Valley town of Weslaco. Shortly after, the FCC agreed to an increase in KRGV-TV's transmitting power from 28.8 kilowatts to 100 kilowatts, and the station won network affiliations with ABC and NBC. During this time, KWTX, a Waco station Johnson had also acquired, bought a half ownership in KBTX-TV, a Bryan, Texas, educational station that the FCC, in an exception to its rule, allowed to convert to commercial use. At the end of April 1956, the LBJ Company had assets of $1,534,381. Nearly three years later, on March 31, 1959, the company's value had reached $2,569,503.

:: BECOMING MINORITY LEADER

By 1952, Lyndon had decided to reach for the Democratic party's Senate leadership post. His plan stemmed from the results of the 1952 Senate elections. The Democrats dropped to 47 seats, and the Republicans were able to organize the upper house. Democratic Majority Leader Ernest McFarland of Arizona was one election casualty, losing to Barry Goldwater, a conservative department-store owner. Although the last two Democratic leaders, Scott Lucas and McFarland had lost their seats in 1950 and 1952 respectively, Johnson decided to try for the job. Unlike Lucas and McFarland, Johnson would not have to carry the burden of unpopular liberal programs advanced by a Democratic President. Rather, as a Minority Leader working with Eisenhower, a popular President, espousing less controversial conservative measures, Johnson could establish a reputation as a Democrat who put country above party and served the wishes of the Texas majority who liked Ike.

For almost two months, from November 5, the day after the 1952 election, to January 3, the day Senate Democrats met to elect their leaders, Johnson devoted himself to winning the Leadership post. He first went after Richard Russell's backing, which promised additional southern support. The exact sequence of events by which Johnson brought Russell and other senators to his side is difficult to reconstruct. But it is clear that Johnson himself masterminded the campaign. He urged Russell to take the post and promised to do the work and let Russell be the boss. But Russell refused. He did not want to be a Minority Leader with little opportunity to lead; nor did he want to abandon his role as Armed Services Committee chairman or as an opponent of civil rights legislation. Moreover, his identification as an anti–civil rights spokesman would have made him unacceptable to northern and some border-state Democrats. Lyndon then asked Russell to support him. Russell already had a high opinion of Johnson, and agreed to support him.

Lyndon pressed his case with other senators as well. Ernest McFarland remembered that "as soon as I was defeated, he [Johnson] called me up. And he had me call all my friends boosting him." Border and western state senators and the six freshman Democrats also received phone calls from Johnson, including John F. Kennedy of Massachusetts. The call to a surprised Kennedy came at dawn, just after his election was confirmed. "The guy must never sleep," Kennedy said to an aide.

When the Democratic caucus met on January 2, 1953, Russell, in what one Johnson aide called "a very wonderful speech," nominated Lyndon, at forty-four, to become the youngest Leader in Democratic party history. He pointed to Johnson's record of party loyalty, his "human values," peerless qualities as a conciliator, and championship of party unity. Russell expressed "complete confidence" in Johnson's ability to serve the "party to which we adhere & [the] country & people we seek to serve." In a show of unity, Theodore Francis Green of Rhode Island, speaking for the East, and Dennis Chavez of New Mexico, speaking for the West, seconded the nomination. The opposition, represented by Murray's candidacy, got just five votes.

Johnson had made his first major move toward consolidating his power as Democratic Leader and restoring the position to the importance it had once enjoyed under Joe Robinson of Arkansas in the 1930s.

:: BIPARTISAN POLITICS

Johnson delighted in the national attention, party influence, and Senate power given him by the Minority Leadership. After only four years, he was on the Senate's center stage, though not yet in the lead role. That part had fallen to Robert Taft of Ohio, the Majority Leader. The son of a former President, a third-term senator, a man described as "Mr. Republican," Taft dwarfed Lyndon in national reputation and prestige. And Lyndon couldn't stand it. When Taft, as he often did, ignored Lyndon's existence, Johnson would lean across the center aisle, pretending he had forgotten his reading glasses, and ask Taft to read the fine print in a bill or committee report to him. When journalists Johnson courted gave Taft more newsprint, Johnson privately referred to them as "piss-ant reporters."

Becoming Minority Leader gave Lyndon a greater sense of self-importance. But he did not seek the job simply for its prestige. He saw the post as carrying responsibilities he welcomed. As a key party figure and a Senate leader, he mapped a strategy that could restore Democratic control of Congress and serve the well-being of the country.

Johnson saw bipartisanship as serving both ends. So did Sam Rayburn. Immediately after the 1952 election, Rayburn had decided to accept the House Minority Leadership and use bipartisanship for both national and self-serving political ends. "Any jackass can kick a barn down, but it takes a good carpenter to build one," he said. He told Eisenhower: "I'll help you on international affairs and defense, if you can get a majority of your own party to go along." Further, if the President wished to extend any existing Democratic program, Rayburn promised to help. Any attempt to jettison New Deal–Fair Deal programs, however, would be resisted.

Johnson saw the wisdom of Rayburn's approach. He was one of a very few people who realized that Eisenhower's 1952 election provided a chance to "convert the fractionalized Democratic Senate group into a cohesive whole" and advance American interests at home and abroad. Our objective should be party harmony, he told a Senate Democratic caucus on January 2. Together, they should fight for a positive program — "a program geared NOT just to opposing the majority but to serving America."

The first and most essential condition of Democratic success under a popular Republican President was party unity. Johnson was mindful of Will Rogers's observation: "I am not a member of any organized political party. I am a Democrat." He also remembered the old saw that a Democrat would rather fight a Democrat any time than fight a Republican. In the winter of 1953, the Democrats seemed more divided than ever among conservatives, liberals, and moderates: segregationists like Harry Byrd of Virginia and Richard Russell of Georgia seemed incapable of cooperation with southern and midwestern liberals like Estes Kefauver of Tennessee, Paul Douglas of Illinois, and Hubert Humphrey of Minnesota. These competing factions could swamp senators in the middle like Johnson.

Johnson began his unity efforts by turning the Senate Democratic Policy Committee into a unified party voice on legislation. He broadened the composition of the Committee to consist of four conservatives, two moderates, and three liberals, and he made it an effective party voice on bills before Congress. To ensure that differences among committee members did not turn into open fights on the Senate floor, he won agreement to a "unanimous consent rule" — 90 percent of Committee members had to support legislative recommendations to win party approval.

Johnson also convinced a more representative Senate Democratic Steering Committee to consider criteria other than seniority for committee assignments. With Russell's backing Johnson made a convincing case to the Steering Committee for relaxation of the seniority rule. As Lyndon told Adlai Stevenson, "We have old members who have everything, and want more, and the younger, abler men sit under the trees and do nothing. We are opening up 9 to 10 committee assignments for the younger men."

Lyndon also promoted unity by muting ideological differences between liberals and conservatives. Hubert Humphrey was a principal case in point. By appointing Humphrey to the Foreign Relations Committee, Lyndon recognized his worth, flattered his ego, and inhibited Humphrey from agitating domestic issues that divided Senate Democrats. Humphrey had to resign from the Labor and Public Welfare and Agriculture committees to accept Foreign Relations. He was reluctant to do it. "'My gosh, Mr. Leader, you know at home my constituency is Democratic farmer-labor party. You're asking me to give up labor. You're asking me to give up . . . Agriculture.' . . . 'Now listen,'" Johnson told him, "'this is one time where you're going to serve your country and your party. . . . You've just got to take another look at yourself here. You can fight for the farmers down here on this [Senate] floor and you can fight for the laboring man, but we've got some serious foreign policy issues coming up and they're going to be major.'"

Along with party unity, Johnson considered a bipartisan foreign policy essential for renewed Democratic majorities in the Congress and the well-being of the country. Opposing Eisenhower on foreign affairs at the start of his term would have been political suicide. Besides, Old Guard, isolationist Republicans were going to do it for the Democrats, and allow them to score political points by backing Ike. Lyndon saw this as not only good politics, but also good national policy.

Eisenhower considered Democratic support of his foreign and defense policies essential. In his State of the Union address on February 2 he called for bipartisanship; and in a private meeting with Republican legislators on February 16, he insisted that it be "firmly established as soon as possible," or before "a major crisis came along." The President then introduced regular defense briefings for Democratic and Republican congressional leaders.

In his State of the Union address, Eisenhower "hammered" the Democrats for having made secret agreements at Yalta in 1945 which permitted Soviet "enslavement" of Eastern Europe. His remarks implied that he would ask Congress to repudiate the Yalta commitments. But a resolution he sent to the Hill on February 20 only criticized the Soviet Union for interpreting Yalta "to bring about the subjugation of free peoples." Isolationist Republicans led by Joseph McCarthy attacked Eisenhower's failure to repudiate the agreements and called for action to free Eastern Europe. Eisenhower urged Republican leaders not to amend his statement. He feared that repudiation would cancel American occupation rights in Berlin and Vienna and alienate the Democrats, who saw it as an attack on FDR. When it became clear that the Republican Old Guard would not back down, Lyndon made the Democrats the defenders of a constructive Eisenhower foreign policy. On February 24 the Democratic Policy Committee commended the President's resolution as containing "no trace of the partisanship that could lead to discord and disunity." The Committee urged unanimous Senate approval as a demonstration of united American opposition to Soviet tyranny.

Domestic affairs was a less promising arena for Johnson's bipartisan strategy. As George Reedy observed, "Eisenhower was an economic conservative and, on domestic legislation, his heart belonged to the moderate right wing of the Republican party." Yet even on domestic issues, Johnson made it seem that the President and the Senate Democrats were joined in a struggle against reactionary Republicans. Johnson held "Democratic" legislation to a minimum, and turned Eisenhower's bills into "New Deal-ish" laws with amendments spawned by the Democratic Policy Committee. By leaving Eisenhower's stamp on the bill, Johnson accurately calculated that the President wouldn't intervene in the Senate debate or veto the measure.

On no issue did Johnson score more effectively for bipartisanship than the Senate's repudiation of Joe McCarthy. Johnson understood that defeating McCarthy would require a conservative-liberal coalition and when McCarthy began attacking traditional institutions, like the U.S. Army, it gave Johnson the opening he sought. From April to June 1954, while McCarthy held hearings on Communist infiltration of the Army, Johnson arranged for television coverage that undermined McCarthy's credibility. As Johnson put it, the day to day exposure allowed people to "see what the bastard was up to." Lyndon then consulted "key Senators," the White House, and Chief Justice Earl Warren before setting up a bipartisan committee that condemned McCarthy. It was a piece of masterful politics that assured McCarthy's demise.

The reward for all Johnson's efforts was restoration of Democratic control of Congress in the 1956 elections. Though Eisenhower would decisively defeat Stevenson for the presidency, the Democrats gained a 17-seat advantage in the House and a two-seat margin in the Senate. Johnson, at the age of 46, now became the youngest Majority Leader in Senate history.

:: MAJORITY LEADER

In January 1955, Johnson's election as Majority Leader promised few advantages. True, the post gave him national prominence as a spokesman for the

Democratic party, but party misadventures could be laid at his doorstep, and with a popular Republican in the White House, Lyndon's danger of negative publicity was considerable. Moreover, if past experience was any guide, the Leader's job would be a source of frustration and a burying ground for hopes of higher office. Most earlier Senate Leaders had faced insurmountable difficulties in effectively bringing other senators into line on party programs. While senators usually have a strong party identification, and party affiliation has a major influence on voting behavior, they are much more beholden to their constituents than to party leaders. "Senators are like a hundred barons," one observer of the upper house said. "They do not owe each other a damned thing. Except insofar as they find it expedient to work together, they are completely independent of one another." One former Senate Leader complained: "I didn't have anything to threaten them with, and it wouldn't have worked even if I had tried . . . sure as hell, someone would have gotten up on the floor and accused me of trying to become a dictator."

Only one Senate Democratic Leader in the twentieth century, Joseph T. Robinson of Arkansas, had made much of a mark. Oscar Underwood of Alabama, the first formally to hold the post, from 1920 to 1923, quit out of frustration with Senate rules and a desire to run for President. Robinson, his successor, held the position for fourteen years, but only asserted himself effectively from 1933 to 1937, when the Democrats enjoyed large majorities and FDR's New Deal proposals had widespread national appeal as an answer to the Depression. Alben Barkley of Kentucky became Vice President after eleven years as Senate party Leader, but his legislative victories were few and far between. Scott W. Lucas and Ernest McFarland, Lyndon's two immediate predecessors, lost their seats after each served two unproductive years. The party's most powerful senators in the fifties, Walter George and Richard Russell, wanted no part of the assignment. Lyndon's effectiveness as Minority Leader suggested that he might prove to be a cut above earlier Majority Leaders, but the slim two-vote Democratic margin in the Senate and a popular Republican President added to the normal limitations a Democratic floor leader faced in making much of a legislative record.

But Lyndon established a system of control over the upper house that made him the most effective Majority Leader in Senate history. Why did he succeed when others had failed? Bryce Harlow, Ike's aide, says that Johnson had a special gift, an undefinable talent for leadership that created fear, admiration, and a desire in others to follow. His leadership consisted of intellectual force, discipline, and indefatigability. It was a mixture of being like other people and different from or superior to them at the same time. "You're one of the boys, but you're bigger than any of them. You're different from them." Above all, it was Lyndon's unequaled "domination of people by sheer force of personality. Never seen his equal," Harlow says, "and I've rubbed up against the greatest people this country has produced for twenty years running." Johnson's presence in the Senate, Florida senator George Smathers recalls, was like "a great overpowering thunderstorm that consumed you as it closed around you."

Central to Johnson's power were the political debts owed him by other senators, particularly for coveted committee assignments. Since a senator "makes his reputation with his colleagues and leaves his mark on legislation" in committees, his place in the "committee caste system" is of paramount importance. First as Minority and then Majority Leader, Lyndon chaired the Democratic Steering Committee, the body responsible for committee appointments. Having increased the seats on major committees—by reducing the number on minor ones—and having guaranteed one good committee assignment to each senator, regardless of seniority, he was able to create a set of political IOUs that came due during future legislative struggles.

In making committee appointments in 1955, Johnson reached out to nearly all Democratic senators. Operating from a back room in the Capitol, he made over 200 phone calls, touching all bases and conferring especially with Russell, George, Symington, and Humphrey. According to John Steele of *Time*, when Johnson finished, he had covered himself "with glory by throwing (for a second time) strict seniority rules to the wind and parcelling out committee assignments in a manner to please." All Democratic newcomers got at least one good appointment, while Alben Barkley and Joe O'Mahoney, former senators who had regained their seats and could have been treated like freshmen, got exactly what they wished. "The move not only was magnanimous," Steele said, "it was smart politics—and Lyndon excels at both. An angry, hurt Barkley . . . would have provided a potential rallying point for any northern liberals who chaff under Johnson's reins this year. But now Alben is in Lyndon's corner and he's acting kittenish." The same was true of O'Mahoney. When another journalist complained about Johnson's appointments in a syndicated column, Hubert Humphrey suggested that he compare the Republicans' "miserable record with the Democratic leadership's action. . . . I worked day and night for better than ten days with Senator Johnson and others on these committee assignments. I can honestly say that . . . the Senate Democratic liberals were given a mighty good deal." Sam Rayburn agreed, writing Lyndon to say what a wonderful job he had done on committee appointments. "You have shown real leadership."

Lyndon made certain to tell senators what he had done for them. Telephone calls reporting Steering Committee decisions were a way of driving home the point. If he didn't reach the senator, his wife would do as well. When he called John Stennis to report his appointment to the Appropriations Committee and Mrs. Stennis said he wasn't there, Lyndon laid it on thick: John had received a great honor, and the Senate had honored itself by selecting "a great American" and one of its finest members to this high post. Lyndon also sent each senator a laudatory press release about their committee appointments with a note saying they were free to distribute it in any manner they considered advantageous. Wayne Morse, for one, found it "very helpful" and put it to use in Oregon, where the press now, unlike 1954, had "difficulty in belittling" his committee assignments.

Lyndon had to disappoint some, but he usually found alternative means to satisfy them. When he couldn't appoint Jack Kennedy to Appropriations, Foreign Relations, or Finance, he wrote a placating letter saying he couldn't "overcome seniority completely" and promised future amends. When he denied liberal Illinois senator Paul Douglas a slot on Finance, he made him chairman of the Joint Economic Committee. With Tennessee's Estes Kefauver, however, who was a Johnson rival and an uncooperative liberal, Lyndon was not so forthcoming. In January, after Kefauver asked to be on the party's Policy Committee, Lyndon bluntly told him: "I have never had the particular feeling that when I called up my first team and the chips were down that Kefauver felt he ought to be . . . on that team. If you feel you . . . want to be, it is the best news I have had. I will meet you more than 50% of the way. I will push you into every position of influence and power that you can have." In short, when Kefauver was ready to become a "Johnson man," Lyndon would be more receptive to his demands. Kefauver preferred to remain his own man.

Lyndon's acquisition of political debts extended to other favors valued by senators. Help with getting a bill passed was one. As chairman of the Democratic Policy Committee, Lyndon had the power to initiate a legislative fight when and on the terms he wanted. Several requests a day came into the Leader's office from senators asking that he speed up or delay a legislative proposal. And Lyndon mastered the tactics for doing both. "Timing can make or break a bill," he told Doris Kearns. "The first weeks provide the best opportunity to fight off a filibuster, the last weeks to avoid a conference committee, and the middle weeks to explore the issue. Sometimes the best tactic is delay—allowing time for support to build up and plunge—moving immediately to take advantage of momentum. Still other times the best timing inside the Senate depends on what's going on outside the Senate, such as primaries or elections or marches or something."

Johnson also used his control over legislative scheduling to choose between competing bills and select the one that caused senators the least political problems. As one Senate aide described it, "No Southern Senator—except perhaps the two from Alabama—can afford to vote for a public housing bill. The Northern Democrats can't afford to vote against one. You can't ask a Senator to slit his own throat. So you bring up the bill in such a way that the Southerners can vote for it because it provides less housing than the alternative (or because it does not contain an FEPC provision) and the Northerners vote for it because it is better than nothing." Senator J. William Fulbright of Arkansas remembers Lyndon as very cooperative in helping pass bills coming out of the Foreign Relations Committee. Johnson "used to say, if anything came out of the committee, just let him know, and he would see that it was passed, and he pretty well did. . . . He was the manager of the Senate. He could make it function. He got action!" Stuart Symington recalled, "If he knew somebody wanted a dam badly, or a new military installation, he would tell him he would do his best to help him get it." But ultimately a favor was expected in return: He would say later, "'I would like you to help me.' He was a master inside negotiator with his colleagues on such matters."

Offices and parking spaces also counted with senators. One chief Senate clerk called them "the keys to happiness. Morale in the Senate depends on those two things." Recognizing their importance as a source of influence, Johnson shifted authority for making office and parking assignments from the Rules Committee to the Majority Leader. The first one he satisfied with his newly acquired power was himself. Grover Ensley, the executive director of the Joint Economic Committee, remembered how Lyndon came to visit the attractive offices of his committee one evening in January 1955. "I had the fire going in the fireplace. I was getting ready to go home about quarter til six . . . and the door opened. Lyndon Johnson came in. . . . He looked around the office—he noted the beautiful chandelier, the John, and the view from the windows. He sat down and we visited a while. He was always looking around the office." The next day Ensley received word that Johnson needed the offices. Ensley then spoke to all the Democrats on the committee, John Sparkman, Paul Douglas, Fulbright, and O'Mahoney. Lyndon had already seen each of them. In return for giving him the Joint Committee's offices, Johnson gave Sparkman an additional hideaway office; Douglas the chairmanship of the Joint Committee; Fulbright a promise of help to become chairman of Foreign Relations; and O'Mahoney a seat on the Joint Committee that five other Democrats had superior claims to. Ensley said later: "Lyndon Johnson had covered *every* possible angle on securing the space!"

Committee and office assignments and help with legislation went far to establish Johnson's influence. But there was a host of other favors and courtesies that his colleagues valued as well: appointments to special committees and as delegates to international conferences, appropriations for subcommittees, information about the consequences of a bill for a senator's constituents, and help in finding an administrative assistant, scheduling a Senate speech, or identifying a pair on a particular bill. Recording the birth of William Knowland's fourth grandchild in the *Congressional Record*, attending the funeral of a senator's relative, noting birthdays and wedding anniversaries, passing along an expensive box of cigars, all were courtesies that were not forgotten and strengthened Johnson's influence.

De facto control of the Senate Democratic Campaign Committee gave Lyndon additional leverage with his party colleagues. But Republicans were not neglected. "I have always been told that no man can be a successful Leader unless he has personal friends on both sides of the aisle," Johnson wrote Republican Karl Mundt of South Dakota in April 1955. Maine's Republican senator Margaret Chase Smith recalled that Johnson played fairly with the membership, whether it was Republicans or Democrats. "He learned what they wanted, what they were interested in. It might be some little bill that affected their district or their state. It might be some personal thing. It might be of little importance to the Senate generally." But it counted with individual senators, who responded by forgetting about party line and ideology when Lyndon needed their help.

All Johnson's wheeling and dealing in behalf of other senators was a prelude to his exercise of personal influence—daily, constant efforts to persuade colleagues to follow his lead. The "only real power available to the leader is the power of persuasion," Lyndon said in 1960. "There is no patronage; no power to discipline; no authority to fire senators like a President can fire [Cabinet] members." Lyndon made persuasion into a science that played the largest part in passing laws. Under his direction, Senate legislation became less a matter of floor debate or open argument and more a case of behind-the-scenes arrangements. Historian Paul Conkin points out that Johnson "had little sympathy for those who wanted to air points of view, to use speeches as a vehicle of public education. Debate tended to sharpen differences or allow senators to posture for audiences back home. . . . Success required a masking of issues, not sharpening them through debate." Johnson worked "through informal personal techniques and numerous small caucuses to build the temporary alliances necessary to pass a bill. These alliances were often years in the making, were tied to numerous small revisions or excisions in ever more complex bills, and in the end reflected numerous bargains or trade-offs among senators. Johnson was a master at bringing this complex process to a final climax at the exact time he had the majority required for victory."

Johnson used what journalists called "the treatment" to deal effectively with individual senators and small caucuses. Evans and Novak described it as "supplication, accusation, cajolery, exuberance, scorn, tears, complaint, the hint of threat. It was all of these together. It ran the gamut of human emotions. Its velocity was breathtaking, and it was all in one direction. Interjections from the target were rare. Johnson anticipated them before they could be spoken. He moved in close, his face a scant millimeter from his target, his eyes widening and narrowing, his eyebrows rising and falling. From his pockets poured clippings, memos, statistics. Mimicry, humor, and the genius of analogy made The Treatment an almost hypnotic experience and rendered the target stunned and helpless."

Benjamin Bradlee of the *Washington Post* compared it with going to the zoo. "You really felt as if a St. Bernard had licked your face for an hour, had pawed you all over. . . . He never just shook hands with you. One hand was shaking your hand; the other hand was always someplace else, exploring you, examining you. And of course he was a great actor, bar fucking none the greatest. He'd be feeling up Katharine Graham and bumping Meg Greenfield on the boobs. And at the same time he'd be trying to persuade you of something, sometimes something that he knew and I knew was not so, and there was just the trace of a little smile on his face. It was just a miraculous performance." Hubert Humphrey said: "He'd come on just like a tidal wave. . . . He went through the walls. He'd come through a door, and he'd take the whole room over. Just like that. . . . There was nothing delicate about him."

Doris Kearns believes that "the treatment" was more calculated and subtle. Johnson usually designed his approaches to other senators to seem wholly spontaneous—an accidental encounter in a Senate corridor leading to a private talk. In fact, they were carefully planned. He "would practice his intended approach, often in the presence of one of his aides. He sorted out in rambling fashion the possible arguments pro and con, experimented with a variety of responses, and fashioned a detailed mental script from which he would speak . . . when the meeting took place." The physical contact was "the product of meticulous calculation": it created a sense of genuine and benign intimacy and affection. Johnson's rhetoric was also carefully scripted to create an illusion that the outcome of the pending legislation depended on the actions of this one senator. "Johnson's argument invoked country and party, loyalty to the leadership, reminders of past services and hints of future satisfactions—but always in a form that disavowed any intention that there was a debt to be paid or trade being offered. There was the welfare of the Senate to be considered and a casual mention of certain powerful interests. All of these mingled arguments were set forth as if they constituted a unitary motive for action, and this was all presented as if Johnson's object were not persuasion, but to 'reason together' in hopes of clarifying the considerations that would help a man to make his own informed decision."

Johnson himself discounted the descriptions of "the treatment" as "nonsense" perpetrated by "intellectuals." He complained that they pictured him performing "a back-alley job . . . holding the guy by the collar, twisting his arm behind his back, dangling a carrot in front of his nose, and holding a club over his head. It's a pretty amazing sight when you think about it. I'd have to be some sort of acrobatic genius to carry it off, and the Senator in question, well, he'd have to be pretty weak and pretty meek to be simply standing there like a paralyzed idiot." Johnson contended that his powers of persuasion rested on his talent for debate and the extensive preparation that went into it.

Great preparation unquestionably preceded Johnson's conversations with his colleagues. He made certain to master the details of the bill under consideration and to marshal the facts either for or against the measure. More important, he knew "every personal interest of every member of the Senate just like he knew the palm of his hand," William Fulbright said. "He knew how to bring people together, because he could appeal to their different interests." Johnson took account of the power groups in each senator's state and who supported and opposed him. According to Henry Jackson, "He understood fully . . . the philosophy, the ideologies, of the senators. He was keenly aware of what would fly with them and what would not."

Doris Kearns says that Johnson "shaped a composite mental portrait of every Senator: his strengths and his weaknesses; his place in the political spectrum; his aspirations in the Senate, and perhaps beyond the Senate; how far he could be pushed in what direction, and by what means; how he liked his liquor; how he felt about his wife and his family, and, most important, how he felt about himself." Johnson told Kearns: "When you're dealing with all those Senators—the good ones and the crazies, the hard workers and the lazies, the smart ones and the mediocres—you've got to know two things right away. You've got to understand the beliefs and values common to all of them as politicians, the desire for fame and the thirst for honor, and then you've got to understand *the* emotion most controlling that particular Senator when he thinks about this particular issue."

Johnson also consciously manipulated journalists. Because William S. White of the *New York Times* admired subtlety, Johnson tried to be subtle with him. Because columnist Stewart Alsop cared "a lot about appearing to be an intellectual and a historian," Johnson played down "the gold cufflinks which you play up with *Time* magazine, and, to him, emphasize your relationship with FDR and your roots in Texas. . . . You learn that Evans and Novak love to traffic in backroom politics and political intrigue, so that when you're with them you make sure to bring in lots of details and colorful description of personality. You learn that Mary McGrory likes dominant personalities and Doris Fleeson cares only about issues, so that when you're with McGrory you come on strong and with Fleeson you make yourself sound like some impractical red-hot liberal."

To Johnson, information was power. His "search for information was ceaseless," Kearns says. "Each encounter, whatever its purpose, was also a 'planned interview,' in which Johnson probed, questioned, and directed the conversation according to *his* ends. Whether in the office or the cloakroom, over lunch or over drinks, Johnson somehow made others feel that every conversation was a test in which they were expected not only to come up with the answers but to score 100 percent, resulting in a tension that often brought forth additional information." Johnson would frequently get staff people together from different Senate committees and pick their brains. He wasn't going around their bosses, William Darden, Richard Russell's aide, remembered, but just getting them to report on the current state of things in their respective committees. Mostly, however, Johnson depended on what the journalist Stewart Alsop called "the biggest, the most efficient, the most ruthlessly overworked and the most loyal personal staff in the history of the Senate" for intelligence gathering.

The principal figure in this operation was Bobby Baker. Johnson made him secretary to the Senate Majority Leader. At the age of twenty-six, Baker had a matchless knowledge of Senate operations and its members. One senator, who "never liked him very much," said that "if you wanted to know what was going on, Bobby was the guy you called. He had the head count. He knew who was drunk, who was out of town, who was out sleeping with whom. He knew who was against the bill and why, and he probably knew how to approach him to get him to swing around. Bobby was it." George Reedy says that the senators "liked Bobby because he was useful, very useful. He'd trade information back and forth. . . . He could deliver money to them during political campaigns. . . . He'd count votes. God, he could count votes. . . . The most important part of Johnson's operation was really sort of an intelligence operation that kept feeding in things with a scale and an efficiency the CIA never dreamed of. Bobby was a very important element of that operation."

Some marveled at Baker's success in mastering so much information. Baker himself said there was no "magic in it. I was industrious, hard working, ambitious . . . I was not bashful in seeking Senators out to ask their views on bills and issues, to learn who influenced who. It was simply a matter of watching, listening, and doing one's homework." But there was more to it than that. Baker haunted the Senate Democratic cloakroom, which he called "the Central Intelligence Agency of the Senate." It was the place where "senators opened up their heads and their hearts—especially as the day wore on and flasks were nipped. . . . It was here I first heard direct from the horse's mouth what senators were considered to be for hire, and to what extent, and to whom." Baker catalogued their preferences and dislikes, their jealousies, class differences, and clashing personal goals. He paid special attention to Senate staffers, read committee reports, and provided senators with numerous favors. "You'd go down in Bobby's office," a member of the Capitol police force recalls, " . . . and on his desk were stacks of money. On his desk. Drawers full of money." Campaign contributions, help in arranging Senate junkets, or in getting a particular desk on the Senate floor, "the mule work," as Baker called it, stored up "residues of goodwill for the future."

While Baker was at the beck and call of all Democratic senators, he was principally Lyndon's man. "We were so well atuned to each other, we could almost read each other's minds," Baker told an interviewer. Some called him the "ninety-seventh Senator," but most referred to him as "Lyndon, Jr." or "Little Lyndon." When he wanted something, Baker would often say, "We want" or "Lyndon wants." And Johnson valued him greatly. "Thank you for sending me the 'run-down' on Democratic Senators," he wrote Baker during a period of indisposition in 1955. "I'm going to be needing more and more as time goes on. I haven't had such a complete round-up of the news in a mighty long time."

Johnson's mastery of the Senate came not only from knowledge of other senators but also a skillful use of Senate rules. Unanimous consent agreements, aborted quorum calls, night sessions, and periods of inaction alternating with bursts of frenetic activity were Johnson's principal weapons in driving bills through. Consent agreements set a time limit on debate; drawn-out quorum calls that replaced traditional brief recesses and were suspended when Johnson was ready to have the Senate resume gave him time to cut deals in the cloakroom; night sessions and stop and go legislating exhausted senators, discouraged prolonged debate, and promoted backroom agreements as the principal device for passing laws. Johnson told reporters that he "talked less and passed more bills than anyone else."

And the outcome was a Senate following Lyndon's lead. On bill after bill, resolution after resolution, Lyndon dominated the 84th Congress. Successful opposition on January 6 to a proposal for changing the Senate rule on curbing filibusters gave a first hint of his mastery of Democratic colleagues and the upper house. Eighteen liberal Democrats, led by Herbert Lehman of New York, met to discuss a rules' fight. Hubert Humphrey argued against "a frontal assault." He urged liberals to "abandon the devil theory of history" that made all southern senators their enemies and to give Lyndon "a chance to see what he could do with the South." Humphrey persuaded fellow liberals to fight for civil rights legislation through the regular committee route. "Behind Humphrey," John Steele told his editor, "stood the off-stage figure of Lyndon Johnson, who wants nobody and nothing to rock the Democratic cockle-shell." Walter White, the head of the NAACP, publicly complained that "shrewd horse trading over committee memberships . . . caused abandonment of the proposed change of Senate rules." Although Humphrey denied it, he told White that "the liberal position on the committees this year is far better than it has been in recent years." He sent Lyndon copies of his correspondence with White and asked if he had "any room in Texas for a displaced liberal."

The bills passed during the 1955 session demonstrated Lyndon's masterful leadership. Although meeting twenty days and two hundred hours fewer than the first session of the 83rd Congress, the initial meeting of the 84th passed nearly two hundred more bills than the 83rd. In addition, the first session of the 84th Congress had no filibusters or heated exchanges over several days that engendered long-term feuds. At the same time, it tackled and passed some of the most controversial legislation the Congress had confronted in seven or eight years. As a memorandum celebrating Lyndon's achievement put it, despite the Democrats' slim, two-vote advantage, "as long as Lyndon was on the Senate floor, the Democrats lost only one party vote during the entire session."

There was some hyperbole in Lyndon's claims. The first half of 1955 witnessed an economic boom that discouraged the creation of new Federal programs. Moreover, as Eisenhower biographer Stephen Ambrose wrote, "the combination of a Democratic Congress and a Republican administration meant that precious little in the way of domestic legislation could be passed. Both parties were jockeying for position for the 1956 presidential election; neither party was willing to give the other credit for major legislation." Nevertheless, Lyndon skillfully drove more than 1,300 bills through the Senate, including major trade, wage, and housing laws.

Johnson's success in leading a closely divided Senate through a productive session stimulated discussion of his suitability for higher office. In June and July 1955, *Newsweek, The New Republic,* and the *Washington Post* speculated on his nomination for the presidency in 1956 or 1960. A *Post* column described him as "the first party leader in modern times to tame the independent Senate," and as a man who was riding "a presidential boom." Columnist Joe Alsop told George Reedy that Adlai Stevenson would probably offer Lyndon the vice-presidential nomination in 1956. If he accepted and the Democrats lost, Stevenson would support Johnson for the presidency in 1960.

:: HEALTH PROBLEMS

A serious heart attack in the summer of 1955 discouraged talk of his running for higher office. The attack had been in the making for a long time because of the furious pace he set during the first half of 1955. "$E = mc^2$ is Albert Einstein's world-shaking formula for energy," one journalist wrote. "But in Washington, D.C., there is a simpler, more understandable formula. In that city of energetic men, energy in its purest political form is expressed in the letters $E = LBJ$."

Johnson's stressful schedule, terrible diet that drove his weight up to 225 pounds, and three pack-a-day cigarette habit were a formula for disaster. On Saturday, June 18, he ate lunch with Florida Senator George Smathers in the Senate dining room, where "he ate his usual double meal and gulped the food." Later in the afternoon, on the way to George Brown's estate in Middleburg, some forty miles from the District, Lyndon grasped his chest and complained of indigestion. A coke and bicarbonate of soda didn't relieve the discomfort. Although he said he felt better the next morning, Smathers didn't think he looked any better and urged him to see a doctor when he got back to town. A cursory exam by the Capitol physician on Monday morning turned up nothing and Lyndon resumed his normal schedule. In fact, he had suffered a heart attack and was on the verge of a more severe one.

On the weekend of July 4, he had to be hospitalized. As they put him in an oxygen tent, he went into shock and turned gray, "just about the color of pavement." He was "motionless as stone and cold to touch. His blood pressure dropped to zero over forty." He had suffered a coronary occlusion and the doctors gave him a fifty-fifty chance of survival.

His condition was touch and go for the next forty-eight hours, but by Wednesday, the fourth day after his attack, prospects brightened. During the next month, he struggled to adjust to the limitations imposed on him by his heart disease — a ban on smoking, a strict diet to reduce weight, and a period of relative inactivity. Lady Bird called it the "Battle of Patience," and though she thought Lyndon might "get along all right, I don't know whether I'll make it or not." The thought of breaking the smoking habit and following a "dismal low-calorie/low-fat diet" filled him with a sense of deprivation. Walter Jenkins remembered how after his recovery "he would take a cigarette and lick it or hold it in his mouth" without lighting, and Lyndon later told Lady Bird that he had missed smoking every day of his life. He despised the hospital food and Lady Bird had to bring him some home-cooked meals. He took to eating a lot of cantaloupe, which is low in calories, and he satisfied his craving for desserts with tapioca. "I'm either going to have to turn registered chemist or jump out of the window," Lady Bird told a reporter.

Politics and thoughts of running for President continued to preoccupy him and helped spur his recovery. In September, he began urging Senate colleagues to visit him at the ranch, and on the 24th, news that Eisenhower had suffered a heart attack fixed his attention on the President's health. He spoke to James Hagerty, Ike's press secretary, two or three times a day for the first three days, and then Jerry Persons, the White House staff man for congressional relations, called Lyndon once a day. Eisenhower's illness opened up a five-month period of uncertainty about who would be the Republican nominee for President in 1956. George Reedy at once sent Lyndon a series of memos on how the President's illness might affect the Democrats, and Lyndon in particular.

A visit to the ranch by Adlai Stevenson and Sam Rayburn on September 28–29 put Lyndon back in the national spotlight. And by the middle of October, Johnson had created the impression that he was as vigorous as ever and once again at the center of Democratic party activities. His appearance at the Dallas State Fair, where he made a twenty-minute speech before an enthusiastic audience and toured the grounds shaking hands, convinced people that he was in good physical condition. He also considered going to Washington, D.C., for a meeting with Dulles before the Secretary left for a

Foreign Ministers conference in Geneva. Even though the trip would have publicized his recovery, his doctors vetoed the plan.

:: THE 1956 PRESIDENTIAL RACE

A meeting with Dulles would also have advanced Johnson's presidential candidacy. Throughout the fall, George Reedy sent him a series of memos on how to build support and convince the country that he was the "man in the saddle." Reedy, for example, saw the addition of Grace Tully—an FDR secretary and a symbol of New Deal liberalism—to Lyndon's staff as an opportunity to induce the representatives of minority groups in Texas— Hispanics, Catholics, Jews, and blacks—"to let their northern brethren know they have a favorable opinion of Lyndon B. Johnson." Above all, he needed to persuade people that a southerner and a man with a heart condition could be nominated and elected. If he could be seen as more of a westerner than a southerner and identified with a program off-setting anti-southern bias, it would go far to meet the first problem. If he could compile an impressive record in the first few weeks of the second session, he could show the country that he was "the same 'miracle man' he was before the heart attack."

The most intriguing offer to help him become President came from Joseph P. Kennedy, father of Senator John F. Kennedy. During a meeting in New York with Joe and Robert Kennedy—John's younger brother—Joe asked Tommy Corcoran to carry a message to Lyndon. If Johnson would announce his intention to run for President and promise privately to take Jack Kennedy as his running mate, Joe would arrange financing for the ticket. During a visit to the ranch in October, Corcoran put the proposition before Lyndon, who turned it down. "Lyndon told me he wasn't running and I told Joe," Corcoran recalls. "Young Bobby . . . was infuriated. He believed it was unforgivably discourteous to turn down his father's generous offer." It was the beginning of a long-term Bobby Kennedy–Johnson feud that intensified as the two men gained greater power and prestige. Corcoran remembered Jack as "more circumspect. He called me down to his office. . . . 'Listen Tommy,' Jack said, 'we made an honest offer to Lyndon through you. He turned us down. Can you tell us this: Is Lyndon running without us?' . . . Is he running?" Corcoran replied. "Does a fish swim? Of course he is. He may not think he is. And certainly he's saying he isn't. But I know God damned well he is. I'm sorry that he doesn't know it." Joe Kennedy then called Johnson to ask his intentions. Lyndon said he was not a candidate.

Lyndon saw it as premature to reveal his intentions. Any commitment to run, even one made confidentially to the Kennedys, seemed certain to leak out and jeopardize chances for the strong legislative record he and Reedy believed vital to a presidential bid. "If his colleagues thought he was pushing all those programs to get a track record for a presidential race," Corcoran said, "they'd scatter every time he called a caucus." Moreover, it was entirely possible that Eisenhower would run again, and if he did, it would make greater sense for Lyndon to seek the presidency in 1960 rather than in 1956. Johnson understood that the Kennedys wanted to use him as a stalking horse for Jack's White House ambitions. Joe Kennedy made it clear to Corcoran that the ultimate aim was to make Jack Kennedy President. From the Kennedy perspective, a losing Johnson campaign against Ike, with Jack as Lyndon's running mate, was a fine way to launch Kennedy's campaign for the presidential nomination in 1960.

Lyndon's refusal to acknowledge his candidacy or run in state primaries weakened his presidential candidacy. Avoiding the primaries did not necessarily bar someone from becoming the nominee. Adlai Stevenson, for example, was very reluctant to enter them. "If the party wants me, I'll run again," he had told a supporter in the fall of 1955, "but I'm not going to run around like I did before and run to all those shopping centers like I'm running for sheriff." In the end, however, he felt compelled to make a substantial effort in some of the states. After losing to Kefauver in New Hampshire and Minnesota, Stevenson ran successful campaigns in Florida, New Jersey, Oregon, and California. When Kefauver subsequently announced his withdrawal from the race and his support of Stevenson, Adlai approached the Democratic Convention in Chicago as the clear front runner.

Throughout the spring, despite his unwillingness to make an open bid for the nomination, Lyndon nurtured vague hopes of winning and took indirect steps to advance his candidacy. In June and July, he began making formal plans for the convention, arranging for a campaign headquarters and a floor demonstration to follow the nomination. His activities encouraged journalists to believe that he was doing more than "merely corralling the Texas votes for Adlai Stevenson." In late July, when NBC television offered a campaign roundup, the reporter suggested that people keep their eyes on Johnson at the Democratic Convention in August. He "is the man to whom both camps of the Democratic party [southern conservatives and northern liberals] look, to play the role of a contemporary Henry Clay—to be the great compromiser at Chicago." As the convention neared, other journalists predicted that if Stevenson didn't make it on the first ballot, the nominee might be Lyndon Johnson.

Stevenson in fact had the nomination locked up. The first ballot put him over the top with 905½ votes to 210 for Harriman, 80 for Lyndon, and 45½ for Symington. By refusing to release Texas and Mississippi delegates who voted for him, Johnson scored points with Texas conservatives who opposed Stevenson. To secure his hold on Texas and other southern conservatives, Johnson had also persuaded Richard Russell to spend a day and a half with him at the convention, where they would be seen sitting, talking, and eating together.

None of Johnson's close advisers could ever say with certainty what he had hoped to accomplish in Chicago. But he was probably aiming at 1960. On the eve of the convention, Rowe had urged against seeking either the presidential or vice-presidential nomination in 1956. Since Eisenhower was likely to win big that year, Lyndon would only lose by being on the ticket. Rowe proposed instead that he now "hold himself apart" and devote the next four years to winning the nomination and the White House.

When a fight for the vice-presidential nomination erupted at the convention, Lyndon did a balancing act which ingratiated him with both wings of the party. Lyndon initially told Stevenson that he had no interest in the vice presidency, and would not lobby for any other candidate. After Stevenson had won the nomination, however, Lyndon, encouraged by Richard Russell and Tommy Corcoran, sent Jim Rowe to tell Adlai that he wanted the job. In his conversation with Rowe, Stevenson was noncommittal. Lyndon responded by telling Adlai that "no Texan wants to be vice president." Stevenson then added to the confusion by deciding to let the delegates choose his running mate. Johnson and Rayburn opposed the plan, believing it would lead to a Kefauver candidacy unacceptable to the South. Stevenson, however, insisted on it.

Lyndon encouraged several senators to think that he favored them. John Kennedy later said that "Maybe Hubert thought that Lyndon was for him and maybe Symington thought the same thing and maybe Gore thought that too and maybe Lyndon wanted them all to think that. We never knew how that one [Johnson] would turn out." Under Lyndon's prodding, Texas voted for Gore on the first ballot, who came in third behind Kefauver and Kennedy. Southerners, including Texans, were opposed to Gore as too liberal. Johnson then told Humphrey that he would try to swing the delegation to him. While this raised Johnson's stock with Hubert, it got no where in the Texas delegation. Lyndon then swung his state to Kennedy, announcing on the second ballot: "Texas proudly casts its fifty-six votes for the fighting sailor who wears the scars of battle. . . ." Although Kefauver gained the nomination on a third ballot, Lyndon had shrewdly satisfied southerners by opposing Estes and northerners by backing Gore, Humphrey, and Kennedy in succession.

By working hard for Stevenson in the general campaign, Johnson emerged from the 1956 election as the Democratic party's dominant national figure. While an Eisenhower landslide buried Stevenson, it left the Democratic congressional majorities intact and made Rayburn and Johnson the party's undisputed leaders. More than ever, a successful presidential bid by Lyndon seemed to be a realistic possibility. But nothing could be taken for granted. Johnson needed some kind of track record in foreign affairs and an accommodation with party liberals if he were to make an effective bid for the 1960 nomination.

Although Lyndon wouldn't abandon bipartisanship on foreign policy issues that dogged Eisenhower during his second term, he believed that his political future partly rested on taking some greater distance from the Eisenhower White House which could mute tensions with liberals. These political considerations would have a large impact on Johnson's leadership of the 85th Congress. In 1957–58, politics and public need would produce landmark legislation affecting the country for years to come.

:: CIVIL RIGHTS

At the start of 1957, Johnson understood that he needed some dramatic public achievement to advance his political fortunes for 1960. Civil rights was the ideal issue. A major legislative gain arranged by Lyndon would strengthen his standing as a national rather than a regional leader and disarm liberals, who were the greatest obstacle to his nomination as the party's presidential candidate. Developments in 1956–57 had put civil rights at the center of domestic concerns. During 1956 the Supreme Court had ordered integration of the municipal bus systems in Columbia, South Carolina, and Montgomery, Alabama. In February 1957, *Time* put Martin Luther King, Jr., on its cover and praised him as the leader of the Montgomery movement and organizer of a Southern Leadership Conference seeking desegregation through nonviolent means. It was clear to Lyndon that pressure from southern blacks made change in the region inevitable. Renewed pressure for legislation that would implement the Supreme Court's 1954 *Brown* decision on school desegregation and enforce black voting rights made these matters ripe for action in Congress. With the House likely to pass a bill, as it did in 1956, the Senate would be the focus of attention. If he could lead a major civil rights bill through the Senate, it would be the first Federal legislative advance in this field in eighty-two years. Such an achievement would have multiple benefits; not the least of which would be a boon to his presidential ambitions.

Men as politically removed from one another as Richard Russell and Jim Rowe shared the understanding that Lyndon could not become President unless he did something significant to protect black rights in the South. "We can never make him President unless the Senate first disposes of civil rights," Russell told George Reedy in the fall of 1956. Jim Rowe advised Johnson: "Your friends and your enemies . . . are saying that you are trapped between your southern background and your desire to be a national leader. . . . If you vote against a civil rights bill you can forget your presidential ambitions in 1960." Rowe urged him to "get all the credit for . . . a compromise . . . , with the emphasis in the South on compromise, and emphasis in the North on getting a bill."

The importance of civil rights was impressing itself on Republican presidential aspirants as well. Nixon and Knowland, who had unimpressive voting records on civil rights, suddenly became champions of legislative advance.

Several other considerations influenced Lyndon's support of a civil rights law in 1957. A noticeable shift of black votes from Democrats to Republicans in the 1956 elections gave the issue a political urgency Lyndon and other Democrats had not felt before. Further, Democratic unity required that southerners and northerners find a way to compromise on the question and mute it as a divisive force in party affairs. Administration sponsorship of a civil rights bill in 1956 demonstrated that the South could no longer rely on Republicans to block reform. As George Reedy told Johnson, "The South is now *completely without allies.* In this situation, the South can stave off disaster only by appealing to those men who wish to see a civil rights bill enacted but *who are willing to listen to reason.*" Reedy urged an alliance between southern and moderate western Democrats like O'Mahoney of Wyoming, Clint Anderson of New Mexico, and Mike Mansfield of Montana to put across "reasonable and prudent legislation."

Arthur Schlesinger, Jr., gave Lyndon another reason to support a civil rights bill. He thought such a law would remind voters that the Democrats had not abandoned their "determination to use affirmative government as a means of serving the people and enlarging their rights and opportunities." Lyndon agreed: "I believe . . . that it is going to be difficult to obtain affirmative action until the Civil Rights issue is disposed of in some manner," he replied. " . . . There must be action on it, because . . . it is a road-block to the positive, constructive steps from which our party does gain advantages. . . . I hope that we can find a just and equitable solution that will enable us to put an end to the present internecine warfare."

Lyndon also believed that the future well-being of the South depended on Federal civil rights legislation that reduced racial strife. This was something he had known since the thirties when he had used the NYA and New Deal agricultural and housing laws to ease the suffering of black Texans and give them a greater measure of economic equality with whites. Harry McPherson, a liberal Texas attorney on his staff in the late fifties, believed that "Johnson felt about the race question much as I did, namely, that it obsessed the South and diverted it from attending to its economic and educational problems; that it produced among white Southerners an angry defensiveness and parochialism; that there were, nevertheless, mutually rewarding relationships between many Southern whites and Negroes; and that it should be possible to remove the common guilt by federal law while preserving the private values."

Doris Kearns reached a similar conclusion about Johnson's view of how segregation hurt the South. Johnson told her that by 1957 "the Senate simply had to act, the Democratic Party simply had to act, and I simply had to act; the issue could no longer wait." Inaction would injure the Senate's prestige, erode black support for the Democratic party, and "brand him forever as sectional and therefore unpresidential." Moreover, he believed that southern opposition to civil rights legislation made it impossible for the region "to act on its most fundamental problem—economic growth. Johnson argued, and he probably believed, that the South was on the verge of new possibilities for rapid expansion. However, the realization of these possibilities was far from certain. Decisions made by the leadership and people of the South could determine whether it would become one of the most prosperous areas of the country or whether it would remain an economic backwater. . . . Among the most significant determinants of Southern prospects would be the willingness of Southern leadership to accept the inevitability of some progress on civil rights and get on with the business of the future, or its continued insistence on conjuring the ghost of Thaddeus Stevens."

Johnson's sympathy for greater racial equality also moved him to support civil rights reform. To be sure, he could talk comfortably to other southerners in the vernacular. "Sam, why don't you all let this nigger bill pass?" he asked Rayburn during 1957. Even as late as 1965, when, as President, he appointed the first black Associate Justice to the United States Supreme Court, he privately used the same pejorative term to describe his appointee.

When a young Texas attorney joining his staff suggested a fine but obscure black federal judge for the position, Johnson said, "Son, when I appoint a nigger to the court, I want everyone to know he's a nigger." The attorney never heard him speak about blacks that way again and felt that Johnson was playing a part and trying to create a kind of rapport between two "good old Southern boys" at their first meeting.

This posturing aside, Johnson, according to Harry McPherson, was "your typical Southern liberal who would have done a lot more in the field of civil rights early in his career had it been possible; but the very naked reality was that if you did take a position . . . it was almost certain that you would be defeated . . . by a bigot. . . . But Johnson was one of those men early on who disbelieved in the Southern racial system and who thought that the salvation for the South lay through economic progress for everybody." George Reedy echoes the point: "The man had less bigotry in him than anybody else I have ever met. Much less than I had. As a kid, I was brought up in an Irish section of Chicago where we'd get out and beat up all the Polack kids whenever we could, or all the Italian kids. . . . And I grew up thinking that dumb Swede was one word. . . . But Johnson had none in him. . . . He had others, but not racial, ethnic, or religious prejudices." And liberal Democrat Clark Clifford, who got to know Johnson well in the fifties, feels that Johnson's sincerity could be in doubt on some matters but not racial equality. He looked at blacks and Hispanics, "looked at their lives, and saw they really did not have a chance. They did not have a decent chance for good health, for decent housing, for jobs; they were always skating right on the edge, struggling to keep body and soul together. I think he must have said to himself, 'Someday, I would love to help those people. My God, I would love to give them a chance!'"

In December 1956, Johnson had decided to pass a civil rights law. Publicly, Johnson denied he was doing anything of the kind. During the first months of 1957, after the White House had reintroduced its 1956 civil rights bill, Lyndon made several trips to Texas to discourage the idea that he was betraying Texas and the South by lining up with proponents of a law.

But that is exactly what he was doing. And more: He was orchestrating its passage. Between January and June the House proceeded deliberately on a bill, passing the administration's proposal on June 18. While Lyndon gave no public indication during this time of how he would respond to House approval, he was actively preparing the Senate for the event. He began holding a series of conversations with Richard Russell about the need to avoid a filibuster that the South might lose. With the Republicans backing Eisenhower's bill, it was entirely possible that a two-thirds majority might be assembled to vote cloture. Johnson persuaded Russell to accept the likelihood of a bill and to work instead to transform it into a measure more acceptable to the South than the one proposed by the White House.

Russell and Lyndon agreed to two major changes in Eisenhower's bill. First, they aimed to eliminate Section III, which would allow the Federal government to take a more active part in integrating southern schools. Second, they wished to ensure that anyone cited for contempt of court in a civil rights case would receive a jury trial. Such an amendment would have the practical effect of nullifying the law: White juries, the only kind southerners then had, would not convict other whites for violating black rights. With these revisions, the bill would turn into a voting rights law which would be largely unenforceable. In Lyndon's view, the South would buy the bill not only because it would be a weak law but also because conservative southern senators found it difficult to justify blatant constitutional violations of black voting rights. They were Constitutionalists who could not fight a voting rights measure with the same fervor they battled school desegregation or fair employment practices. Civil rights advocates would accept the measure as a limited, symbolic, but nevertheless important, first step toward greater Federal protection of black rights.

Getting a bill passed required a series of behind-the-scenes maneuvers largely arranged by Johnson. When the House bill arrived in the Senate on June 18, its advocates fought to put it on the calendar for floor debate or keep it from going to Eastland's Judiciary Committee where it would once again be buried. On June 20, Republican Minority Leader Knowland and liberal Democrat Paul Douglas joined forces to win the procedural fight by a vote of 45 to 39. Johnson, knowing proponents of the bill would win, sided with the southerners and insulated himself from criticism in Texas that he had joined the civil rights camp.

More surprising, four liberal western senators—Wayne Morse, Warren Magnuson, Mike Mansfield, and Jim Murray—voted to give Eastland the bill. They were trading their votes on civil rights for southern votes on public power. They had promised to help Johnson and Russell on civil rights in return for passage of a bill financing the Hells Canyon Dam on the Snake River in Idaho. In 1956, private power advocates had prevailed by 51 to 41 in turning back the Hells Canyon bill. The westerners seized the opportunity to switch conservative southern votes to their side. The southern maneuver to keep the civil rights bill from coming to the floor failed, but they honored their commitment anyway by helping pass the Hells Canyon bill, 45 to 38, on June 21. Five southerners, Russell, Eastland, Sam

Ervin, Russell Long, and George Smathers, all of whom had previously voted against the dam, now favored it.

Compared with the previous year, when Johnson gave no appreciable support to Hells Canyon, he now pulled out all stops. Johnson relied on a southern-western coalition to finance the dam and pass a civil rights bill without a filibuster, Frank Church of Idaho recalled. "He knew the western interest in Hells Canyon, and it was through his intervention with key southern senators, I'm sure, that enabled us to pass the bill."

On July 2, Richard Russell began the debate on the civil rights bill with a speech attacking all of Part III authorizing "the reimposition of post–Civil War Reconstruction" and portion of Part IV sanctioning trials by Federal judges without juries to punish defiance of the law. The speech was revealing less for what Russell said than what he didn't say. His attack was not on the entire bill but on two of its principal provisions, signaling that their elimination could lead to passage of a watered-down bill.

Johnson and Russell got unexpected help from Eisenhower on the next day. At a press conference, when the President was asked to comment on opposition to his bill, he replied that he wished only to protect and extend the right to vote. Was he willing to rewrite the bill to limit it to voting rights? a reporter asked. He refused to answer, "because I was reading part of that bill this morning, and there were certain phrases I didn't completely understand. So, before I made any more remarks on that, I would want to talk to the Attorney General and see exactly what they do mean." "It was a stunning confession of ignorance," according to Eisenhower biographer Stephen Ambrose. Ike "had been pushing the bill for two years . . . and yet now said he did not know what was in it. Eisenhower's admission was an open invitation to the southern senators to modify, amend, emasculate his bill, and they proceeded to do just that." On July 10, Russell visited Eisenhower at the White House to ask support for amending the bill. The President expressed his willingness "to listen to clarifying amendments to the Bill as it stands." The President's secretary noted in her diary: "He is not at all unsympathetic to the position people like Senator Russell take; far more ready than I am, for instance, to entertain their views. He always says 'I have lived in the south, remember.' The President also expressed himself as adamant on the right to vote, however, which was just what Russell and Johnson wanted to hear."

Lyndon responded to these developments by emphasizing the need for reasonableness and compromise. On July 11, he described the debate in the Senate as "of great value to our country," and inserted a *New York Times* editorial in the *Congressional Record* urging that the bill be restricted to voting rights. "It would in no way prejudice the inexorable forward march of school desegregation in the South to make it clear that this bill deals exclusively with voting rights, which is what almost everybody had thought all along it deals with," the *Times* said. "Integration of schools is quite another matter . . . it is the part of wisdom to take one step at a time and concentrate now, in this law, on the basic right of a free ballot."

Eisenhower's remarks at another press conference on July 17 gave further impetus to those who wished to limit the bill to voting rights. Asked if "it would be a wise extension of federal power at this stage to permit the Attorney General to bring suits on his own motion, to enforce school integration in the South," the President replied that action without any request from local authorities was not a good idea. "I personally believe if you try to go too far too fast in laws in this delicate field that has involved the emotions of so many million Americans, you are making a mistake."

Eisenhower's comments convinced Senate liberals that it would be difficult to keep an unamended Part III in the bill. The opinions of several Washington attorneys, including former Secretary of State Dean Acheson and FDR advisers Ben Cohen and Jim Rowe, that Part III was unconstitutional reinforced this view. "It [Part III] would be hopeless confusion — just madness," Acheson told Johnson. " . . . We have got to convince these damn fool Northern liberals not to nail their flag to the mast. They are defending the wrong thing [in Title III]." But the liberals' strategy was to compromise only after forcing a vote on Part III. When Gerry Siegel, one of Lyndon's staff attorneys, privately proposed a revised Title III that Russell had already agreed to, Paul Douglas and liberal attorney Joe Rauh refused to consider it. The liberals wanted to vote for the original Part III, and if it was defeated they would then support a modified version.

But they never had the chance. After listening to the floor debate for two days, Clinton Anderson of New Mexico, a civil rights supporter, suggested to Johnson that Part III be removed from the bill. It would ease southern fears of Federal military intervention to enforce school desegregation and would allow the Senate to pass a voting rights bill. Lyndon, who was "very receptive" to the idea and "very, very anxious to help," urged Anderson to find a moderate Republican co-sponsor who commanded bipartisan respect. When Anderson won the agreement of Vermont Senator George Aiken to help, it allowed Lyndon to put together a moderate-southern coalition which eliminated Title III on July 24 by a vote of 52 to 38.

Some hard work to put across a jury trial amendment remained. Johnson now worked around the clock, sleeping in his office and getting fresh clothes from Lady Bird each morning. To impress upon civil rights supporters his eagerness for a bill, he invited Eleanor Roosevelt, who was visiting Washington, to come see him at the Capitol. He sent his car with Grace Tully to bring her to his office. During their meeting, he told the former First Lady, who felt he had been slow to act on civil rights, "I'm here every night all night, day and night, but where are all the liberals?" Tully remembered Mrs. Roosevelt as "so interested" in what Johnson had to say. But, like other liberals, she had mixed feelings about the jury trial amendment.

Although liberals worried that a jury trial in cases arising out of civil rights violations would mean certain acquittal for southern offenders, some of them found the argument for a trial by jury irresistible, especially when Lyndon, supported by distinguished liberal attorneys like Ben Cohen and Abe Fortas, offered civil rights advocates certain concessions. Relying on an argument set forth by a Wisconsin law professor in a liberal magazine, the *New Leader*, Johnson agreed to omit jury trials in civil contempt cases but require them in criminal contempt proceedings. To draw labor support, he had the amendment include a requirement for trial by jury in criminal contempt cases involving unions. Major segments of organized labor, led by George Meany of the AFL and John L. Lewis of the UMW, agreed to support a bill that would ensure jury trials in criminal contempt cases resulting from violations of labor injunctions. Meany and Lewis hoped that the amendment would help protect labor from the indiscriminate use of injunctions by arbitrary judges. Walter Reuther of the CIO, however, opposed the amendment as nothing more than a means to continue denying black southerners the right to vote.

To answer this assertion, Johnson had Frank Church offer yet an additional amendment, guaranteeing "the right of *all* Americans to serve on [Federal] juries, regardless of race, creed or color." On the evening of August 1, just before the final vote on the jury trial amendment, Lyndon advised Church when to offer his "addendum; and he staged and timed that drama at the end of the long debate . . . in such a way as to attract maximum attention to this modification of the amendment, in the hopes that it would pull over . . . undecided votes." Although the addition pulled some swing votes to Lyndon's side, it temporarily made some of the southerners waver. Richard Russell felt "sold down" by Clint Anderson and Johnson. On August 2, he complained in a handwritten memo to himself that he had "allowed himself to be stampeded by Clint Anderson on threats of reviving Part III." With ten senators who had voted to eliminate Part III ready to vote against jury trials and nine who had supported retention of Part III prepared to back jury trials, "a little shaking and the house could come down."

Anderson himself tried to impress on Russell how weak his commitment to the jury trial amendment was by saying that he would vote for it "only to please L.B.J."

The administration fought hard to block the jury trial provision. Knowland and Vice President Nixon pressed Republican senators to stick by the White House, holding out offers of patronage to bring some of the waverers into line. Lyndon also pulled strings. After the jury trial amendment had been introduced, he felt the need for some "histrionics" supplied by Rhode Island's John Pastore. "Now you just watch the little Italian dancing master and see what happens here," Johnson told some of his aides. Pastore got up and started arguing against jury trials for criminal contempt. But a few minutes into his speech, he suddenly asked, "Wait, is that right?" And after analyzing what he had said, he concluded that he was wrong and came out strongly for the proposed amendment. Lyndon also promised Republican senators from Kansas and Maryland the right to fill newly created Federal district judgeships in return for their votes. Knowland, who thought he could count on thirty-nine Republicans, in fact had only thirty-three on his side. Late in the evening of August 1, after it was clear that Johnson had enough votes to win, Nixon told him in the Senate cloakroom, "You've really got your bullwhip on your boys tonight, Lyndon." "Yes, Dick," Johnson answered, "and from the way you've been trying to drive your fellows, you must have a thirty-thirty strapped to your hip, but it's not doing you any good." Nixon acknowledged that Johnson had won for the time being, but predicted that the long run would produce a different result. Shortly after midnight on August 2, at the end of a fourteen-hour legislative day, the Senate voted 51 to 42 for inclusion of the jury trial provision. The following day senators gave unanimous consent not to introduce additional amendments.

White House opposition jeopardized final passage of the bill. Nixon described the Senate action on the jury trial amendment as "a vote against the right to vote," and declared it "one of the saddest days in the history of the Senate." Reports described the President as "bitterly disappointed" and "damned unhappy," while House Minority Leader Joe Martin said the bill was "dead for the session." In response, civil rights advocates expressed "bitter disappointment" over the Senate changes in the bill, but urged its passage nevertheless as providing "some progress in this area." On August 7, the Senate voted 72 to 18 to pass the amended bill. But House members of a conference committee refused to accept the Senate changes. They won agreement to jury trials in criminal contempt cases only when a judge's sentence exceeded a $300 fine or 45 days in jail. Strom Thurmond of South Carolina staged a record-setting twenty-four-hour eighteen-minute filibuster against the compromise bill on August 28–29. He embarrassed other southern senators and momentarily deterred final passage of a bill most of them saw as a victory over civil rights advocates. Thurmond's action provoked Richard Russell to describe it as "a form of treason against the people of the South." Passing both houses on August 29, the President signed the bill into law on September 9.

Johnson was closely identified with the law, which received a mixed reception. Critics objected to the bill as a sham, a false promise of increased opportunity for southern blacks to vote. Eleanor Roosevelt complained that Lyndon was "trying to fool the people" with a law she called a "mere fakery." Republican and Democratic civil rights advocates echoed her complaint. Eisenhower's Deputy Attorney General William Rogers compared the law to "handing a policeman a gun without bullets." Prominent black leaders Ralph Bunche and A. Phillip Randolph thought it would have been better to have no bill or considered it worse than no bill at all. Senator Paul Douglas said the bill "was like soup made from the shadow of a crow which had starved to death." To Joseph Rauh of the Americans for Democratic Action, "Johnson's triumph was so tarnished that it proved his unfitness for national leadership." Johnson's critics had a point. The 1957 law did little to increase black voting and nothing to protect other civil rights. Two years after the bill had become law, for example, there were only 205 black voters on the rolls in four Alabama counties with large black populations, and not a single southern black had been added to the voting rolls.

Nevertheless, at the time, many civil rights proponents considered the bill a significant advance on where the Congress and the country had been. Benjamin Cohen called it "a great, historic event . . . the first time in over three-quarters of a century that the Senate has taken positive action on a civil rights bill." The theologian Reinhold Niebuhr saw the law as "a great triumph of democratic justice . . . because it . . . made some progress in reconciling a recalcitrant South to a higher standard of justice." Black civil rights leader Bayard Rustin thought it was a weak but "very important" law "that would establish a very important precedent." Civil rights leaders "were right in claiming that it contained only limited substance . . . ," George Reedy said. "But they failed to recognize the irrelevancy of the point. The act was a watershed. . . . A major branch of the American government that had been closed to minority members of the population seeking redress for wrongs was suddenly open. The civil rights battle could now be fought out legislatively in an arena that previously had provided nothing but a sounding board for speeches. . . . In less than a decade, a body of civil rights legislation was placed on the statute books to a degree that outstripped anything conceived in 1957." Reedy was right. The 1957 law was more symbol than substance, but it worked a radical change in legislative behavior: Enacting an effective civil rights bill was no longer out of reach.

Lyndon himself called the law "a great step forward." He saw it as an inducement to Americans everywhere to recognize that "nothing lasting, nothing enduring has ever been born from hatred and prejudice—except more hatred and prejudice." One columnist believed that Johnson had made himself "a—if not the—principal spokesman of the Democratic party in the country. Because he voted for and is an architect of the right-to-vote law, he is the first Southern Democratic leader since the Civil War to be a serious candidate for Presidential nomination and, if nominated, to have a fair chance of winning." Bobby Baker wrote him: "Your labors are being recognized in the American press. It is gratifying to know that the record made by you is acceptable to the great majority of Americans."

Johnson's hope that the civil rights law would mean a significant advance in southern race relations received a sharp jolt from a crisis in Little Rock, Arkansas. On September 3, Governor Orval Faubus had called out the National Guard to prevent the integration of Central High School. After a Federal court enjoined Faubus from using the Guard to keep black students from attending the school, Faubus withdrew the troops. In response, howling mobs appeared at the high school on September 23 and 24 to prevent attendance by nine black pupils. On the 24th, Eisenhower federalized the Arkansas Guard and sent additional Federal troops to enforce the law.

Southern political leaders were outraged. Senator Eastland called it "an attempt to destroy the social order of the South"; Richard Russell complained of "highhanded and illegal methods," "Hitler-like storm-trooper tactics," and "bayonet-point rule." Although the black students were able to attend the school and the crisis slowly faded during the next month, it showed that the 1957 Civil Rights Act had done little to advance the cause of reasonable race relations in the South. "I only hope that the magnificent work that you accomplished last summer has not been destroyed by the events in Arkansas," the historian C. Vann Woodward wrote Lyndon. "I confess that those events make me less hopeful for the future of the Democratic party as well as for a solution to the integration problem."

During the conflict, Lyndon tried to keep a low profile. Gerry Siegel, George Reedy, and Jim Rowe all advised Johnson not to "be involved either directly or indirectly." Lyndon saw the political wisdom in their advice, but he worried that the lack of constructive leadership or solutions would injure the entire nation. "The Arkansas situation is deeply disturbing," he wrote Dean Acheson. " . . . It is difficult to see a terminal point to a situation which is basically intolerable, and I am afraid that this country is headed for some real moments of trouble." "The task of responsible leadership . . . is to avoid irreconcilable positions," he wrote Chester Bowles. "The emotional tensions that have been created cannot be confined to one part of the country." Publicly, Johnson deplored the use of troops to maintain law and order and counseled self-restraint and prudence. When matters had calmed down in October, Jim Rowe urged him to become an intermediary between Faubus and Eisenhower. But the White House, which also considered discussing the situation with Johnson, sent him word that any conversation would "bring a bombardment for a statement . . . and this naturally had some of the potentialities of a trap." Convinced they were right, and seeing no political gain for either the nation or himself, Lyndon allowed the crisis to run its course without intervention on his part.

:: NASA

A crisis over a Soviet-launched man-made earth satellite, *Sputnik I*, became Johnson's principal public concern during the last months of 1957. The successful Soviet space launch sent a tremor of fear through the American Congress, press, and public. Although the device weighed less than 200 pounds and carried no military or scientific equipment, the country saw it as a demonstration of Soviet superiority in missiles and scientific education. Eisenhower assured the country that the satellite did not raise any apprehensions in him and that he saw nothing "significant in that development as far as security is concerned." But the country was unconvinced. Despite the President's assertion that the United States held the lead in a race for intercontinental ballistic missiles (ICBMs), Americans, spurred by Soviet boasting, now feared that Moscow had the capacity to send nuclear warheads across the ocean to strike their homeland. The Soviet accomplishment initiated a sharp debate in the United States, where "interservice rivalry, underfunding, complacency, disparagement of 'egghead' scientists, inferior education, [and] lack of imagination in a White House presided over by a semiretired golfer" received blame for America's second-class status in space.

Democrats attacked the Eisenhower administration for allowing the United States to fall behind the Soviets. Lyndon also saw the potential for enhancing his candidacy. "The issue *[Sputnik]* is one which, if properly handled, would blast the Republicans out of the water, unify the Democratic party, and elect you President," George Reedy wrote him. Johnson saw the political advantage to himself and the Democrats in seizing the space issue. But he feared a witch hunt that might further undermine confidence in the country's military strength and reveal the administration as unable to meet the Soviet challenge. He believed that a restrained, nonpartisan investigation would best serve the country and himself.

Richard Russell agreed. He asked Johnson to gather information from the Defense Department on the state of America's missile program before deciding on an appropriate course of action. The Pentagon was eager to cooperate. "We very much appreciate the way you are approaching this," Ike's Secretary of Defense Neil McElroy told Johnson on October 21. ". . . If through your efforts it is kept out of partisan politics, it will be for the good of the public and we want to work with you." Yet McElroy had no illusions about the politics involved. As one assistant told him, "No sooner had *Sputnik*'s first beep-beep been heard—via the press—than the nation's legislators leaped forward like heavy drinkers hearing a cork pop."

On November 3, the Soviets launched a second, much heavier satellite carrying a dog. Two days later, Lyndon told Dulles that "the country was scared. Something had to be done. He himself was not panicky and did not want to engage in a search for a scapegoat but did feel that there was a need for a searching and constructive inquiry by Congress. On the same day, he told Republican Senator Styles Bridges that Russell was very upset. Russell felt that Johnson and Bridges should use the Preparedness subcommittee for an investigation. Johnson also said that he was putting together a top-notch staff. Johnson advised Bridges to tell the press that he was "in complete agreement with Senator Johnson and that this should be a national investigation instead of a partisan one; that we are going to ask the people in charge to tell us . . . how we can regain the leadership."

Johnson set up a series of ground rules to insulate the investigation from becoming too political. First, the only guilty parties in the inquiry were Joe Stalin and Nikita Khrushchev. Second, the Committee's only interest in the past would be as a guide for future action. Third, the inquiry's sole objective was securing the defense of the United States. And fourth, the party identification of witnesses was irrelevant; what mattered was their knowledge on how the United States could produce better missiles at a faster rate.

During the two months of hearings, Lyndon largely stuck to his design. Yet he was not simply a selfless patriot. He also took partisan advantage of the hearings, but in subtle ways. The facts emerging from the investigation demonstrated the administration's ineptness in mounting an effective missile and space program. It also allowed Lyndon to identify himself as the country's leading congressional advocate of a stepped-up effort in space. He dominated the hearings, introducing witnesses, leading cross-examinations, and making himself the principal spokesman to the press. When an attempt to launch an American missile on December 6 ended in failure, Lyndon declared: "How long, how long, oh God, how long will it take us to catch up with the Russians' two satellites?"

The two-month investigation from November to January represented only the first phase of Lyndon's effort to make the country the world's leader in space. He believed it essential to set up a permanent Federal space agency and a standing congressional committee. On February 6, he led a resolution through the Senate setting up a Special Committee on Space and Astronautics which was to frame legislation for a national space program. On the 20th, he became chairman of the 13-member committee, and on April 14, he and Styles Bridges co-sponsored the administration's bill creating a National Aeronautics and Space Agency (NASA).

Lyndon was the architect of the new organization. He was eager to give the military a large say in the country's space effort, but he saw good reasons for putting the program in civilian hands. If the task had been assigned to one of the military services, it would have created a budgetary imbalance between them. It seemed wiser to create a civilian-controlled space agency that could call on all three services for support. It also made good political sense. Lyndon and the White House knew that peaceful rather than military uses of space were more palatable to domestic and foreign opinion. He received his most favorable publicity when identified with the international aspects of outer space, aides told Johnson. In historian Walter A. McDougall's words, "The space program was a paramilitary operation in the cold war, no matter who ran it," but civilian control headed off a significant imbalance between the services and met the political needs of American officials at home and abroad.

Two other goals for the space program eluded Lyndon. He wanted the legislation to include a nine-member Space Council that would set comprehensive space policy and designate specific programs. But Eisenhower, who thought it would become another National Security Council, urged that the Space Council be a purely advisory body. After Lyndon acceded to Ike's wishes at a White House meeting on July 7, the way was cleared for the measure to become law on July 29. Lyndon also wanted senators to dominate a joint congressional space committee. But House members led by Majority Leader John McCormack refused, and separate committees were created.

By September 1958 Lyndon had entered the small circle of men from whom the nation picks its chief executives. Yet he was hardly the unanimous choice of other Democrats, especially liberals. Despite his leadership on civil rights, they saw Johnson as too highhanded or overbearing and too self-aggrandizing or hungry for power and control. "I despised the guy" from the early days in the Senate, one of them said. "He was a hypocritical s.o.b. . . . He was a typical Texan wheeler-dealer with no ethical sense whatever, but a great pragmatic ability to get things done." Doris Fleeson, the liberal columnist, distrusted Johnson's professions of public service. She saw him as subordinating the interests of his party and country to his personal ambitions, and his overpowering style irritated her: Told that another journalist had written a favorable piece about Johnson to keep Lyndon talking to him, she responded, "How could you stop him?" Critics also joked about a sixty-foot flagpole at Johnson's ranch flying Old Glory, the ensign of the Lone Star state, and a personal pennant with LBJ set in the middle of five white stars on a blue field. Antagonism to his grandiosity expressed itself in quips on the eve of the 1958 and 1959 State of the Union addresses: Lyndon Johnson "will resent Ike's interference in governmental affairs"; "Senator Lyndon Johnson entered the House chambers to a sustained rising ovation. He was accompanied by the President."

John Kennedy entertained audiences in 1958 with the story that the Good Lord in a dream told him he would be the Democratic party's nominee and would then be elected President. He told Stu Symington about his dream, who said it was funny that he had the same dream himself. When they both told Lyndon their dreams, he said, "That's funny. For the life of me I can't remember tapping either of you two boys for the job."

Yet for all this antagonism to him, no one could deny that Johnson had become one of the country's most formidable political figures with a powerful claim on the presidential nomination of his party. Although Johnson made blanket denials in 1957–58 that he was a candidate, few people believed him, and many assumed that despite certain handicaps, his ability, drive, and energy might well carry him to the nomination and the White House.

4 :: THE VICE PRESIDENT

:: THE MAKING OF A V.P.

From the fall of 1958 to the Democratic Convention in July 1960 the struggle for the party's nomination was front-page news. At the beginning of 1959, political pundits agreed that Senators Hubert Humphrey, Lyndon Johnson, John Kennedy, and Stuart Symington, New York Governor Averell Harriman, and Adlai Stevenson were the front runners. The start of the year was a crucial time in the fight for the nomination. Jim Rowe urged Lyndon to launch a campaign at once. Johnson said he couldn't get the nomination and wouldn't run. Rowe didn't believe him. "He wanted the thing. I think he wanted it so much his tongue was hanging out. Then this other part of him said, 'This is impossible. Why get my hopes up? I'm not going to try. If I don't try, I won't fail.'"

Doubts about winning gave Lyndon some hesitation. But he had been in the race since 1956. His refusal to mount an organized public campaign was part of a strategy for getting the nomination. Johnson believed that any public declaration of his intent to run would have defeated him. He told Rayburn: "All this talk about my candidacy is destroying my leadership. I'm trying to build a legislative record over there. The Senate already is full of presidential candidates. If I really get into this thing, they'll gang up on me and . . . I'll be disqualified for the nomination."

In the spring of 1959, Lyndon arranged changes in Texas election laws that advanced primaries from July and August to May and June and allowed a candidate to run for two national offices at the same time. Were Lyndon renominated for the Senate in the spring, he could still become the party's presidential or vice-presidential nominee in the summer and run for both offices simultaneously.

During 1959 Lyndon believed that his strategy was working. In March, Reedy told him that columnists accepted his denials as "genuine and sincere," but he continued to be "in the Presidential picture. . . . You are the only national Democratic leader who has a record of achievement."

Johnson attributed his viability as a candidate to his identification as a political moderate, a pragmatic southwesterner capable of good working relations across the political spectrum. In a time of intense racial and sectional strife, Johnson saw himself as perhaps the only politican who could substantially ease black-white and North-South tensions. Moreover, as a visceral New Deal liberal who had worked effectively with southern and western conservatives and Eisenhower moderates, he thought he could accommodate the various special interests in the nation as no elected official had since FDR. Finally, as a consistent advocate of a strong defense, he viewed himself as someone around whom the nation could rally in foreign affairs. He believed that the party and country would turn to him as a consensus builder, a moderate nationalist who could more effectively hold the nation together and address its domestic and international problems than any politician, Democrat or Republican, on the national scene.

At the close of the congressional session in September 1959 questions arose about Lyndon's intentions in the 1960 campaign. Publicly and privately he continued to deny his candidacy. Asserting that his health would not permit him to run and that a southerner could not get the nomination or be elected, he refused to acknowledge that he was in the chase. Other political leaders didn't believe him. Adlai Stevenson thought he was a candidate; and Jack Kennedy said that Lyndon was "running very hard." Jack sent his brother and campaign manager Bobby Kennedy to Johnson's ranch to ask him directly. Lyndon said he wasn't running and wouldn't oppose or help Jack, but urged against a third nomination for Adlai. During the visit, Johnson insisted that they hunt deer. Bobby was knocked to the ground and cut above the eye by the recoil of a powerful shotgun Johnson had given him to use. Reaching down to help the thirty-four-year-old Bobby up, Lyndon said: "Son, you've got to learn to handle a gun like a man." The incident was an indication of Johnson's small regard for Jack Kennedy's claim on the White House.

People close to Johnson at this time believed that his heart condition and fear of defeat inhibited him from an all-out fight for the nomination. These concerns account in part for his undeclared candidacy. But, more important, his non-candidacy continued to serve his political ends. An announced bid for the presidency would likely make him the immediate front runner and the object of a powerful, and probably successful, stop-Lyndon movement. He saw no other Democrat with an equal claim to the nomination and White House. Stevenson had had his chances, and party leaders would shun him. Humphrey was too liberal to be an effective national candidate. Symington lacked the sort of track record that would inspire the party and country to make him President. That was even more the case with Jack Kennedy, however appealing his style and personality. Lyndon told Bobby Baker that he knew ten times more about running the country than Jack did. "That kid needs a little gray in his hair." He called him a "playboy" and a "lightweight," who was "smart enough," but had shown little capacity for the sort of hard work required of an effective President.

Johnson's obtuseness about Kennedy speaks volumes about Lyndon's limited understanding of how important style was in a presidential candidate and successful White House occupant. Franklin Roosevelt's patrician bearing, Harry Truman's plain spoken honesty, Dwight Eisenhower's benign, nonpartisan demeanor, and John Kennedy's charm and intelligence served to endear each of them to great numbers of Americans. Johnson's deserved reputation for crudeness and wheeling and dealing cast a long shadow over his many legislative achievements and undercut his chances of winning over a majority of Democrats and the nation's voters.

By the spring of 1960, Lyndon's fight for the nomination was an open secret. Publicly, Lyndon had restated his unwillingness to run. "I have been asked about my Presidential candidacy from Phoenix, Arizona, all the way to Washington, D.C.," he announced on January 6. "My answer has been the same in every instance. I am not running for anything other than a successful session of this Congress and United States Senator from Texas." Yet he left the door ajar by declaring: "I do not pretend to know what I will be doing next summer or next fall."

To no one's surprise, on July 5, Lyndon formally announced his candidacy. He predicted that he would win on the third ballot. He explained that he had not been able to declare his candidacy while Congress was in session. As Majority Leader, he could not miss the hundreds of votes other active candidates missed. As for the nomination, the issue before the convention was experience and capacity to lead. World Communism would show "no mercy for innocence, no gallantry toward inexperience, no patience toward errors."

By the time the convention began in earnest on the evening of July 11, Lyndon knew that Kennedy had the nomination locked up. Two days before, after seeing Hubert Humphrey and Governor Robert Meyner of New Jersey, Johnson had told an aide, "It is all over with. It is going to be Kennedy by a landslide."

On the night of July 13, after Kennedy won the nomination on the first ballot, 806 to Lyndon's 409, Kennedy was not happy at having to choose a running mate in twenty-four hours. But he already had given the question some thought. Several weeks before the convention, Theodore Sorensen and other campaign advisers had given him lists of potential vice-presidential nominees. Johnson's name headed several of the lists, but Kennedy did not think Lyndon would give up the Senate Leadership. "I wouldn't want to trade a vote for a gavel, and I certainly wouldn't want to trade the active position of leadership of the greatest deliberative body in the world for the part-time job of presiding," Lyndon had said. Meanwhile, the Kennedy campaign had assured labor leaders and liberal delegates they were wooing that Lyndon would not be on the ticket. On Monday, July 11, however, columnist Joe Alsop and *Washington Post* publisher Phil Graham urged Kennedy to pick Johnson. "He immediately agreed, so immediately as to leave me doubting the easy triumph," Graham remembered, "and I therefore restated the matter, urging him not to count on Johnson's turning it down but to offer the VPship so persuasively as to win Johnson over. Kennedy was decisive in saying that was his intention, pointing out that Johnson would help the ticket not only in the South but in important segments of the Party all over the country."

Graham and Alsop weren't the only ones active in Lyndon's behalf. According to Arthur Krock, Governor David Lawrence of Pennsylvania, speaking for Mayor Richard Daley of Chicago and Carmine DiSapio of New York, recommended that Kennedy put Johnson on the ticket.

Johnson was eager to do it. On the morning of the nomination, when Sam Rayburn discussed the matter with House Majority Leader John McCormack and Massachusetts congressman Tip O'Neill, Rayburn said, "Well, if Kennedy wants Johnson for Vice President . . . then he has nothing else he can do but to be on the ticket." Rayburn gave McCormack and O'Neill his phone number, and asked them to tell "Jack Kennedy that if he wants me to talk to Lyndon Johnson, I'll tell him exactly that. . . . If Jack Kennedy is interested in Lyndon Johnson being the vice-presidential nominee, you have him call me and by golly, I'll insist on it." That evening, O'Neill related the message to Kennedy on the sidewalk in front of Chasen's Restaurant in West Hollywood, where Kennedy had gone for a reception. "Of course I want Lyndon Johnson," Kennedy said. " . . . The only thing is I would never want to offer it and have him turn me down; I would be terrifically embarrassed. He's the natural. If I can ever get him on the ticket, no way we can lose. We'd carry Texas. Certainly I want him. I'll call Sam Rayburn. You tell Sam that I'll call him after the convention tonight." O'Neill gave Rayburn the message at the convention later that night. O'Neill didn't see Rayburn again until they returned to Washington. When they met in the House lobby, Sam said, "Well Tom . . . I guess we played a part of history that will never get in the history books."

In addition to Rayburn's conversation with McCormack and O'Neill, there is other evidence that Lyndon was eager for the vice-presidential nomination if he couldn't get the top spot. In March 1960, as Johnson and several friends had driven in his limousine to a wedding in New Jersey, they discussed Kennedy's qualifications for the presidency. When everyone agreed that Jack had the class, education, instincts, and guts to do the job, Lyndon suddenly said: "A fellow from my part of the country couldn't be anything more than another John Nance Garner." Johnson seemed to be thinking about what he could make of the vice presidency. As with the Majority Leader's post, could he make it into something more than it had traditionally been? In June, Bobby Baker had "cautioned" Ted Sorenson "not to be so certain that his boss would reject a Kennedy-Johnson ticket." At the same time, Reedy gave Johnson a memo justifying a decision to take the vice presidency. Further, on July 5, when a reporter pressed him to say if he would consider taking the vice presidency, he replied: "I would never reject something that hasn't been offered to me. . . . I have been prepared throughout my adult life to serve my country in any capacity where my country thought my services were essential." Clark Clifford says that on the night of July 13, after Kennedy's nomination, Rayburn urged Jack to take Lyndon as his running mate. Eliot Janeway remembers that Johnson "was very anxious to get out of the Majority Leadership. Johnson would have paid for the vice presidency."

Johnson in fact had good reason to want the vice-presidential nomination. In Arthur Schlesinger, Jr.'s view, Johnson had "a deep sense of responsibility about the future of the South in the American political system. He used to lament the fact that so much southern political energy was diverted from constructive political channels to the defense of the past . . . fighting for lost causes. If the Democratic party did not give a southerner a place on the ticket in 1960, it would drive the South even further back on itself and into self-pity, bitterness and futility. He may well have seen in the Vice-Presidency a means of leading the South back into the Democratic party and the national consensus."

It was also clear to Johnson that he could no longer control the Senate as he had in 1955–58. In 1959 and 1960, party liberals and Eisenhower's assertiveness had undermined Johnson's effectiveness as Leader. "Johnson felt he had lost control," Janeway says. "He had lost emotional control of the Senate. And he was very bitter against a good third of the Democratic caucus." Theodore F. Green of Rhode Island told Tommy Corcoran that "Lyndon was finished as an effective majority leader. . . . If he went back, Green said, they might give him the title again but they wouldn't follow him." Lyndon didn't need Janeway to tell him what he already knew. His best days as Majority Leader had passed. If Kennedy won the presidency, the White House would set the legislative agenda and Lyndon would be little more than the President's man in the Senate. If Kennedy lost the election, Lyndon would be left to cope with another assertive Republican President, as Ike had been in 1959–60, and hostile Democratic liberals, who would surely say that Lyndon's bipartisanship or failure to publicize differences between Democrats and Republicans had contributed to a Nixon victory. If he ran with Kennedy and they lost, he could still go back to the Senate and be in a stronger position than ever to seek the presidential nomination. Should Kennedy and he win, Lyndon might use his political magic to convert the vice presidency, as with the Senate Leadership, into something more than it had been before.

It is impossible to reconstruct the exact sequence of events on July 14 leading to Johnson's selection as the vice-presidential nominee. "The full story of how Kennedy selected Johnson as vice president will never be told," Myer Feldman, a special counsel to President Kennedy, said. When Feldman asked the President what the true story of the selection was, Kennedy replied: "Well, you know, I don't think anybody will ever know."

What seems clear is that Kennedy wanted Johnson on the ticket to help him win southern states and because Johnson seemed transparently qualified to be President. And so despite opposition from Jack's brother Bobby and from labor and other liberal leaders, Kennedy made Johnson his running mate.

On the evening of the 14th, Lyndon's name went before the convention. The balloting began, and when the roll call reached Massachusetts, John McCormack proposed a voice vote on Johnson's nomination. Eager to avoid embarrassing objections, the Kennedys arranged with McCormack and Governor LeRoy Collins of Florida, the convention chairman, to suspend the rules and permit the voice vote. When Collins put the proposition to the delegates, the shouted "ayes" and "nays" seemed about evenly divided. But Collins declared that two-thirds of the delegates had concurred and Senator Lyndon B. Johnson had been nominated for the vice presidency by acclamation.

In the six weeks before the traditional Labor Day start to the presidential race, Kennedy and Johnson made campaign plans. The Kennedys wanted

Lyndon to focus on the South and West and Jack on the industrial states. Johnson was to be a "regional candidate" who would "solidify the South ... attract the conservatives and ... give an atmosphere of soundness" to the ticket. Johnson's advisers urged him instead to be a "national candidate" who went into all sections of the country and faced elements in the party and the electorate that viewed him with suspicion. Likewise, they felt that Kennedy should go into the South and meet the religious issue head on.

At the end of July, Lyndon went to the Kennedy Compound at Cape Cod to discuss campaign strategy and the congressional session beginning on August 8. Some of Kennedy's aides privately criticized Johnson's overbearing manner and verbosity during the two days of talks, but Kennedy considered the meeting a success. Lyndon's ebullience at a joint press conference, in which he did most of the talking, pleased Kennedy, who felt it dispelled talk of any incompatibility between them. Johnson encouraged the picture of mutual congeniality in a press release to Texas papers: Texans like Johnson and New Englanders like Kennedy shared a sense of pride, tradition, and fearlessness that Texans would see for themselves when Kennedy came to the Lone Star state.

The principal issue Johnson confronted in the campaign was Kennedy's religion. By early August, Johnson had received so much mail questioning a Catholic's suitability for the presidency that he had asked the Kennedy campaign for suggestions on a reply. Texas friends also predicted a tough fight for the state and said religion was the main problem. "We are just catching hell on that issue," one observer told Walter Jenkins.

Lyndon hammered on the religious bigotry behind the opposition to Kennedy. In September, after Kennedy effectively told a group of Protestant ministers meeting in Houston that his religion would have no impact on his performance as president, Johnson began attacking Nixon for failing "to publicly repudiate those raising" the religious question. White House counsel Bryce Harlow told Nixon that he was "being religioned right out of this campaign." While Nixon wouldn't discuss the matter directly, "Lyndon is talking religion at every stop, all over the country . . . And you're just flat losing the campaign on religion, and that's wrong. You should attack it, the hypocrisy of it. . . . It's a calculated stance. Kennedy can't talk it. Lyndon can and Lyndon's talking it."

A lot of Johnson's calculated talk on religion came in a five-day whistle-stop tour of the South beginning October 10. Former President Harry Truman, who had used the back platform of a train so effectively in the 1948 campaign, urged Lyndon to do the same thing. Starting in Virginia, Johnson's tour covered 3,500 miles across eight states, where he gave sixty speeches. The eleven-car train, the *LBJ Victory Special*, or "Cornpone Special," as some journalists dubbed it, was met by governors, senators, congressmen, and other state and local officials who shared the back platform with Lyndon for a few stops along the way. The trip was good political theater. Aides to Texas congressmen dressed in coveralls positioned themselves throughout the crowd in Culpeper, Virginia, and led the cheers for Johnson. Lindy Boggs, wife of Louisiana congressman Hale Boggs, led an advance team of five other women dressed in blue blazers, white pleated skirts and blouses, and red hats. They flew from city to city to meet the train, where their presence helped discourage opponents from more overt displays of antagonism to Kennedy and Johnson. Using southern songs played over loudspeakers and homespun speeches to disarm audiences, Lyndon celebrated Democratic achievements, decried Nixon's unreliability, and compared the attack on Kennedy's Catholicism to prejudice against the South.

Hecklers with signs declaring "LBJ Is a Friend of Socialism" and "The *Yellow* Rose of Texas" showed Lyndon the limits of his influence in the South. He worried especially about Texas, where the election was a toss-up. At the end of September, he wired Fort Worth newspaper publisher Amon Carter, "I need you as I have never needed you before." Former congressman Lloyd Bentsen told Walter Jenkins that Texas Democrats were broke and weren't getting money from their usual sources. In mid-October, Lyndon told John Connally he was "deeply disturbed about Texas. . . . We just must not win the nation and lose Texas. Imagine when we win how the next Administration will look upon us."

Jim Rowe remembered that Johnson "was wound up tight like a top and I think the ever haunting fear of losing Texas never left him for a second." Johnson's tension over the outcome of the campaign spilled over into private tirades at his staff. Almost anything could touch him off: a disappointingly small crowd, a tight speaking schedule, a schedule with too much free time, an encounter with someone he didn't like, a podium that didn't meet his exact specifications for reading a speech or being seen by his audience, a failure of the loudspeaker system, a missing change of clothes, or practically anything that other less temperamental or intense personalities would have ignored.

Yet whatever the difficulties with him in private, "he ran a tremendous public campaign," Jim Rowe said. He celebrated "the Boston-Austin Axis," the union of North, South, and West; attacked Nixon and religious prejudice; praised Kennedy; pressured southern Democrats into working for the ticket; and mustered all possible support in Texas. Johnson gave the Kennedys reason to feel that they had chosen an effective running mate.

No single incident in the campaign involving Johnson did more to help the ticket than the public abuse of Lyndon and Lady Bird by right-wing opponents in Dallas four days before the election. Lyndon confronted a mob of angry protestors at a downtown hotel on November 4. Led by Dallas congressman Bruce Alger, Texas's only Republican representative, they carried signs denouncing Johnson as a Carpetbagger controlled by Yankee Socialists. As Lyndon and Lady Bird walked across the street from the Baker to the Adolphus Hotel and then through its lobby to an elevator, the crowd, partly of Junior League women, "the Mink Coat Mob," some called it, verbally and physically assaulted the Johnsons, hitting Lady Bird on the head with a picket sign and spitting at them.

Although Lyndon was genuinely outraged by the abuse, he immediately saw the political advantage in Texas and throughout the South in the televised pictures of a shrieking mob assaulting an unprotected vice-presidential candidate. Indeed, as they inched forward through the crowd, Johnson asked the police to leave: "'If the time has come when I can't walk through the lobby of a hotel in Dallas with my lady without a police escort, I want to know it.'" When Lady Bird lost her temper and started to answer one of the hecklers, "Mr. Johnson kind of put his hand over her mouth and stopped that and brought her right along." The Johnsons could have made their way through the Adolphus lobby in five minutes, one observer recalls. But they "took thirty minutes . . . and it was all being recorded and photographed for television and radio and the newspapers, and he knew it and played it for all it was worth." Bill Moyers said that Johnson "could never have calculated that scene or fixed that situation or arranged for it. He didn't know how he was going to carry Texas. . . . If he could have thought this up, he would have thought it up. Tried to invent it. But the moment it happened, he knew." He used the incident to tar the Republicans as extremists and persuade Richard Russell to do some last minute speaking for the ticket in Texas and South Carolina.

On November 8, Kennedy won the presidency by 112,881 votes out of 66,832,818 cast. The electoral college showed a more decisive margin of 303 to 219. Seven of the old Confederate states—Alabama, Arkansas, Georgia, Louisiana, North and South Carolina, and Texas—went Democratic. Florida, Tennessee, and Virginia voted Republican, while Mississippi gave a plurality to an independent segregationist ticket. Texas favored Kennedy and Johnson by only 46,233 votes out of 2,311,670 cast. At the same time, Lyndon won his Senate race against Republican John Tower, but by only 56.5 percent to 43.5 percent, 1,210,000 to 936,000 votes.

Kennedy's effectiveness as a campaigner was indisputable. But no one in the Kennedy camp discounted the importance of Lyndon's contribution, especially in the South, where he skillfully emphasized all the Democrats had done for the region without publicly using racist appeals to win white votes. As Joseph Kennedy had predicted immediately after Jack had chosen Johnson as his running mate, "Don't worry, Jack. . . . Everyone will be saying that this was the smartest thing you ever did." If it was not the smartest, it certainly was one of the shrewdest. It is doubtful that a midwestern running mate would have given him the help he needed in the South.

Lyndon responded to their victory with mixed feelings. He was exhilarated by the important part he played in the campaign, and particularly at having helped put Texas in the Democratic column for the first time since 1948. Yet he also had a sense of frustration at being elected Vice President rather than President. On election night, after he knew they had won, he "looked as if he'd lost his last friend on earth. . . . I don't think I ever saw a more unhappy man," one of his secretaries recalls. He expressed his distress and rivalry with Kennedy during a telephone call: "'I see you are losing Ohio,'" he said to Jack. "'I am carrying Texas and we are doing pretty well in Pennsylvania.'" "Doesn't that sound like him?" Jim Rowe told Hubert Humphrey.

As the Vice President–elect in 1960, Johnson hoped to provide a measure of leadership uncommonly associated with that largely symbolic office. He knew how little his predecessors had accomplished in what John Adams called "the most insignificant office that ever the invention of man contrived or his imagination conceived." But as a congressional secretary, an NYA administrator, a congressman, and a senator, he had achieved things others had not thought possible. He aimed to convert the vice presidency into a vehicle for gains the country would not soon forget. And should the presidency be within his reach after a vice-presidential term, he would challenge the country to fulfill its boldest dreams. For Lyndon Johnson, politics had been a difficult, sometimes dirty business. But most of all, it was a vocation in which a fallible man could rise from the obscurity of the Texas Hill Country to the second office of the land and along the way do extraordinary things.

:: "THE MOST INSIGNIFICANT OFFICE"

Lyndon was a reluctant Vice President. He had hoped and planned for the presidency, but fate or the limitations of his time, place, and personality had cast him in the second spot. And he despised it. As Vice President, he found himself in a dead-end job. Or so the 172-year history of the office suggested. There were no notable achievements by a Vice President to give him comfort, and no Vice President had succeeded to the presidency by election since Martin Van Buren in 1836. Johnson was mindful of the observation made by Thomas R. Marshall, Woodrow Wilson's V.P., that the Vice President "is like a man in a cataleptic state. He cannot speak. He cannot move. He suffers no pain. And yet he is conscious of all that goes on around him." John Adams, the first occupant of the office, wrote: "I am Vice President. In this I am nothing, but I may be everything." Johnson recalled: "Every time I came into John Kennedy's presence, I felt like a goddamn raven hovering over his shoulder."

John Kennedy added to Johnson's sense of being eclipsed and useless. The son of a famous father, Joseph P. Kennedy, Harvard-educated, handsome, charming, urbane, a northeastern aristocrat with all the advantages, JFK appeared to be everything LBJ was not. As painful to Johnson, Kennedy's claim on the presidency seemed unmerited alongside of his own. "It was the goddamnedest thing," Johnson later told Kearns, "here was a whippersnapper. . . . He never said a word of importance in the Senate and he never did a thing. But somehow . . . he managed to create the image of himself as a shining intellectual, a youthful leader who would change the face of the country."

When the forty-three-year-old Kennedy, the youngest man ever elected to the presidency, declared in his Inaugural speech that "the torch has been passed to a new generation of Americans," Johnson saw the reference as applying not only to Eisenhower, at age seventy, the oldest man then to have served in the White House, but also to himself. To be sure, he had established a record as an exceptional Senate leader and had made a significant contribution to JFK's election. But whatever his political savvy as a legislator and a campaigner, he was now an outsider, a marginal figure in a Kennedy White House taking its distance from familiar faces and programs as it sought to conquer "the New Frontier."

:: DEFINING THE JOB

Johnson had no intention of remaining a fringe player in a Kennedy administration. In accepting the vice-presidential nomination, he had high hopes of transforming the office. Presiding over the Senate and casting rare tie-breaking votes—a Vice President's only constitutional duties— were not Johnson's idea of how to achieve a second four years as Vice President and a record to win the presidency. A promise from Jack Kennedy to

Sam Rayburn that he would give Lyndon "important domestic duties and send him on trips abroad," if he agreed to become Vice President, was music to Johnson's ears. During the 1960 campaign one of Johnson's aides told him that the Founding Fathers "intended the Vice President to be the number two man in the government" and that a larger executive role for the Vice President should complement a significant part for him in rallying Congress behind the President's program. Johnson wanted the memo published in a national magazine.

Johnson's plan to make himself a powerful Vice President ran into insurmountable obstacles. On January 3, seventeen days before taking office, he tried to assure himself of an unprecedented congressional role. At a Democratic Senate caucus, Mike Mansfield of Montana, Johnson's hand-picked successor as Majority Leader, asked the 63 Democratic senators to let Johnson preside over future caucuses. The proposal angered several senators, who saw this as a power grab and a challenge to the traditional separation of congressional-executive authority. Liberal Senator Albert Gore, Sr., of Tennessee spearheaded the opposition: "This caucus is not open to former senators," he declared. Although a vote of 46 to 17 gave Johnson a large majority, it left no doubt in his mind that most senators opposed the plan. "You could feel the heavy animosity in the room, even from many who voted for Lyndon," Gore asserted. The reaction of his Senate colleagues humiliated and enraged Johnson. "I now know the difference between a caucus and a cactus," he told someone who leaked his remark to reporters. "In a cactus all the pricks are on the outside."

Johnson suffered another humiliating defeat within days after becoming Vice President. In his eagerness to establish an important role for himself, Johnson proposed that Kennedy sign an Executive Order giving the Vice President "general supervision" over a number of government agencies, including NASA, and directing Cabinet heads and department chiefs to give Johnson copies of all major documents sent to the President. Knowing a power grab when he saw one, Kennedy simply ignored the memo. But White House aides, determined to put Johnson in his place at the start of the new administration, leaked the incident to the press and compared Lyndon to William Seward, Lincoln's Secretary of State, who had made a similar unsuccessful proposal.

Yet in turning aside Lyndon's reach for power, Kennedy did not want to alienate him and destroy his usefulness to the administration. Indeed, Kennedy was sensitive to Lyndon's plight: The powerful Majority Leader of 1955–60, whom the younger, less experienced JFK had to court for favors, was now the supplicant asking for a share of power. Kennedy had no intention of letting Lyndon become a dominant figure or more than a well-controlled functionary in his government. But neither did he wish to provoke him into becoming a covert opponent, as John Nance Garner, FDR's first Vice President, had been. "I can't afford to have my Vice President, who knows every reporter in Washington, going around saying we're all screwed up, so we're going to keep him happy," JFK told White House aide Kenneth O'Donnell. Having won the presidency by a paper-thin margin over Nixon and needing southern Democratic support to pass significant legislation and win reelection to a second term, JFK saw LBJ as a useful political ally.

Kennedy tried to assuage Johnson's huge ego with the trappings of power. He raised no objection to letting Lyndon hold on to his Majority Leader's office, a seven-room suite across from the Senate floor, known as the "Taj Mahal" or the "Emperor's Room." Decorated in royal green and gold with crystal chandeliers and plush furniture, the office featured a lighted full-length portrait of Johnson leaning against a bookcase and two overhead lamps projecting "an impressive nimbus of golden light" as Lyndon sat at his desk. In addition, although Kennedy rejected a request from Johnson for an office next to the President's, he assigned him a six-room suite on the second floor of the Executive Office Building (EOB) next to the White House. Since many, including Presidents Truman and Eisenhower, believed that the Vice President was a member of the legislative rather than the executive branch, Johnson's presence in the EOB had significant constitutional implications. Kennedy also invited Lyndon to attend Cabinet meetings, weekly sessions with House and Senate Leaders, pre-press conference briefings, and National Security Council meetings, as required by law.

Kennedy insisted that his staff treat Johnson with the same respect they would have wanted shown him were their positions reversed. "You are dealing with a very insecure, sensitive man with a huge ego," JFK told O'Donnell. "I want you literally to kiss his fanny from one end of Washington to the other." Kennedy also asked Angier Biddle Duke, White House Chief of Protocol, to take care of the Johnsons. "'I want you to . . . see that they're not ignored, not only when you see them but at all other occasions.'" Kennedy explained that everyone in the administration eventually would be so busy they would forget about Johnson, and he wanted Duke "to remember." And so during White House photo sessions, when Lyndon "would always hang in the back as if he felt he was unwanted," Duke "would say in a loud voice, 'Mr. Vice President, Mr. Vice President,' and then the president would look around and say, 'Where's Lyndon? Where's Lyndon?' Johnson liked that, and he'd come up front."

New York Times columnist Arthur Krock remembered Kennedy "often" expressing concern about Lyndon, saying, "'I've got to keep him happy somehow.'" To appease Johnson, who would descend on him with personal complaints, Kennedy worked out a routine with O'Donnell. JFK would first hear Lyndon out, and then call in O'Donnell for a tongue-lashing about Johnson's problem. Johnson would then "go away somewhat happier." Johnson told Secretary of State Dean Rusk that he "had been treated better than any other Vice President in history and knew it."

Johnson's satisfaction was hardly Kennedy's first priority. His problems with the Soviet Union, Cuba, Southeast Asia, the domestic economy, black pressure for equal rights, and the political survival of his administration left him little room to fret over a discontented Vice President. Yet he had genuine regard for Johnson as a "political operator" and even liked his "roguish qualities." More important, he viewed him as someone who, despite the limitations of the vice presidency, could contribute to the national well-being in foreign and domestic affairs and, by so doing, make Kennedy a more effective President.

JFK gave some careful thought to Johnson's role in the administration. He did not want him managing its legislative program and creating the impression that the President was following the lead of his Vice President, a more experienced legislator. Kennedy was happy to have Johnson gather intelligence on what senators and representatives were thinking, but he had no intention of allowing him to become the point man or administration leader on major bills. Besides, he understood that Johnson no longer had the means he used as Majority Leader to drive bills through the Senate. Instead, he wanted Johnson to head a new Committee on Equal Employment Opportunity (CEEO), chair the National Aeronautics and Space Council, and represent the United States on trips abroad.

Kennedy knew that civil rights was going to be a major issue during the next four years. The campaign in the fifties by Martin Luther King, Jr., and the Southern Christian Leadership Conference against racial segregation made civil rights a compelling question for JFK's administration. He doubted, however, that a cautious Congress dominated by southern Democrats would be favorably disposed to a bill assuring black Americans the right to vote and access to public facilities across the South. Consequently, he planned to rely on executive action as an immediate device for advancing black equality. He wanted the CEEO to combat discriminatory hiring practices in the Federal government and by private businesses with federal contracts. Lyndon was to be one of the principal figures implementing this strategy. As a southern moderate who had led the 1957 civil rights law through the Congress and who believed the national well-being required equal treatment for blacks, Johnson could be invaluable in advancing a rational response to a highly charged issue and preventing southern alienation from the administration.

At the same time, Kennedy wanted Johnson, the legislative father of NASA, to have a significant part in shaping space policy. Again, he would not let Lyndon eclipse him on an issue given high public visibility by Soviet space shots, but he was eager to use Johnson's expertise on a matter of vital national concern. Moreover, in giving Johnson some prominence as an architect of America's space program, Kennedy was making him a political lightning rod. Should an effort to catch and pass the Soviets in space technology fail or suffer a well-publicized defeat, Lyndon would be out front taking some, if not much, of the heat. As for trips abroad, this was a ceremonial given of the Vice President's office, but Kennedy also saw them as an outlet for Johnson's restless energy.

None of what Kennedy asked him to do made Johnson happy. He resented the President's unwillingness to rely on his legislative expertise, telling people that his knowledge and contacts on the Hill were not being used. "You know, they never once asked me about that!" he complained privately about administration dealings with Congress. He had little enthusiasm for foreign travels that would be more symbolic than substantive. Although he saw some political benefits coming to him from chairing CEEO and the Space Council, he also saw liabilities that could work against his having another vice-presidential term or ever getting to the presidency. As important, he viewed both jobs as relegating him to a distinctly secondary role in the administration, which, of course, they did.

:: GOODWILL AMBASSADOR

Initially, one of the hardest assignments for Johnson to accept was that of goodwill ambassador. In the nearly three years he served as Vice President, he spent almost two and a half months making eleven trips to thirty-three foreign lands. Most of it consisted of showing the flag. But Kennedy saw it as a good way to fill Johnson's time and improve his disposition. Kennedy told Smathers, "I cannot stand Johnson's damn long face. He just comes in, sits at the Cabinet meetings with his face all screwed up, never says anything. He looks so sad." Smathers suggested that the President send

Johnson "on an around-the-world trip . . . so that he can get all of the fanfare and all of the attention and all of the smoke-blowing will be directed
at him, build up his ego again, let him have a great time." Kennedy thought
it "a damn good idea," and in the spring of 1961 he sent Johnson to Africa
and Asia.

Johnson was reluctant to spend his time on what he saw as mostly frivo-
lous business. But his craving for center stage, which he could have traveling abroad but not at home, quickly made him an enthusiast of foreign
trips. Indeed, they became a kind of theater in which he could act out his
zany, irreverent, demanding, impetuous characteristics that amused and
pleased some and offended and amazed others. They also gave him an
opportunity to bring a message of hope to needy people in distant lands. In
Africa and Asia his trips partly became a crusade for the New Deal reforms
that had transformed America. Eager to combat Communist appeals to
poor developing nations, Johnson pointed to economic change in his
native South as a model for Third World advance.

A four-day trip to Senegal in April 1961 was part comic opera and part
serious diplomatic mission. Kennedy's decision to send Lyndon there
largely rested on a desire to compete with Communist efforts to woo emerging nations. For Johnson, it immediately became a chance to play the great
man offering enlightened guidance to an impoverished people. He insisted
that a seven-foot bed to accommodate his six-foot-three-and-a-half-inch
frame, a special shower head that emitted a needlepoint spray, cases of
Cutty Sark, and boxes of ballpoint pens and cigarette lighters with L.B.J.
inscribed on them travel with him to Dakar.

There, he ignored the diplomatic niceties urged upon him by the U.S.
Embassy. One morning at 4:30 he and Lady Bird traveled to a fishing village, where the American ambassador refused to leave his limousine. "It
was too smelly a town for him," a Johnson traveling companion recalls. The
ambassador counseled Johnson against any contact with these people,
whom he described as dirty and diseased. But the Vice President strolled
among the villagers handing out pens and lighters, shaking hands with
everyone, including a few fingerless lepers, and advising the bewildered
natives that they could be like Texans, who had increased their annual
income tenfold in forty years. The trip was a microcosm of Johnson's
career: a grandiose, temperamental man doing outlandish things simultaneously to get attention and improve the lot of the poor.

A two-week trip to Asia in May had a similar design. With Communist
insurrections threatening to overturn pro-Western governments in Southeast Asia, Kennedy sent Johnson and Jean and Stephen Smith, JFK's sister

and brother-in-law, to visit government chiefs in Laos, South Vietnam, Taiwan, the Philippines, Thailand, India, and Pakistan. The principal business of the trip was in Saigon, where Johnson was supposed to encourage Ngo Dinh Diem, the President of South Vietnam, to introduce social reforms and increase his military effort against the Communists.

Most recollections of this trip, however, focus on Johnson's outlandish behavior. In Saigon, while security people responsible for the Vice President's safety fretted and everyone sweated in the stifling heat, Johnson repeatedly stopped a motorcade from the airport into the city to shake hands with South Vietnamese onlookers and give them pens, cigarette lighters, and gold and white passes to the U.S. Senate gallery. "Get your mamma and daddy to bring you to the Senate and Congress and see how the government works," he told bewildered children. In downtown Saigon he made a passionate arm-waving speech in which he called Diem the Winston Churchill of Asia. "He was totally carried away by the occasion," one journalist remembered. At his hotel, during a press conference that included several foreign correspondents he didn't know, he disrobed, toweled himself off, and climbed into fresh clothes.

In Bangkok he held a press conference in his pajamas at three in the morning to respond to some misinformation published by a newspaper. Cautioned that touching people, and particularly anyone's head, would offend the Thais, Johnson strolled the streets of Bangkok shaking hands and jumped on a bus, where he patted children on the head. One American diplomat who accompanied the Vice President cabled the State Department: "Saigon, Manila, Taipei, and Bangkok will never be quite the same again."

India was next on Johnson's agenda. In New Delhi Johnson had what he called "a belly-to-belly talk" with Prime Minister Jawaharlal Nehru, a neutralist in the Cold War. A want of "appreciable business" between the two produced long silences on Nehru's part until Johnson hit on the subject of rural electrification, a matter on which they were in fervent agreement. The conversation impressed American Ambassador John Kenneth Galbraith as innocuous: "Both Nehru and Johnson spoke rather formally on education, which they favored; poverty, which they opposed; freedom, which they endorsed; and peace, which they wanted."

The rest of Johnson's stay in India consisted of brief trips outside New Delhi, where he campaigned as if he were running for Congress. Johnson rode on a bullock cart, drew water from a well, laid a cornerstone at an engineering institute, shook hands all around, handed out pencils with the inscription, "Compliments of your Senator, Lyndon B. Johnson—the

greatest good for the greatest number," and recounted the triumphs of electrification in rural America. At the Taj Mahal in Agra, he tested the monument's echo with a Texas cowboy yell.

In Pakistan Johnson made headlines with his campaign-style diplomacy.
On his way into the city from the Karachi airport, he stopped to shake
hands with some of the applauding, enthusiastic crowd lining the streets.
Spotting a barefoot man standing with a camel at an intersection, Johnson
stepped across a muddy ditch to greet him and urge, as he had done repeatedly on the trip, "y'all come visit me in the United States." The next day a
Karachi newspaper lauded Johnson for reaching out "to the man with no
shirt on his back" and for inviting Bashir Ahmad, the camel driver, to come
to America. Not long after Johnson returned home, the American Embassy
in Pakistan reported that Bashir's visit to America had become a cause
célèbre and that, if it didn't happen, "the Vice President was going to look
like the biggest four-flusher in history." Johnson arranged Bashir's trip to
the United States, where with the help of a sophisticated Pakistani transla-
tor, who turned much of what Bashir said into "beautiful little homilies,"
the camel driver made a triumphal tour and received a pickup truck
donated by the Ford Motor Company.

Johnson's behavior abroad makes it easy to poke fun at him as a comic
figure or some sort of fabulous Texas character, a man with a monumental
ego whose priority was more the selling of Lyndon Johnson than the
advancement of any foreign policy goal. There is, of course, a certain truth
to this, but Johnson was also someone who never lost sight of bold public
designs.

Johnson's trips to Africa and Asia, and especially Vietnam, where the
competition with the Communists had turned violent, was a kind of New
Deal crusade. It was an attempt to get out and meet the people and sell
them on the virtues of American democracy and free enterprise. For Johnson, Vietnam, and Southeast Asia more generally, was less a geopolitical
balance-of-power contest with Communism than a giant reclamation
project—a campaign to sell his beloved New Deal liberalism to Asians as
superior to Communism's economic and political command systems or
even their own less productive and less stable economic and political institutions. However parochial it may have been, Johnson, like Woodrow Wilson and other evangels of democracy, was a crusader for the American
dream, an exponent of the idea that inside of every impoverished African
and Asian there was an American waiting to emerge.

Kennedy, most professional diplomats, and journalists saw Johnson's
behavior as cornball diplomacy that had limited value in foreign relations.

Kennedy lodged no protest against Johnson's actions, but it confirmed Kennedy in an impulse to keep Johnson at arm's length in the management of foreign affairs. Indeed, during the Bay of Pigs crisis in April 1961, when CIA-supported anti-Castro Cubans staged an abortive invasion of their homeland, Johnson, at JFK's request, had entertained West German Chancellor Konrad Adenauer at his Texas ranch. Nevertheless, Johnson had some influence on foreign affairs. His trip to Vietnam gave him a chance to speak his mind on what the administration saw in 1961 as the threat to U.S. interests in Southeast Asia. French defeat at the hands of the Viet Minh in 1954 had stirred American fears of Communist gains throughout the region and moved the Eisenhower administration to back the pro-Western Diem government in South Vietnam. A civil war in neighboring Laos heightened concern at the start of the Kennedy presidency that Communist-sponsored wars of national liberation in Asia would represent a major challenge to the United States in the next four years. If America faltered, Kennedy warned, "the whole world, in my opinion, would inevitably begin to move toward the Communist bloc."

Yet Kennedy's actions in Vietnam contrasted sharply with his rhetoric. Although he encouraged the U.S. military to develop a program of counterinsurgency warfare, he was reluctant to make any significant commitment of American forces to Laos or Vietnam. Consequently, he struggled to find a middle ground between a significant U.S. military effort and non-involvement that might allow Communist success. Johnson's trip to Saigon in May was meant to reassure Diem and the South Vietnamese people that the United States would not abandon them to the Communists. Johnson carried a letter from Kennedy promising more military advisers and aid which would allow Diem to increase the size of his forces. On his return to the United States Johnson pressed the case for a greater commitment to the defense of South Vietnam. "I cannot stress too strongly the extreme importance of following up this mission with other measures, other actions, and other efforts," LBJ told JFK. "The basic decision in Southeast Asia is here," Johnson asserted. "We must decide whether to help these countries to the best of our ability or throw in the towel in the area and pull back our defenses to San Francisco and a 'Fortress America' concept."

Johnson's view of Vietnam represented the prevailing wisdom in the administration, the Congress, and the press. Defeat in Vietnam would mean the loss of all Southeast Asia and worse. In the grip of the World War II experience, when one uncontested Hitler aggression led inevitably to the next, most Americans, including JFK, shared Johnson's exaggerated fear that a Communist victory in Vietnam would become the prelude to a Red tide sweeping across the Pacific. In consequence, between 1961 and 1963, the Kennedy administration expanded the number of U.S. military advisers from 692 to 16,700 and increased matériel aid to a level that marked a "transition from advice to partnership" in the war. When Diem's repressive rule in his country produced ever greater instability in South Vietnam, the Kennedy administration agreed to a military coup that toppled Diem's rule and took his life. Johnson thought the decision to oust Diem "very unwise," but, as with other foreign affairs questions, he had no significant impact on administration actions.

Nothing underscored Johnson's limited role in foreign policy-making more than his silence during White House deliberations on the Cuban missile crisis in October 1962. During the two weeks that JFK held meetings on how to settle the greatest post-1945 crisis in Soviet-American relations, LBJ was a shadow figure. The one instance in which LBJ played more than a peripheral role in foreign affairs was during a crisis over Berlin in August 1961.

An exodus of many of the best-trained citizens from East Germany through Berlin moved the Communists to build a wall sealing off the eastern part of the city. Unclear as to whether this was a prelude to more aggressive action against West Berlin, unwilling to order an assault against the wall, as some in Germany asked, and eager to counter demoralization in the American, British, and French zones, Kennedy ordered Johnson to make a symbolic trip to Berlin.

Johnson took on the assignment with characteristic energy and preparation. He stayed up all night on his trans-Atlantic flight discussing his itinerary and speeches that would give meaning to his trip. Landing in Bonn, Johnson gave the West German crowd greeting him a message from President Kennedy that America was "determined to fulfill all our obligations and to honor all our commitments."

Johnson's trip to West Berlin was a triumphal tour. After an eighty-minute flight to Tempelhof Airport, LBJ rode to the city center in an open car cheered by 100,000 spectators. Stopping repeatedly to shake hands with the people lining the curbs, he was greeted with unmistakable enthusiasm. At City Hall, where 300,000 Berliners had gathered, he declared himself in Berlin at the direction of President Kennedy to convey the same commitment that "our ancestors pledged in forming the United States: 'Our lives, our fortunes, and our sacred honor.'" The moment was the capstone of what LBJ saw as his most successful vice-presidential mission abroad.

:: OUTER SPACE

During the 1960 campaign Kennedy had attacked the Eisenhower administration for allowing the Soviets to get ahead of the United States in missile technology and the space race. The issue to JFK and most Americans was not just a concern that the Soviets were gaining a military advantage but the sense that America was losing the global contest for "hearts and minds." In 1961–63 few things in the Cold War counted more to Kennedy and Johnson than the wish to convince people everywhere that America's institutions and industrial and scientific capacity were superior to Russia's.

In April 1961, after a Soviet cosmonaut became the first man to orbit the earth and the failure at the Bay of Pigs had embarrassed the United States, JFK asked Lyndon to make "an overall survey of where we stand in space. Do we have a chance of beating the Soviets by putting a laboratory in space, or by a trip around the moon, or by a rocket to land on the moon, or by a rocket to go to the moon and back with a man?"

Johnson replied that the Soviets were ahead of us "in world prestige attained through technological accomplishments in space." And other nations, identifying space gains as reflections of world leadership, were being drawn to the Soviets. Johnson recommended "manned exploration of the moon" as "an achievement with great propaganda value."

Kennedy needed no prodding from Johnson to make the case for some dramatic space venture. At the end of May, he told a joint session of Congress: "If we are to win the battle that is now going on around the world between freedom and tyranny, the dramatic achievements in space which occurred in recent weeks—a sub-orbital flight by astronaut Alan Shepard—should have made clear to us all . . . the impact of this adventure on the minds of men everywhere. . . . It is . . . time for this nation to take a clearly leading role in space achievement, which in many ways may hold the key to our future on earth." Kennedy asked the country to commit itself to the goal of landing a man on the moon and returning him safely to earth before the decade was out.

Yet Kennedy worried that a highly publicized American space effort that ended in failure would further damage the nation's prestige and inflict a political wound that could jeopardize his hold on the presidency. Shepard's flight had encouraged Kennedy's hopes that America might catch and pass the Soviets, but he remained concerned about future mishaps. In June, when Shepard drove with the President, LBJ, and Newton Minow, head of the FCC, to speak before the National Convention of Broadcasters, Kennedy poked Johnson and said: "You know, Lyndon, nobody knows that the Vice President is the Chairman of the Space Council. But if that flight had been a flop, I guarantee you that everybody would have known that you were the Chairman."

The possibility that he would be a sacrificial political lamb for a faulty space effort did not dampen Johnson's enthusiasm for a manned mission to the moon. In 1963, when criticism from academics, journalists, and political conservatives began to be heard against "the moon-doggle," Johnson told Kennedy: "The space program is expensive, but it can be justified as a solid investment which will give ample returns in security, prestige, knowledge, and material benefits."

Johnson saw other, more selfish benefits flowing from the space program. Convinced he was backing a winner, he made strong efforts to identify himself with every aspect of its work. Not only did he crisscross the country in publicized visits to space installations, he also gave a series of "factual space reports to the public" on the work of NASA and his space council. The ostensible objective was to educate the country, but it had the added advantage of keeping his name in the news. And then there were the pork-barrel gains that served the economic interests of Texas and the South and strengthened his political hold on the state and the region, especially at a time when his support of civil rights for blacks was undermining it.

Johnson's thousand days as Vice President demonstrated his effectiveness in building a national consensus for a space program. As NASA Director James Webb later said: "When President Kennedy asked him to prepare a memorandum as to what our space program should be, . . . he called in some businessmen. . . . Then he called in Werner von Braun and General Schraver from the Air Force and a large number of technical people and sort of had hearings." After that "he called in the political leaders . . . in Congress and . . . said to them: 'We ought to go forward but we don't want to go forward unless you are going to commit yourself to stay with us.' . . . So he developed this commitment of certain leaders . . . and this . . . made it a lot easier for the rest of the country to come along."

:: THE COMMITTEE ON EQUAL EMPLOYMENT OPPORTUNITY

Johnson's greatest challenge as Vice President was chairing the CEEO. The goal of helping black Americans win equal access to jobs appealed to his sense of fairness and compassion for a disadvantaged minority. The CEEO chairmanship had the added advantage of disarming northern liberal hostility, which Johnson saw as a potential obstacle to a presidential bid in 1968.

Yet Johnson also feared that chairing the CEEO might trap him into antagonizing northern liberals, who would complain he did too little, and southern conservatives, who would attack him for doing too much. At the start of Kennedy's term all agreed that civil rights was a political liability. Kennedy, who had backed the Democratic party's platform of equal access to "voting booths, schoolrooms, jobs, housing, and public facilities" and seemed ready to put a major civil rights bill before the Congress, initially did almost nothing about the problem, except to promise action through Johnson's committee. Whatever the committee might achieve—and few were optimistic that it would be much—Kennedy was primarily using it as an expedient between advocates of bold legislative proposals and southern defenders of the status quo.

Although he saw political liabilities resulting from almost anything he did at the CEEO, Johnson was determined to get something done. This was partly a matter of personal temperament and ego; the assignment was a fresh challenge, a test of his capacities as a leader. At the same time, he believed that racial discrimination had no legitimate place in American life. Charles Boatner, a Johnson aide, remembers that the Vice President collected statistics on the number of black college graduates working in their fields. When he learned that practically none were—that a black B.A. in electrical engineering had to work as an electrician—he described it "as a tremendous waste of manpower . . . we were just throwing aside, through prejudice, one of our great assets, . . . brainpower."

Kennedy and Johnson believed that the CEEO could make a difference in giving blacks a fairer chance at more and better jobs. A federal work force of over two million and government contracts paying the salaries of another 15.5 million Americans gave the government considerable leverage to advance the interests of black wage earners. In particular, Johnson insisted that all contractors doing business with the government sign statements denying discriminatory practices and that the committee be free to cancel contracts with businesses violating their commitments.

At the same time, though, Johnson was the soul of caution. Discrimination against "Negroes" was wrong; it violated the spirit and letter of American ideals; it limited the country's economic output and injured its prestige abroad. But it was part of the southern landscape, and moving too vigorously to break old habits would produce social divisions and political losses that neither Kennedy nor Johnson were prepared to accept, at least not in 1961–62.

Johnson, therefore, was reluctant to compel southern accommodation to his committee's equal employment demands. "This is not a persecuting committee or prosecuting committee," he announced in March 1961. "In most cases, we believe and hope the situation can be straightened out through persuasion and . . . appeals to good will."

But Johnson had an excessive faith in volunteerism. To increase black employment, he principally relied on "Plans for Progress." The scheme originated with Robert Troutman, an Atlanta attorney and businessman reacting to a series of complaints by the NAACP against the Lockheed Aircraft Corporation plant in Marietta, Georgia. Lockheed was eager to reach an accommodation with the NAACP and avoid jeopardizing its agreements with the Air Force, which made it the federal government's largest contractor. Likewise, Georgia officials and New South entrepreneurs like Troutman, who had helped make Lockheed the largest employer in the state and saw desegregation of businesses in the South as essential to the region's economic well-being, were eager to resolve the conflict.

When Lockheed removed "White" and "Colored" signs from its Marietta plant and promised more and better jobs for blacks, Troutman hailed it as a model of what could be done with other corporations across the South. Moreover, using his ties to the White House, which included an acquaintanceship at Harvard with the late Joe Kennedy, Jr., and an early commitment to JFK in the 1960 campaign, Troutman won appointment as chairman of a CEEO "Plans for Progress" subcommittee.

A great self-promoter and charming personality with a knack for negotiating deals and ingratiating himself with influential people, including the President, Troutman quickly persuaded dozens of the country's major defense contractors to join "Plans for Progress." He described the operation as based on voluntary agreements that would open "doors of job opportunity" without making the CEEO into "an employment agency or a policeman with a nightstick chasing down alleged malefactors." Troutman also emphasized his opposition to quotas, hiring people for reasons of "race, creed, color, or national origin." The objective was to remove all such considerations from job selection and use merit as the only criterion. Troutman himself, however, acknowledged that such an approach promised little change: Blacks, he said, lacked the training to qualify for the best jobs or even good ones.

Johnson was not especially happy about Troutman's central role at CEEO. He was Jack Kennedy's man, who had opposed LBJ in the 1960 campaign, and with his talent for self-advertising he seemed likely to win credit for gains that Lyndon craved. On the other hand, he also served

Johnson's purposes: Should things go wrong, he could be a lightning rod protecting JFK, Lyndon, and the CEEO from critics; he also had a moderate, voluntary program that Johnson warmly favored.

By the summer and fall of 1961, tensions inside the CEEO over the value of "Plans for Progress" had become an open secret. The *New York Times* reported that, despite White House ceremonies lauding voluntary agreements with contractors, solid evidence of greater black employment was hard to come by. White House praise for Troutman's program was arousing public suspicion that the administration was simply engaged in posturing.

The doubts led in 1962 to Troutman's resignation. Johnson was relieved to see him go. Even before he had decided to quit, LBJ, distressed by the committee's poor press and stumbling efforts, had asked Theodore Kheel, a prominent New York labor negotiator and civil rights advocate, to survey and evaluate the CEEO's activities. In his report to Johnson in July, he recommended a shift from voluntary to compulsory compliance and a staff reorganization that would include appointment of an executive vice chairman who eliminated internal squabbles and ran day-to-day operations. Johnson seized upon Kheel's suggestion by replacing Troutman with Hobart Taylor, Jr., a black Michigan attorney and son of a longtime Texas friend, as executive vice chairman.

But Johnson had won a Pyrrhic victory. His more direct control over the CEEO came at a time when nothing his committee did could satisfy explosive pressure for genuine advance toward black equality.

In 1962–63 Lyndon used the CEEO to expand black job opportunities in the government and the private sector. Federal jobs held by blacks increased 17 percent in fiscal 1962 and another 22 percent in fiscal 1963. In addition, Johnson's committee directed private contractors to correct nearly 1,700 complaints lodged against them by black employees, doubling the rate at which the CEEO had required "corrective actions" in one year. Yet these CEEO gains barely made a dent in black unemployment or satisfied the demand for comprehensive civil rights legislation that would challenge the whole Jim Crow system of segregation across the South.

:: CIVIL RIGHTS

By 1963 the pressure to do something about black rights in the South had reached fever pitch. In the spring of 1961 black and white freedom riders challenging segregated transportation in Alabama suffered beatings at the hands of mobs unrestrained by local police. When Bobby Kennedy asked civil rights leaders for a "cooling-off period," which could save the President from embarrassment on a European trip, James Farmer of CORE replied: "We've been cooling off for 100 years. If we got any cooler we'd be in a deep freeze." In the summer and fall, Martin Luther King led an unsuccessful campaign to desegregate public facilities in Albany, Georgia, where the local police chief averted violence by jailing civil rights workers who had broken no laws. In 1962 James Meredith's effort to become the first black to enroll at the University of Mississippi in Oxford resulted in mob violence that forced the dispatch of hundreds of federal marshals, the federalizing of the Mississippi National Guard, and the deployment of U.S. troops. Meredith's registration left two people dead and numerous injured, including several marshals attacked with bricks and bottles.

In response to the strife, the Kennedys exercised greater executive leadership in behalf of civil rights than any administration in American history. They won judicial orders enjoining local police forces and anti–civil rights groups like the Ku Klux Klan from interfering with interstate travel. They persuaded the Interstate Commerce Commission to end segregation in interstate bus terminals. They filed forty-two lawsuits in behalf of black voting rights, and helped win congressional approval of the Twenty-fourth Amendment to the Constitution—prohibiting a poll tax. They also appointed forty blacks to important administration posts, and put Thurgood Marshall, the winning counsel in the landmark 1954 school desegregation case, *Brown v. Board of Education*, on the federal Circuit Court of Appeals in New York.

Yet most civil rights advocates saw the Kennedy administration's response to the struggle for black equality as inadequate. Above all, Kennedy refused to take on the Congress, and particularly its southern power brokers, by asking for a major civil rights law. The Kennedys justified their inaction by pointing out that not even a 1962 literacy bill guaranteeing voter registration for anyone with a sixth-grade education could overcome a southern filibuster. The argument carried little weight with civil rights advocates, who pointed to JFK's timidity in issuing an Executive Order desegregating federally supported housing. When the President finally acted in November 1962, making the simple "stroke of a pen" he had promised in the 1960 campaign, his order was limited to future housing. Moreover, his refusal to lobby the Senate for a change in Rule 22 from a two-thirds vote to a three-fifths vote to end filibusters confirmed the view that he would not risk any part of his legislative program for the sake of civil rights.

In the spring and summer of 1963, the pressure on Kennedy to provide bold leadership on civil rights became irresistible. In February, JFK had asked Congress for limited reforms affecting voting rights and school desegregation. But there was little indication that the White House would make a strong push for even these modest proposals and no one in the civil rights movement anticipated significant gains without a renewed crisis in the South.

As a consequence, Martin Luther King launched a campaign in April to desegregate Birmingham, Alabama — the largest segregated city in America. The response by police chief Eugene (Bull) Connor shamed the nation. Showing no regard for the constitutional rights of demonstrators, Connor's men beat protestors with nightsticks, herded them into vans with the help of electric cattle prods and snarling police dogs, and turned high-pressure fire hoses on them that ripped the bark off trees. Kennedy told a delegation of Democrats at the White House that the scenes he witnessed on television made him sick. When a confrontation with Governor George Wallace over admitting black students to the University of Alabama at Tuscaloosa coincided with continuing turmoil in Birmingham, Kennedy gave an emotional speech to the nation decrying the oppression of its black citizens a hundred years after emancipation and asked Congress to enact the most comprehensive civil rights law in history.

Kennedy's decision represented a turning point in his presidency. As Theodore Sorensen, White House aide and later JFK biographer, said: "The decision to ask for legislation . . . was a very, very important decision for him." It put his presidency in political jeopardy.

The extent of the risk came home to the White House during the next three months when Congress showed little disposition to act on or even take up other administration bills. Kennedy's popularity showed a steady decline during these months: People complained that he was pushing integration too fast, and they expressed increasing preference for Republican Governor George Romney of Michigan as the next President.

:: ROBERT KENNEDY

No one in the administration was more upset by developments than Robert Kennedy, the Attorney General. Bobby was fiercely loyal to Jack; he was like "a tigress protecting her cubs," JFK Assistant Secretary of State Averell Harriman remembered. Columnist Joseph Alsop said: "Bobby never diverged for one instant from his brother's views, nor did he ever really consider anything except his brother's interest."

In 1963 Bobby believed that unless the administration delivered on greater equality for blacks it would miss a chance to advance simple justice for an oppressed minority, lose liberal support, and put off the mass of voters by appearing ineffective and weak. Convinced that the administration needed to prevent racial tensions from exploding into further violence and that his brother's reelection was at stake, he began pressuring everyone on civil rights.

Few got more heat from Bobby than Johnson. But more than civil rights was involved. There was bad blood between them going back to 1955. In the spring of 1960, Peter Lisagor, a *Chicago Daily News* reporter, enflamed Bobby's antagonism to Lyndon by repeating a conversation he had with Johnson on a plane. "All of the enmity and hostility he held for the Kennedys came out." Johnson described Jack as "a 'little scrawny fellow with rickets' and God knows what other kind of diseases." Johnson predicted that Jack's election would give Joe Kennedy control of the country and would make Bobby Secretary of Labor. When Lisagor finished, four-letter words and all, Bobby turned to the window and said: "'I knew he hated Jack, but I didn't think he hated him that much.'"

"No affection contaminated the relationship between the Vice President and the Attorney General," Arthur Schlesinger writes. "It was a pure case of mutual dislike. . . . Johnson was seventeen years older, six inches taller, expansive in manner, coarse in language, emotions near the surface. It was southwestern exaggeration against Yankee understatement; frontier tall tales, marvelously but lengthily told, against laconic irony. Robert Kennedy, in the New England manner, liked people to keep their physical distance. Johnson, in the Texas manner, was all over everybody—always the grip on the shoulder, tug at the lapel, nudge in the ribs, squeeze of the knee. He was a crowder, who set his great face within a few inches of the object of his attention and, as the more diffident retreated, backed them across the room in the course of monologue."

For all their differences, Kennedy and Johnson shared characteristics that made them antagonists. In 1968, after years of rivalry, Lyndon told Bobby in their last meeting, "Bobby, you and I weren't made to be Vice President," alluding to their similar temperaments.

Both men were powerful, at times overbearing, tyrannical characters who did not treat opponents kindly. They were alley fighters, knee in the groin, below-the-belt punchers, hell-bent on winning at almost any cost. Dirty tricks, intimidation, hard bargains were weapons in their political arsenals they carried into campaigns for high office and for legislative and political gains needed to keep them or, in Bobby's case, Jack there. They

also shared bold, indeed, noble dreams for the country of better race relations, less poverty, and more security from external threats. They held a
common regard for the national system that had allowed them both to gain
prominence and power. But each self-righteously saw the other as less capable of achieving the great ends bringing them together in the same party
and the same administration.

The issue dividing them in 1963 was Johnson's performance at the
CEEO. In the first five months of the year, when the press reported that
"Plans for Progress" was "largely meaningless," the President urged Johnson
to "keep after the companies" and to publicize what had been achieved.
Although the compliance rate was much higher than indicated in the newspaper accounts, Bobby believed the stories, and they enraged him. He saw
Johnson's committee as "mostly a public relations operation" with no real
leadership from the Vice President. In the end, Bobby believed that the
President, not the Vice President, would pay the price for the committee's
failure: "I could just see going into the election of 1964, and eventually these
statistics or figures would get out. There would just be a public scandal." It
was bad enough that blacks weren't getting jobs but "what concerned me,"
Bobby said, was the thought of "this coming out in 1964." When Bobby
spoke to his brother about the situation, Jack "almost had a fit."

Bobby gave clear expression to his feelings about Lyndon's performance
at the CEEO. In May and July, he attended the committee's meetings,
where one high administration official remembers Bobby treating Lyndon
"in a most vicious manner. He'd ridicule him, imply he was insincere."
Secretary of Labor Willard Wirtz shuddered "at the way those two men
would cut each other up in meetings." At the May session, in the midst of
the Birmingham turmoil, Kennedy "asked a lot of questions that were
impatient, very impatient; I could see," Burke Marshall said, "it made the
Vice President mad."

At the July meeting, with the civil rights bill before Congress and the
issue hotter than ever, Kennedy went after Johnson again. "It was a pretty
brutal performance, very sharp," one participant recalled. "It brought tensions between Johnson and Kennedy right out on the table and very hard.
Everybody was sweating under the armpits."

Johnson felt unfairly abused. The CEEO's record wasn't as bad as some
made it out to be. Moreover, the voluntary approach, which was receiving
such bad press, had originated with Jack's man, Troutman. Nevertheless,
what Bobby and the White House saw was a Vice President unable to convince people that his effort to advance black job equality was anything more
than a sham.

Johnson also felt that he had been ignored and then unappreciated for what he had done in behalf of the 1963 civil rights bill. The bill had been drafted without consulting him, and he resented it. He was also angry that, despite a JFK injunction to include Johnson in White House discussions with congressional leaders, he was rarely invited. On June 3, after newspapers reported that Kennedy would send a civil rights bill to Congress, Johnson told Ted Sorensen in a telephone conversation: "I don't know who drafted it. I've never seen it. Hell, if the Vice President doesn't know what's in it how do you expect the others to know what's in it? I got it from the *New York Times.*"

Unable to get in to see the President about the bill, Johnson used his conversation with Sorensen and discussions with two Justice Department officials to say his piece. He believed it a mistake for Kennedy to put legislation before the Congress without first doing more homework. If he sent a bill up now, it wouldn't be enacted and would be "disastrous for the President's program." Believing it "a very wise suggestion" to do some more work in Congress, the White House delayed sending up the bill for nine days. Then it arranged a series of meetings with influential groups to generate support in the country and pressure on Congress to pass the law. Many of the participants at these sessions remembered Johnson as the strongest, most passionate voice for the legislation.

Yet none of this sat very well with Bobby Kennedy. Although he acknowledged the wisdom of Johnson's advice on dealing with Congress and the support he gave the bill after it went forward, he saw the Vice President as "opposed to sending it up" and as generally unhelpful.

Without question, Johnson underestimated the importance of Kennedy's civil rights proposal compelling equal access to public accommodations. He minimized the need to force an end to legal segregation as a prelude to economic and educational gains. Injured pride or his absence from the drafting process may partly account for his coolness to the bill. He also was insensitive to how besieged the Kennedys felt about the civil rights struggle. Nevertheless, for the Attorney General to see Johnson as more of an obstructionist than a facilitator in the battle for civil rights is a distortion that tells more about the animus between the two than Lyndon's part in trying to advance the cause of black equality. More than civil rights or personal differences, however, had Bobby on edge about Lyndon. In 1962–63 public scandals involving Billie Sol Estes, a Texas wheeler-dealer, and Bobby Baker, the secretary to the Senate Majority Leader, threatened to reveal unsavory connections to Johnson that would embarrass the administration and make it vulnerable to charges of corruption in the 1964 campaign.

John Kennedy had taken account of Johnson's reputation before offering him the vice presidency and had concluded that Lyndon would be more of an asset than a liability. Nevertheless, given Johnson's public image as a Texas wheeler-dealer, any fresh hint of corruption was bound to make the Kennedys take notice and prepare themselves for the worst.

The Kennedys paid close attention to the allegations about Johnson and Baker. Larry O'Brien, JFK's special assistant for congressional relations, remembers that the President had a "keen interest" in the Bobby Baker case. The Attorney General closely followed the Justice Department's investigation, including inquiries into Johnson's possible part in Baker's corrupt dealings. Despite wrongdoing on Baker's part that would eventually send him to prison, Johnson believed that Bobby Kennedy instigated the investigation in hopes of finding something that could knock him off the ticket in 1964.

In the fall of 1963, when the press began reporting that JFK was considering a replacement for LBJ, it confirmed what Johnson had been convinced of for over two years. Jack and Bobby, however, emphatically denied that they ever had a plan to drop Lyndon. Privately, JFK told journalists and political associates that it "was preposterous on the face of it. We've got to carry Texas in '64 and maybe Georgia," he said. At a press conference in October, Kennedy stated his determination to keep Johnson on the ticket.

Was there any basis to Johnson's suspicions? The question of whether Robert Kennedy or people close to him discussed throwing Johnson off the ticket is open to dispute. In 1968, Evelyn Lincoln, JFK's secretary, published a book in which she recounted a conversation with the President in November 1963. Kennedy told her that he intended to replace Johnson with Governor Terry Sanford of North Carolina as his running mate, saying, "it will not be Lyndon." People close to JFK and prominent journalists thought it unlikely that Kennedy had any plan to do this.

Yet there are reasons to believe that the Kennedys discussed replacing Johnson. With the Bobby Baker case on the front pages and links to LBJ a distinct possibility, it seems reasonable to assume that the Kennedys considered contingency plans for 1964. Yet once it seemed likely that Johnson would ride out the Baker scandal, the Kennedys believed it wise to keep Johnson in place. And so denials by the Kennedys of plans to dump Lyndon was shrewd politics. While public speculation on dropping Johnson helped make it possible, denials that it was intended served the greater likelihood that Lyndon would again be Jack's running mate.

:: KENNEDY'S ASSASSINATION

On November 22, 1963, Lee Harvey Oswald, a ne'er-do-well drifter, assassinated President Kennedy as he rode in a motorcade through the streets of Dallas, where he had come to do some political fence mending. The nation and people around the globe fell into a state of grief and anguish. Johnson remembered himself in a state of shock with a rush of emotions ranging from anguish, bewilderment, and distress to compassion and deep concern for Mrs. Kennedy and her children. Yet Johnson must have felt some guilt as well. But not because, as some books, dramas, and films would later allege, he was part of a conspiracy to kill the President. He had absolutely nothing to do with Kennedy's death. It was more the guilt of a competitive older brother, a sibling or close associate who suddenly displaces his younger, more successful rival. For all his genuine regard for Jack Kennedy and sense of terrible loss at the President's demise, Johnson surely felt some elation at having gained the office he had said he deserved more than JFK. Five days later, when he spoke before Congress, he began, "All I have I would have given gladly not to be standing here today." It was the new President's way not only of expressing his grief but also of publicly unburdening himself of the inner guilt he felt at having eclipsed his great collaborator and rival.

Other concerns tore at Johnson as well. He believed it essential to provide the nation with a convincing explanation of why and how Kennedy was killed. "A troubled, puzzled, and outraged nation wanted to know the facts," he writes in his memoirs. But on November 24, when Jack Ruby, a Dallas nightclub operator, shot and killed Oswald in the garage of the Dallas jail on his way to a court hearing, the incident, Johnson said, turned the nation's "outrage to skepticism and doubt."

Suspicions now abounded about a conspiracy perpetrated by right-wing fanatics or Russia or Cuba or the CIA or the FBI or the Mafia or even Johnson himself. To quiet these rumblings and to investigate the President's death, on November 29, Johnson appointed a bipartisan panel that included Chief Justice Earl Warren, former CIA Director Allen Dulles, former U.S. High Commissioner of Germany and prominent foreign policy adviser John J. McCloy, Democratic Senator Richard Russell of Georgia, Republican Senator John Sherman Cooper of Kentucky, Republican Congressman Gerald Ford of Michigan, and Democratic Congressman Hale Boggs of Louisiana. They were all men with reputations for integrity and devotion to the country. They inspired confidence in the belief that an honest assessment of what happened would result from their work.

During the next ten months, while the Warren Commission studied the information put before it by government investigators, Johnson pressed for a report as soon as possible so as to quiet public suspicions of a conspiracy. In September 1964, the commission concluded that Oswald and Ruby each acted alone. And though the CIA and FBI had held back information which would have undermined their respective reputations for effectiveness, the report's fundamental proposition about Oswald and Ruby has never been persuasively refuted.

Though Johnson himself had doubts about the accuracy of the Commission's findings, he wanted no public discussion of his concerns. Not because, as *New York Times* columnist Anthony Lewis said, "The search for conspiracy only increases the elements of morbidity and paranoia and fantasy in this country." Rather, Johnson believed that increased speculation about a conspiracy could threaten international stability and undermine his authority by encouraging allegations about his possible role in killing JFK. Instead, he thought it better to repress such divisive discussions and concentrate on bold domestic reforms, which he instinctively understood could now be made in Kennedy's name. And once he had paid proper homage to the fallen President, he wanted to seize the opportunity that had unexpectedly come to him and turn the country in directions few expected him to take.

5 :: FROM JFK TO LBJ

Only one other President in the century, Theodore Roosevelt, had come to power after an assassination. And the passive, unspectacular William McKinley, T.R.'s predecessor, was no John Kennedy. Lyndon Johnson faced the toughest transition since Harry Truman succeeded the legendary Franklin Roosevelt. "I always felt sorry for Harry Truman and the way he got the presidency," Johnson told an aide two days after Kennedy's death, "but at least his man wasn't murdered."

Johnson had to confront the grief and despair many people felt over the loss of a beloved leader and their antagonism toward someone who, however much he identified with JFK, seemed like a usurper, an unelected, untested replacement for the man the country now more than ever saw as more suitable for the job. In the first days of his presidency, only 5 percent of the public felt they knew very much about LBJ, while 67 percent said they knew next to nothing about him. Seventy percent of the country had doubts about how it would "carry on without" Kennedy.

Johnson, like T.R. and Truman, understood the essential need for continuity, for reassuring people at home and abroad that the new President would be faithful to the previous administration. The death of a President was trauma enough, but Kennedy's assassination made his passing a national crisis in self-confidence, a time of doubt about the durability of the country's democratic system and its tradition of nonviolent political change. "A nation stunned, shaken to its very heart, had to be reassured that the government was not in a state of paralysis," Johnson later recalled. "I had to convince everyone everywhere that the country would go forward. . . . Any hesitation or wavering, any false step, any sign of self-doubt, could have been disastrous. . . . The times cried out for leadership."

Despite his private fears, Johnson was an inspiration to the country. His public appearances, his use of language, his management of the press promoted feelings of continuity and unity. To be sure, traditions of political stability and shared assumptions about cooperative efforts to advance the national well-being eased Johnson's burden. But an almost uncanny feel for the appropriate word and gesture honed by thirty-two years in the political arena were as important in making him equal to the task.

In the difficult days after Kennedy's death, words were Johnson's weapons in a war on uncertainty and gloom. Like a master therapist, the new President soothed the nation with language that conveyed sincerity and wisdom. Proclaiming a national day of mourning on November 23, Johnson invoked the martyred Kennedy as a source of national strength: "As he did not shrink from his responsibilities, but welcomed them, so he would not have us shrink from carrying on his work beyond this hour of national tragedy."

Few things contributed more to Johnson's successful transition than a national address on the evening of November 27. Speaking to a joint session of Congress from the rostrum of the House, where he could remind Americans that he was a seasoned and successful political leader with thirty-two years of experience on Capitol Hill, Johnson's demeanor and language struck exactly the right tone. Dressed in a dark suit and tie reflecting the country's somber mood, he humbly asked the help of all Americans in shouldering "the awesome burden of the Presidency," which "I cannot bear . . . alone."

Invoking memories of FDR, who in another time of crisis began his administration with a call for action, Johnson urged the country "to do away with uncertainty and doubt" and show "that from the brutal loss of our leader we will derive not weakness, but strength; that we can and will act and act now." Johnson described Kennedy's dreams of a better America and a more peaceful world and reminded the country of JFK's words, "'let us begin.' Today, in this moment of new resolve, I would say to all my fellow Americans, let us continue." Thirty-four bursts of prolonged applause interrupted Johnson's twenty-five minute speech. The enthusiasm for his words in Congress reflected the national response.

His objective, LBJ candidly told a press conference, was to create a sense of continuity and unity in the country. By the first of the year, Johnson could not have been more pleased with his success. The press, George Reedy told him, had never before been so completely on his side: "They are in a mood now where they are merely looking for historical indications that you are going to be a good President and a strong President." Gallup polls showed Johnson with a 79 percent approval rating, with only 3 percent disapproving of his performance.

:: THE KENNEDY LEGACY

Between November 1963 and the 1964 election, LBJ identified himself with JFK not only as a means of winning public support but also because he saw Kennedy's unfinished liberal agenda as essential to the national well-being. In his November 27 address, for example, he had told the country that "no . . . eulogy could more eloquently honor President Kennedy's memory than the earliest possible passage of the civil rights bill for which he fought so long. Johnson also urged passage of an $11 billion tax cut Kennedy had urged as a device for expanding a sluggish economy.

In pressing the case for JFK's domestic reforms, Johnson was on comfortable ground. His idea of the presidency was picking up where FDR's New Deal had left off—expanding prosperity, opening doors of opportunity to poor folks, and honoring the country's rhetoric about equal treatment under the law. On November 23, when he met with Walter Heller, chairman of the Council of Economic Advisers, Johnson stated his eagerness for reforms that could help the 22 percent of Americans living in poverty. The publication of Michael Harrington's small but powerful book, *The Other America*, and literary critic Dwight Macdonald's review of it, "Our Invisible Poor," in *The New Yorker* had spurred interest in the issue in 1962–63.

Johnson was mindful of the many Americans, especially the elderly and blacks, who lived "on the outskirts of hope" in "inherited, gateless poverty." He told Heller about antipoverty plans Kennedy had intended to implement in a second term: "That's my kind of program. We should push ahead full-tilt on this project."

Johnson's eagerness for a poverty program did not mean that he had a well-formulated plan. Initially, he thought of such a program as a revival of FDR's National Youth Administration: an attack on poverty focusing on poor youths in inner cities and depressed rural areas. Heller urged instead that they ease poverty by relying on "Community Action" by which poor people would be given command of federal educational and jobs programs. But Johnson didn't see how Community Action would provide education and create jobs, the essentials he saw for any successful attack on poverty.

Despite the uncertainties, a war on poverty, as they agreed to call it, excited Johnson's attraction to grand visionary plans. "We were moving into uncharted territory," Johnson later wrote. "Powerful forces of opposition would be stirred. . . . But the powerful conviction that an attack on poverty was right and necessary blotted out any fears that this program was a political land mine." Johnson wanted something that would "be big and bold and hit the whole nation with real impact." "When I got through," he told a journalist, "no one in this country would be able to ignore the poverty in our midst."

Announced with a flourish in his January 1964 State of the Union address, the War on Poverty was pure Johnson—bigger, bolder, grander in concept than any reform proposal in the country's history. "This Administration today, here and now, declares unconditional war on poverty in America. . . . Our aim is not only to relieve the symptoms of poverty, but to cure it and, above all, to prevent it," he said. He wanted Congress to pass a parcel of laws that would give the government the wherewithal to fight and win the war.

Johnson's pronouncement on curing poverty was of a piece with other bold proposals he urged on Congress. He asked the next session to do "more for civil rights than the last hundred sessions combined"; to enact "the most far-reaching tax cut of our time"; to achieve "the most effective, efficient foreign aid program ever; and . . . to build more homes, more schools, more libraries, and more hospitals than any single session of Congress in the history of our Republic. All this and more can and must be done. It can be done by this summer," Johnson said. It would be no more than fulfilling the faith that John Kennedy had in his fellow Americans to create "a nation that is free from want . . . for our time and for all time to come."

:: THE LEGISLATOR

Although Congress and the public gave Johnson's speech a warm reception, no one familiar with the slow almost tortuous means by which major bills become laws expected Johnson to get most of what he asked. Johnson himself had few illusions about the difficulties he faced in Congress. As he told one aide shortly after becoming President, "Everything on my desk today was here when I first came to Congress" twenty-six years ago.

But in calling for so much reform so quickly, Johnson wasn't posturing for history. Johnson had every hope that JFK's tax cut, the civil rights bill, and the war on poverty would translate into concrete laws. He believed that the sympathy for proposals identified with JFK would make them irresistible. Years later, Johnson told Doris Kearns: "Everything I had ever learned in the history books taught me that martyrs have to die for causes. John Kennedy had died. But his 'cause' was not really clear. That was my

job. I had to take the dead man's program and turn it into a martyr's cause."
In addition, he believed that a tax bill that would spur a sluggish economy,
a rights law that would end the injustices of southern segregation, and an
attack on economic suffering that might benefit all Americans made his
appeal a realistic call to congressional action.

As important, he had every confidence that these were the right proposals at the right time and that he was the one who could enact them. In
dealing with Congress, he had three decades of experience and the knowledge that as Senate Majority Leader he had exercised more effective control in the Upper House than any senator in American history. This had not
been the result of chance or circumstance but of considered actions and
hard work. Though it was clear to Johnson that his role as President was different from that of Majority Leader, he nevertheless saw useful similarities
that could help him pass laws.

In the Senate he had exchanged favors for votes. As President, he had a
greater variety of gifts that could be traded for congressional backing. Further, he had asserted his power in the Senate by learning the needs and
wants of his colleagues and playing to them at every turn. As President, he
had greater means to measure legislators' wants and more ways to satisfy
them; he expected the Johnson "treatment" to be more effective than ever
in bending Congress to his will.

Johnson also understood that mastering Congress meant having a first-
rate staff. As President, he could not interact with senators as he had as
Majority Leader, though this was difficult for him to accept. One aide
remembers holding the President back from involving himself too much
in the hour to hour management of pending bills. "There was no time day
or night he wasn't prepared to charge in." Early one morning, after a losing
all-night struggle in the House, the aide called Johnson to report the defeat.
"When did this happen?" Johnson asked. In the middle of the night, the
aide replied. "Why didn't you call me?" Johnson said. "You should have
called me and told me about it. You know, when you're up there bleeding,
I want to bleed with you. We have to share these things."

Initially, Johnson's legislative staff consisted of the Kennedy aides manning the office of congressional relations. Lawrence F. O'Brien, a public
relations expert who had worked for JFK since 1952, was its principal figure. An amiable and soft-spoken man with roots in the liberal wing of the
Democratic party, O'Brien shared with the Kennedys an Irish background,
a warm sense of humor, and an unsentimental astuteness about politics
that had made him an effective campaign organizer and a skilled liaison
with Congress.

Johnson never confined legislative work to designated specialists. "The Johnson people, no matter what their assignments were," O'Brien says, "joined me at his urging in participating in the legislative effort. That applied to every Johnson person in the White House over the years that I was there." The principal Johnson men were four Texans and a Midwesterner whom Johnson liked to describe as "valuable chunks of humanity who can do anything."

Johnson had no official chief of staff. He "ran the White House as he had his Senate office, under his hat," one aide said. Though no assistant had overall supervisory powers, Walter Jenkins was the first among equals. The forty-five-year-old Jenkins had been with Johnson since graduating from the University of Texas in 1939. Described as gentle, quiet, and the only one who had "total rapport" with the President, Jenkins was a man Friday who enjoyed everyone's trust and presided over the details of daily operations at the White House.

George Reedy was Johnson's second longest serving aide. The son of a Chicago *Tribune* crime reporter, Reedy was something of a child prodigy who attended the University of Chicago, where he became a socialist and developed an interest in journalism. After college and a stint in the Army Air Force as an intelligence officer during World War II, he became a Capitol Hill reporter for United Press International. In 1951 he gave up journalism for a job on Johnson's Senate staff. The forty-six-year-old Reedy was a shrewd political analyst who counseled Johnson on everything from his public image to legislative maneuvers and election campaigns. His work for Johnson as Vice President focused on press relations, and when Pierre Salinger, JFK's press secretary, left that post in March 1964, Reedy replaced him.

Horace Busby was another "triple threat man," as Johnson liked to describe his aides. At the University of Texas in the 1940s Busby, or "Buzz," as his friends called him, established a reputation as a crusading student journalist devoted to reform politics. In 1948, Busby worked in Johnson's Senate campaign and then served him on and off over the next fifteen years as a speech writer and legislative and political analyst. As soon as LBJ became President, the forty-year-old Busby became an official member of Johnson's staff. His duties were speech writing and "special projects," which meant feeding the President ideas about domestic change and the political repercussions of anything he might attempt.

Bill Moyers was the youngest, and in many respects the most extraordinary, member of Johnson's staff. A poor boy from Marshall in northeast Texas, Moyers began his forays into journalism as a student at the University of Texas that won him a job at LBJ's Austin television station KTBC. After study at the University of Edinburgh and at Baptist Theological Seminary in Fort Worth, Moyers had worked for Johnson in his 1960 vice-presidential campaign. During the next three years, he had served as deputy director of the Peace Corps, where he functioned as an "idealist-operator," mixing "the nineteenth-century American missionary instinct with twentieth-century managerial attitudes and cynicism." The twenty-nine-year-old Moyers entered Johnson's White House as an appointments and scheduling secretary and part-time speech writer. But his talent and devotion to the President quickly projected him into the front rank of Johnson's aides.

Jack Valenti, a forty-seven-year-old Houston advertising man, whom one journalist described as "the most enigmatic and the most omnipresent of the Johnson men," had first met LBJ in 1956 at a businessmen's reception. Impressed with the strength of the senator's personality, Valenti had written a flattering newspaper column about him and then in 1960 managed the Kennedy-Johnson advertising campaign in Texas. After he became President, Johnson brought Valenti to the White House, where he began serving as everything from a "glorified valet" to a chief of staff. He did "whatever needed to be done." He "was a major liaison with Senate Minority Leader Everett Dirksen; soothed the feelings of congressmen whose districts had lost an appropriation; moved projects through the bureaucratic web; and functioned as Johnson's ambassador in telling important people things they did not want to hear."

Johnson's agenda was so ambitious he needed a "two-shift day" to achieve it. Rising at 6:30 or 7:00 each morning, he began his workday in bed, where he read newspapers, the *Congressional Record*, and documents prepared by aides who conducted early morning business in the bedroom. Johnson thought nothing of placing early morning phone calls to congressmen and senators. "I hope I didn't wake ya," LBJ told Ohio Congressman Wayne Hayes one morning at 6 a.m. "Oh, no," Hayes replied. "I was lying here just hoping you would call." Reaching the Oval Office at about nine, Johnson worked until 2 p.m., when he exercised by vigorously walking around the White House grounds or taking a swim.

The second half of his "day" started at 4 p.m. after a nap in his pajamas, a shower, and fresh clothes. It lasted until at least midnight and often until one or two o'clock in the morning. Sometimes the two shifts turned into an uninterrupted fourteen or sixteen hours. It was his means for not only doing good but also making a record that served his sense of self. If he could get Kennedy's program passed, he said, "Kennedy would live on forever and so would I."

:: LEGISLATIVE GAINS: THE TAX CUT AND WAR ON POVERTY

The first test of Johnson's plan was enacting Kennedy's $11 billion tax cut. A debate between conservatives and liberals had kept it bottled up in the Senate for ten months. Conservatives, complaining that Federal budget deficits were a drag on the economy and would become more of an economic impediment with a tax cut, dismissed liberal arguments that lower taxes would fuel an economic expansion and "full employment." Liberals also asserted that growth and fewer tax loopholes, including a reduced oil depletion allowance, would provide additional revenues to cut deficits. As Vice President, Johnson had been publicly silent on the bill, but his orthodoxy about balanced budgets and sympathy for oil and gas made him unsympathetic to JFK's proposal.

As soon as he became President, however, he changed his mind. If he were to make his commitment to Kennedy's legacy believable, he needed to sign on to the tax cut. Moreover, the argument of distinguished economists that cutting taxes would mean a $30 billion expansion of the gross national product in 1964 rather than $12 billion made the reform almost irresistible. A warning from economic advisers that without a tax cut a slowdown and a rise in unemployment would occur next year clinched the argument.

Relying on every device he had learned as Majority Leader, Johnson engineered a lopsided Senate margin of 77 to 21 for the tax cut, which was a prelude to congressional approval at the end of February.

Johnson's victory became an opportunity to create additional momentum for the administration's legislative program. In nationally televised remarks, the President praised House and Senate leaders for their support, and emphasized that if the tax cut worked as anticipated, it would expand the country's prosperity and benefit all Americans. He portrayed his administration as a nonpartisan agency devoted strictly to the national well-being.

In encouraging views of himself as no group's special advocate, he had his eye on the antipoverty campaign. If he were going to sell Congress and the country on fighting poverty, he believed it essential to advertise it as of benefit to all Americans—not just the poor and especially inner city blacks, who made up a significant part of the country's disadvantaged.

From late November to the middle of March, when he put a poverty bill before Congress, Johnson's several public references to fighting poverty emphasized that this was a "sound investment: $1,000 invested in salvaging an unemployable youth today can return $40,000 or more in his lifetime." Poverty was costing the government billions of dollars annually in welfare costs and the lost tax revenues of unproductive citizens. In private, Johnson cautioned aides against including anything in the poverty program that could be seen as a "dole" or an attempt at redistribution of wealth. He wanted the program to be seen as a "hand up" not a "hand-out."

The columnist Walter Lippmann saw clearly what Johnson intended: "A generation ago it would have been taken for granted that a war on poverty meant taxing money away from the haves and turning it over to the have nots. . . . But in this generation a revolutionary idea has taken hold. The size of the pie can be increased by intention, by organized fiscal policy and then a whole society, not just one part of it will grow richer."

Establishing the ultimate goal of an antipoverty crusade — abolishing poverty — was much easier than figuring out how to make it work. "I'm gonna put $500 million in this budget for poverty, and a good deal of it ought to go to your people," Johnson told Roy Wilkins in January. "But we ought to have some better ideas about how" to do it.

First of all, Johnson decided to give the program an independent base, making it like the National Youth Administration or Civilian Conservation Corps, separate New Deal agencies that made significant gains for the needy in the thirties. Johnson believed that if you put a new agency into an old-line bureaucracy, it would kill it.

To keep JFK's name associated with the war on poverty, Johnson asked Sargent Shriver, JFK's brother-in-law, to head it. As head of Kennedy's Peace Corps, Shriver had turned what many, especially in Congress, thought would be an overly idealistic crusade for foreign hearts and minds into a practical, highly appealing program for aiding Third World countries. Shriver impressed Johnson as a sensible idealist who knew how to get along with Congress, make the Peace Corps work, capture the public imagination at home and abroad, and counter Cabinet officers who would try to keep a poverty agency from taking away any of their authority.

In an appointment letter, Johnson made less than clear how Shriver would carry on the fight. Shriver was to direct the activities of all executive departments involved in the program, and he was to act as Johnson's representative to Congress in advancing necessary legislation. He was also to coordinate all government and private activities across the nation and attend Cabinet meetings, where the war on poverty was to become a regular part of their business. But Johnson left it up to Shriver to implement his directive. Specifically, Shriver was to design a program described in a bill Johnson wanted before Congress by the middle of March.

In selecting Shriver, Johnson had made the right choice. They shared an evangelical enthusiasm for conquering seemingly insoluble problems.

Also like Johnson, Shriver had a huge appetite for work, sometimes calling aides at three and four in the morning. He told the chairman of AT&T that he imagined a telephone system that "had us all plugged in like an umbilical cord so we could never get away." Lest enthusiasm for the job at hand flag, Shriver hung motivating mottos on his office walls. "There is no place in this club for good losers," one said. "Bring me only bad news; good news weakens me," another advised.

Shriver faced a daunting assignment, as discussions about the content of the poverty program made clear during February and March. A task force of advisers, which Shriver began assembling twenty-four hours after being appointed by Johnson, experienced "chaos and exhaustion," or what one participant called "the beautiful hysteria of it all." One member of the Council of Economic Advisers remembered how "bewildered" they were "by the complete disarray of the nominal professionals in the field of poverty."

Shriver struggled to make sense of his assignment. At a luncheon with Michael Harrington, Shriver said: "Now you tell me how I abolish poverty." Harrington replied: "You've got to understand right away that you've been given nickels and dimes for this program. You'll have less than a billion dollars to work with." Ever the optimist, Shriver saw the glass as half-full: "I don't know about you, Mr. Harrington, but this will be my first experience at spending a billion dollars, and I'm quite excited about it." When Shriver convened representatives of the federal agencies listed in a three-inch book identifying government programs to aid the poor, "the infighting over who would do what got so bitter that it appeared the whole project might be wrecked. Johnson wasn't much help to Shriver. His interest was principally in having a bill he could sell to Congress. He had a general preference for a program that would focus on helping young people through education and job training. But beyond that, he wanted Shriver to manage the details of how the program would be organized.

The Economic Opportunity Act (EOA) Johnson sent to Congress on March 16 was a blend of several things. It proposed the creation of a Job Corps and work training and work-study programs—all aimed at giving impoverished youngsters the opportunity to complete their education and develop salable skills. It outlined a Community Action Program, which would "give every American community the opportunity to develop a comprehensive plan to fight its own poverty—and help them to carry out their plans." Third, it asked funding for VISTA, Volunteers in Service to America, a domestic Peace Corps for those ready to enlist in the war against poverty. Fourth, it proposed a loan program to provide incentives for those who would hire the unemployed. And last, it urged the creation of the Office of Economic Opportunity as a vehicle for coordinating the war on poverty.

At the same time, however, Johnson, like everyone else, had no clear idea how to overcome poverty. Neither he nor Shriver had much faith in Community Action; when Shriver heard the suggestion during the task force deliberations, he said privately: "It'll never fly." But he and Johnson were sold on the idea by the prevailing wisdom of poverty experts, who believed strongly in overcoming the "culture of poverty" by the largely untried but promising means of "maximum feasible participation."

In trying to sell Congress on legislating a fight against poverty, Johnson could rationalize his public rhetoric by private hopes that, even if what he proposed did not work, there would be ample opportunity in the next eight years to find the means that would. Moreover, he understood from past experience that, once a major government program had been put in place, it would be easier for supporters to modify its workings than for opponents to dismantle it.

:: THE GREAT SOCIETY

On March 15, the day before he sent the poverty bill to Congress, Johnson gave an interview to representatives of the three television and radio networks. Eric Sevareid of CBS asked whether the President had settled on a catch phrase like the New Deal or New Frontier to describe his administration. Johnson answered that he had been too busy to think of "any slogan, but I suppose all of us want a better deal, don't we?" Although saying he didn't believe in labels, Johnson described himself as a prudent progressive.

A better deal and a prudent progressive were two of the phrases Johnson had come up with in an avid search for a "big theme" to characterize his presidency. Despite his protestations about being too busy and not believing in labels, Johnson had been "badgering" Richard Goodwin, a JFK aide and now LBJ speech writer, to find a popular slogan that would resonate with voters in the 1964 campaign and give his administration its historical identity.

Goodwin consulted with Eric Goldman, a Princeton historian who had joined Johnson's White House in December as the organizer of a "quiet brain trust." Goldman's duties included suggesting goals and specific programs. He thought that the President should use "a full-dress speech to place his Administration in the perspective of the long-running American experience." Goldman believed that Johnson's presidency could mark the transition from a generally affluent America to one in which the nation attended "not only to the quantity but to the quality of American living. . . . I suggested," Goldman recalled, "that in terms of a popular slogan, the goal of 'post-affluent' America was probably best caught by the title of Walter Lippmann's book of some years back, *The Good Society*."

Preferring "the Great Society" to describe Goldman's idea, Goodwin used the phrase and concept in a draft speech. Johnson liked the feel and language of Goodwin's draft so much that they wanted "to build a whole speech around it." They believed they "could fit a lot of what we were trying to do within the curve of this phrase." They soon fastened on a May 22 commencement address at the University of Michigan in Ann Arbor as the occasion for using it.

The speech appealed to the best in the American temperament. "For a century," Johnson said, "we labored to settle and to subdue a continent. For half a century we called upon unbounded invention and untiring industry to create an order of plenty for all of our people. The challenge of the next half century is whether we have the wisdom to use that wealth to enrich and elevate our national life, and to advance the quality of our American civilization. . . . For in your time we have the opportunity to move not only toward the rich society and the powerful society, but upward to the Great Society. . . . It is a place where men are more concerned with the quality of their goals than the quantity of their goods."

To reach this promised land, Americans would have to rebuild their cities, eliminating urban decay and providing modern housing and efficient transportation for all and a renewed sense of community. They would also have to recommit themselves to "America the beautiful," the preservation of the country's natural splendor and an unpolluted environment with clean air, clean water, green forests, and usable seashores. Third, they would need to rededicate themselves to educational reform, building school systems across the nation that would offer an escape from poverty and stimulate a love of learning. The twenty-minute speech before more than 80,000 people in the university's stadium on a warm sunny day was a great hit. The jubilant crowd, grateful for the President's attendance at their children's graduation, sensing that they were hearing a landmark address, and, stirred by the President's words, interrupted him for applause twenty-nine times. For Johnson the approval and enthusiasm were intoxicating. On the plane ride back to Washington, he was "manic" or "just . . . absolutely euphoric." Violating a self-imposed rule, he had a scotch highball and joined the pool reporters in the back of the plane. Asking them what they thought and warming to their positive assessment, he "read, with emphasis, portions of the speech to us. He wanted to make sure we got the story."

Few Americans took Johnson's rhetoric at face value. When the Gallup poll asked whether people thought poverty would ever be done away with in the country, only 9 percent said "yes" and 83 percent said "no." Moreover, hardly anyone expected Johnson's administration or subsequent ones to reach the utopian goals LBJ outlined in his Great Society speech.

Johnson himself had little idea of what a Great Society or a war on poverty meant beyond "fulfilling FDR's mission." His objective, Bill Moyers says, was to finish the Roosevelt revolution. Johnson "never really liked the term Great Society," Moyers adds. "It didn't come easily to him." But it gave the press a "bumper sticker. He didn't like it as much as he liked the New Deal. That's really what he saw himself doing."

Though there were no polls saying start a war on poverty or a community action program or environmental protection, people didn't object to Johnson's grand designs. To the contrary, his positive outlook on the nation's future was a welcome antidote to the grief and dejection so many Americans continued to feel over Kennedy's assassination. In short, Johnson's enthusiasm and confidence that the country could reach unprecedented heights made Americans feel better about themselves. Never mind that he was overstating and overselling his vision of where he hoped the country would go. It was enough that he forecast a better day when pride in the nation's accomplishments would replace recrimination and doubt about a violent America doomed to national decline.

:: THE IRONY OF FATE

The principal area in which Americans had doubts about their new President was foreign affairs. From the start of his term, commentators saw him as uncomfortable with overseas questions and less adroit at juggling international challenges than domestic ones.

To refute this image, Johnson told reporters in January 1964: "I am spending more time on foreign affairs than on any other subject. I have had 175 separate meetings . . . ; and I have made 188 telephone calls. . . . I've met twice with the National Security Council. I've had Secretary McNamara at the White House 30 times. I've met with the Joint Chiefs of Staff three times in 60 days. I've had Secretary Rusk here 51 times. . . . I have instructed my staff to notify me immediately when something important happens anywhere in the world. . . . I am often called in the middle of the night . . . with late information on developments abroad."

Despite the substantial time and energy Johnson gave to foreign issues, he could not mask his preference for and greater competence in domestic matters. Like Woodrow Wilson, who believed "it would be the irony of fate if my administration had to deal chiefly with foreign affairs," Johnson hoped that external demands would not distract him from what needed to be done at home. As one aide put it, LBJ "wishes the rest of the world would go away and we could get ahead with the real needs of Americans." Johnson himself said half-jokingly: "Foreigners are not like the folks I am used to."

Johnson's congressional service had not given him a sure feel for mastering overseas events the way it had for legislative challenges. Nor had his travels abroad given him a clear sense of what he should aim for there. To be sure, containing Communism and avoiding a nuclear holocaust were obvious goals. But beyond these generalizations Johnson did not have the sort of keen interest in the world Kennedy had brought to the White House. Johnson's uncertainty about charting the right course for the varied and confusing challenges pressing in on him daily from all over the world made him dependent on JFK's foreign policy advisers, especially Secretary of State Dean Rusk, Defense Secretary Robert McNamara, and, most of all, McGeorge Bundy, the National Security Adviser.

Rusk was an enormous comfort to Johnson. He was almost the perfect man in the right place at the right time. He was a rock-solid adviser on foreign and national security policy. After serving as an army colonel in the China-Burma-India theater in World War II and a staff officer in the Pentagon, he was Assistant Secretary of State for United Nations Affairs and then for the Far East during Truman's presidency. In 1952 he had become head of the Rockefeller Foundation in New York, where he was serving when he became JFK's compromise choice for the State Department. As secretary, he had been a tireless and generally faceless diplomat, working, as one colleague in the Kennedy administration described him, "as long and as hard as anyone in Washington. There was much else in Rusk's background and personality that appealed to Johnson. A Georgian with a soft southern drawl, Rusk was a self-made man who shared LBJ's passion for helping the poor, ending segregation, and opening avenues of opportunities for all peoples regardless of race or social background. Rusk's attendance at Oxford University as a Rhodes scholar, his professorship of government at Mills College in California, and his service as president of the Rockefeller Foundation also gave him standing with LBJ.

Robert McNamara's presence in the Defense Department also reassured Johnson, who viewed him as an ideal complement to Rusk. The forty-seven-year-old McNamara held degrees from Berkeley and the Harvard

Business School, where his brilliance as a student had won him a faculty position teaching accounting. During World War II he had served as an officer in the air force, applying "proven business methods to war" and making a reputation that landed him a postwar job at the Ford Motor Company. By 1961 his managerial skills had made him the chief executive officer. His talent for administering a huge bureaucracy persuaded Kennedy to appoint him Secretary of Defense. McNamara's faith in rational solutions to vexing problems gained him the title of "the can-do man in the can-do society in the can-do era." After Johnson met McNamara for the first time, he described him — "that fellow with the Staycomb" in his slick black hair — as Kennedy's smartest Cabinet member: You could almost hear the computers clicking away, Johnson said. Like Johnson, he loved the idea of using power to do good.

The third member of Johnson's foreign policy and defense triumvirate was Mac Bundy, as his friends called him. He was a descendant of the Boston Lowells, who made a fortune in New England textiles and played a central part in the development of Harvard. He was a man of impeccable background and supreme self-confidence. At Groton, a leading prep school, his brilliance and self-assurance moved a fellow student to say he was ready to be dean of the school at the age of twelve. An essay he wrote as an undergraduate at Yale was, in the judgment of his teacher, a distinguished historian, better than anything all but a few faculty members could have achieved. After service in the army during World War II and a brief period teaching in the Harvard government department, Bundy, at the age of thirty-four, became the youngest Dean of Faculty in Harvard's history. Eight years later he joined Kennedy's administration as Special Assistant for National Security Affairs, and quickly established himself as a dominant figure in a universe of powerful, brilliant men.

Despite his reliance on Rusk, McNamara, and Bundy, Johnson wouldn't let on that he was anything less than their boss. As Bundy puts it, Johnson's "problem in foreign affairs at the beginning was . . . 'I'm going to show these guys I'm not a Texas provincial. I'm a world statesman. I can talk to De Gaulle.'" But Johnson found it difficult. Foreign affairs "wasn't his own home country in the same way that proving to Larry O'Brien that he could count the Senate better than O'Brien. That was easy," Bundy said.

Nevertheless Johnson was determined to set his own course in world affairs. It is "total baloney" that we, Rusk, McNamara, and Bundy, were running the government, Bundy said. We "understood that we were working for a President who . . . insisted on making his own decisions. It's baloney that we were running, defining" Johnson's actions abroad.

:: THE PERILS OF FOREIGN POLICY: VIETNAM

Johnson's determination to set his own course in foreign affairs did not translate into mastery of overseas problems. Vietnam was a telling case in point. As in domestic affairs, Johnson saw a need initially to continue Kennedy's policy. But just what that meant was difficult to know. Kennedy had repeatedly stated his determination in public to prevent a Communist takeover in South Vietnam. He had backed this up by increasing arms shipments to Saigon and expanding the number of military advisers from less than 700 to 16,700. Moreover, he had deepened American involvement by acquiescing in the military coup that toppled Diem.

Yet at the same time, Kennedy gave strong indications that the American commitment would go only so far. Repeated requests from U.S. military chiefs for combat troops in Vietnam had received a blanket refusal from JFK. Further, he had told a number of political associates that he intended a total withdrawal of American military personnel from Vietnam after the 1964 election. If, instead, he had expanded U.S. military involvement in Vietnam, it may be assumed that it would have left open the possibility of withdrawal without an appearance of defeat. "No one can say what JFK would have done" in Vietnam, Bundy says. "But that it would have been different and it would have been less than Johnson are I think safe generalizations."

Johnson, however, partly to assure public backing, described his actions as largely in line with Kennedy's. In a conversation on November 24 with Ambassador to Saigon Henry Cabot Lodge, CIA Director John McCone, Rusk, McNamara, and Bundy, Johnson stated his determination to fulfill Kennedy's goal of not losing Vietnam. As Bundy stated it later, Johnson was "simply not going to accept the notion that he's going to be the man who can't hold the Alamo. . . . It's an unfair jump in the sense he knows it's not the Alamo, but the judgment he's going to have rendered on him is not going to be that he lost Vietnam.

Bill Moyers remembers Johnson telling him after the meeting: Lodge "'says it's going to be hell in a handbasket out there. . . . If we don't do something, he says, it'll go under. . . . They'll think with Kennedy dead we've lost heart. So they'll think we're yellow and don't mean what we say. . . . I'm not going to let Vietnam go the way of China."

Johnson saw Vietnam as a test of American resolve abroad. But he also thought it had the potential for disturbing consequences at home. He wanted quick and effective action against the Communists in Vietnam as a way to head off losses overseas and stalemate on domestic reform. But the whole business unnerved him. "Right now I feel like one of those catfish" in your part of Texas, LBJ told Moyers. "I feel like I just grabbed a big juicy worm with a right sharp hook in the middle of it." The bait was so tempting, but was he the one being hooked?

Even if Johnson had answered "yes," it is nearly inconceivable that in 1963–64 he would have walked away from Vietnam. Given existing assumptions about the Cold War—about a long-term struggle between capitalism and Communism—and public feeling in America about the imperative of meeting global challenges from Moscow and Beijing to assure the survival of the United States, no President, especially an unproven, unelected one, could simply have withdrawn without some real hope that the South Vietnamese could have held off a Viet Cong–North Vietnamese takeover. Retrospective thinking, colored by later results, should not ignore or distort this reality.

Vietnam became a matter that Johnson wished to subject to his irresistible political will. He sent Lodge and General Duong Van Minh, Diem's successor, letters urging them to get on with the job of beating the Communists. He pressed Minh "to act now to reverse the trend of the war."

A coup at the end of January 1964, in which General Nguyen Khanh replaced Minh, opened the way to yet greater instability and likelihood of Communist success in Vietnam. But it did little to discourage Johnson from a growing resolve to meet the challenge. He urged Khanh to see "the necessity of stepping up the pace of military operations against the Viet Cong."

He also tried to strengthen America's effort in the war by organizational changes and rhetoric. He told Bundy that with 15,000 U.S. advisers and 200,000 South Vietnamese troops, we should be able to maintain the status quo for six months. From Johnson's perspective, this meant being able to put Vietnam on hold until after the November election, when other decisions could be made.

A major McNamara speech on Vietnam at the end of March indicated what these might be. McNamara emphasized America's determination to keep helping South Vietnam. The country and the region were described as having "great strategic significance in the forward defense of the United States." Further, McNamara pictured Vietnam as "a test case for the new Communist strategy"—wars of national liberation or "covert aggression or insurgency." In a meeting the following week with congressional leaders, the President and McNamara explained that they were considering "taking the war to . . . North Vietnam," a policy the Joints Chiefs believed essential for success in the south.

During April and May Johnson confronted a growing crisis when Communist aggression in Laos and Cambodia joined with continuing advances by the Viet Cong in Vietnam. LBJ now asked Congress for an additional $125 million in military and economic assistance to Vietnam, and the White House called a meeting of top advisers on Vietnam in Honolulu for June 1–3. Johnson instructed the participants to discuss plans for "selected and carefully graduated military force against North Vietnam . . . after appropriate diplomatic and political warning and preparations."

The officials also were to consider asking Congress for a resolution supporting future military actions. He set Bundy to work drafting a congressional resolution that could take care of the problem. But Johnson saw it as premature to ask Congress to act. In the spring of 1964 a Gallup survey showed 63 percent of the public giving little or no attention to the fighting in Southeast Asia, while in another opinion poll 25 percent of Americans had heard nothing about the conflict. Although a majority of those attentive to the problem favored stronger action, this amounted to only a small percentage of the public.

The strongest inhibitions Johnson saw on pushing a resolution were the 1964 election and pending bills in Congress. Johnson believed that a war fever in Congress and the country would undermine his chances of getting the civil rights bill passed and might cause his defeat in the presidential election. He believed it essential first to educate Americans about the stakes in Vietnam as preludes to a resolution and greater involvement in the war.

:: CIVIL RIGHTS

In the spring of 1964 Johnson's focus was principally on winning passage of JFK's civil rights bill. From the moment he had assumed the presidency, he saw a compelling need to drive Kennedy's bill through Congress with no major compromises that would weaken the law.

As a southerner who had accommodated himself to segregation through most of his career, Johnson seemed like an unreliable advocate of a civil rights statute that would force an end to the system of racial separation in public facilities across the South. He could not fully divest himself of attitudes instilled by a southern upbringing. But he was determined to rise above his own limitations on race and to bring the country with him. "I'm going to be the President who finishes what Lincoln began," he said to several people.

A few days after he became President, he asked Senator Russell to come talk to him about the civil rights bill. "The President sat in a wing chair.

The Senator sat at one end of a small couch. Their knees almost touched."
As Jack Valenti remembered it, Johnson said: "'Dick, you've got to get out
of my way. I'm going to run over you. I don't intend to cavil or compro-
mise.' 'You may do that,' he replied. 'But by God, it's going to cost you the
South and cost you the election.' 'If that's the price I've got to pay,' said the
President, 'I'll pay it gladly.'"

The following week Johnson told labor leaders that "the endless abra-
sions of delay, neglect, and indifference have rubbed raw the national conscience. We have talked too long. We have done too little. And all of it has
come too late. You must help me make civil rights in America a reality."
Two days later, in a well-publicized meeting at the White House, he gave
the same message to the country's principal black leaders. "This bill is
going to pass if it takes all summer," he told them. "This bill is going to be
enacted because justice and morality demand it."

He had several reasons for wanting to make good on civil rights. First,
he felt that passing Kennedy's bill would help heal the wound opened by
his assassination. To Johnson's thinking, the President's murder resulted
from the violence and hatred dividing America and tearing at its social fab-
ric. As important, there was the moral issue or the matter of fairness that
Johnson felt with a keenness few could fully understand. Johnson, the most
powerful political leader in the world, was also Johnson, the poor boy from
Texas, who identified with and viscerally experienced the suffering of the
disadvantaged.

He repeatedly told the story of Zephyr Wright, his cook, "a college graduate," who, when driving the Vice President's official car with her husband
from Washington to Texas, couldn't use the facilities in a gas station to
relieve herself. "When they had to go to the bathroom," Johnson told Mississippi Senator John Stennis, "they would . . . pull off on a side road, and
Zephyr Wright, the cook of the Vice President of the United States, would
squat in the road to pee." He told Stennis: "That's wrong. And there ought
to be something to change that. And it seems to me that if people in Mississippi don't change it voluntarily, that it's just going to be necessary to
change it by law."

His sense of outrage was even more pronounced toward Alabama Klansmen who had killed four black youngsters by setting off a bomb at a Birmingham church in September 1963. He urged FBI Director J. Edgar
Hoover to leave no stone unturned in finding the perpetrators. He also
asked Hoover to step up his investigations of several other Birmingham
bombings tied to racial intolerance.

Yet all Johnson's rhetoric could not entirely disarm the suspicions of civil rights advocates. If he had felt so strongly about the issue, why had it taken him so long to act on it? Why was he going to make an all-out fight for the civil rights bill now? Roy Wilkins asked him at their December meeting. Johnson thought a minute, wrinkled his brow and said: "You will recognize the words I'm about to repeat. Free at last, free at last. Thank God almighty, I'm free at last." Borrowing from Martin Luther King's speech to the civil rights advocates who had marched on Washington in the summer of 1963, Johnson was describing himself as liberated from his southern political bonds or as a man who could now fully put the national interest and moral concerns above political constraints imposed on a Texas senator.

At the same time, Johnson saw civil rights reform as essential to the well-being of his native region. He had known for a long time that segregation not only separated blacks and whites in the South but also separated the South from the rest of the nation, making it a kind of moral, economic, and political outsider, a reprobate cousin or embarrassing relative the nation could neither disown nor accept as a respectable family member. An end to southern segregation would mean the full integration of the South into the Union, bringing with it economic progress and political influence comparable to that of other regions. And though many in the South would abandon their roots in the Democratic party in response, Johnson was determined to administer the unpleasant medicine that would cure the region's social disease. The election of Presidents from Georgia, Texas, and Arkansas during the next thirty years testifies to the region's renewed influence in the nation anticipated by LBJ.

Johnson also saw personal political gain from pressing ahead with civil rights legislation. In the fall of 1963, 50 percent of the country had felt that Kennedy was pushing too hard for integration. Only 11 percent wanted him to go faster, while 27 percent were content with his pace. By February 1964 the number opposing more vigorous civil rights efforts had dropped to 30 percent, and the percentages favoring more aggressive action and what Johnson was doing had increased to 15 percent and 39 percent, respectively. By the last week of April, 57 percent of the public said they approved of the way Johnson was handling the civil rights problem, and just 21 percent disapproved.

It was welcome news to LBJ, who believed his election to the presidency depended in significant part on his firm advocacy of a civil rights law. "I knew that if I didn't get out in front on this issue the liberals would get me," he later told Doris Kearns. "I had to produce a civil rights bill that was even stronger than the one they'd have gotten if Kennedy had lived. Without this, I'd be dead before I could even begin."

Yet Johnson also had reason to think that a forceful stand on civil rights might ruin him politically. Black civil rights leader Andrew Young said that, while Johnson knew that support of the civil rights bill was the way to assure his place in history and "the way to really save the nation, he knew it was not politically expedient."

Johnson also worried that an all-out push for a bill that didn't pass could be a serious blow to his political standing. And he saw defeat as a distinct possibility. When he asked Hubert Humphrey to lead the civil rights act through the Senate, Johnson said: "This is your test. But I predict it will not go through." Partly because he believed it and partly to light a fire under Humphrey, Johnson launched into a diatribe about the ineffectiveness of Senate liberals. "You bomb-throwers make good speeches, you have big hearts, you believe in what you say you stand for, but you're never on the job when you need to be there. You spread yourselves too thin making speeches to the faithful."

Because they would be up against Russell, who knew all the Senate rules better than the liberals, Johnson expected Humphrey to lose the battle. It was a "speech" Humphrey had heard repeatedly from Johnson, but it was less a cry of despair than a summons to do better. He firmly promised to back Humphrey to the hilt. "As I left, he stood and moved toward me with his towering intensity: 'Call me whenever there's trouble or anything you want me to do,'" Johnson said.

To guard against some of the political fallout from a possible congressional defeat, Johnson told Robert Kennedy: "I'll do . . . just what you think is best to do on the bill. We'll follow what you say. . . . I'll do everything that you want me to do in order to obtain passage of the legislation." Johnson sent word to Senate Democratic leaders to get Bob Kennedy's approval on everything. Why did he do that? an interviewer asked Kennedy. "He didn't think . . . we'd get the bill," Bobby answered. And if that were the case, "he didn't want . . . to have the sole responsibility. If I worked out the strategy, if he did what the Department of Justice recommended . . . —and particularly me—then . . . he could always say that he did what we suggested and didn't go off on his own." Kennedy believed that "for political reasons it made a great deal of sense." Johnson couldn't lose this way, because if the bill passed, he would still get "ample credit."

At the outset, Johnson's legislative strategy was the same as Kennedy's: First, get a bill through the House. In the five months before his death, JFK had convinced House leaders from both parties to agree on a compromise law that concentrated its fire on giving southern blacks access to public accommodations and public schools and all citizens equal employment opportunities. This bill had received the approval of the House Judiciary Committee in October and was before the Rules Committee in November when Johnson became President.

On November 25, Johnson told the nation's governors that he expected bipartisan approval of the bill in the House. "The real problem will be in the Senate," he advised congressional leaders. But he took nothing for granted in the House, where Howard Smith of Virginia, Chairman of the Rules Committee, seemed determined to delay matters as long as possible. To put some heat on Smith, Johnson launched a campaign for a discharge petition that would bypass his committee. Republican supporters, seeing this as a liberal Democratic bid to take exclusive credit for the bill, resisted Johnson's pressure. Moderate Democrats, eager not to jeopardize bipartisan support, did the same. On January 30, after he had agreed to drop the petition, the Rules Committee approved the bill by an 11-to-4 vote.

Although Johnson and Larry O'Brien were fairly confident that the bill would pass the House, they worried that some of the Republicans might not stay committed and that various amendments, which could dilute the bill, might pass. Consequently, during the next eleven days, Johnson was constantly on the phone, bargaining with Democrats and Republicans alike. "We let them, the Congressmen, know that for every negative vote there was a price to pay," Jack Valenti recalls. "There were many times on that floor when even, Republican leader Charlie Halleck, in spite of his commitment, would vote for crippling amendments, which we had to beat down," civil rights leader Clarence Mitchell remembers. "And there were many times when if it had not been for the Johnson intercession, we wouldn't have had enough votes on the floor to hold things."

On February 10, within minutes after the bill passed the House 290 to 110, Johnson was on the phone to congressmen praising their action. "We're rollin' now with tax and civil rights if we can just get this through the Senate," he told one of them. "I don't know how we'll ever do it, but we sure gonna try."

At about 2 a.m. the next morning, Johnson reached Texas Congressman Jake Pickle, one of only six southerners to vote for the bill. "I didn't want to let the night go by without my telling you how proud I am of you," Johnson said. He reflected on the fact that, as a member of the House, he had lacked Pickle's courage to vote for a civil rights bill.

Johnson carefully considered his role in trying to win Senate approval of the bill. "A President cannot ask the Congress to take a risk he will not take himself. He must be the combat general in the front lines. . . . I gave to this fight everything I had in prestige, power, and commitment." But he understood that it would be a poor idea to become too involved in the day-to-day tactics on the Hill. "I deliberately tried to tone down my personal involvement in the daily struggle so that my colleagues on the Hill could take tactical responsibility—and credit," Johnson said later. Nevertheless, he had no intention of leaving anything to chance or letting Senate allies design a strategy. On February 11, he gave Senate Majority Leader Mike Mansfield marching orders on the telephone and kept in close touch with him on evolving strategy.

Johnson believed that he could best help advance the bill by repeated public appeals. At a February press conference he made clear that he expected a filibuster in the Senate, but that he would oppose any attempt substantially to change the House bill. During the next five months, while the Senate debated civil rights, hardly a week went by without a restatement of Johnson's conviction that a law should be passed just like the one approved in the House. We are "committed" to the bill with "no wheels and no deals," he said. He also made clear that, having won most of his legislative agenda for the session, he was ready for a long filibuster. "They can filibuster until hell freezes over," he declared. "I'm not going to put anything on that floor until this is done."

Yet Johnson did not confine his efforts to public statements. Behind the scenes he continually gave direction and energy to the Senate battle for a bill. In January, he told Roy Wilkins "to get on this bill" and get twenty-five Republican votes for cloture. "You're gonna have to persuade Dirksen why this is in the interest of the Republican party," LBJ said.

He believed that the key to overcoming a filibuster and winning approval for the principal features of the House measure was to weaken resistance among southern senators and to enlist Dirksen in the fight. Kenny O'Donnell remembers Johnson telling the southerners, "You've got a southern president and if you want to blow him out of the water, go right ahead and do it, but you boys will never see another one again. We're friends on the q.t. Would you rather have me administering the civil rights bill, or do you want to have Nixon or Republican Bill Scranton? You have to make up your minds."

Johnson's appeal was effective. Clarence Mitchell remembers the pained expression on one southerner's face when he described the pressure Johnson put on him. While this senator would never have voted for the bill, "he could have hurt us in a lot of ways that he didn't hurt us." Johnson's point registered on Russell as well. "Now you tell Lyndon," Russell told Bill

Moyers, "that I've been expecting the rod for a long time, and I'm sorry that it's from his hand the rod must be wielded, but I'd rather it be his hand than anybody else's I know. Tell him to cry a little when he uses it."

Whatever gains he made with the southerners, Johnson saw Dirksen as the lynchpin in the fight. "They say I'm an arm-twister," Johnson told Roy Wilkins, "but I can't make a southerner change his spots any more than I can make a leopard change 'em. . . . I'm no magician. I'm gonna be with ya, and I'm gonna help everywhere I can." But others needed to join in, especially Dirksen, whom he told could establish a special place for himself in history by recognizing that civil rights reform was inevitable. He used the example of Senator Arthur Vandenberg of Michigan, whose shift from isolationism to internationalism during World War II won him a historical reputation as a statesman. At the same time, Johnson told Humphrey: "Now you know that this bill can't pass unless you get Ev Dirksen. You and I are going to get him. You make up your mind now that you've got to spend time with Ev Dirksen. You've got to let him have a piece of the action."

Humphrey, having arrived at the same conclusion, flattered and courted Dirksen at every turn. "I began a public massage of his ego," Humphrey writes, "and appealed to his vanity. I said he should look upon this issue as 'a moral, not a partisan one.' The gentle pressure left room for *him* to be the historically important figure in our struggle, the statesman above partisanship, . . . the master builder of a legislative edifice that would last forever. He liked it." Humphrey, as he said later, was ready to kiss "Dirksen's ass on the Capitol steps."

Humphrey, in fact, had a better sense of how to manage Dirksen and other senators than Johnson. When Dirksen wanted to schedule a cloture vote at the end of April, after a month's debate, Humphrey, with Johnson's help, convinced him to wait. No Senate filibuster had ever been ended before by cloture, and Humphrey foresaw that additional weeks of debate would be needed before such a groundbreaking development could occur. In addition, against the judgment of Johnson and liberals in and out of the Senate, Humphrey agreed to several amendments Dirksen proposed as a prelude to getting his support on cloture. Since the amendments did nothing to weaken the provisions of the bill as they applied to the South, civil rights proponents accepted them as a necessary but small compromise.

On June 10, after seventy-five days of debate, the Senate took a cloture vote. The night before, Johnson called Humphrey to ask whether he had the sixty-seven votes, or two-thirds needed to end the debate. "I think we have enough," Humphrey replied. Johnson wasn't satisfied. "I don't want to know what you think. What's the vote going to be? How many do you have?" Confident of only sixty-six supporters, Humphrey spent the evening working on three southwestern Democrats whose votes were not certain. Though Johnson largely left the lobbying and head counting to Humphrey, he had promised a Central Arizona water project to Carl Hayden for his backing—a vote which seemed likely to tip several other senators to the administration's side, including the two from Nevada.

Dirksen, who "had a magnificent sense of drama, loved the center stage, and loved the sound of his mellifluous . . . voice," had the last word before a vote. Taking his text from Victor Hugo, Dirksen, who was suffering from a peptic ulcer and whose "face looked like a collapsed ruin, drawn and gaunt," intoned: "Stronger than all the armies is an idea whose time has come. The time has come for equality . . . in education and in employment. It will not be stayed or denied. It is here."

Predicting that they would get sixty-nine votes, Humphrey followed the proceedings with keen anticipation. Senator Clair Engle of California, who was dying of a brain tumor and could not speak, arrived in a wheelchair and pointed to his eye when called to vote. The final tally of 71 to 29 exceeded Humphrey's expectations. He "involuntarily" raised his arms over his head at what he saw as the culmination of a lifetime in politics fighting for equal rights.

Johnson took great satisfaction from this historic gain. Should we have a major signing ceremony or should we do it quietly? Johnson asked legislative aide Lee White. "It's so monumental," White answered. "It's equivalent to signing an Emancipation Proclamation, and ought to have all the possible attention you can focus on it." In a simple, dignified ceremony in the East Room of the White House attended by government officials, foreign diplomats, and black and white civil rights advocates, Johnson signed the bill before a national television audience on the evening of July 2. One panoramic photograph of Johnson at a small table before the more than 100 dignitaries seated in long rows conveys the sense of importance Johnson and his audience attached to the occasion.

"We believe all men are entitled to the blessings of liberty," Johnson said. "Yet millions are being deprived of those blessings—not because of their own failures, but because of the color of their skin. The reasons are deeply imbedded in history and tradition and the nature of man. We can understand—without rancor or hatred—how this happened, but it cannot continue. . . . Our Constitution, the foundation of our Republic, forbids it. The principles of our freedom forbid it. Morality forbids it. And the law I will sign tonight forbids it."

Yet Johnson also had his doubts and anxieties about an act of law that was about to change the social structure of the South. He told Hubert Humphrey in May: "The thing we are more afraid of than anything else is that we will have real revolution in this country when this bill goes into effect. . . . It took us ten years to put this Supreme Court decision into effect on education. . . . Unless we have the Republicans joinin' us and helpin' put down this mutiny, we'll have mutiny in this goddamn country. So we've got to make this an American bill and not just a Democratic bill."

The evening Johnson signed the bill, Bill Moyers visited him in his bedroom, where he found Johnson seated on his bed with several newspapers headlining the civil rights act spread around him. Johnson seemed deflated. Sensing his mood, Moyers asked why he was so glum. "Because, Bill," he replied, "I think we just delivered the South to the Republican party for a long time to come."

Johnson remained concerned that the South might resist the law. He feared it would lead to violence, bloodshed, public anarchy, economic dislocation, and defeat for his administration and the Democratic party in the 1964 campaign. In fact, nothing of the kind occurred, as Russell predicted to Clarence Mitchell after his defeat on cloture. Because the civil rights bill was an act of Congress rather than "judge or court made law," Russell expected the South to accept the outcome with little trouble. It did. By the 1980s access to public facilities across the South for blacks was so commonly accepted that youngsters born in the 1970s could not imagine the segregated society of pre-1964.

But Johnson could not know this at the time. And so civil rights was an uncertain element in the presidential campaign, which by the summer of 1964 was the focus of Johnson's political life.

6 :: "LANDSLIDE LYNDON"

Franklin Roosevelt's idea of the presidency was himself in the White House. Lyndon Johnson's idea of the presidency was FDR, Truman, Eisenhower, and even Kennedy in the office. But LBJ? Despite much talk about eclipsing "the whole bunch of them" as a reformer and a vote-getter, Johnson found it difficult to see himself as Chief Executive. He knew he was as smart, and maybe even smarter, than most of his predecessors. He had no doubt that his thirty years in Washington made him as well prepared to be President as anyone else. But he couldn't shake a constant, nagging concern that he didn't quite measure up.

Throughout his career, inner doubts translated into worries about losing elections, even when every political calculation suggested otherwise. His fears made him back and fill and agonize over withdrawing from races he badly wanted to run and seemed almost certain to make. And when he ran, he was unrelenting, pressing himself and everyone in the campaign into ceaseless, frenzied, exhausting efforts.

The 1964 election put Johnson's self-doubts on display to everyone around him. A constant refrain during his first nine months in the presidency was his uncertainty about running for a full term. Most everyone thought he was being too clever by half. There was no chance Johnson wouldn't run. He was playing a political game, or so they believed. But the day after the Democratic party convention opened in August, he drafted a withdrawal statement. "Our country faces grave dangers. . . . The times require leadership . . . and a voice that men of all parties, sections and color can follow. I have learned after trying very hard that I am not that voice or that leader."

Lady Bird talked him out of quitting. In response to his statement, Mrs. Johnson soothed him with assurances that he was "as brave a man as Harry Truman—or FDR—or Lincoln." She told him that "to step out now would be *wrong* for your country, and I can see nothing but a lonely wasteland for your future. Your friends would be frozen in embarrassed silence and your enemies jeering." When Johnson told Russell that he had decided against running, Russell, "begging forgiveness for frankness, . . . told him he was talking like a child—and a spoiled one at that. . . . I knew he was not serious and my advice was to take a tranquilizer and get a couple of hours sleep."

Johnson's reluctance was irrational. Through the spring of 1964 national opinion was decidedly in his favor. In late March, pollster George Gallup told a White House aide that "the President is doing a fantastic job. We all thought that the honeymoon would last 30–45 days and then the polls would drop off sharply. But this has not been the case. The President still has a fantastically high national rating, and it looks like that rating is going to continue." The only place poll numbers showed the slightest problem was in the South, where LBJ had a 13 percent disapproval rating.

Despite all the good news on his popularity, Johnson believed that if he were going to win in November he needed, first, to enact the liberal agenda—the tax cut, war on poverty, and civil rights—and, second, to demonstrate that he was a President who could rise above politics to serve the national interest. In addition, he believed it essential to map out a strategy against a Republican opponent. His initial list of GOP candidates included Nixon, New York's Governor Nelson Rockefeller, Ambassador to Vietnam Henry Cabot Lodge, Pennsylvania Governor Bill Scranton, and Arizona Senator Barry Goldwater.

Because he found it difficult during the spring to anticipate his opponent in the fall campaign, Johnson tried to prepare himself for a race against either a moderate or a conservative Republican. He thought all of them, as he told Hubert Humphrey, would be vulnerable to the argument that "the reason the Republicans haven't won any elections since Hoover except Eisenhower . . . is because they spend all their time on Roosevelt's boy Jimmy and on his dog, and . . . on Truman and Margaret and the music critics and . . . on Kennedy and his religion . . . and . . . if they don't stand for something, hell, if they just come out here and talk about revival of the corn tassel or come out for Tom Watson watermelons, it'd be something. But they just, by God, are against things, against everything and trying to smear and fear." But Johnson really didn't need to counter the Republicans in the first half of 1964; their intra-party strife was doing it for him.

:: BARRY'S THE ONE

Only sixteen states held primaries in 1964, with the rest choosing delegates to the national conventions at local and statewide party caucuses. By mid-April, some estimates gave Goldwater nearly 450 of the 655 delegates needed for the Republican nomination. When he won the California primary on June 2, he was all but assured of the prize. Barry Morris Goldwater was the envy of a fiction writer's imagination. Born in the Arizona territory in 1909, he was the offspring of Jewish and Protestant pioneers who built the two biggest department stores in the area and played leading roles in the public life of the territory and state beginning in 1912. During World War II, Goldwater left the family business for service in the air force. In 1952, he won a U.S. Senate seat and immediately became an outspoken advocate of ultra-conservative ideas that put him at odds with not only most Democrats but also the Eisenhower administration, which he called "a dime-store New Deal."

A blunt man with little feel for the nuances of traditional American politics, Goldwater did nothing to hide or shade his political views. Well before he began his presidential campaign, he had put himself on record as favoring the withdrawal of recognition of the Soviet Union, freedom for local military commanders to use atomic weapons against the USSR—"Let's lob one into the men's room of the Kremlin," he had said—the sale of FDR's Tennessee Valley Authority, and abolition of the graduated income tax. During the New Hampshire primary campaign, he had urged that Social Security be made voluntary, described welfare recipients as people with low intelligence and little ambition, decried government interference in the economy and Federal aid to education, defended his opposition to civil rights legislation, and advocated the bombing of North Vietnam.

Democrats watching the rise of Goldwater's candidacy were gleeful. "It begins to look as though the Republicans are really going on a Kamikaze mission in November," ADA president John P. Roche wrote Bill Moyers in June. On the eve of the Republican convention in July, Lou Harris released a national survey showing that "on eight out of 10 issues facing the country, the American people feel they are in sharp disagreement with the Arizona senator." But in 1964 conservative Republicans, who had seized control of the party machinery and assured Goldwater's nomination, were more interested in trumpeting their ideology than in winning an election.

Goldwater's acceptance speech at the convention underscored his determination to make his campaign "a choice not an echo." The speech was not a traditional appeal for conciliation and party unity but a preaching to the converted, a call to the faithful to stand with him against "collectivism" and Communism. There could be no compromising these goals. "Extremism in the defense of liberty is no vice! . . . Moderation in the pursuit of justice is no virtue!" Goldwater declared. "My God," one reporter remarked, "he's going to run as Barry Goldwater."

Johnson and his closest advisers puzzled over how to react to Goldwater's nomination. There was an impulse to see Goldwater's candidacy as "absurd" and the Republican party as conceding the election. It was difficult to believe that so right-wing a candidate, espousing such extreme views on both domestic and foreign affairs, could marshal a significant challenge to a popular incumbent, as Johnson was in the summer of 1964.

But taking nothing for granted, Johnson insisted on a tough, hard-driving campaign. He saw "Goldwaterism" as "the outgrowth of long public unrest with Big Government, Big Spending, . . . and feeling that 'Washington doesn't understand our problems.'" He wanted to broaden the Democratic party base by reaching out to Independents and Republicans. Though he would be his own campaign manager and insisted on involving everyone at the White House in the election, he intended initially to act presidential and avoid taking on Goldwater himself.

:: THE "BOBBY PROBLEM"

Despite initial maneuvers against Goldwater and the Republicans, Johnson wasn't yet ready to focus his full attention on the fall campaign. Since early in the year he had been wrestling with questions about who would be his running mate. Initial soundings indicated warm support for Robert Kennedy. National polls showed Bobby holding a four-to-one edge over Hubert Humphrey, his closest rival.

Johnson felt frustrated and trapped by the prospect of having Kennedy on the ticket. It was an open secret that they disliked each other. Someone "very close" to Johnson told Alsop "categorically that Johnson will never under any circumstances choose Robert Kennedy." Three weeks after JFK's death, Johnson himself had told Ken O'Donnell: "I don't want history to say I was elected to this office because I had Bobby on the ticket with me. But I'll take him if I need him."

Throughout the spring Johnson explored possible alternatives to Kennedy as a running mate. Partly, this was an exercise in creating interest in what would otherwise be a cut and dried Democratic convention. First, Johnson floated Sargent Shriver's name. A Catholic, a member of the Kennedy clan, Shriver seemed like a good substitute for Bobby. On consideration, however, Johnson rejected the idea. Shriver's presence on the ticket would still have raised questions about LBJ's capacity to win on his own. At the same time, Johnson considered Hubert Humphrey, Eugene McCarthy, the junior senator from Minnesota, and Defense Secretary Robert McNamara. Johnson wanted Kennedy to take himself out of the running, but Bobby wouldn't do it. He had no illusion about Johnson's wishes, nor did he find the job all that appealing. True, it would make him an heir apparent to the presidency, but it carried a price he didn't want to pay, a Johnson Vice President would need to be a "yes man" who conformed to LBJ's every wish. "Whoever he is," Johnson told people in 1964, "I want his pecker . . . in my pocket."

Knowing all this, Kennedy still wouldn't drop out of the race. The allure of the second spot as a stepping stone to the first remained, but there was also some satisfaction in making Johnson squirm. Even if Bobby didn't run, he wanted to be asked.

By June, however, after Goldwater's victory in California, Johnson began to feel that the vice-presidential nomination would be of little consequence in determining the outcome of the election. Polls early in the month showed him with a 74 percent approval rating and a 77 to 18 percent margin over Goldwater in a trial election. As important to Lyndon, polls began to show that none of the vice-presidential candidates would do anything to strengthen his candidacy.

Yet Johnson couldn't just put Kennedy to one side. So, he now developed a plan to eliminate Kennedy from the running. Johnson put out a statement declaring that no one in the Cabinet or who met with the Cabinet, meaning Adlai Stevenson and Sargent Shriver, would be considered for the vice presidency. It would be too great a distraction from running their respective departments.

An end to Bobby's candidacy freed Johnson to encourage speculation about the vice-presidential nominee. It was a way to baffle reporters, get them writing about Johnson's problem in choosing a Vice President, and stir public interest in what would happen at the Democratic convention beginning on August 24. But before he got to the convention and subsequent campaign, Johnson felt compelled to answer doubts about Vietnam.

:: THE TONKIN GULF RESOLUTION

By June 1964 Vietnam had become a constant low-level irritant to Johnson. At home, the public and many in the Congress seemed indifferent or bewildered by the war; a few senators cautioned against deeper involvement; and

Barry Goldwater complained about the administration's weak response to the Communist challenge. In Vietnam itself there was no immediate prospect of a stable regime capable of resisting attacks without continuing and probably greater U.S. military and economic support.

Johnson's preference in the middle of June was to put the problem on hold until after the November election. He had no intention of letting Vietnam go, but he hoped for a respite from politically distracting decisions during the campaign.

Yet, however much Johnson wished to deemphasize the issue, Vietnam was not a problem that would even temporarily go away. If, for example, the North Vietnamese thought his administration was immobilized during the presidential campaign, Johnson believed it could mean the demise of South Vietnam. Nor did he dare risk having American voters view him as ineffective in dealing with the Communist threat.

On June 12, Johnson made clear that he had no intention of leaving or expanding the war in Vietnam. He seized upon a visit by Germany's Chancellor Ludwig Erhard to announce their mutual opposition to Hanoi's aggression against Saigon and determination to support the South Vietnamese against the Viet Cong.

In the first half of July, Johnson considered making a nationally televised talk on Vietnam that, in Bill Moyer's words, "could defuse a Goldwater bomb before he ever gets the chance to throw it." At the same time Johnson worried about meeting a Goldwater challenge to his Vietnam policy, General Khanh in Saigon pressed him to step up efforts against Hanoi or to "go north." Joint Chiefs of Staff Chairman Maxwell Taylor was so fearful of a Khanh resignation and South Vietnamese overtures to the Communists for a negotiated settlement that he proposed joint contingency planning for bombing North Vietnam. Taylor also asked for several thousand additional military advisers, which Johnson agreed to send.

By the end of July, Johnson was eager to bolster South Vietnamese morale, put Hanoi on additional notice of U.S. determination to stand fast, and deprive the Republicans of any advantage they hoped to gain from Vietnam in the campaign. To help advance the first two goals, the administration increased secret military efforts known as Operation 34-A, raids on the coast of North Vietnam by South Vietnamese commandos and U.S. advisers, and DE SOTO patrols by U.S. destroyers gathering electronic and other military intelligence and making a "show of force" to Hanoi.

During the night and early morning of July 30–31, a 34-A operation took place against two North Vietnamese islands in the Gulf of Tonkin. The following day the USS *Maddox*, an American destroyer, began a DE SOTO

patrol in the same area. On Sunday morning, August 2, three North Vietnamese torpedo boats attacked the *Maddox* in international waters sixteen
miles from the coast. The *Maddox*, supported by planes from an aircraft
carrier, hit back, sinking one and damaging another of the North Vietnamese boats.

George Ball and Senator J. William Fulbright later said that the stepped
up operations in July and August were meant to provoke Hanoi into a
response that would allow the United States to begin air attacks on North
Vietnam. Fulbright, in fact, held this view at the time of the attack. In a
telephone conversation on the morning of August 3, Fulbright told Ball
that "he was a little suspicious and thought probably that the incident was
asked for."

But McNamara and Bundy dispute that. MacNamara told his biographer
Deborah Shapley: "I don't believe that the president, or I, or Dean Rusk, or
Mac Bundy were planning, in the sense of anticipating or embarking upon
'overt war' with North Vietnam in 1964. I know that the president didn't
intend 'overt war' and I didn't intend 'overt war' in 1964. Johnson didn't have
plans for military action other than to continue on as we were." Likewise,
Bundy told Shapley, Johnson "didn't want to take decisions on this issue in
an election year."

Johnson's response to the August 2 attack in the Gulf bears out the
MacNamara and Bundy assertions. Though Johnson was determined to
show Hanoi that the United States would not be intimidated, his initial
impulse was to play down the incident and keep it from escalating into a
confrontation that would agitate unwanted questions about military action
during the presidential campaign.

On the morning of August 2, when he met with State Department and
military advisers, he "sounded bewildered about what had happened; he
couldn't understand why they [the North Vietnamese] had done it. . . . He
certainly didn't say, 'The sons of bitches, what do they think they're doing?'"
The conversation was Johnson's way of saying that he didn't want to turn
the August 2 attack into anything more than it was: an incident in the ongoing struggle between Hanoi, Saigon, and Washington.

On August 2 and 3, when the North Vietnamese said nothing in public
about the attack, Johnson assumed that they also wanted to keep the incident from ballooning into something more. The President and all his principal advisers concluded that Hanoi had made a false connection between
the 34-A operation on July 30–31 and the subsequent *Maddox* patrol. Believing that the *Maddox* had been part of the attacking force against their
Tonkin Gulf islands, the North Vietnamese had felt compelled to attack

the destroyer. Seeing the incident as an error by Hanoi, the White House wanted to let the episode fade from view.

But Johnson and his advisers misread Hanoi. They could not believe that the North Vietnamese would be so foolish as to challenge U.S. military power head-on. Everyone from Johnson on down saw the destroyers in the Gulf as an intimidating force that would discourage Hanoi from further aggression or at least put them on notice that they would have to deal directly with American power if their campaign of subversion continued against the South. The North Vietnamese viewed the American ships not as a deterrent but rather as a target or an opportunity to tell Washington that it would not be inhibited by U.S. power in pursuit of its vital national interest, the unification of all Vietnam under its control.

On August 4, however, when McNamara phoned Johnson with a report that two destroyers were under attack by torpedo boats, Johnson decided to give Hanoi "a real dose." Johnson then told Bundy that the time had come to pass a congressional resolution they had been discussing. Either before or right after seeing Bundy, Johnson arranged for the television networks to give him time in the evening to announce his response to the North Vietnamese attack.

During two midday meetings with his principal national security and foreign policy advisers, Johnson mapped out a military response. They agreed to an air strike against North Vietnamese torpedo boat bases.

But the straight line toward retaliation hit a snag in the afternoon of the 4th when the *Maddox* commander raised doubts that an attack had taken place. At 1:27 p.m. the ship sent word that "a review of the action makes many reported contacts and torpedoes fired 'appear doubtful.' 'Freak weather effects' on radar, and over-eager sonarmen may have accounted for many reports. 'No visual sightings' have been reported by the *Maddox*, and the commander suggests that a 'complete evaluation' be undertaken before any further action."

Though the commander of U.S. Pacific forces quickly assured Washington that an attack had taken place, despite some inaccurate sonar reports, Johnson and McNamara wanted guarantees that they were not responding to a phantom battle. Consequently, Johnson asked McNamara for a prompt report on whether the attack had occurred.

Inquiries to the Joint Chiefs gave Johnson the assurances he demanded and persuaded him to go forward with a retaliatory air strike and a request to Congress for a supporting resolution, which was to endorse not only immediate military action but also a more general policy of firmness in Southeast Asia. On August 7, after two days of hearings and brief debate, the resolution won unanimous approval in the House and passage in the Senate with only two dissenting votes. The two dissenters and some other senators who voted for the resolution worried that they were giving the President a blank check or a pre-dated declaration of war. Though Johnson described the resolution as being "like grandma's nightshirt—it covered everything," he had no intention then of using it to take the country into an undeclared war. He saw the bombing raid against North Vietnam and the resolution as principally serving two short-term purposes. They put both Saigon and Hanoi on notice of American resolve to stay the course in preserving an independent South Vietnam, and they deprived Goldwater of the chance to make Vietnam an issue in the campaign.

Despite a sense of elation at having effectively handled a foreign crisis, the realm in which journalists were saying he didn't excel, his response to the August 4 episode was a time bomb waiting to explode. First, there was the possibility of accusations that the attack in the gulf had never occurred. To be sure, with his Pacific commander and his Secretary of Defense assuring him that it had, Johnson had every reason to assume this was the case. Nevertheless, he had his doubts. As he later told George Ball "with disgust . . . , 'Hell, those dumb, stupid sailors were just shooting at flying fish!'"

Though more than thirty years later no one can state with absolute certainty that an attack occurred, the bulk of the recent evidence suggests it did. Still, Johnson couldn't have known the full details of the case at the time. And so he went ahead, knowing full well that he might be acting on a false premise. But once the report of the attack had come in and he had asked the networks for air time and decided that now was the moment to get the congressional authorization he wanted on Vietnam, he wasn't going to back down.

At the same time Johnson authorized air strikes against North Vietnam and won an endorsement from Congress over an incident he knew was in doubt, he also misled the public about American actions in the gulf. In describing Hanoi's attacks as deliberate, unprovoked aggression, he was conveniently omitting the 34-A operations, which CIA Director McCone had told him were the basis for North Vietnam's attacks.

An even greater mistake on Johnson's part was assuming that the Tonkin Gulf resolution gave him congressional or any other kind of backing for a potentially wider struggle in Vietnam. It is true the resolution gave him a formal endorsement for using American power against Communist subversion in South Vietnam. But there had been no actual debate about committing substantially more American blood and treasure to a war in Southeast Asia. And as a keen student of American politics, who remembered the great debate of 1939–41 over America's response to the European war and FDR's reluctance to do anything without a stable consensus, Johnson should have known that a resolution rushed through Congress under crisis conditions could not be a firm basis for future escalation in an undeclared and ill-defined war.

:: CHOOSING A VICE PRESIDENT

The immediate response in the country to the bombing of North Vietnam and the resolution elated Johnson. Eighty-five percent of Americans endorsed his actions, with 71 percent saying they thought the United States was handling affairs in South Vietnam as well as could be expected. Forty-eight percent of the country favored stronger measures, while only 14 percent wanted to negotiate a settlement and leave.

Johnson now felt temporarily free to ignore Vietnam and focus his attention on the presidential campaign. With the Democratic convention opening on August 24, he needed to decide on a running mate. After the announcement that Robert Kennedy and the Cabinet were out of the running, Hubert Humphrey became the odds-on favorite. Johnson and Humphrey had good relations dating from the 1950s when they had created a bridge between conservative and liberal Democrats. More important, Humphrey's presence on the ticket would give the country a competent second-in-command and would strengthen Johnson's electoral appeal in the Midwest and industrial Northeast.

Humphrey had been campaigning for the job for months. He saw the vice presidency as his only route to the White House. But he had to pay a high price for the privilege of becoming Johnson's lieutenant. Two weeks before the convention, Eric Goldman watched Humphrey eating lunch at the White House mess: "His face was that of a man who was being drained. In public, he handled his awkward situation as unrequited suitor with self-effacing good humor. "Nobody has to woo me," Humphrey told reporters. "I'm old reliable, available Hubert."

Johnson did not acknowledge Humphrey as his choice until August 24, the first day of the convention. The price Johnson demanded was unflagging loyalty. During a White House meeting between them, Johnson emphasized what a terrible job Humphrey would be taking on and how the office would get in the way of their friendship. He wanted Hubert "to understand that this is like a marriage with no chance of divorce. I need complete and unswerving loyalty," Johnson said. Humphrey repeated his vows of fealty, and the bargain was finally sealed.

Sam Ealy Johnson, Jr., ca. 1930.
LBJ Library Collection

Rebekah Baines Johnson, 1917.
LBJ Library Collection

Claudia Alta (Lady Bird) Taylor in 1934,
a few months before marrying Lyndon.
LBJ Library Collection

FDR, Governor Jimmy Allred, and LBJ, at Galveston after LBJ won his congressional seat. *LBJ Library Collection*

LBJ in his Senate office, November 1954, discussing the Senate's reprimand of Senator Joseph McCarthy. *LBJ Library Collection*

With Dwight Eisenhower, John Kennedy, Richard Nixon, and other notables looking on, Lyndon Johnson is sworn in as Vice President. *LBJ Library Collection*

Kennedy, LBJ, and John Connally during President Kennedy's fatal visit to Dallas, Texas, November 21–22, 1963. *LBJ Library Collection*

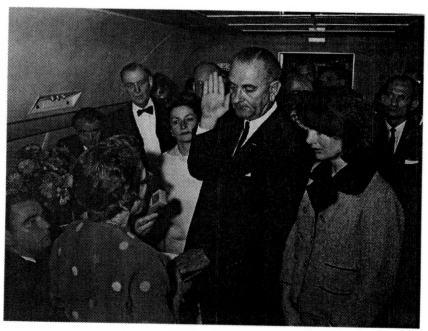

Johnson's grim swearing-in on Air Force One, with Jacqueline Kennedy in bloodstained clothes by his side and Lady Bird to his right. *LBJ Library Collection*

In January 1964, Johnson met with Martin Luther King, Jr., and other black leaders to plot legislative strategy for the most far-reaching civil rights law in American history. The law passed in July. *LBJ Library Collection*

Johnson on the campaign trail in 1964. *LBJ Library Collection*

1965 was the high point of Johnson's influence in passing major reforms. Here he is seen at a Medicare signing ceremony in July 1965 with former President Harry Truman, who had tried and failed to pass such a law in the 1940s. Vice President Hubert Humphrey, a forceful advocate for LBJ's reforms, looks on.
LBJ Library Collection

A conference in Honolulu with Vietnamese President Nguyen
Van Thieu and Prime Minister Nguyen Cao Ky provided no
solution to Johnson's difficulties with the war. LBJ speaks with
Ky. *LBJ Library Collection*

1968 was one of the worst years in American history.
LBJ listens to a tape sent from Vietnam by Captain
Charles Robb, his son-in-law. *LBJ Library Collection*

On March 31, Johnson announced that he would not run again.
LBJ Library Collection

The Democratic convention in Chicago in August 1968 exploded in street
violence. Policemen use their guns to push along youths arrested at
Chicago's Lincoln Park. Hundreds of riot-helmeted, gas mask-clad
policemen sprayed tear gas into thousands of Hippies, Yippies, and antiwar
demonstrators to rout them into Lincoln Park and pursued the fleeing
band through North Side streets. *UPI/Corbis-Bettman*

Johnson died of a heart attack in January 1973. He was buried in a family cemetery at his ranch. *LBJ Library Collection*

important as nailing Goldwater on past statements were attacks on his current campaign statements and actions. On September 2, for example, after Goldwater voted against a Medicare bill, Moyers informed Johnson that he had urged Ken O'Donnell "to pull out all the stops among organizations of older Americans. . . . This is a great opportunity for us to beat him to death among these older people."

The White House organized a sixteen-man committee devoted to demeaning Goldwater. It met twice a day, 9:30 in the morning and 6:00 in the evening. They began developing books that would castigate Goldwater: *You Can Die Laughing*, *Goldwater Versus Republicans*, and a book of cartoons. It prepared statements on major issues on which Goldwater had made himself vulnerable, and distributed them to people who could "get them into the papers in the right places at the best time." They assigned one staffer to feed negative information to LBJ supporters, who would get it in the local press prior to or during Goldwater visits. They prepared rebuttals of Goldwater-Miller statements and assigned committee members to get them published. They fed hostile questions to reporters traveling with Goldwater; they wrote letters to popular columnists like Ann Landers; they made lists of columnists they knew and lobbied them regularly for articles critical of Goldwater; and they pressured mass magazines to attack Goldwater's views on nuclear weapons.

As a major supplement to the committees work, Johnson assigned White House aides to work with the ad agency Doyle Dane Bernbach (DDB) in preparing television and radio spots that Valenti believed can "be a heavy weapon for us . . . our real attack on Goldwater without involving the President." Johnson agreed to devote considerable financial resources to an electronic media campaign — $3 million for local spots and another $1.7 million for network programs. The objective was to convince as many people as possible that Goldwater was an extremist who could do some terrible things. Moyers suggested television ads, saying: If Goldwater became President he could take us out of the United Nations; he "could have his finger — or that of some field commander — on the nuclear trigger; . . . he could . . . destroy the nuclear test-ban treaty; . . . he could . . . make the social security program voluntary. . . . He could do these things — But only if we let him. Vote for President Johnson on November 3. The stakes are too high to stay home."

The DDB ads destroyed any slight hope Goldwater might have had of overcoming Johnson's lead. On September 7, the Johnson campaign broadcast the "Daisy" spot, the most famous political ad ever made. It began with a little girl in a field of flowers picking petals off a daisy while she counted to ten. As a man's voice counted down from ten to one, the film showed a startled look on her face and then a close up of her eye, which dissolved to black and then an atomic explosion. As viewers watched the mushroom cloud, Johnson declared: "These are the stakes—to make a world in which all of God's children can live, or to go into the dark. We must love each other, or we must die." An announcer's voice then urged: "Vote for President Johnson on November 3. The stakes are too high for you to stay home."

The ad was slated to run only once. The White House had a number of others they wanted to use and didn't think repetition was a good idea. The response to the ad convinced Moyers and Valenti to stick to their plan. Moyers remembers that the White House switchboard "lit up with calls protesting it, and Johnson called me and said, 'Jesus Christ, what in the world happened?' and I said, 'You got your point across that's what.'. . . Johnson was very pleased with it," but he had "a wonderful time putting on an act," complaining that he was being accused of a low blow. Despite his protests, Johnson was inclined to run the ad again. Moyers, however, convinced him that it was a poor idea.

Nevertheless, the hullabaloo raised by the "Daisy" ad did not deter Johnson and Moyers from using other negative spots attacking Goldwater. They depicted Goldwater's domestic radicalism. One quoted his wish to "saw off the Eastern seaboard"; another focused on Republican divisions over Goldwater's candidacy; and a third, far harsher spot pictured Ku Klux Klansmen burning a cross and quoted an Alabama Klansman's remark: "I like Barry Goldwater. He needs our help." The most effective and heavily used ad described Goldwater's threat to the Social Security system. It showed two hands ripping up a Social Security card, while an announcer warned that on at least seven occasions Goldwater had declared his intention to change the present Social Security set up. It ended with the reassurance that "President Johnson is working to strengthen Social Security." Johnson had no compunction about hitting Goldwater so hard, partly because the negative attacks seemed to be so effective. In late September, a Gallup poll found that Johnson had a three to one advantage over Goldwater when Americans evaluated their qualifications for the presidency. Moreover, where only 2 percent of the public thought Johnson was reckless, 24 percent described Goldwater that way.

In the last days of October, a report from the University of Michigan Survey Research Center showed that many voters, including Republicans who were deserting to Johnson in unprecedented numbers, thought that Goldwater was a "terrible" candidate who made his party look like "a gang of nuts and kooks." A poll coming to Johnson four days before the election showed him with a 61 percent to 39 percent lead. Everything suggested that he and his aides had made all the right choices in the campaign.

If Johnson had qualms about running so negative a campaign against Goldwater, they were diminished not only by the conviction that this was the sure road to victory but also by the ugly attacks and innuendos Goldwater and the Republicans used against him. Between March and August a series of articles appeared in the *Wall Street Journal*, the *Washington Star*, and *Life* raising questions about how Johnson had amassed a fortune of between $9 and $14 million. After the *Emporia* (Kansas) *Gazette* wrote a scathing editorial describing Johnson as "the most corrupt man ever to enter the White House" in modern times, the Republicans began running it as a campaign ad in newspapers.

As distressing to Johnson, the Republicans began distributing, especially in the South and the West, copies of *A Texan Looks at Lyndon* by J. Evetts Haley. The book was a vicious attack on Johnson, bringing together every negative story ever told about him and questioning his right to be President. It was the most prominent of several right-wing tracts, which Drew Pearson said in August 1964 were outselling lurid novels. In October, the abundance and growing impact of this smear literature became a topic of discussion at the White House. After a tour of Western states, Larry O'Brien reported to the President that "these books are being distributed by the Republican Party as well as by John Birchers and other right-wing organizations. They are available at all newsstands. They are being read and having some impact. At every meeting our campaign leaders agreed the books are hurting. In addition to the outright attacks on Johnson, there were rumors of hidden corruption that Republicans encouraged as a way to undermine his public standing. A former congressional staffer spread the story that the State Department arranged for LBJ to receive a large sum in counterpart funds for his personal use when he visited Hong Kong in 1961. The rumor was so persistent that the department "urgently" asked the Consul General there in October 1964 to provide a full report, which cleared Johnson.

At the same time, rumors also began to circulate that Johnson had kidney tumors that were much more serious than his heart condition. Two Navy radiologists told this to someone who passed it on to an associate of Drew Pearson's. Texas newspapers carried ads about Johnson's medical history and the odds of his surviving another term.

All the rumors and smear books bothered Johnson less than Goldwater's attack on his morals. A spot ad the Republicans ran during the last month of the campaign featured an announcer saying: "What has happened to America? We have had the good sense to create lovely parks—but we're afraid to use them after dark. We build libraries and galleries to hold the world's greatest art treasures—and we permit the world's greatest collection of smut to be freely available."

The Republican assault on Johnson's morals got a big boost during the campaign when a scandal involving Walter Jenkins became public in mid-October. On October 7, after attending a cocktail party in downtown Washington, Jenkins was arrested in a nearby YMCA men's room on a charge of indecent sexual behavior. Although rumors of the incident circulated in Washington during the next week, nothing became public until a *Washington Star* reporter discovered Jenkins's name on a police blotter. When an editor at the paper called the White House with the information, he was told that Jenkins would call back with a denial. Instead, Jenkins went to see Abe Fortas and Clark Clifford, who lobbied the editors of Washington's three newspapers to get more evidence before printing a story that could devastate Jenkins and his family. Jenkins was now so agitated that a doctor hospitalized him.

That evening, after reporters discovered a similar undisclosed charge against Jenkins dating back to 1959, the press published the story. When Johnson, who was campaigning in New York, learned of these developments from Reedy, he responded with glacial calm and instructed Jenkins to resign. The episode bewildered everyone who knew Jenkins. An FBI investigation to determine whether Jenkins had been blackmailed and the source of any security leak turned up only expressions of amazement at Jenkins's behavior. Most everyone the FBI talked to speculated that Jenkins had cracked under the strain of eighteen-hour workdays.

Goldwater himself refused to say anything directly about the Jenkins incident. When reporters on his campaign plane pressed him for a comment, he would only speak "off the record." "What a way to win an election," he said, "Communists and cocksuckers." Goldwater publicly ignored the scandal. Moreover, it was quickly eclipsed by news that Nikita Khrushchev had resigned as Soviet Premier and the Chinese Communists had exploded a nuclear device.

The outcome of the election was everything Johnson had hoped for. Winning forty-four states to Goldwater's six, five in the South and Arizona, Johnson held a 486 to 52 margin in the electoral college. Only FDR's advantage of 523 to 8 electoral votes in 1936 was larger. Johnson's victory was record-breaking in every other respect. His 43,129,484 popular votes against Goldwater's 27,178,188 represented the largest vote, the greatest margin, and the biggest percentage (61 percent) ever received by a President to that point in U.S. history. In addition, voters gave him the largest majorities in Congress since FDR's election in 1936—a Senate with 68 Democrats and 32 Republicans, two more than before, and a House favoring the Democrats by a 295 to 140 margin, a gain of 37 seats.

Would Johnson have done as well if he had run a less combative campaign? Perhaps not. But the election drew a smaller percentage of eligible voters—62.1 percent—than Kennedy and Nixon did—63.8 percent—in 1960. Moreover, where the Kennedy-Nixon campaign had produced a 10 point increase in the percentage of voters going to the polls, the Johnson-Goldwater contest saw a drop of nearly 2 percent. Neither Goldwater nor Johnson generated the degree of enthusiasm that JFK and Nixon had stirred four years before.

Still, Johnson hardly saw that as a blight on what everyone agreed was a spectacular success. Most important to LBJ, he now believed that he had an endorsement for his Great Society, the War on Poverty, and a tough, but not reckless, hold-the-line policy against any Communist advance, particularly in Vietnam. He saw the victory as his; he had carried it off without a Kennedy on the ticket. Now he was free to launch a Johnson administration that was much less in the shadow of JFK.

As many supporters recognized, though, the decisive result was more the product of anti-Goldwater than pro-Johnson or pro-administration sentiments. If there was a mandate in 1964, it was for avoiding extremism of any kind at home and abroad. By failing to make explicit where he intended to take the country in the next four years, Johnson won less than a solid consensus for bold change in either domestic or foreign affairs. But he refused to see it that way. For the moment, he assumed he had national backing for major reforms equal to anything in our history.

7 :: KING OF THE HILL

The autumn and winter of 1964 were a happy time for Lyndon Johnson. He was fulfilling every imaginable fantasy in his political life: He was a highly popular President winning passage of groundbreaking laws, describing broad plans for bold advances in American life, and gaining election in his own right with an unprecedented number of votes. If success gave him a temporary sense of repose, a feeling that at age fifty-six he had indelibly stamped his mark on history and could enjoy the prospect of another four and possibly even eight years achieving great things for the country, it was not evident to anyone around him. Johnson, Bill Moyers says, had "an exquisite hole at his center, which was an unfillable void." He was an inveterate malcontent, a man constantly reaching for new goals.

In August, after his nomination, and again in November and December, after his election, he spent weeks at his Texas ranch, where he was supposed to be relaxing. But a vacation from work, even a brief respite from his normally arduous schedule, was impossible. "Rest for him," Hubert Humphrey said, "was controlled frenzy."

:: CREATING THE GREAT SOCIETY: ENDS AND MEANS

Johnson focused his post-election energy on making the Great Society a reality. He doubted that his smashing victory was a mandate or an unqualified national commitment to any specific legislative program. To be sure, the country understood that he intended to "move ahead," but it hadn't endorsed a particular set of bills or given him unqualified support for bold measures advancing radical change.

Look, he told his congressional liaison men in January 1965, "I was just elected President by the biggest popular margin in the history of the country—16 million votes." But he was convinced that he had already lost about three million of those supporters now that Barry Goldwater wasn't around to scare the hell out of people. "After a fight with Congress or something else, I'll lose another couple of million. I could be down to 8 million in a couple of months." In addition, Johnson expected Congress to assert itself against him in due course. "I've watched the Congress from either the inside or the outside, man and boy, for more than forty years," he told presidential adviser Eric Goldman, "and I've never seen a Congress that didn't eventually take the measure of the President it was dealing with."

For all his caution, Johnson nevertheless saw his electoral victory and current popularity as an unusual opportunity to get a lot of important bills through Congress. The initial key to building a Great Society, Johnson believed, was managing and controlling the 89th Congress. He was gleeful at the challenge; he felt as if he had spent his career preparing for it. His nearly twenty-four years in the House and the Senate gave him a special advantage. But Johnson knew that his expertise and ties to House and Senate members would go only so far; taking Congress for granted would be a mistake. It would have to be stroked, cuddled, made to feel that it was the center of the political universe.

The effort to sell Congress on the Great Society began in the summer of 1964, well before a single proposal went to the Hill. In August, he held a "Salute to Congress" at the White House for all members of both Houses and their wives. "This is the first recognition of this kind ever given by a President to the Congress and its members," House Speaker John W. McCormack wrote him afterward.

A crucial element in getting congressional cooperation was to keep anyone from getting "mad." To this end, Johnson wanted no talk of a miracle "Hundred Days," a whirlwind of activity producing a host of major bills that would challenge Congress to do more than seemed achievable. By mid-November, however, Johnson had already begun planning for big legislative gains. But reluctant to give too much advance notice of his agenda, which might stir organized opposition, he muted his plans for as long as possible.

Johnson's State of the Union message was the opening statement of his intentions. It was also a demonstration of his skill at managing the Congress. The message asked for action on Great Society measures—laws that would enrich the quality of American life. And though he spoke of the cities, the environment, the schools, the arts, and the people's health, he avoided the sort of details that arouse opponents to action. He emphasized his eagerness for government savings that would exceed the $3.5 billion in eliminated waste his administration had achieved last year. He promised a cut in excise taxes and a balanced budget that would free up money for his national agenda.

:: FEDERAL AID TO EDUCATION

Johnson's highest Great Society priority was to broaden educational opportunities and enrich the quality of school offerings. He had an almost mystical faith in the capacity of education to transform people's lives and improve their standard of living. He shared with earlier generations of Americans an evangelical faith in educational opportunity as a public good. "He was a nut on education," Hubert Humphrey said. "He felt that education was the greatest thing he could give to the people; he just believed in it, just like some people believe in miracle cures."

Public education had been Lyndon's ticket out of poverty in rural Texas, and he wanted all children in the country to have the same chance to advance themselves. He was confident that federal funds could make a significant difference in expanding and improving education at every level. Indeed, with the postwar baby boom causing overcrowded classes in run-down schools short of competent teachers, Johnson believed that there was no choice but for Washington to take the initiative in meeting the problem. The increase in school population had created an unusual opportunity: Middle-class parents in every region of the country would welcome federal efforts to improve education for the poor as well as their own children.

While education was primarily the responsibility of states and localities, the federal government needed to assure that the basic needs of local schools were met. Every President from FDR to JFK had worked toward that goal, Johnson announced. "I plan to get on with the task."

Johnson said nothing about the frustration all Presidents had suffered since Roosevelt when asking for federal aid to education. To be sure, the Lanham Act in 1940 had begun support for school districts with military bases or "impacted areas," the G.I. bill had helped World War II veterans attend colleges, the National School Lunch Act in 1946 had provided a hot meal for school children, and the Cold War had promoted science, math, engineering, and foreign language study through the National Science

Foundation and National Defense Education Act; but more general attempts to aid elementary and secondary education had repeatedly failed.

The three Rs—race, religion, and Reds—had blocked action: To many Americans, federal aid meant enforced integration, unconstitutional support of parochial schools, and excessive government control of people's lives.

Johnson needed a strategy that could overcome the three Rs and neutralize conservative Rules Chairman Howard Smith, whose committee was known for its "no rules for schools." A House reform diluting Smith's power took care of the latter. Further, the 1964 civil rights bill, barring segregation in federally supported programs, eliminated race as a reason to oppose federal aid to education. Moreover, two-to-one margins in both houses of Congress for Democrats espousing a liberal faith in government activism weakened the appeal of objections to federal interference in local affairs.

The church-state issue, however, remained a formidable stumbling block. After consulting administration officials and educational and religious leaders, Commissioner of Education Francis Keppel found an answer. Instead of proposing general aid to public schools, which would reignite "a bitter battle" over helping parochial students, Keppel suggested "categorical aid" to poor children in city slums and depressed rural areas. Partly inspired by *Everson v. Ewing Township*, a 1947 U.S. Supreme Court ruling that federal aid to parochial students was constitutional if it went to children rather than schools, Keppel urged help to needy children regardless of whether they attended public or private schools. The money, moreover, was to go to impacted districts described in the 1940 Lanham Act, assuring the distribution of federal funds to well-off and impoverished schools.

Understanding that Keppel's approach would mute debate over aiding parochial schools and help generate a national consensus for federal aid to education, Johnson warmly endorsed his plan. In addition, Johnson resisted proposals from HEW, the Bureau of the Budget, and the Office of Education to assure that money under Lanham would go more to poor than prosperous school districts, which had been receiving the lion's share of the grants. Although advertising the bill as aimed at educating the underprivileged, Johnson believed it would have a better chance to pass if it also gave substantial sums to middle-class and well-to-do children.

On January 12, Johnson sent Congress a Message on Education. He announced "a national goal of Full Educational Opportunity," reminded Congress that the country spent "seven times as much on a youth that has

gone bad" as on one who stayed in school, and asked for a doubling of federal spending on education from $4 billion to $8 billion.

The reaction to his message on education was everything Johnson could
have asked. Leading newspapers warmly endorsed the President's proposal.
Yet Johnson knew that press support was no assurance of congressional
action, especially on a ground-breaking measure, without constant pressure.
His aides would need to monitor the many twists and turns the Elementary
and Secondary Education Act (ESEA) seemed certain to take in Congress,
and he would have to lobby or stroke pivotal congressmen and senators.

Johnson had no hesitation about involving himself directly in the fight.
In February, after he met privately with National Education Association
(NEA) leaders, they voted to endorse ESEA. At the end of the month, he
made a symbolic visit to the Office of Education. "Nothing in the world
could have done our cause more good or raised morale higher," Keppel
said. Johnson then invited 200 NEA officials to the White House on March
1 to underscore his eagerness for federal aid to education.

Over the next six weeks, while Congress completed its work on the bill,
Johnson pressured House and Senate leaders with a series of phone calls,
and kept tabs on the likely congressional votes. The House rewarded his
efforts with a margin of 263 to 153 on March 26. He now insisted that the
Senate enact the same law and avoid the need for a conference committee,
which might cause mischief. Republican Senator Winston Prouty of Vermont complained that the issue before the nation was not education, but
"the future of the Senate as a co-equal partner in the legislative process."
Ignoring Prouty, the Senate passed the House bill by 73 to 18 on April 9.

Eric Goldman described Johnson's performance as an astonishing piece
of political artistry. In only eighty-seven days, "the Congress had passed a
billion-dollar law, deeply affecting a fundamental institution of the nation.
. . . The House had approved it with no amendments that mattered; the
Senate had voted it through literally without a comma changed."

Johnson was euphoric. He said: "Since 1870, almost a hundred years
ago, we have been trying to do what we have just done—pass an elementary school bill for all the children of America. . . . We did it, by all that's
good we did it, and it's a wonderful proud thing. . . . This is the most important bill I will ever sign."

On April 11, in a ceremony outside a dilapidated little building a mile
and a half east of his ranch, where he had first gone to school, Johnson
signed the law in the presence of Katie Deadrich Looney, his first teacher;
a classmate; some of the Mexican-Americans he had taught in Cotulla,

Texas, in 1927–28; four debate team members he had coached in Sam Houston High School in 1929–30; and a number of Washington dignitaries. "Take it from me," he declared at a White House ceremony two days later, "I worked harder and longer on this measure than on any measure I have ever worked on since I came to Washington in 1931—and I am proud of it."

Johnson knew that enactment of ESEA was only the beginning of wisdom. Yet Johnson's reach in administering the law was limited. Beyond delegating the work to administration officials, his preoccupation with passing other bills and managing foreign affairs left him little time and inclination to pay close attention to how ESEA was working. More important, the bill dictated that local school districts rather than the federal government have the greatest say in spending ESEA funds. And they chose to use them on conventional ends and means. Moreover, Federal spending under Johnson's reform amounted to only 6 percent of the cost of elementary and secondary education.

"Lyndon Johnson thought Title I [of ESEA] was an antipoverty program," historian Allen J. Matusow writes. "Local officials made sure it never was. A 1977 sample survey revealed that nearly two-thirds of the students in programs funded by Title I were not poor; more than half were not even low achievers; and 40 percent were neither poor nor low achieving." Eight years later, and twenty years after ESEA had passed, the National Institute of Education estimated that about half the funds spent under the law had gone to children living above the poverty line.

Moreover, as studies shortly began to make clear, Johnson's hopes that education could improve the lives of poor youngsters far outran the reality. Educators found that poverty had more to do with family background and general social context than the quantity and quality of education a child received. And even where studies suggested initial improvements for poor kids helped by ESEA reading and math programs, later assessments indicated that benefits faded quickly and left students little better off than those not in the programs.

Still, as Johnson anticipated, the aid to education mandated under ESEA contributed to the national well-being. Though the law never provided either the equal education or the educational opportunity Johnson hoped it would, it went far to spur state governments to become more involved in educational questions, shape new teaching techniques such as small-group instruction, fix attention on the importance of early childhood schooling, benefit students at near-average achievement levels, speed desegregation of schools, and assist handicapped and non-English-speaking pupils who previously had received no special attention. Finally, it led to the creation of a Cabinet-level Department of Education in 1980 and the enduring hope that additional studies and efforts may yet bring our understanding of elementary and secondary instruction to a point that will more fully assure the educational opportunity Johnson considered a birthright of all Americans.

In November 1965 Johnson signed a Higher Education Act (HEA). The law established college and university community service programs designed to assist in the solution of urban and suburban problems. It provided monies to support library acquisitions at colleges and universities and to train librarians and specialists in information sciences. It instituted a program for "strengthening developing institutions," which meant aid to poor black colleges. Its Title Four, the law's most important and expensive part, provided scholarships, loans, and more spending on federal work-study programs to aid students.

By 1970, in five years, one out of every four college students in America was receiving some form of financial assistance provided by HEA. The law facilitated a huge expansion of college enrollments. In 1970, 34 percent of the eighteen-to-twenty-one age group in America attended some college degree credit program; up from 15 percent in 1950. By 1990, the number had grown to 52 percent.

The fact that the country's educational system works as well as it does has something to do with the federal support Johnson initiated in 1965. If his educational reforms did not lead to a Great Society, they have at least made for a better society. It is an achievement for which Johnson deserves the country's continuing regard.

:: MEDICARE

For Johnson, there could be no Great Society—no improved quality of national life—without greater access for all Americans to health care and special efforts to conquer the country's most disabling diseases and common killers, heart attack, cancer, and stroke.

Johnson had been an advocate of federally supported health care delivery and research since the 1940s when he had backed the Hill-Burton law assisting states to build hospitals. In 1956, he had attached an amendment to a Social Security bill making it possible to provide federal health insurance to the elderly.

In the first months of his presidency, Johnson sent a message to Congress announcing his determination to make "the wonders of modern medicine" available to all Americans. He urged hospital insurance for the aged, more modern hospitals, increased and better medical manpower, and greater spending on mental health and ways to prevent and cure heart disease, cancer, and strokes, the country's leading causes of death.

Johnson's highest initial health care priority in 1964 was not Medicare or hospital insurance for the elderly but the creation of a Commission on Heart Disease, Cancer and Strokes (HDCS). In April, when he introduced the members of the commission in a White House ceremony, he announced his "keenest," "greatest," and "most personal interest" in their work, and urged them to spare no effort in bringing America's three great killers and cripplers under control.

Buoyed by Johnson's evangelism and by the medical advances of the 1940s and 1950s that had produced cures for infectious diseases, especially polio, the commission issued a report in December that promised "miracles" in the near future. A $2.8 billion program implemented over five years could bring the "ultimate conquest" of heart disease, cancer, and strokes. Swept up in the euphoria of overcoming the diseases that had accounted for 71 percent of the country's deaths in 1962, Johnson declared the world on "the threshold of a historic breakthrough. Heart disease, cancer, and stroke [can] be conquered—not in a millennium, not in a century, but in the next few onrushing decades."

During 1964–65 Johnson increasingly focused on hospital insurance for the aged under Social Security. Although it had been on liberal reform agendas since the 1930s and had failed to win passage in four successive Congresses beginning with the 85th in 1957, it had gained widespread public appeal by the summer of 1964 as the most desirable change in the country's system of financing and delivering health care.

Johnson saw a Medicare law as a realistic goal of the 89th Congress. With two-to-one margins in both Houses, it seemed likely that some kind of hospital insurance for Americans over sixty-five would be approved. Larry O'Brien believed that passage of a Medicare bill was now "as inevitable as tomorrow morning's sunrise." He predicted Senate passage by a vote of 55 to 45.

The key figure in passing Medicare was Arkansas Congressman Wilbur Mills, the chairman of the Ways and Means Committee. Mills and his committee had been staunch opponents of government-sponsored hospital insurance. A fiscal conservative, Mills worried that Medicare would lead to large federal deficits. He was also reluctant to back any controversial legislation that might fail or pass by a small margin. In July 1964, when Cohen had asked the President to get a commitment from Mills on Medicare,

Johnson replied that "he hadn't been successful in getting Mills committed to anything."

For all Johnson's vaunted talent at persuasion, Mills was not susceptible to presidential pressure. Nor was he very responsive to national opinion favoring Medicare legislation. Holding a safe seat and seeing himself as a man of principle who would not jeopardize the country's fiscal future for the sake of a social reform, however worthy, Mills and his committee had been an insurmountable obstacle to Medicare in 1961–64.

Yet, as Johnson appreciated, Mills was a political realist. With the Democratic landslide in November 1964, Mills understood that he would no longer command a conservative majority on Ways and Means and that it would be difficult, if not impossible, to resist passing Medicare. Consequently, on November 11, 1964, and again on January 1, 1965, he publicly acknowledged that his committee "would be able to work something out" on Medicare, though he continued to insist on the importance of a sound financing plan.

Mills's comments convinced Johnson that he could get a Medicare law passed in the first session of the 89th Congress. In his State of the Union address on January 4 and more fully in a special message to Congress on the 7th, Johnson made the case for hospital care under Social Security: Since "four out of five persons 65 or older have a disability or chronic disease," since hospital stays and costs for folks over sixty-five are twice what they are for younger people, since "almost half of the elderly have no health insurance at all," and since "the average retired couple cannot afford the cost of adequate health protection under private health insurance," the President asked that Social Security "be extended to finance the cost of basic health services" through "regular, modest contributions during working years."

Johnson was so confident now that he could get Medicare passed, he agreed to put the bill at the top of his legislative agenda; the House and Senate labeled the bill H.R.1 and S.1. But to assure against creating new grounds for opposition, he proposed a narrowly focused bill, which would cover the aged for hospital, but not physicians' costs. By omitting doctors' fees, Johnson hoped to avoid charges of "socialized medicine."

As designed by Mills and Wilbur Cohen and approved by the President, Medicare provided 60 days of hospital coverage, 180 days of skilled nursing home care, and 240 days of home health visits for Social Security recipients sixty-five and older. A Hospital Insurance Trust Fund created with small payroll deductions and employer contributions amounting to 0.076 of 1 percent of wages was to finance the program. The outlook for the bill seemed so bright that seventy House members and forty-three Senators offered themselves as co-sponsors. Moreover, Speaker McCormack advised the White House that Mills and the House leadership saw no need for hearings.

Yet it quickly became apparent that conservative Republicans and the American Medical Association might be able to sidetrack the administration's bill with alternative proposals. To disarm this opposition, Mills proposed incorporating their principal features into Medicare. At a closed session of his committee on the afternoon of March 2, Mills made the "ingenious" suggestion that Medicare become "a three-layer cake": hospital insurance under Social Security; a voluntary insurance program for doctors' bills subsidized out of general federal revenues; and an expanded medical welfare program for the indigent administered through the states and known as Medicaid.

Johnson needed no prodding to accept Mills's proposal. He saw it as a significant advance on the administration's bill and as certain to fly through the House. When Cohen told him that Part B insurance for doctors' bills would cost the government about $500 million a year, Johnson dismissed the cost as cheap for so desirable a reform. "'Five hundred million. Is that all?' Johnson exclaimed with a wave of his big hand. 'Do it. Move that damn bill out now, before we lose it.'" When Ways and Means reported the bill and the House passed it on April 8 by a 110-vote margin, a group of senior citizens feted Mills at a luncheon. "We've seen the promised land," the delegation chairman told the gathering.

But "the promised land" lay through the Senate. And despite every expectation that the upper House would also pass a Medicare bill, Johnson wisely took nothing for granted. It was to take over 500 minor Senate amendments and some hard bargaining in a conference committee before Congress passed Medicare on July 28.

Johnson's central concern now was to assure that AMA members would not refuse to participate in the Medicare and Medicaid programs. He believed "the medical profession's cooperation was absolutely crucial to Medicare's success." But "predictions that hospitals, clinics, and doctors' offices would be flooded with hordes of elderly patients, [and] that the system would collapse under its own weight," discouraged health professionals from cooperating. Worse yet, some conservatives, like the actor Ronald Reagan, saw Medicare as the advance wave of socialism, which would "invade every area of freedom in this country." Reagan foolishly predicted that Medicare would compel Americans to spend their "sunset years telling our children and our children's children what it was like in America when men were free."

Some members of the administration were so worried about winning the cooperation of the AMA that they urged a meeting with AMA leaders at which the President appealed to doctors to support a law favored by the people and worked out "in the most painstaking way in accordance with the exacting rules of our democracy."

Johnson did not think that the AMA and most physicians would find it easy to oppose Medicare without serious damage to their public standing. But he was worried enough to invite AMA leaders to the White House, where he could compel a public acknowledgment of their support. In a July 30 discussion with eleven AMA officers Johnson asked the physicians for help in getting doctors to rotate in and out of Vietnam for a few months to serve the civilian population. Appealing to their patriotism, Johnson declared, "Your country needs your help. Your President needs your help." The doctors responded almost in unison with promises to start a program immediately. "Get the press in here," Johnson told Moyers. When they arrived, Johnson described and praised the AMA's readiness to help the Vietnamese. But the reporters, undoubtedly primed by Moyers, wanted to know whether the doctors would support Medicare. Johnson, with mock indignation, said: "'These men are going to get doctors to go to Vietnam where they might be killed. Medicare is the law of the land. Of course, they'll support the law of the land. Tell him,'" Johnson said, turning to the head of the delegation. " . . . 'Of course, we will,'" the AMA president responded. "'We are, after all, law-abiding citizens.'" A few weeks later the AMA announced its intention to support Medicare.

Within a decade Medicare had become a widely popular entitlement that no President dared oppose. During his eight years in the White House from 1981 to 1989, Reagan, despite vigorous efforts to contain Medicare and Medicaid costs, never proposed the dismantling of either program. The elderly, who had become a powerful voting bloc and had reduced their chances of falling into poverty with the help of Medicare, were ready to punish anyone at the polls who attacked a program they cherished almost as much as Social Security.

Yet all was not perfect with the Johnson health care reforms. Eager to assure the cooperation of hospitals and physicians, the measures included no real controls over either of them. Hospitals were entitled to be reimbursed for reasonable costs, which was whatever hospitals said they were. Physicians were to be paid customary fees, which would be based on past billing history. There was no inhibition on the freedom of doctors to raise charges each year and submit their higher fees as "billing history."

The results of this generosity were staggering increases in medical costs to the entire society. Where total Medicare expenditures were $1 billion in the first year of the program, they had risen to $237 billion by 2001, despite repeated attempts by the government to rein them in. The approximately 6 percent of gross national product Americans spent on health care in 1965 had increased to 13.5 percent by 1997. Though advances in medical technology drove some of this expense, much of it resulted from the increasing use of health care and lack of medical cost controls. The benefits to the elderly and the indigent from Medicare and Medicaid are indisputable. But they did not solve the problem of care at reasonable cost for all Americans. Nor did Medicare provide drug coverage, which by 2002 had become a significant part of caring for the elderly. Johnson's reforms were only a partial and imperfect solution to a dilemma that other industrialized societies had addressed more successfully.

:: SELMA AND VOTING RIGHTS

Johnson's vision of a Great Society included an unprecedented degree of racial harmony, with blacks granted equal opportunities to advance their well-being. He hoped that the 1964 civil rights act would begin the process of integrating African Americans into the mainstream of southern life. At the very least, he hoped that all sides in the region's racial strife would give the act a chance to work and relieve the federal government of the need to take new steps to right historic wrongs. This meant not only southern acceptance of desegregation in public facilities but also full participation by blacks in southern politics. In Johnson's view, allowing blacks to vote and hold local, state, and federal offices would give them the same political influence other groups had used to serve their interests.

Yet Johnson knew that southern accommodation to desegregation under the 1964 law might not be enough to give blacks, who had been systematically excluded from the polls, the franchise. In Mississippi and Alabama, for example, only 6 and 19 percent, respectively, of voting-age blacks were on the rolls, and office-holders, whose power rested on the existing political customs, would not voluntarily alter a system that served their interests.

To make southern leaders understand that the alternative to regional reform was federal intervention, Johnson demanded an end to unconstitutional limits on black voting in his January State of the Union address. He asked for the elimination of "every remaining obstacle to the right and the opportunity to vote" and declared that "opportunity for all" must include the end to "barriers to the right to vote" by "Negro Americans." At the same time, he privately asked Nicholas Katzenbach, the acting Attor-

ney General, to draft legislation that would enforce constitutional guarantees to vote.

Johnson was ambivalent about putting a voting rights bill before Congress early in 1965. Not because he doubted the value of giving blacks the
ballot. He considered such a law "in many ways . . . even more critical
than" the civil rights act. Rather, he saw prospects for congressional passage
as "unpromising," and he was reluctant to force another confrontation with
the South.

But in the first three months of 1965, King and the Southern Christian
Leadership Conference masterminded a campaign in Selma, Alabama, that
persuaded Johnson to sponsor a voting rights act. King and the SCLC leadership saw no prospect of black enfranchisement flowing from recent laws
and actions. Efforts by a variety of civil rights organizations to register black
voters under a "Freedom Summer" project in 1964 had brought little more
than violence and intimidation. King saw black enfranchisement in the
South coming only when the federal government made it happen. And this
would require another Birmingham or some fresh demonstration of repressive police action against black demonstrators peacefully asking for the vote.

Selma, the "most oppressive" city in the South, where less than 1 percent of potential black voters was registered, became the focus of King's
campaign. It also had a law enforcement officer who was a caricature of
himself. Pinning a "Never!" button to his lapel, surrounding himself with
deputies carrying electric cattle prods, Jim Clark, a heavyset, jowly man
who called blacks "the lowest form of humanity," lived up to his advanced
billings as a violent southern sheriff. After an attack on demonstrators that
aroused national sympathy for their campaign and stiffened their resolve to
fight on, civil rights organizations voted Clark "an honorary member of
SNCC, SCLC, CORE [and] the N-Double A-C-P."

Beginning on January 18, a series of demonstrations by black residents
asking to register captured national attention. Jim Clark played into King's
hands by arresting numerous protestors, including hundreds of school children, and committing acts of violence that made the front pages of newspapers across the country. On February 3, King sent Johnson a message asking
him to send a personal emissary to Selma to evaluate the situation, make a
statement supporting the voting drive campaign in Selma, and take appropriate legislative and executive action to secure the right to vote in all elections, including those controlled by individual states.

Johnson responded cautiously. At a press conference on February 4, he
urged all Americans to "be indignant when one American is denied the
right to vote. The loss of that right to a single citizen undermines the free-

dom of every citizen." He also cited federal efforts to use the courts to eliminate voting discrimination.

Because Johnson refused to say if he would ask for a voting rights bill,
King now publicly declared his intention to press for one. The next day,
Johnson announced his support of King's proposal. Before he sent a bill to
Congress, however, civil rights advocates in the House introduced two bills
on February 8. Despite these developments, Johnson was still not ready to
act. He did agree to a fifteen-minute meeting with King at the White
House, which convinced King that further action in Selma would be
needed before Johnson would ask Congress for a voting rights law.

Violent confrontations over the next several weeks, including the death
of a twenty-six-year-old demonstrator shot in the stomach by a state trooper,
and King's announcement on March 3 that he would lead a walk from
Selma to the state capital of Montgomery beginning on March 7, still did
not win a firm commitment from Johnson. At another meeting on March
5 between him and King, the President refused to say "exactly what would
be in the voting proposal and . . . offered no promises." Johnson also apparently warned King against mistakes by civil rights groups that could drain
off national interest in voting legislation.

All the mistakes now came from Alabama officials. On March 6, Governor George Wallace banned the March 7 walk as likely to endanger the
public safety. But 600 demonstrators, without King, who remained in
Atlanta after being warned of a plot against his life, set out on the march
anyway. After crossing the Edmund Pettus Bridge over the Alabama River,
they confronted some fifty state troopers and dozens of Clark's deputies barring their path on U.S. Highway 80. After warning the marchers to disperse
and giving them two minutes to leave, the troopers rushed forward, beating them with clubs and driving them back across the bridge into town.
Besieged by tear gas, clubs, whips, and mounted horsemen, seventeen
marchers needed hospitalizing and forty required treatment for minor
injuries and tear gassing.

The national reaction to what the press called "Bloody Sunday" was
everything advocates of a voting rights law could have wished. Johnson
issued a statement "deploring the brutality with which a number of Negro
citizens of Alabama were treated when they sought to dramatize their deep
and sincere interest in attaining the precious right to vote." He also
announced his intention to send a voting rights bill to Congress in the following week.

Johnson now came under strong pressure to intervene with federal
troops. Sympathy marchers in cities around the country urged the Presi-

dent to protect the protestors in Alabama, while pickets outside the White House carried signs denouncing Johnson's inaction: "LBJ, just you wait . . . see what happens in '68."

Johnson needed the cooperation of Alabama Governor George Wallace, who also wanted to prevent further bloodshed. Wallace had national ambitions and the sense to see that more violence would mark him as simply a racist rather than an opponent of federal authority, which he rightly believed could be made into a popular political issue.

To escape his dilemma, Wallace asked Johnson to see him. Johnson agreed at once, and they met at the White House on the afternoon of March 13. Johnson's objective was to make clear that he would back the legitimate demands of the marchers and insist that Wallace protect peaceful demonstrators from police violence.

Johnson orchestrated every aspect of the meeting. He received Wallace in the Oval Office, where he sat him on a couch with soft cushions that placed him some three or four feet above the floor. Johnson positioned himself in a rocking chair "and leaned toward the semi-recumbent Wallace, his towering figure inclined downward until their noses almost touched." After Johnson let Wallace say his piece against outside agitators stirring up trouble and his opposition to federal intervention in the affairs of his state, Johnson gave him the "treatment." "I know you're like me, not approving of brutality," Johnson said, and handed the governor a newspaper with a picture of a state trooper kicking a black protestor. Then raising the issue of black disenfranchisement, Johnson asked Wallace to persuade Alabama registrars to give blacks their constitutional right to vote. Wallace protested that he didn't have the wherewithal to sway these local officials. "Don't shit me about your persuasive power, George," Johnson replied. "I saw you . . . attacking me [on television] George. And you know what? You were so damn persuasive that I had to turn off the set before you had me changing my mind."

"'Why don'tcha just desegregate all your schools?'" he asked Wallace. "'You and I go out there in front of those television cameras right now, and you announce you've decided to desegregate every school in Alabama.'" Wallace replied: "'Oh, Mr. President, I can't do that, you know. The schools have got school boards; they're locally run. I haven't got the political power to do that.' Johnson said, 'Don't you shit me, George Wallace.'"

After nearly three hours of hammering at the governor, Johnson appealed to his sense of history. He urged Wallace not to "think about 1968; you think about 1988. You and me, we'll be dead and gone then, George. Now you've got a lot of poor people down there in Alabama, a lot of ignorant people. You can do a lot for them, George. Your president will help you. What do you want left after you when you die? Do you want a Great . . . Big . . . Marble monument that reads, 'George Wallace—He Built'? . . . Or do you want a little piece of scrawny pine board lying across that harsh, caliche soil, that reads, 'George Wallace—He Hated'?" After their meeting, Wallace remarked: "Hell, if I'd stayed in there much longer, he'd have had me coming out for civil rights."

Johnson's immediate concern was to mobilize congressional action on voting rights. He didn't think it was enough simply to send a proposal to the Hill with a special message describing the historical record of constitutional violations of black rights. Rather, he felt compelled to go before Congress, where he could command the attention of the nation and the world and emphasize the importance and urgency of remedying this national insult to law and democracy.

It was Johnson's greatest speech and one of the most moving and memorable presidential addresses in the country's history. Comparing Selma to Lexington and Concord, to Appomattox, Johnson described it as "a turning point in man's unending search for freedom. . . . Rarely in any time does an issue lay bare the secret heart of America itself. . . . Rarely are we met with a challenge . . . to the values and the purposes and the meaning of our beloved Nation. The issue of equal rights for American Negroes is such an issue. And should we defeat every enemy, should we double our wealth and conquer the stars, and still be unequal to this issue, then we will have failed as a people and as a nation."

The issue, Johnson said, was democracy, the right of the individual, regardless of race or color, to vote. "There is no constitutional issue here," Johnson asserted. "The command of the Constitution is plain. There is no moral issue. It is wrong—deadly wrong—to deny any of your fellow Americans the right to vote in this country. There is no issue of States rights or national rights. There is only the struggle for human rights."

And, Johnson declared, measuring every word, "what happened in Selma is part of a far larger movement which reaches into every section and State of America. It is the effort of American Negroes to secure for themselves the full blessings of American life. Their cause must be our cause too. Because it is not just Negroes, but really it is all of us, who must overcome the crippling legacy of bigotry and injustice. And," Johnson paused, raising his arms for emphasis, "We shall overcome."

A moment of stunned silence followed, as the audience absorbed the fact that the President had embraced the anthem of black protest. And then almost the entire chamber rose in unison, "applauding, shouting, some stamping their feet." Tears rolled down the cheeks of senators, congress-men, and observers in the gallery, moved by joy, elation, a sense that the victor, for a change, was human decency, the highest standards by which the nation was supposed to live.

Johnson did not wish to conclude before giving African Americans their full due. "A century has passed, more than a hundred years, since the Negro was freed. And he is not fully free tonight. . . . A century has passed, more than a hundred years, since equality was promised. And yet the Negro is not equal. . . . The real hero of this struggle is the American Negro," the President added. "His actions and protests, his courage to risk safety and even to risk his life, have awakened the conscience of this Nation. . . . He has called upon us to make good the promise of America. And who among us can say that we would have made the same progress were it not for his persistent bravery, and his faith in American democracy?" Martin Luther King, Jr. watching on television in Birmingham, cried.

Johnson had every indication that the bill would pass both houses quickly by wide margins. Though administration representatives in the Senate had to break a conservative filibuster and fend off liberalizing pro-visions that jeopardized the bill, by May 26, after only two and a half months, the Senate passed the bill by a lopsided 77 to 19 count. In the House, where conservative maneuvering presented a challenge, the bill won passage on July 9 by an overwhelming 333 to 85 vote. On August 6, in remarks in the Capitol Rotunda, Johnson emphasized the historical impor-tance of the measure he was about to sign and promised that he would move swiftly to enforce its provisions.

The impact of the law across the South was evident at once. By the end of 1966, only four states of the old Confederacy had less than 50 percent of their voting-age blacks registered, and in three of these, registration had reached 47 percent. Only Mississippi, with 33 percent of blacks on the voting rolls, was well short of the law's requirement. At the end of 1967, Georgia, Louisiana, and Virginia had also exceeded the 50 percent target, and Mississippi had 45 percent of its black citizens registered. By the 1968 election, Mississippi was up to 59 percent, and black registration in the eleven Confederate states averaged 62 percent. In 1980, ten million blacks were on the nation's voting rolls, only 7 percent less than the pro-portion of voting-age whites.

Black office-holding now also expanded dramatically, with the number of black officials multiplying in six Deep South states during the next four years nearly sixfold. Between 1968 and 1980, moreover, the number of southern black elected state and federal officeholders nearly doubled. As important, white politicians seeking black votes abandoned the region's traditional racist demagoguery. In the words of one historian, "a new generation of moderate governors, putting aside the ancient obsession with race, gave the South enlightened leadership." The act also made a large difference in numbers of black elected officials nationally; by 1989, the few hundred black officeholders of 1965 had grown to 6,000.

The momentum for legislation supporting black advance ground to a halt in August 1965 with five days of rioting in Watts, the black ghetto of Los Angeles. Outwardly the most benign black inner city in the country, Watts, with its tree-lined, unlittered streets and neat single-family cottages, seemed like an unlikely place for an explosion of protest against the conditions of deprivation and despair common to black ghettoes. But it was as full of joblessness, crime, suffering, and hopelessness about escaping the miseries of black urban life as any other ghetto in America.

Because the disorders, which cost thirty-four lives and $35 million in property damage, agitated fears that black anger would now turn into mass upheavals in the country's cities, white America responded to Watts with diminished sympathy for black suffering and LBJ's agenda.

Johnson now approached the issue of black rights with greater caution than had been the case in the first two years of his term. He wanted the discussion of black rights temporarily put aside. He intended to come back to these matters, but he believed that a tactical pause would now serve the larger cause of long-term advance.

8 :: FOREIGN POLICY
   :: DILEMMAS

The Gulf of Tonkin Resolution in August 1964 gave Johnson a temporary respite from unpleasant choices in Vietnam. Having hit back at the North Vietnamese and having rallied Congress and the country behind a promise not to abandon South Vietnam, he wished to mute discussion about Southeast Asia. But he knew the problem would not go away. On August 10, he told national security advisers that the next challenge from Hanoi, which he expected soon, would have to be met with firmness. He had no intention of escalating the conflict "just because the public liked what happened last week," he said. But he wanted planning that would allow us to choose the grounds for the next confrontation and get maximum results with minimum danger.

Still, he wanted no significant change in policy before the November election. Having "stood up" to Communist aggression, he now wished to sound a moderate note. In speeches during the campaign, he emphasized giving Vietnam limited help: He would "not permit the independent nations of the East to be swallowed up by Communist conquest," but it would not mean sending "American boys 9 or 10,000 miles away from home to do what Asian boys ought to be doing for themselves."

:: VIETNAM: THE FORK IN THE ROAD

In December, after the elections, Mike Mansfield wrote Johnson that we were on a course in Vietnam "which takes us further and further out on a sagging limb." In time, he predicted, we could find ourselves saddled with "enormous burdens in Cambodia, Laos, and elsewhere in Asia, along with those in Viet Nam." In reply, Johnson objected to Mansfield's suggestion that "we are 'overcommitted' there. Given the size of the stake, it seems to me that we are doing only what we have to do." In a conversation with columnist Walter Lippmann later that month, Johnson complained that he was not eager for American involvement, "but this is a commitment I inherited. I don't like it, but how can I pull out?" Moreover, though polls revealed no well-defined majority in favor of escalation, a substantial plurality supported military action against the Communists, with only between 26 percent and 30 percent opposed.

Johnson remained determined not to abandon Vietnam. Remembering Munich, he saw weakness overseas as leading to World War III. Moreover, if he held his hand and South Vietnam fell, it could work havoc with his political influence and power to achieve domestic advance. A new Joe McCarthy might come on the scene to pose rhetorical questions about how Vietnam had been lost, or so he feared.

A decision for stronger action Johnson had been creeping toward came in the last week of January when another change of government occurred in Saigon. On January 27, the day after the coup, Bundy and McNamara told Johnson that "our current policy can lead only to disastrous defeat. . . . Bob and I believe that the worst course of action is to continue in this essentially passive role which can lead only to eventual defeat and an invitation to get out in humiliating circumstances. . . . The time has come for harder choices."

Johnson now agreed to follow a more aggressive policy. The combined pressure of events in Saigon and the unequivocal advice that he needed to act decisively persuaded him to strike at the North Vietnamese. The trigger for action was a Viet Cong attack on an American base at Pleiku in the central highlands, which killed eight U.S. advisers and wounded dozens of others. He agreed to an air strike against North Vietnam to demonstrate that Hanoi "could not count on continued immunity if they persisted in aggression in the South."

This retaliatory attack was the opening salvo in a systematic air campaign against the North. Though Johnson had made up his mind to initiate sustained bombing, he did not wish to launch the campaign until Soviet Premier Aleksei Kosygin, who was visiting Hanoi, had left. Consequently, on February 10, when the Viet Cong struck another U.S. base at Qui Nhon on the central coast of South Vietnam, killing twenty-one Americans, Johnson authorized only a retaliatory attack. No mention was to be made of "continuing action" for the time being.

"Rolling Thunder," as the sustained bombing campaign was named, was initiated on February 13, after the Joint Chiefs had identified a series of targets to be attacked during the next eight weeks. "We will execute a program of measured and limited air action jointly with GVN against selected military targets in DRV," the White House informed the embassy in Saigon. "We will announce this policy of measured action in general terms." In fact, no public statement was issued. As columnist James Reston described it in the *New York Times* the following day, the United States had entered "an undeclared and unexplained war in Vietnam."

Johnson's refusal to make the expanded air war clear to the public partly rested on a concern not to distract Congress and the country from his reform agenda. But ambivalence about the policy also motivated him. "He had no stomach for it," Mrs. Johnson told me, "no heart for it; it wasn't the war he wanted. The one he wanted was on poverty and ignorance and disease and that was worth putting your life into. . . . And yet every time you took it to the people, every time you said anything in a speech about civil rights your audience would begin to shift their feet and be restive and silent and maybe hostile. But then the moment you said something about defending liberty around the world—bear any burden—everybody would go to cheering."

:: "A CLOUD OF TROUBLES"

In agreeing to an air campaign against the North, Johnson had only vague hopes of what would be gained. The most optimistic proponents of bombing believed it would immediately boost Saigon's morale and stiffen its resolve to fight. There was also an expectation that steady escalation would force Hanoi to rein in the Viet Cong and ask for a halt to the attacks. The United States could then continue air raids until the North ceased backing the Communist insurgency in the South.

At the same time Johnson heard positive estimates of what an air campaign could achieve, he also received warnings that it would lead only to more fighting. The Joint Chiefs themselves, mindful that they were bombing a country without an industrial infrastructure or a capacity to produce its own war matériel, doubted that air strikes could significantly alter Hanoi's behavior. George Ball and Ambassador to Moscow Llewellyn Thompson urged Johnson to understand that Hanoi would never give up the struggle for control of South Vietnam unless it faced "a crushing military defeat."

Johnson himself had substantial doubts that an air campaign would force Hanoi to end its aggression. But he saw immediate gains. It could forestall a Communist victory in South Vietnam and the rest of Southeast Asia and a domestic ruckus over who "lost Vietnam."

Although he agreed to let the military bomb North Vietnam on a regular basis, he still didn't see himself as committed to a war in Southeast Asia. The United States was now clearly doing more than before, but he didn't want to describe it that way. He wanted the freedom to turn the air campaign off when he saw fit, and, if need be, take the United States out of the conflict without any sense that there had been an embarrassing defeat.

To assure himself of the greatest possible flexibility, Johnson insisted on saying little in public about what he was doing. Others told him this was a bad idea. They wanted him to prepare the country for substantial sacrifices by publicly stating what an air campaign might mean. Bundy, for instance, urged LBJ to understand that "at its very best the struggle in Vietnam will be long. It seems to us important that this fundamental fact be made clear . . . to our own people and to the people of Vietnam." Hubert Humphrey also tried to persuade Johnson that he might be making "the most fateful decisions of your Administration" and needed to assure public backing.

The warnings from Bundy and Humphrey that escalation posed potential problems for Johnson heightened rather than weakened his determination to say little publicly about the expanding war effort. First, he couldn't bring himself to acknowledge that the bombing made an ever larger U.S. role in the struggle inevitable. Second, since the question of America's role in the fighting remained opened, he shunned discussion of commitments that could easily distract Congress from passing landmark reforms. Third, opinion polls suggested to him that for the time being he didn't need openly to discuss escalation.

From late February to the end of March, while he continued to say little publicly about the war, he searched for additional means to influence developments in Vietnam. Now that he had agreed to sustained bombing, he wanted everyone in the government to figure out how to make it work. But as LBJ understood, injunctions to his generals and advisers were not enough to change conditions in Vietnam. "Light at the end of the tunnel," Johnson told Bill Moyers about the bombing. "Hell, we don't even have a tunnel; we don't even know where the tunnel is."

On March 6, Bundy, McNamara, and Rusk gave him the bad news that "chances of a turn-around in South Vietnam remain less than even; the brutal fact is that we have been losing ground at an increasing rate in the countryside in January and February. The air actions have lifted morale, but . . . there is no evidence yet that the new government has the necessary will, skill and human resources which a turn-around will require." Bundy now urged consideration of sending in ground forces.

Yet Johnson was reluctant to deploy ground forces. He was not against doing it. To the contrary, he believed that ground troops would do far more good against the Viet Cong and North Vietnamese than air strikes and would not directly risk a confrontation with Peking or Moscow, which an error in the air war might provoke. And so at the end of February, he had agreed to send U.S. Marines to guard an American air base at Danang. But he was not ready to put them directly into combat and risk the casualties that would expand U.S. involvement. Only defensive operations on the perimeter of the base were permitted. But conditions were now in place for a ground war that could mean the commitment of hundreds of thousands of U.S. troops.

:: VIETNAM: PEACE ON OUR TERMS

In March, Johnson told Eric Goldman that Rolling Thunder, about which he had so many doubts, would force North Vietnam into a settlement in twelve to eighteen months. He compared it to a "filibuster — enormous resistance at first, then a steady whittling away, then Ho [Chi Minh] hurrying to get it over with."

The fog of uncertainty that plagued Vietnam policy-making troubled Johnson. His highest priority was to settle on a well-defined, consistent policy that held out prospects of ending the conflict. Public opposition to administration policy following the onset of Rolling Thunder heightened LBJ's sense of urgency about resolving the crisis. In the weeks after the bombing began, criticism erupted in Congress, the press, on university campuses, and in White House correspondence.

Johnson was determined to disarm his critics and unify the country behind his Vietnam policy. His objective at the beginning of April was to answer complaints about American resistance to a negotiated settlement by proposing talks on terms the North Vietnamese would find hard to resist. Johnson doubted that Hanoi would come to the peace table. How dare his critics call him a "war-monger," he said, when it was the Communists who wouldn't negotiate.

But Johnson believed that he had majority opinion on his side. An opinion poll showed that 60 percent of Americans felt that only U.S. troops would be able to stop the Communist infiltration of South Vietnam. Forty-six percent of the sample wanted Johnson to "hold the line" in Vietnam. An additional 20 percent wanted an expansion of the war in the North. But

31 percent favored negotiations, "with a view to getting out." The country was evenly split for and against sending in large numbers of U.S. troops.

In late March Johnson decided to give a speech at the Johns Hopkins University, which had three aims. First, it would demonstrate that administration policy toward Vietnam was not confused and erratic but in line with what had been in place for ten years. Second, it would offer "unconditional discussions" for peace that would silence critics calling the President a "warmonger." Third, if there were no productive result from a proposal for talks, it would clear the decks for a steady escalation acceptable to most Americans and likely to force a negotiated peace assuring independence for South Vietnam.

Johnson's speech before a university audience critical of an expanded effort in Vietnam began with the background and basis for American involvement in the struggle. A ten-year pledge to South Vietnamese independence dating from the Eisenhower presidency and running through Kennedy's meant that the Johnson administration had "a promise to keep." The loss of Vietnam would be a prelude to new aggressions in Asia and across the world. Consequently, in the struggle for Vietnam, Johnson said, "We will not be defeated. We will not grow tired. We will not withdraw, either openly or under the cloak of a meaningless agreement."

Because "our patience and our determination are unending" in defense of Vietnam, Johnson urged Hanoi to begin peace talks before thousands more died and North Vietnam suffered the devastation of what it had "built with toil and sacrifice." If Hanoi guaranteed South Vietnamese independence, it could look forward to a cooperative effort, backed by a billion-dollar American investment, to develop all of Southeast Asia. "The vast Mekong River can provide food and water and power on a scale to dwarf even our own TVA. The wonders of modern medicine can be spread through villages where thousands die every year from lack of care. Schools can be established to train people in the skills that are needed to manage the process of development."

Johnson's appeal convinced neither critics at home nor opponents abroad. His assumptions that a Communist victory in Vietnam would extend to all of Southeast Asia, that the area was vital to U.S. security, and that a failure to fight in Vietnam would undermine our influence around the world and might even lead to a war with China and Russia seemed no more persuasive after his speech than before.

Moreover, though Johnson told Bill Moyers that "Ho will never be able to say, 'No,'" to a billion-dollar development program, the North Vietnamese leader did just that. Johnson's New Deal evangelism, his experience

with the transformation of rural Texas and the South, and his underestima-
tion of Ho's commitment to the unification of all Vietnam and distrust of
what he saw as neo-colonialism, a Western capitalist state exploiting Vietnam, clouded Johnson's judgment about Ho's response. Yet Johnson himself, in a moment of greater realism about Southeast Asia, had declared: "If
I were Ho Chi Minh, I would never negotiate." Ho, in fact, said the same
thing. The war could end only if the United States totally withdrew from
the South and ceased attacking the North, and Saigon shared political
power with the Viet Cong.

If Johnson didn't get the response from Hanoi he wished, his speech nevertheless put him in a stronger position with Congress, the press, and the
public. In the main, all responded positively to what the *Washington Post*
called the "skillful brandishment of both the sword and the olive branch,"
and Smathers described as "the glint of iron" alongside "the velvet in the
speech." A State Department survey of American opinion concluded that
the President's "adroit exposition of U.S. policy" received "wide acclaim."
And though some like Walter Lippmann saw little gain resulting from
Johnson's speech, Johnson himself believed that the address now gave him
a stronger basis on which to fight a wider war.

:: THE DOMINICAN REPUBLIC

In 1961, the assassination of Rafael Trujillo had ended a thirty-one-year military dictatorship and led to the election of Juan Bosch in December 1962.
The Bosch regime lasted only seven months, when a coup replaced him
with a military junta. Bosch's departure produced few regrets in Washington, where he was viewed as "a dangerous demagogue" who might inadvertently open the way to a Communist government.

The Johnson administration, especially Thomas Mann, in charge of
Latin America, was far more comfortable with the "nontotalitarian" dictatorship of Donald Reid Cabral, a pro-American businessman, whom U.S.
Ambassador William Tapley Bennett, "a courtly southern gentleman [and]
career foreign service officer of the old school," called "Donny." Under
Bennett's and Mann's guidance, the Reid Cabral government received
more money, $100 million, in direct and guaranteed loans than any regime
in Dominican history.

The eruption of a constitutionalist countercoup on April 24, 1965, dis-
comforted the U.S. Embassy in Santo Domingo and the State Department,
which feared a restoration of Juan Bosch's presidency. In response, the
embassy began encouraging the Dominican government's military chiefs

"to forestall a leftist takeover." An alarmed Bennett cabled the State Department on the 28th: "The issue here now is a fight between Castro-type elements and those who oppose. I do not wish to be over-dramatic but we should be clear as to the situation." Four hours later, he reported a rapid deterioration in the situation and urged landing U.S. Marines to protect American lives.

Throughout the crisis, Johnson, who had remained closely in touch with developments, saw no alternative to sending in armed forces. In a public statement on the 28th, Johnson explained his use of troops as necessary to assure the safety of Americans. He had not sent in the troops to prevent a possible Communist coup, Johnson said. But of course this was his principal concern. Already under attack for his actions in Vietnam, he didn't wish to open himself to additional criticism as a knee-jerk anti-Communist who saw a military solution to every left-wing threat around the globe.

Johnson tried to establish a consensus for his policy with a live radio and television broadcast on the evening of the 30th. He explained that violence and disorder were increasing in the island, that foreign nationals and Dominicans themselves remained in danger, and that "people trained outside the Dominican Republic are seeking to gain control." He announced an OAS mission to the island to arrange a cease-fire and help promote a democratic solution to the conflict.

Two days later, with no letup in the crisis, Johnson increased the number of troops to the island and stepped up his efforts to convince people at home and abroad that he was doing the right thing with additional public comments. "At stake are the lives of thousands, the liberty of a nation, and the principles and the values of all the American Republics," he declared. He also said that the revolt had taken "a tragic turn. Communist leaders, many of them trained in Cuba . . . took increasing control. And what began as a popular democratic revolution . . . was taken over and really seized and placed into the hands of a band of Communist conspirators."

Although the mass of Americans approved of the President's policy, influential critics in Congress, the media, and the universities disputed his description of events. They did not believe that the Communist threat in the island was what Johnson represented it to be or that the U.S. government was so ready to stand aside while the Dominicans determined their political fate. Their skepticism was warranted.

Johnson, in fact, shared his critics' doubts. He knew that the evidence of Communist subversion was less clear and the dangers to foreign nationals less pronounced than he said. But with the embassy in Santo Domingo warning of dangers to Americans and a Communist threat and pressing for troops to solve both problems, Johnson couldn't say no. If a number of Americans were killed and/or a left-wing government came to power, conservative critics in the United States would have denounced his "failure" to act.

Because the situation in the Dominican Republic was too murky to lend itself to clear demonstrations of any kind, Johnson was vulnerable to criticism he couldn't refute. As a consequence, he began to overstate the case for intervention.

In meetings with reporters, he described embassy warnings that without U.S. troops blood would have run in the streets. In fact, he said, "some 1,500 innocent people were murdered and shot, and their heads cut off, and six Latin American embassies were violated and fired upon over a period of 4 days before we went in. As we talked to our Ambassador to confirm the horror and the tragedy and the unbelievable fact that they were firing on Americans and the American Embassy, he was talking to us from under a desk while bullets were going through his windows and he had a thousand American men, women, and children assembled in the hotel who were pleading with their President for help to preserve their lives." Since none of this was strictly true, it deepened rather than eased doubts about Johnson's response to Dominican developments. Moreover, when the Santo Domingo embassy released a list of fifty-four "Communist and Castroist leaders" of the rebels, some of whom turned out to be conservatives, it further undermined Johnson's case for intervention. His hyperbole won few converts and provoked additional criticism of him as either misinformed or a "liar."

Happily for Johnson the Dominican crisis lasted only a short time. Under prodding from the OAS and the U.S. government, the Dominican factions signed a cease-fire agreement on May 5. Two days later a Dominican general set up a five-man "Government of National Reconstruction." But the rebels refused to accept it as a legitimate expression of the popular will. They did, however, agree to cooperate with an OAS committee in trying to arrange for a democratically elected regime. While negotiations proceeded, the OAS sent in an Inter-American Peace Force, which included U.S. troops, to prevent a renewed outbreak of fighting. On August 29, the OAS committee won agreement to an "Act of Dominican Reconciliation" providing for a provisional government and the promise of free elections within nine months.

On June 1, 1966, after a period punctuated by continuing acts of violence, particularly against the left, Joaquin Belaguer defeated Juan Bosch by a vote of 57 percent to 39 percent in an election largely free of fraud. Though the left saw the outcome as the product of U.S. intimidation, the Johnson administration hailed the result as a victory for constitutional government.

One of the chief consequences of the Dominican crisis for Johnson was a heightened sense of urgency about identifying and following an unwavering course in Vietnam. He believed it essential if he were to convince supporters and opponents at home and abroad that he had an effective strategy for meeting the challenge in Southeast Asia.

:: VIETNAM: "THE WINNING STRATEGY"

Even before the crisis in Santo Domingo intensified Johnson's desire for a long-term solution to the problem of South Vietnam, he had begun moving toward the only means he saw for rescuing the country from Communist control—great numbers of American ground troops who could inflict substantial losses on the Viet Cong and North Vietnamese regulars. An agreement at the beginning of April to broaden the mission of the Marines from strictly defensive to offensive operations and to plan for the introduction of two additional divisions had opened the way to the escalation of the land war. By the middle of June, the total of U.S. ground forces in Vietnam was to be 82,000, a 150 percent increase.

As concerned as ever not to stir public debate, which could distract Congress from Great Society bills, Johnson hid his decision, preferring "to announce individual deployments at appropriate times." Yet the escalation was an open secret. On April 21, Hanson Baldwin, the military correspondent of the *New York Times*, reported that U.S. ground forces were shifting from defensive to offensive operations. Rusk had tried and failed to squelch the story. Johnson complained that Rusk had been "too gentle" in trying to kill it.

Yet the President had no intention of unilaterally escalating the American ground effort in Vietnam. He believed it essential to have congressional support. To get it, he asked a supplemental $700 million appropriation for Vietnam and the Dominican Republic. This was "no . . . routine appropriation," he said. "For each member of Congress who supports this request is voting to continue our effort to try to halt Communist aggression."

The Congress, where voices of dissent over the escalating war had been heard in greater numbers since March, was surprisingly pliant. In two days, with next to no debate and no amendments in either chamber, the House approved the request by a 408 to 7 vote and the Senate by a margin of 88 to 3. With U.S. forces already in the field, the congressmen and senators saw no way to deny them what Senator John Stennis of Mississippi described as "the tools with which to fight."

During the rest of May, while the Dominican crisis played itself out, Johnson made no additional commitments to expand the war in Vietnam. This was in spite of growing concern about Saigon's capacity to survive. Political instability brought the collapse of a civilian government and the return in early June of military rule under Nguyen Van Thieu as Chief of State and Nguyen Cao Ky as Prime Minister.

At the same time, a Communist offensive beginning in mid-May inflicted a series of defeats on South Vietnamese forces and threatened a military collapse. By the beginning of June, the Saigon embassy reported that the bombing offensive against North Vietnam was changing nothing in the South, where we faced an impending disaster. "It will probably be necessary to commit U.S. ground forces to action." For the time being, however, the North Vietnamese and Viet Cong seemed more likely than ever to sustain their war effort. On June 7, the U.S. military command in Saigon reported the disintegration of ARVN and the likely collapse of the government unless U.S. and third-country forces came to the rescue. General William Westmoreland asked for an increase of U.S. troops from 82,000 to 175,000 — 41,000 immediately and another 52,000 over the next several months, a total of forty-four battalions. He wanted to abandon a "defensive posture" and "take the war to the enemy."

In three meetings over the next seventy-two hours, Johnson struggled to define a response. He settled on the idea that an increase to about 100,000 men would allow the South Vietnamese to hold the line through the summer without turning the conflict into an American or, as George Ball put it, "a white man's war."

Except for Ball, all of Johnson's advisers now agreed on the necessity of preserving the independence of South Vietnam from a Communist takeover. The "wise men" — ten prominent, former foreign policy officials, including Dean Acheson and Clark Clifford — told Johnson that he had no choice but to expand the war to prevent a Communist victory that would jeopardize America's national security around the world. He also needed to create national backing for the war by publicly explaining his decisions.

At a news conference on July 9, Johnson stated that casualties were increasing in Vietnam on all sides and that things were likely to get worse before they get better. "Our manpower needs there are increasing, and will continue to do so." Seventy-five thousand U.S. troops "will be there very shortly. There will be others that will be required. Whatever is required I am sure will be supplied." Four days later, in another press conference, he declared that increased aggression from the North may require a greater American response on the ground in the South.

The question he posed to himself in the second half of July was not whether to put in additional troops but how many and at what pace. He wished to send enough men initially to prevent a South Vietnamese collapse and then to change the course of the war. But he also intended to make a commitment that would be compatible with domestic goals.

At the end of a meeting on July 21, Johnson stated what he felt had to be done. "Withdrawal would be a disaster, a harsh bombing program would not win and could easily bring a wider war, and standing pat with existing forces ('hunkering up'—as he called it) was only slow defeat. Only . . . doing what McNamara urged was left," putting in a large number of ground forces. "It was the end of debate on policy," one participant recalls, "and the beginning of a new debate on tactics and above all on presentation to the country. In his own favorite phrase, the President had decided to 'put in his stack.'"

Johnson's focus was now on how to put the decision for a wider war before the country. "How would you tell the American people what the stakes are?" Johnson asked his military chiefs in a meeting on the 22nd. "The place where they will stick by you is the national security stake," one general replied. "Do all of you think the Congress and the people will go along with 600,000 people and billions of dollars 10,000 miles away?" the President asked. "Gallup poll shows people are basically behind our commitment," Army Secretary Stanley Resor declared.

At a smaller meeting three hours later, Johnson searched for a formula to announce escalation without suggesting a major change in policy. He feared it would agitate Congress and the public and encourage Moscow and Peking to increase support of Hanoi.

The President was determined to avoid a public explosion over Vietnam. To mute his decision, Johnson announced the expansion of the war at a press conference rather than in a speech to a joint session of Congress. Moreover, all he would say was that troop commitments were going up from 75,000 to 125,000, with additional forces to be sent later when requested. Nor would he call up reserve units now, though he would give it careful consideration in the future. His decision did "not imply any change in policy whatever," he also told reporters. To further downplay the action, Johnson surrounded it with talk of his Great Society goals, which he would not allow to be "drowned in the wasteful ravages of cruel wars," and announcements of Abe Fortas's nomination to the Supreme Court and John Chancellor's appointment as director of the Voice of America.

"If you have a mother-in-law with only one eye and she has it in the center of her forehead," Johnson joked privately, "you don't keep her in the living room." Yet Johnson knew that he could only hide the full meaning of his larger military commitment for so long. For he had no illusion that his administration was undergoing a sea change resembling FDR's shift in the 1940s from Dr. New Deal to Dr. Win-the-War.

:: DR. WIN-THE-WAR

Johnson did not reach his decision casually to fight a land war in Asia. He and his advisers had made exhausting reviews of their options. The defeat of the French in a similar struggle, the difficulty of fighting a guerrilla war with conventional forces, the determination of the North Vietnamese to make it long and costly, the likely hesitation of the American public once the price in blood and treasure began to register, and the likelihood that a protracted conflict would divert resources from the Great Society all gave Johnson pause.

But the conviction that a Communist victory would have worldwide repercussions for America's national security, especially in Southeast Asia, and would provoke a right-wing reaction in the United States that would wreck Johnson's administration overwhelmed his doubts. Moreover, he and most of his advisers thought it unlikely that the Viet Cong and North Vietnamese would be able to hold out forever against America's massive air, land, and sea power. True, it was going to cost American lives to accomplish the goal, but the extent of that sacrifice was not assumed to be large or anything like the Korean losses, which ran to 30,000 men. Before any such development, the Communists would have to come out and fight, and when they did, American forces, in the words of one general, would "cream them."

Johnson had few illusions about what escalation of the war would mean at home. He knew that wars had sidetracked Populism, Progressivism, and the New and Fair Deals. "Losing the Great Society was a terrible thought," Johnson later told Kearns, "but not so terrible as the thought of being responsible for America's losing a war to the Communists. Nothing could possibly be worse than that."

Yet at the time, Johnson had every hope that escalation would not mean the end of reform. On the contrary, by the time Johnson was "putting in his stack," his legislative program was largely in place. True, he would put additional reforms before the second session of the 89th Congress, but it did not match the proposals of the first in importance. Johnson believed that, even if future reforms were sidetracked, he had already gained enough major legislation to put foreign affairs on an equal and possibly even higher footing than domestic ones.

But if Johnson had largely created the legislative framework for his Great Society and was ready to devote himself to Vietnam, why was he so reluctant to speak more openly to the country about expansion of the war? Because until October 1965, Congress was still at work on his reforms. After that, however, he was ready to see the war come front and center. By then, the most important Great Society laws would be fixtures on the national scene. World War II had not destroyed the major elements of the New Deal, and Johnson expected it to be the same with the Great Society and Vietnam. True, some of the programs would not get the full financing they needed, but this would come in time, when the struggle in Vietnam ended. And so to Johnson, fighting in Vietnam meant not destroying the Great Society but delaying its full impact on American life.

Indeed, for all his anguish over Vietnam, Johnson saw positive developments flowing from the war: It was an opportunity to combat Communist hopes of advancing their cause through wars of national liberation. It was also another in a series of brave responses to Cold War challenges faced by America since 1945. It was one more opportunity to show the Chinese and the Soviets that we could not be intimidated. They would then be more receptive to détente or a peaceful standoff with the West.

As he saw matters in the summer and fall of 1965, he was meeting the challenge to presidential greatness at home and now he hoped to do the same abroad. For the war in Vietnam was a chance not only to promote long-term international stability but also to allow Johnson to make a great mark in foreign affairs. He had not gone looking for a fight. He was not contriving an international conflict for the sake of his historical reputation. But confronted by a foreign challenge that seemed to pose a major threat to the national well-being, Johnson intended to do his duty. If it added to his presidential greatness, all to the good. But it was no more than a secondary, comforting reason to fight.

Yet however many constructive reasons Johnson saw for fighting, he could not quiet a fear that the war might ultimately ruin his presidency. There were no guarantees that U.S. military pressure would bring the Communists to negotiate a settlement or that the American right wouldn't mount an effective attack against a political compromise in Vietnam or that the domestic left wouldn't be able to stir mass opposition to a long war.

In 1965, Johnson was more concerned about the right than the left. "George," he told Ball, "don't pay any attention to what those little shits on the campuses do. The great beast is the reactionary elements in the country. Those are the people that we have to fear."

But he could not ignore the power of antiwar dissenters to sway public opinion. True, opinion polls in the spring and summer of 1965 showed the country to be generally sympathetic to his course in Vietnam. In mid-May, Americans favored the use of military force in Southeast Asia by a two to one margin, 52 percent to 26 percent. At the end of June, 62 percent of the country thought the President was doing a pretty good or excellent job in Vietnam.

Yet at the same time, the public was sharply divided over the fighting. At the end of April, 20 percent supported carrying the war to the North, while 28 percent wanted negotiations and 43 percent urged holding the line. In July, a quarter of the country supported a complete withdrawal or a halt to fighting and the start of negotiations. A like number wanted stepped-up efforts and/or a declaration of war. Sixteen percent were content to continue on the present course, but the largest number, 33 percent, had no set view of how to proceed. The uncertainties were reminiscent of the discontent during the Korean war, which had eroded Truman's public standing.

In this context, Johnson feared the damage opposing voices in the press and among the country's intellectuals might have on the war effort. "Every student anti-U.S. policy demonstration is priceless gold for the Viet Cong," Jack Valenti told LBJ in April. The campus teach-ins, columnists, and public marches denouncing the bombing of a weak third-world country greatly troubled Johnson. Attacks on him personally for a "credibility gap"—for exaggerating the dangers in the Dominican Republic and for failing to tell the truth about America's growing involvement in Vietnam—further incensed him. "How do you know when Lyndon Johnson is telling the truth?" a joke began to make the rounds. "When he pulls his ear lobe, scratches his chin, he's telling the truth. When he begins to move his lips, you know he's lying." The journalist Hugh Sidey said that to Johnson "the shortest distance between two points was a tunnel."

:: VIETNAM: HEARTS AND MINDS

In the four months after Johnson made his July 28 announcement, he focused on the need to solidify support for the war effort in Vietnam and the United States without public debate.

With over 200,000 U.S. troops deployed by the end of October, he believed that the conduct of the war would now take care of itself. Unlike the bombing, which Johnson constantly worried might provoke the Chinese and Soviets into a confrontation with the United States, LBJ largely left the U.S. military to determine how ground forces were to be used in the war. By contrast, he paid substantial ongoing attention to targets and the minutiae of bombing as a way to guard against a wider conflict.

In the autumn of 1965 Johnson's principal focus was on signs that the Communists would now limit or even end their aggression in Vietnam. There was a belief among Johnson and his associates, Bill Moyers says, "that if we indicated a willingness to use our power, they [the Communists] would get the message and back away from all-out confrontation. . . . There was a confidence . . . that when the chips were down, the other people would fold."

General Maxwell Taylor told LBJ: "By the end of 1965, the North Vietnamese offensive will be bloodied and defeated without having achieved major gains. Hanoi may then decide to change its policy. 1966 could be a decisive year." In short, the very presence of so much U.S. power in Vietnam was enough to do the job without additional planning on Johnson's part as to exactly how those forces would be used. Indeed, the President assumed that the next big decision about land forces in Vietnam would not be how they would operate but whether more would be needed to achieve our ends.

Johnson was more focused now on encouraging political stability in a country where divisions and coups had become a way of life. He partly took his cue from an August 1965 paper on "Politics and Victory in Vietnam" by Walt W. Rostow, the head of the State Department's Policy Planning Council. Success in the war, Rostow argued, required "some effective political expression of South Vietnamese anti-Communist nationalism. . . . We must turn to the problem of the political life of South Vietnam with a seriousness which matches that now accorded to military and diplomatic aspects of the crisis." All America's efforts in behalf of the South Vietnamese, Johnson believed, would come to naught unless we effectively encouraged the development of a viable political system commanding the loyalty of the people.

Yet the struggle for hearts and minds in Vietnam commanded much less of Johnson's attention in the summer and fall of 1965 than the one he fostered in the United States. Accurately believing that a stable consensus at home was essential for a sustained war effort, he mounted an unacknowledged campaign to refute the arguments of war critics and discredit them as sensible exponents of America's national interest.

In the second half of 1965 the White House expanded upon steps begun in the spring to justify the war in general and Rolling Thunder in particular. The State Department and national security advisers had taken the administration's case to campus teach-ins; friendly academics and journalists had been enlisted to write favorable articles; Hubert Humphrey and Averell Harriman had been sent to speak to university audiences as well as gatherings of business and labor leaders; national organizations had been lobbied to pass approving resolutions; a committee of prominent citizens had been set up to speak out in defense of the war in newspaper ads and letters to the editor; and a White House speechwriting team had begun "to provide the fodder for congressional support for Vietnam policy."

To win the political war over Vietnam at home, Johnson took aim at three targets: the media, Congress, and the mass public. He saw the press as particularly troublesome. In general, the media supported Johnson's decisions to fight. Like most Americans at this time, they believed the national interest required an independent South Vietnam. But this was not enough for Johnson. He wanted to control the flow and content of the news and bend the media to his designs. Johnson refused to be passive toward media criticism. He and his principal press aides believed that "poisonous and sour" reporting seriously undermined the war effort. Enraged by press attacks, Johnson complained that "subversives" had "infiltrated the press corps." "The Viet Cong atrocities never get publicized," he said. "Nothing is being written or published to make you hate the Viet Cong; all that is being written is to hate us."

Johnson also saw Congress as vital to any successful war effort. And not primarily because they controlled the purse strings. He knew that, once U.S. forces were deployed, Congress would feel compelled to provide the funding, which, in fact, it did. More important, the President understood that a congressional majority would consistently support the war but that some of it would be grudging or soft. And this worried him.

Johnson accurately saw congressional opposition as a spur to press and public skepticism about the wisdom of fighting. Consequently, in September 1965, when Fulbright raised his voice against Johnson's actions in the Dominican Republic and Vietnam, it sent a chill through the White House. Though Fulbright wrote Johnson that he believed his dissenting view would help the administration and the country come to grips with foreign policy questions, Johnson saw it only as an impediment to a successful war effort.

In mid-September, however, the *Washington Post* reported that Johnson had "more solid support for his policies in Viet-Nam than at any other time since the fighting began to escalate in February." Seventy-five percent wanted Johnson to hold the line or carry the war north, and only 25 percent, a drop of 11 percent from May, preferred negotiations.

In November, the Gallup poll reported that, "in sharp contrast to recent public demonstrations, survey evidence indicates that American public opinion is moving toward greater support of U.S. military action in Vietnam." Sixty-four percent, compared with 52 percent in May, believed the United States should have become involved in the war, and only 21 percent thought not. Harris's November survey continued to give Johnson a 66 percent approval rating. In December, Harris recorded a ten-to-one margin against withdrawal from Vietnam.

Yet all this "scientific sampling" did not convince Johnson that the public was reliably behind the war. One NSC staff member had it right when he declared in December: "The polls give the President high marks on Vietnam—but I have a vague feeling that this support may be more superficial than it is deep and committed (many people probably do not even understand what it is that they are supporting)."

Like the NSC official, others in the administration, including Johnson, had a sense of unease about the national commitment to the fighting. The President and others around him couldn't put their finger on it, but they knew this wasn't like World War II, with a powerful and transparently immoral enemy opposed to fundamental American values. Nor was it the same as Korea, which had occurred at the height of the Cold War and seemed a more serious test of American resolve to meet the Communist challenge in Asia and around the globe.

When dissenters raised questions about the wisdom of fighting Third World Communists who had no power to directly injure the United States, it registered on Americans in ways that made Johnson and his advisers uncomfortable. For they also sensed that Vietnam did not have the hold on the public imagination that would allow for a long war. Hence, the administration's impulse to press the case for Vietnam regardless of what the polls said.

Johnson would have done well to have encouraged a wide-open debate in Congress and the press on what to do about Vietnam. Perhaps some Great Society legislation would have been shelved as a consequence, but given liberal majorities in Congress it is hard fully to credit Johnson's fears about a debate playing havoc with domestic reform

What seems reasonably sure, however, is that an expanded war following a debate would have meant a stronger, more stable commitment to the fighting. This by no means guaranteed an enduring consensus in the face of stalemate, defeat, and substantial casualties, but it would have put Johnson in a much stronger political position. Complaints about his credibility, objections to "Lyndon Johnson's war," with all the political difficulties these attacks entailed, could have been avoided. More important, escalation of the fighting by national agreement rather than Johnson's unilateral decisions would have placed him in a position to escape the war if and when it turned sour. As matters stood at the end of 1965, Johnson had committed the prestige of the country and his administration to a conflict that great numbers of Americans now felt we could not afford to lose.

9 :: RETREAT FROM THE
:: GREAT SOCIETY

By the winter of 1965–66 Johnson had a government in place of his own making. A number of Kennedy's appointees still held high office, most notably, Rusk at State, McNamara at Defense, and Larry O'Brien as principal legislative liaison. But no one could doubt that the Kennedy officials had now become Johnson's men, officeholders who worked comfortably in behalf of the President's domestic and foreign policies.

Most of the aides Johnson had appointed in November 1963 were still at their posts two years later. But Jack Valenti and Bill Moyers had become firsts among equals. Valenti continued to be a man Friday. He kept the President's calendar, coordinated work on presidential statements, prepared LBJ's correspondence, and oversaw "special presidential projects," which meant everything from liaison with Senators Dirksen and Mansfield to day-to-day dealings with the State Department. Valenti was as loyal to Johnson as anyone in the administration: "I sleep better at night knowing Lyndon Johnson is President," he told the press. But two and a half years with LBJ had exhausted him, and in April 1966 he decided to accept appointment as president of the Motion Picture Association of America.

Bill Moyers would also leave at the end of 1966, complaining later that "after you've worked with LBJ, you can work with the Devil." The strains of serving Johnson and a chance to return to journalism decided him to become the publisher of the Long Island newspaper *Newsday*. But for three years he had been one of Johnson's most devoted special assistants. And Johnson had rewarded him: In October 1964 he had become Chief of Staff with responsibility for task forces that had shaped so many of the landmark reforms during 1965. In July 1965, Johnson had made him George Reedy's successor as press secretary. Though Moyers's principal activity was the care and feeding of the press, Johnson had announced that he would also "be working on anything I want him to from time to time."

As press secretary, Moyers struggled with a number of problems. Johnson was never happy with his media coverage, and Moyers became the object of LBJ's hostility for not getting the press more fully behind the administration on Vietnam. Johnson and other aides saw the credibility gap as the consequence of Moyers's deviousness rather than the President's. "Bill was never overly scrupulous about the truth," George Reedy said later. "It was no accident that the President's popularity started to fall very abruptly as soon as Bill took over." Jake Jacobson, another White House aide, shared Reedy's judgment: Moyers answered too many questions, Jacobson believed, and never replied, "I don't know. . . . Whether it was the President's answer or him, you never did know that." However much Moyers may have contributed to the credibility gap, it was the President's own deceitfulness that stood at the center of the distrust that congressmen and senators, journalists, and ultimately people all over the country felt toward him.

Moyers's difficulties with Johnson also stemmed from what the President saw as the excessive press attention given to a member of his staff. Other aides complained that Moyers was ready to step over them and the President in the service of his own ambitions. If all these in-house problems were not enough to drive Moyers to retire, he also had to cope with journalists who saw him as the President's defender and an obstacle to information he denied them. When he took the press secretary's job, Moyers remembers telling his wife, "This is the beginning of the end, because no man can serve two masters," meaning Johnson and the press. By the summer of 1966, all these burdens put Moyers in the hospital with a case of bleeding ulcers.

During 1966, as Valenti and Moyers made their exits, other aides filled the vacuum. Domestic affairs became the principal responsibility of Joseph Califano. When Moyers began his press duties, he recommended that Johnson shift Califano to the White House from Defense, where he was serving as McNamara's special assistant. A graduate of the Harvard Law School and a brilliant systems analyst, the thirty-four-year-old Califano was asked to take on Moyers's job of preparing and coordinating domestic legislation.

On the first day in his new position, Califano learned what working for LBJ would mean. Getting up at 3 a.m. to fly to the President's ranch, he joined the President at his pool for a swim. "Are you ready to come help your President?" Johnson shouted at him from one end of the pool. Saying it would be an "honor and a privilege," Califano plunged into a three-and-a-half-year whirlwind of activity. Day and night, Califano ate more meals with Johnson than his own family, frequently seeing him "early in the morning in his bedroom and late at night as he fell asleep. He barked orders at me over the phone at dawn and after midnight, in the formal setting of the Oval Office and as he stood stark naked brushing his teeth in his bathroom."

Califano was such a quick study and so devoted to the Great Society programs that, within six months of coming to the White House, he sometimes became a surrogate President. Early in 1966, as Johnson was about to go abroad, he called Califano to his bedroom, where he said: "'You're going to be the President. . . . We have to get all this legislation passed. We have to do this, we have to do that.' And then he . . . gave me cufflinks. He gave me an electric toothbrush with the Presidential seal on it. He gave me a tie clasp, he gave me cigarette lighters and I ended up walking with my arms full of all these presents, to say goodbye to him. . . . I don't think I slept . . . for all the time he was away. I worked so hard because all these bills were on the Hill," and Johnson called him every night at three in the morning.

The other principal figure to join Johnson's domestic staff was Marvin Watson. A Texas businessman and wheelhorse in the state Democratic party, Watson was a Johnson loyalist who in 1960 had established one of the first Johnson-for-President clubs. In 1964, he had served as LBJ's coordinator at the Democratic Convention. The following January, Johnson made him a special assistant in charge of appointments, management of the White House office, and liaison with Democratic governors, the Democratic National Committee, and various state and local political groups. One journalist described him as the "White House's No. 1 Hatchet Man." Responding to Johnson's insistence on a leak-proof administration, he required that White House operators record all incoming and outgoing calls, including the names of the parties speaking to each other. He insisted that White House chauffeurs report on the destination of any staff member using official transportation.

Watson also served as Johnson's liaison to the FBI, which led some reporters to call him a "mystery man" or "gum shoe" operator. Watson denied that he was any sort of mystery man, just a faithful presidential servant. One White House coworker described him as a stickler for details, "the greatest nit-picker around," "the master of the paper clip." Judging from the FBI record of a meeting on White House physical security, Watson deserved his reputation. He provided Deke DeLoach with the precise number of White House guests during 1965 and the fact that 65,873 tradesmen or workmen also came to the mansion during that time. He passed along detailed information on how many White House, Executive Office, and press passes had been issued and the number of times the building had been picketed last year. Watson was Johnson's bureaucrat par excellence.

The greatest change in Johnson's foreign policy staff was the replacement of Mac Bundy by Walt W. Rostow as National Security Adviser. In the spring of 1965, as Johnson expanded American commitments in Vietnam, Bundy urged a public debate to convince the country that the administration was following the right course. In April, Bundy agreed to debate Hans Morgenthau, a prominent international relations expert from the University of Chicago. When Johnson learned this, he sent Bundy to the Dominican Republic to report on the crisis. Later that year, when Bundy rescheduled the event, the President sent word through Moyers that he didn't want Bundy to debate. Believing that he had lost the President's confidence and doubting the wisdom of escalation based largely on the Gulf of Tonkin Resolution and questionable public opinion polls, Bundy decided to resign. He asked Harvard President Nathan Pusey about a professorial appointment, but, before Pusey could reply, Bundy agreed to become president of the Ford Foundation beginning in April 1966.

The forty-nine-year-old Rostow was seen as a strong choice for Bundy's post. Rostow had been a Rhodes Scholar at Oxford; held a Ph.D. in economics from Yale; had taught at MIT's Center for International Studies for ten years; published a famous book, *The Stages of Economic Growth: A Non-Communist Manifesto*; and served since 1961 as the head of the State Department's Policy Planning Council. In 1964–65 he had helped persuade the President that only a strong public stance, including direct military pressure, against North Vietnam could stop the insurgency in the South.

Johnson saw Rostow as the right man for the job in all respects but one. He was too prolix, too verbose. Johnson instructed Valenti to talk to Rostow about how he liked to work with an adviser. Valenti sat down with him before LBJ announced the appointment and told him how to write a memo and how to conduct himself in a meeting with the President. Valenti explained that Johnson liked the crispness with which Bundy or MacNamara presented a case. "I told him that . . . if he were opening a meeting to state the issue and briefly, very briefly, maybe state the pros and cons and then shut up." Memos "ought to be very spare, very lucid." Rostow took Valenti's instruction "with amazing good grace and great humility," and largely gave Johnson what he wanted.

As with all his aides, Johnson began their new relationship with some abuse, which was calculated to intimidate and subordinate someone whose natural talents might make him too independent. The President never wanted toadies working for him but he wanted people who were entirely responsive to presidential commands. A press leak about Rostow's appointment threw Johnson into a rage, or at least Johnson acted as if it did. He called Rostow late at night to chide him for abusing the President's confidence. Rostow, who had done no such thing, emphatically denied the charge. Johnson slammed the phone down with no indication of whether this meant he had changed his mind about appointing him. Without further discussion or notice to Rostow of his intentions, he announced the appointment the next day to the press.

It is more than likely that Johnson himself was the source of the leak on Rostow's selection. Califano recalls more than one instance in which Johnson orchestrated a situation that subjected an aide to a presidential tirade. "With the guy that was something before he came to him," Califano says, "he [LBJ] always seemed to have to break him in some way or get him to agree to do something, or even in the worse sense he'd humiliate him in some way to make him totally his man, . . . to make sure he was totally loyal."

The cast of characters close to Johnson at the White House included three other highly talented men who worked tirelessly to make the Great Society a reality. Douglass Cater, a forty-one-year-old Alabaman with two degrees from Harvard, joined LBJ's administration in 1964 after serving for fourteen years as the Washington and national affairs editor of the *Reporter* magazine. Initially hired as a speech writer and "idea" man whom the President instructed to "think ahead," Cater focused his attention on health and education issues. By the beginning of 1965 he had become Johnson's "expert" on these matters and played a central role in shaping and passing some forty health and education bills in the next two years.

Harry McPherson, a thirty-six-year-old native Texan and University of Texas law graduate, joined Johnson's staff in August of 1965. His acquaintance with the President dated from 1956 when he had worked as assistant counsel to the Senate Democratic Policy Committee. A thoughtful and well-read man, McPherson served as assistant secretary of state for educational and cultural affairs from July 1964 to August 1965. With Bill Moyers's support he became counsel to the President for six months, succeeding to the post of special counsel in the following February. Though he worked as the President's personal lawyer for the next two years, he principally served as Johnson's top speech writer. An evocative writer with a keen feel for Johnson's style of speaking and desire for terse, spare prose that included "a little poetry" and some alliteration, McPherson crafted all the President's major addresses beginning in the summer of 1966.

The oldest and most famous of Johnson's special assistants was Robert Kintner. Born in 1909, by the time Kintner had come to the White House he had established himself as a prominent journalist and network television executive. In the 1930s he had been a reporter for the *New York Herald Tribune* and had coauthored the widely read column "Capitol Parade" with Joe Alsop. After service in World War II, he had become a vice president at the American Broadcasting Company, succeeding to the presidency in 1950. In 1956, he had left ABC for NBC, where he was president from 1958–65, and chairman of the board in 1966.

Kintner and Johnson had a friendship dating back to the late thirties. As someone who had "no political ambition, no need for money and no desire for publicity," the fifty-six-year-old Kintner was, according to one journalist, "better geared psychologically to serve the President than any member of the inner circle." Kintner's assignment was to advise on top-level appointments, help Democratic candidates in 1966, and improve the President's public image.

:: THE STATE OF THE UNION

In the winter of 1965–66, Johnson struggled to define what the coming political year would bring. He had no doubt that Vietnam would dominate his conduct of office, but he had no intention of saying so publicly or of acknowledging that the surge of domestic reform would now have to take a back seat to the war. Though he understood the impossibility of maintaining the momentum of domestic change while fighting so large a war in Vietnam, he refused to acknowledge this publicly.

His eagerness to do right by the nation and political calculation convinced him to promote the fiction that the country was rich enough and committed enough to have guns and butter. We knew, Califano says, that "we had to pay incredible attention to the economy both to figure out what was . . . right . . . but also [to] do it in a way that did not jeopardize the continuation of the Great Society programs."

At the end of the 1965 congressional session Johnson had written Mike Mansfield to praise him and Congress for their great accomplishments, but he also pointed to "23 major items of legislation" that were still to be enacted. Mansfield responded by recommending a slow down in 1966 and an emphasis on implementing the many major bills just passed. Harry

McPherson urged much the same, proposing the creation of a commission to assure the proper administration of the new laws.

Johnson was of two minds about how to proceed. He knew Mansfield and McPherson were giving him sound advice, but he couldn't let go of a determination to make the second session of the 89th Congress another watershed moment in the country's history. Nor did he believe it made good political sense for him to shift his emphasis from enacting laws to administering existing ones.

His State of the Union address on January 12, 1966, reflected the dual commitments he urged the nation and Congress to reach for in the coming year. He acknowledged at the start of his address that Vietnam "must be the center of our concerns." But he refused to accept that the Communists in Vietnam could "win a victory over the desires and the intentions of all the American people. This Nation is mighty enough, its society is healthy enough, its people are strong enough, to pursue our goals in the rest of the world while still building a Great Society here at home."

Johnson challenged the country and Congress "to carry forward, with full vigor, the great health and education programs that you enacted into law last year." He urged Americans to "prosecute with vigor and determination our war on poverty" and to "rebuild completely, on a scale never before attempted, entire central and slum areas of several of our cities." He asked a commitment to attack the poisons in our rivers, with an eye to "clean completely entire large river basins." He called for an expansion of federal efforts against crime in the streets; he decried the continuing abuses of civil rights, asking for additional legislation to ensure nondiscrimination in federal and state jury selection and in the sale and rental of housing; he recommended modernizing and streamlining "the federal government by creating a new Cabinet-level Department of Transportation and reorganizing several existing agencies," including reforms in the civil service to make it more efficient and productive; he recommended consumer protection bills requiring truth in selling and truth in lending; and he suggested a constitutional amendment extending the terms of congressmen to four years, concurrent with the President's.

"Because of Vietnam," which took up half of his speech, Johnson said that "we cannot do all that we should, or all that we would like to do." But he outlined how much could be accomplished nevertheless. By attacking government waste and inefficiency, preventing labor strikes, holding down inflation, and maintaining the economic growth of the last five years, which had raised after-tax wages by 33 percent, corporate earnings by over

65 percent, and farm income by nearly 40 percent, the administration could find the means to continue building the Great Society.

In an emotional appeal that brought the largely liberal congressmen and senators to their feet, Johnson asked "the representatives of the richest Nation on earth, you, the elected servants of a people who live in abundance unmatched on this globe, . . . [to] bring the most urgent decencies of life to all of your fellow Americans." He urged Congress not "to sacrifice the children who seek the learning, or the sick who need medical care, or the families who dwell in squalor" to false economies not required by the war. The *Washington Post* described the President's message as, "U.S. Can Continue the 'Great Society' and Fight in Vietnam . . . —LBJ Hands Congress Massive Work Load."

Despite his rhetoric, Johnson was too much of a political realist to think that he could achieve all this. But he saw three reasons to try or at least give the appearance of trying. First, he genuinely wanted to ease suffering among the poor and enrich the lives of the middle class. And even if he couldn't do as much as he liked in 1966, bold pronouncements about marching toward Eden would increase the likelihood that he could get part of what he put on the agenda. Second, he believed it politically essential to declare his determination to reach the promised land. He saw any indication of a slowdown in reform efforts as an invitation to conservatives to attack the whole enterprise as unaffordable and unreachable. Third, it was remotely possible that a series of administration actions affecting the economy might provide enough money to combat the Communists in Vietnam and public problems in the United States. And so, even if a new round of reform efforts fell short, he was determined to try.

:: ADVANCING THE GREAT SOCIETY:
THE DEPARTMENT OF TRANSPORTATION

Johnson loved the idea of being the most prolific reform leader in presidential history. The second-year Great Society agenda he had unveiled in his State of the Union address consisted of 113 separate measures on everything from child, consumer, and environmental protections to urban renewal. It was a grand follow-up to the stunning achievements of the first session of the 89th Congress.

It also commanded his determination to get it passed. At the end of May, after most of the agenda had been introduced, the President called in the Cabinet secretaries. The job now, Johnson told them, was to raise "legislative promises into full-grown realities. . . . If we approach it half-heartedly or over-confidently, we will fail. . . . I do not intend to fail. I do not intend to waste a single chance, or break the smallest promise."

Yet for all Johnson's devotion to another round of reform legislation, his 1966 proposals were a pale imitation of those of 1965. To be sure, Congress would approve 97 of LBJ's 113 bills. But compared with the educational, health, and voting rights acts of 1965, the reforms of 1966 were relatively limited. Child nutrition, truth in packaging, rent supplements, the teacher corps, clean rivers, child, mine, and tire safety, and the Freedom of Information Act did not have the impact that the earlier laws had on the country. This is not to say that they were inconsequential; each of them had a significant effect on various groups, but none of them had the reach and resonance of the earlier measures.

Except for reforms embodied in a new Department of Transportation. The role of the federal government in managing the country's transportation systems was a microcosm of Johnson's view of federal authority. Since the start of the Republic, the government had played a significant part in drawing the nation together through road, canal, railroad, and airport construction. By the 1960s more than thirty agencies, most of them under congressional control, regulated the nation's road, river, sea, and air transit. In a country as vast as the United States, with a mid-sixties population of nearly 190 million people, Johnson, ever the New Dealer faithful to the conviction that consolidation of control in the executive assured greater economy and efficiency, intended to create a Department of Transportation responsible for all phases of national mobility and safety.

Beginning in 1965, Johnson had made clear to his task force on transportation that he wanted a program that would improve conditions "radically, looking not only to next year, but to 1980, the year 2000 and beyond." Johnson saw a transportation department as not only a chance to "invigorate" and "modernize" the country's transit systems but also to do "major things" without costing much money.

Aware that a transportation department might arouse strong opposition from the automobile, truckers, railroad, airline, and maritime industries, Johnson had White House aides talk to as many interested parties as possible. When Califano reported that the head of the American Trucking Association was an enthusiastic supporter, the President brightened and said: "'Joe, we're going to get our Department of Transportation! You know why?' I had no idea. He gave me a patronizing look, and almost whispered, 'Because of the truckers. When the truckers deal on the Hill, they deal one on one'—Johnson paused for effect and leaned toward me—'and only in cash.' He slapped his leg approvingly."

On March 2, Johnson sent a bold transportation message to Congress outlining what he saw as the problems and solutions. The country's expenditures on transportation accounted for one-sixth of the American economy—$120 billion. But there was terrible waste caused by time-consuming road, airport, and harbor congestion, highway accidents costing 50,000 lives a year; a reliance on "aging and often obsolete plant and equipment, networks chiefly designed to serve a rural society"; and "the failure to take full advantage of new technologies." The country needed an enlightened government agency that would serve "as a full partner with private enterprise in meeting America's urgent need for mobility."

The new department was to be a catch-all agency. It was to include the Commerce Department's office of transportation, the Bureau of Public Roads, the Federal Aviation Agency (FAA), the Coast Guard, the Maritime Administration, the safety functions of the Civil Aeronautics Board (CAB) and the Interstate Commerce Commission consolidated under a new National Transportation Safety Board, and the agencies responsible for the Great Lakes, the St. Lawrence Seaway, and the Alaska Railroad. In addition, the new department was to assume shared responsibility with the CAB for subsidies to local airlines, with the Army Corps of Engineers for river and harbor construction projects, with the State Department and the CAB for international aviation routes and fares, and with Housing and Urban Development for urban transportation.

Johnson also asked Congress to pass a Traffic Safety Act to reduce the carnage on America's highways. Since the introduction of the automobile, 1.5 million Americans had died in car crashes—"more than all the combat deaths suffered in all our wars." Under the act, the President proposed to increase federal grants to the states for highway safety, compel improved auto safety performance, and create a national highway safety research and test center.

Despite considerable enthusiasm in most quarters for a department performing the functions Johnson described, the legislation ran into objections threatening its passage. In the Senate, where John McClellan of Arkansas chaired hearings on the bill, questions were raised about shifting the Coast Guard and the FAA into the new department and the criteria that would be required for approval of new Corps of Engineer navigation projects. Under a new rule, some $3 billion to $4 billion in projects might be sidetracked.

McClellan, who saw the new standards blocking projects he favored, resisted the change. The President was willing to accept his demand for the old standard on advancing river construction, but he didn't want to write it into the bill.

To force McClellan's hand, Johnson told Califano to leak a rumor to the press that McClellan was holding up the transportation act "'because he wants the Corps of Engineers to build a dam on land he owns so he'll get a lot of money when the government buys the property.' 'Is that true?'" Califano asked. Johnson leaned back in his chair and described how his former boss Congressman Dick Kleberg publicly accused a competitor for his House seat of taking "'female sheep up into the hills alone at night. Well,' the President said, 'I jumped up and shouted, Mr. Kleberg, Mr. Kleberg, that's not true. And you know what Mr. Kleberg did?' Johnson asked . . . 'He just looked down at me and said, "Then let the son of a bitch deny it."' Johnson and I both laughed, then he paused and said quietly, 'You just let John McClellan deny it.'"

Though no such pyrotechnics were necessary to bring McClellan into discussions of passing the bill, some tough negotiations followed on the language that went into the act on navigation projects. After Califano thought he had reached an agreement with the senator, he brought it to Johnson, who dismissed it as no bargain at all. Johnson told Califano to check under his fly, "'because there's nothing there. John McClellan just cut it off with a razor so sharp you didn't even notice it.'"

Though McClellan and the White House reached a compromise that assured Senate passage of the bill, the House leadership frustrated Johnson by excluding the Maritime Administration from the new department. Shipowners and maritime labor unions supported by a bipartisan majority in the House wanted to create an independent Maritime Administration that would give special attention to the problems of an ailing industry.

Johnson tried to prevent a development that he thought would seriously undermine the proposed Cabinet office. If maritime interests could preserve their autonomy, it would boost the case for an independent FAA. "Altogether," Budget Director Charlie Schultze told him, this could "begin a wholesale gutting of the Department bill." To counter such a result, the President promised to give a maritime administrator in a transportation department authority to build "a modern, efficient merchant marine fleet." If the maritime industry went its separate way, it "would be the only major transportation mode not represented in the new Department" and would "not have a voice at the Cabinet table or as a powerful voice in the policymaking councils of Government."

Johnson instructed Califano to work out a settlement with the shipping interests urging maritime autonomy. Promises were made to include a maritime subsidy board and give "a special statutory delegation of authority" to a Maritime Administration in the department. But this still failed to meet labor and industry objections, and AFL-CIO President George Meany effectively pressured House members into excluding merchant shipping from department control. Senator Henry Jackson told the White House that if the maritime provisions had remained in the bill, "the House would have rejected the conference report and 'there would be no Department of Transportation during this Congress.'"

In a signing ceremony at the White House on October 15, Johnson celebrated the birth of a department that would untangle America's lifeline. "Today we are confronted by traffic jams. Today we are confronted by commuter crises, by crowded airports, by crowded airlanes, by screeching airplanes, by archaic equipment, by safety abuses, and roads that scar our nation's beauty." The department "we are establishing will have a mammoth task—to untangle, to coordinate, and to build the national transportation system for America that America is deserving of."

Johnson was incensed at the exclusion of the Maritime Administration and refused to invite representatives of the shipping industry and unions to the bill signing. He also urged Congress to "reexamine its decision to leave this key transportation activity alone, outside" the jurisdiction of the department. Fifteen years later, in 1981, the Congress saw the wisdom of Johnson's advice and moved the Maritime Administration into the department.

The month before the transportation bill became law, Johnson had signed the National Traffic and Motor Vehicle Safety Act and the Highway Safety Act. Together with the new Transportation Department, the clean air and water acts of 1965, the 1966 clean rivers law, the Fair Packaging and Labeling Act, and the other safety laws for children, mines, and tires, Johnson began a process of regulation that improved the environment and reduced the hazards that had injured and killed millions of Americans. At the same time, it touched off an ongoing debate about the value of government intrusion into people's daily lives and demands for greater freedom from government controls. Did the gains in safety and product quality outpace the costs and problems generated by regulation? There are no simple answers to these questions. Johnson himself, when signing the transportation bill, felt compelled to declare: "Our transportation system was built by the genius of free enterprise. And as long as I am President, it will be sustained by free enterprise."

Yet one thing seems clear: The failures of a free enterprise system provoked an outcry for tough regulations, which, according to safety experts, have played a crucial role in reducing highway deaths and injuries. Since the safety and regulatory measures Johnson put in place more than thirty years ago have largely remained and been expanded, despite creating some limits on economic growth, it seems reasonable to conclude that the reforms of 1965–66 did significantly more good than harm.

:: THE GREAT SOCIETY IN RETREAT: CIVIL RIGHTS

As the war in Vietnam expanded and resources for Great Society–War on Poverty programs diminished, Johnson had to confront the problem of what more his administration could do to advance civil rights for blacks and open wider avenues of opportunity. The riots in Watts followed by upheavals during the summer of 1966 in thirty-eight cities, including Chicago, Cleveland, Milwaukee, Atlanta, Philadelphia, and Minneapolis, aroused concerns that black militants were intent on driving the country into a race war. Television pictures of black youths shouting "burn, baby, burn" sent waves of fear through suburban America and turned sympathy for helping an oppressed minority into hostility toward suggestions of making additional special efforts to right past wrongs.

In July 1966 one congressional survey of 12,000 constituents revealed a majority in favor of cutting poverty programs, welfare, urban renewal, and rent subsidies to finance the Vietnam War. Strong support was voiced for pollution programs and safety legislation, but an amazing 90 percent opposed additional civil rights legislation.

During 1965–66 Johnson tried to sustain black gains through the courts and additional legislation that would require little or no increases in spending. He also tried to keep the political costs to a minimum. In the summer and fall of 1965 he had pressed the case for school integration, ordering daily reports on the progress of southern school districts in complying with requirements that they submit desegregation plans. Though Johnson was ready to push desegregation across the South, where he felt he now had little left to lose politically, he had no intention of pressing the issue beyond the bounds of political reason in the North, where he feared provoking more of a backlash than was already evident.

Despite the landmark civil rights laws of 1964 and 1965, Johnson believed that significant legislative reforms further assuring equal treatment and expanding federal jurisdiction to combat civil rights crimes were possible at small cost to the government. Since all-white southern juries continued to ignore miscarriages of justice in race crimes, the President believed that Congress would give a sympathetic hearing to a civil rights bill including provisions for impartial jury selection. Second, since bias in the sale and rental of housing had contributed to the creation of black ghettos, where festering problems erupted in riots, Johnson hoped Congress would agree to prohibit housing discrimination. Finally, Johnson wanted Congress to expand the Attorney General's authority to bring suits to desegregate schools and public facilities and to protect civil rights workers.

The most controversial part of another civil rights bill was the attack on housing discrimination. In October 1965, Califano told the President that there was "tremendous pressure from civil rights leaders" to take additional executive action on the issue. If he acted without Congress, Califano told him, he might provoke a drawn out court fight and "be accused of over-extending your authority." If he asked for legislation, it would have the advantage of reducing a possible defeat in court, would be more broadly applicable than an Executive Order, and would put the political burden as much on Congress as himself. On the other hand, a legislative proposal would confront strong congressional opposition fueled by constituents fearful of reduced property values following integrated housing.

Johnson chose the politically more expedient and legally surer course. In his State of the Union address, he urged Congress to enact a civil rights bill with housing, jury selection, and crime enforcement provisions. Everett Dirksen immediately announced his opposition to the ban on housing discrimination. During the first four months of 1966 Johnson struggled to find ways to build support for his proposal. In early March, White House aides felt that congressional contacts were still "inadequate" and that more time was needed to discuss matters with Dirksen, who, as with the 1964 and 1965 acts, seemed likely to be crucial to Senate passage. Though Dirksen would not endorse the fair housing provision and one legislative aide told the President that the "housing proposal will be impossible to enact," Johnson refused to abandon what he saw as the core of the bill.

At the same time, however, he felt compelled to deemphasize the importance of another civil rights act. To be sure, his message to Congress on April 28 rang with strong language about injustice, equality, opportunity, and fairness. Moreover, he did not mince words about the extent and destructiveness of unfair housing codes. "The time has come for the Congress to declare resoundingly that discrimination in housing and all the evils it breeds are a denial of justice and a threat to the development of our growing urban areas. . . . The truly insufferable cost of imprisoning the

Negro in the slums is borne by our national conscience. When we restrict the Negro's freedom inescapably we restrict a part of our own."

But the President also wanted to make clear that no civil rights act at this time would make a definitive difference in solving the problems of racial discrimination. Johnson asked that several paragraphs be added to his message to make clear that "no amount of legislation, no degree of commitment on the part of the national government, can by itself bring equal opportunity and achievement to Negro Americans. It must be joined by a massive effort on the part of the states and local governments, of industry, and of all citizens, white and Negro." It was now up to black Americans "to take full advantage of the improved education and training . . . to use the opportunities for orderly progress that are now becoming—at last—a reality in their lives."

To underscore the limited importance Johnson attached to the bill, he considered releasing his civil rights message to Congress when he was out of town. "It will be difficult to get any decent coverage for the message because the White House Press Corps will go with you," Joe Califano told him. "Who wants more coverage?" Johnson asked rhetorically.

Johnson knew that getting the bill through Congress intact was a long shot. A White House poll of Democratic congressmen and senators in the spring on what they considered the most important issues in their districts and states put civil rights well down the list behind Vietnam, inflation, and the war on poverty. The housing section of the bill was so controversial that the House subcommittee separated it from the rest of the proposal. The full committee defeated a motion to kill the housing provision by only 17 to 15. A coalition of liberals and southerners then defeated several amendments that would have weakened the bill.

Southerners believed that a strong law would not pass the House. To their surprise, the House approved the legislation on August 9 with limitations on what constituted housing discrimination. The President issued a statement praising the House action and putting the best possible face on the fair housing provision.

The Senate could not be persuaded to act. The Judiciary Committee bottled up the bill. When one liberal senator tried to put the measure on the Senate's calendar for floor action, it was blocked. A motion to set aside consideration of a pending bill and begin discussion of the civil rights act produced a twelve-day filibuster. Cloture petitions in September netted only 54 and 52 of the 60 necessary votes. Dirksen, despite pressure from Attorney General Katzenbach and Johnson himself, refused to back a bill with a housing title, and predicted that even a change in his position would not assure the votes for cloture. Katzenbach advised against seeking a bill without the housing provision, which civil rights groups and House conferees insisted remain in the law. He also urged the President to see Dirksen as a way of making "it clear that we had done everything we could to get a civil rights bill and that our failure to do so was the responsibility of the Republican leadership."

Johnson now decided to abandon the fight for the time being. And even if he had wanted to continue the struggle, it was clear to him that the summer riots and divisions in the civil rights movement between traditional leaders such as A. Philip Randolph, Roy Wilkins, Whitney Young, and Martin Luther King and younger leaders of CORE and SNCC, like James Farmer, Floyd McKissick, Stokely Carmichael, and H. "Rap" Brown, made the task very difficult.

At the same time, he understood that he himself remained closely identified with civil rights and that he could not simply stand aside and let differences between blacks and whites deteriorate into a race war. As Harry McPherson told him, "you cannot shake off that leadership. You are stuck with it, in sickness as in health. The very fact that you have led the way toward first-class citizenship for the Negro, that you are identified with his cause, means that to some extent your stock rises and falls with the movement's." The President needed more than ever to point the way toward "peaceful change" by helping pass social reforms that opened additional opportunities to blacks and by persuading moderate black leaders to "speak out for order."

Johnson didn't need prodding to remain attentive to civil rights issues and search for strategies that could promote integration and black gains. A Gallup poll in September, as the civil rights bill failed, described "racial problems" as America's biggest domestic issue.

:: THE GREAT SOCIETY IN RETREAT: THE WAR ON POVERTY

During 1966 the war on poverty faltered. It was a victim of expenditures on Vietnam, threatened inflation and economic disarray, and its own internal contradictions.

Johnson could not admit publicly that the antipoverty crusade was in trouble. He knew full well by the end of 1966 that his public pronouncements trumpeting the coming end of want in America were unrealizable. If he still had hopes of reaching that exalted goal, Harry McPherson urged him to see matters as they were. "There is no real agreement on how to go about improving the job situation, or education, or family income in the slums," McPherson told him in December. "I think we have about all the social programs we need—already authorized. We may have too many. . . . You need to ask: What is this program trying to accomplish? How well has it done? What should we be trying to accomplish in this area?"

Yet Johnson himself didn't think of the overall war on poverty as a "failure," certainly not in 1966. In public, he had nothing but praise for the achievements of OEO and the whole poverty fight. And he had reasons to believe that much good was being done. At the end of 1965, Walter Heller had urged him not to skimp on the Great Society: "A billion or two extra invested in better training, education, and housing—especially for the poor and the Negro—will give America a *far bigger payoff than if we add that billion or two to already-swollen private consumption and investment,*" Heller told him.

But even without the additional money, by the beginning of 1967 Johnson saw a record of accomplishment that spelled much more success than failure. For one, federal spending on the poor had increased in every relevant category—education and training, health, and cash benefits like social security and unemployment insurance—and government services provided by the OEO and the Community Action Program (CAP) had raised government outlays for the poor from nearly $13 billion in 1963 to almost $20 billion in 1966.

In December 1966, budget analysts told the President that the administration's best weapon in the poverty war was jobs. An increase in employment of 8.4 million from 1960 to 1966 helped explain why the number of poor Americans had declined from 22 percent to 17 percent. In addition, the government's policies and general prosperity had helped keep a "large number of people . . . from falling into poverty" and raised the standard of living for even those who remained below the poverty line. "What have we learned?" a paper presented at a Cabinet meeting asked. "Poverty in America Can Be Eliminated." The 38 million poor of 1959 had come down to 25.9 million by 1967; the 14 percent of whites and 47 percent of nonwhites in poverty had declined to 10 percent and 35 percent, respectively.

Johnson spoke repeatedly in public during 1966 about the gains being made against want. Spending on Great Society programs had nearly doubled in three years: Federal outlays for health and education were up 59 percent; spending on cities had leaped 76 percent; and unemployment was sharply down, by 32 percent for whites and 34 percent for blacks.

Nevertheless, it was an open secret that the President's commitment to Great Society–War on Poverty programs had waned and that hopes were being disappointed. In November 1966, Charlie Schultze told Johnson that "states, cities, depressed areas and individuals have been led to expect immediate delivery of benefits from Great Society programs to a degree that is not realistic. This leads to *frustration, loss of credibility, and even deterioration* of State and local services as they hang back on making normal commitments in order to apply for federal aid which does not materialize."

Johnson did all he could to combat the impression of a slowdown in the antipoverty campaign. "We just have to keep hammering home our side of the question every time we get a chance," Bill Moyers told the President. But Johnson knew that there was a gap between his public declarations and private actions. For one, he was at war with the Community Action Programs around the country. Under the flag of "maximum feasible participation," CAPs challenged local political leaders for control of poverty funds. They put the poor on local poverty boards, "neighborhood service centers," which fought with established institutions—schools, welfare agencies, and housing authorities—about the ways in which they served inner city residents. "Local governments didn't bargain for all this—being sued, being demonstrated against, having sit-ins in their offices," one proponent of CAP said.

The growth of community action challenges to local political organizations worried Johnson. During 1964 and much of 1965, however, he had been reluctant to intervene. He took some pleasure in seeing poor folks have a say in local affairs and bend political machines to their will. He believed that the pressure generated by the CAPs might make the war on poverty more effective. As long as squabbles between city officials and CAPs didn't endanger other Great Society programs, Johnson was content to placate complaining politicians with sympathetic words about the difficulties of reining in out-of-control agencies.

By late 1965, however, with congressmen and senators growing reluctant to provide money for activities challenging local political allies, and an emerging White House conviction that organizing efforts among the poor would become a launching pad for a Robert Kennedy presidential campaign, Johnson took steps to check "maximum feasible participation." When he was told about an attack on Democratic party leaders in the District of Columbia by CAP protesters, for example, he instructed Bill Moyers: "For God's sake get on top of this and put a stop to it at once." As other complaints came in, Johnson told his aides to quash the political organizing of CAP radicals.

A year later, a White House task force on reorganizing HEW recommended shifting all of the OEO programs to appropriate Cabinet departments, except community action. OEO would then "be set up as a separate agency outside the Executive Office of the President to run CAP and to develop and demonstrate new programs which would be ultimately turned over to on-going departments as they matured."

Johnson was clearly looking for a way to neutralize the OEO. He saw everybody at OEO as "disloyal to him." He complained repeatedly to Wilbur Cohen at HEW that "the OEO people were always trying to undermine him." Shriver, who now offered to resign, urged Johnson to replace OEO with a domestic National Security Council chaired directly by the President and including the Vice President and all the major Cabinet officers. Shriver wanted his departure to give no suggestion of bad blood between himself and the White House, or so he said. Concerned that the reorganization of OEO and Shriver's resignation would be seen as a downgrading of the whole war on poverty, Johnson persuaded Shriver to stay as head of the OEO, which was also to remain intact.

Yet in spite of maintaining the status quo, Johnson was in fact crimping the war on poverty. Throughout 1966 his struggle to hold down federal expenditures partly revolved around trimming antipoverty costs and discouraging Congress from adding funds to his appropriation requests.

By the beginning of 1967, Johnson had few qualms about holding down antipoverty spending. But not because he was ready to give up the fight against want. On the contrary, as far as he could tell, the war on poverty was succeeding with only modest expenditures of $1.5 billion to $1.75 billion. All the statistics he saw indicated a steady decline in the numbers of indigents. Just how this was happening was not clear to him, though he understood that this was partly the consequence of an expanding economy generating more and better-paying jobs.

Less obvious was the fact that Community Action Programs across the country, but particularly in major cities, were promoting greater awareness of welfare rights, which brought substantial numbers of poor onto the welfare rolls. "Since the federal government picked up half the tab for Aid to Families with Dependent Children (AFDC)," one analyst says, "welfare was often the cheapest way to give poor blacks something they needed— . . . money. Nor were there powerful white voting blocks competing for welfare dollars or resisting black demands, as there were in education, housing, and employment."

Between 1960 and the early 1970s, there was a fourfold increase in AFDC, with much of the expansion coming after 1964. "The federal government accomplished little in the ghetto save opening up the welfare rolls," this analyst concludes. Some of the Great Society programs gave modest numbers of poor a hand up rather than a handout. "But in the ghetto—where schooling was poor, where the family was already in serious trouble, and where crime was becoming a way of life for many young men—the successful policies were irrelevant. The real impact was on welfare, and thus on dependency and on the black family."

:: THE ELECTIONS OF 1966

The domestic difficulties, coupled with growing frustration about Vietnam during 1966, spelled trouble for Johnson and the Democrats in the congressional and state elections. Even in good times, the incumbent party and President usually suffer some losses in mid-term contests. And with the uncommonly large margins the Democrats held in the House (295 to 140), the Senate (68 to 32), and the statehouses (33 to 17), they seemed certain to lose some ground.

For more than a year before the November voting, the White House had been tracking the decline of Democratic party fortunes. Analysts predicted a loss of between twenty and thirty-six House seats. Moreover, the Republicans seemed certain to win several gubernatorial campaigns. Johnson and the party received more bad news in February and March when polls showed a decline in the President's popularity to 56 percent, a drop of five points in just one month and the lowest level since he had assumed office in November 1963.

Johnson now considered what role to play in the upcoming campaign. His identity as a lifelong Democrat encouraged him to fight for his party. In addition, Democratic defeats would be seen as partly a personal repudiation and would weaken his ability to lead in the next two years.

At the same time, however, he had an aversion to excessive partisanship. In the fifties, during Eisenhower's presidency, he had built his national reputation as a moderate southerner and an advocate of bipartisanship, particularly in foreign affairs. His appeal in the 1964 campaign had been to both parties, urging Democrats and Republicans alike to join him in opposing extremism of the left and the right. Johnson also had a history of tension with northern Democratic party leaders and labor unions, whom he described as "a bunch of damn crooks" and "racketeers." As for the Democratic National Committee, he considered it largely superfluous. Hubert Humphrey said, "Legend to the contrary notwithstanding, when it came to party politics, he [LBJ] was not good.

Johnson approached the 1966 elections with great caution. Remembering FDR's failure in the 1938 primaries to oust conservative Democrats and seeing it as accepted "policy" to remain neutral, he made clear to party candidates that he would "stay completely away from any of the [primary] campaigns until these are over and the General Contest is on."

As for the fall elections, he took a wait-and-see attitude. If he were to involve himself in the campaign and the Republicans made significant gains, he would be the biggest loser. If he largely stood aside, he would likely shoulder less of the responsibility for Democratic defeats. One aide advised him in early May that if things took "a turn for the better in Vietnam, you should go on the campaign trail. . . . If, however, things get worse, . . . the best policy would be for you to remain in the White House."

At the end of May Johnson saw reason to sit out the elections. A chart on results from presidential efforts in off-year campaigns gave no reason to get significantly involved. Moreover, current polls suggested little that he could do to reverse party fortunes. His popularity continued to fall. Worries about inflation, Vietnam, and his proposal to bar racial discrimination in the sale or rental of private housing were further reducing his attractiveness to voters. Likewise, the Democrats, who had a twenty-one-point advantage over the Republicans in November 1965 as the party best able to handle national problems, held only a seven-point edge over the GOP in May. It was the closest the margin had been since August 1960, when the two parties had been nearly even. The results of this question over the years had been a good indicator of voter sentiment and suggested that the Republicans might gain as many as fifty or even sixty House seats and two in the Senate, where there were thirty-five races.

When the President's approval rating slipped to between 46 and 50 percent in June, the White House began focusing not on how to cut Democratic losses in Congress but how to improve Johnson's public appeal. "Our standing is down and likely to drop further," Bill Moyers told Johnson on June 9. Consequently, Johnson decided against any special effort to save the seventy-five Democratic congressmen who were "most vulnerable in their reelection bid." When Cliff Carter at the DNC asked the President to film one- to five-minute conversations with these congressmen for use in their campaigns, Johnson refused.

Instead, the White House began an intense effort to staunch the President's political bleeding. Though in February he had declared himself "sick of having to offset any [unfavorable] image," Johnson now instructed aides "to disseminate more affirmative polls" and arrange to enter positive editorials in the *Congressional Record*. At a meeting of the President's top staff members, they discussed speech themes and other means of boosting his standing. All agreed that Vietnam, peace, inflation, and agriculture were the concerns of the moment. But the real problem was not finding themes but humanizing a President who seemed too humorless and too intent on a search for consensus. Greater candor and consistency also seemed essential to creating some momentum for his political resurgence.

In July, Johnson took up the challenge by making two trips to the Midwest and holding background meetings with journalists. By the middle of the month, the President's aggressive defense of his administration and stepped-up bombing against North Vietnam caused a surge in his popularity, jumping ten points to 56 percent from his low point in June. Johnson's second tour demonstrated to the columnist Marianne Means that he had not "lost his fire on the stump nor his ability to mesmerize a crowd, particularly when he discusses such dramatic events as the war in Viet Nam."

Yet in spite of this surge, Johnson continued to keep his distance from the congressional campaigns. When Tommy Corcoran suggested that the DNC turn the election into a referendum on LBJ with the slogan, "A vote against Johnson is a vote for Hanoi," he vetoed it. He also rejected a suggestion to bring in the freshmen Democrats for a meeting and pictures. A proposal that he campaign for "a number of marginal Democrats" in Pittsburgh and Dayton or Cincinnati on his way to Indiana in late July was no more convincing to him.

Though the President made two more "nonpolitical" trips in August to the Northeast and West, his public standing took another downturn. By September, his approval rating had fallen back to 48 percent, with people expressing diminished confidence in his ability to manage the economy in general and inflation in particular. A trial presidential heat between LBJ and Michigan Governor George Romney gave Johnson a slight 51 to 49 advantage. A Harris poll also showed the Democrats losing more ground in the congressional and gubernatorial races.

Because Johnson now feared losing as many as sixty seats in the House and 6 to 8 seats in the Senate, he approved a plan for some sixty administration officials—the Vice President, Cabinet, and subcabinet secretaries—to coordinate visits to congressional districts across the country. The worst thing that could come out of this, Kintner told Johnson, were newspaper stories saying "the President fears a major defeat in the election and has rallied his appointees to political activity to try to offset it." Johnson now also agreed to meet with Democratic incumbents at the White House and make a three-and-a-half-minute film for use by Democratic candidates.

Yet at the same time, the President continued to refuse to become overtly partisan. In late September, he told reporters that he had no plan to travel widely in the states before the election. He also refused to get into a public dispute with the Republican House leadership over Vietnam. And when he did get out on the hustings, he said, "We haven't been talking party matters. We have been talking people matters; problems of people."

On financial support for Democratic candidates as well, he was not very forthcoming. Because of Republican accusations that big contributors to Johnson's principal fund-raising committee, the President's Club, were receiving favored treatment for government contracts, Johnson largely closed down the operation in the last months of the campaign, when money was badly needed. Partly to distance himself from the election, Johnson decided to make a seventeen-day trip to Asia from October 17 to November 2. Shortly before he left, he said that he had no plans to campaign when he returned.

In October, Marianne Means told readers of her column that the President has "displayed an indifference toward practical politics which dismayed and perplexed party leaders. He seldom left the White House. He sharply restricted money-raising endeavors and forbade solicitation of new members for the President's Club. He let the Democratic National Committee flounder uselessly."

Privately, Johnson was torn about what to do. He saw a substantial Republican victory coming, and he wished to insulate himself from it as much as possible. As important, he saw some advantage to replacing liberal Democrats with Republicans. True, it would make it harder, if not impossible, to win significant legislative victories. But it would give him stronger support in Congress to fight in Vietnam. And by the fall of 1966, this was his highest priority. Indeed, the periodic reports he requested from aides on the congressional races during 1966 included assessments of candidates' views on Vietnam as the lead item.

Still, Johnson didn't want to let the Republicans win without a fight. It galled him to think that a President with his record of achievement should be identified with any kind of political defeat. "I am willing to let any objective historian look at my record," he told aides in an Anchorage, Alaska, hotel room the evening before he returned to Washington from Asia. "If I can't do more than any[one else]to help my country, I'll quit. The week before he left for Asia he mapped plans for a four-day campaign blitz carrying him to eleven states all over the country. During his Asia trip, six more states were added to his itinerary. More important, detailed plans were made for Johnson to sign various bills in appropriate settings.

But sensing a strong Republican showing, regardless of what he did, Johnson canceled the trip at the last minute. When he publicly denied that he had ever planned such a campaign swing, it hurt him and the Democrats more than if he had followed through on his plan. On November 8, the Republicans gained 47 House seats, reducing the Democratic margin to 248 to 187, three Senate seats, making the division 64 to 36, and eight governorships for a 25 to 25 split of the states.

As the year ended, Johnson's credibility, his willingness to be honest with the press, the public, and Congress, had become a bigger issue than his extraordinay legislative gains or Democratic party defeats. And central to so many doubts about the President's reliability was his direction of the war in Vietnam, which was becoming the country's greatest concern.

10 :: "LYNDON JOHNSON'S WAR"

By the winter of 1965–66 nearly 60 percent of the country saw the Vietnam War as America's most urgent problem. The number had more than doubled since the presidential campaign in 1964. Two out of three Americans considered it essential to take a stand in Vietnam, with only 20 percent favoring a pullout over an expanded role for U.S. forces. Seventy-five percent of a sample poll viewed the war as "part of our worldwide commitment to stop Communism."

There were also growing indications that as the war went, so would Lyndon Johnson's public standing. At the end of 1965, his approval rating remained impressively high at 64 percent. Moreover, for the third year in a row, Americans chose him as the most admired man in the world, with Dwight Eisenhower second and Robert Kennedy third. Some three-fourths of the country endorsed the President's handling of Vietnam and expressed antagonism to antiwar demonstrators.

Yet at the same time, the public's support had distinct limits. It had little appetite for a long, expanded war. Bill Moyers told Johnson in December that most Americans hoped that stepped-up military actions would facilitate "a negotiated, compromise peace." Escalation was acceptable because it would bring "peace more quickly." But impatience and frustration were also evident: Only 25 percent of the country thought "we are making any progress" in Vietnam and 43 percent complained that the administration was not doing enough to end the fighting.

Sentiment in the United States, although important, was only one element shaping Johnson's judgments on the war. In November, Vietnam Ambassador Henry Cabot Lodge told the President that "we are beginning to master the technique of thwarting and eventually overcoming the Viet Cong main force units and military redoubts." Lodge warned against a cease-fire or anything that might demoralize Saigon and collapse the government.

The Joint Chiefs urged LBJ to expand the American military effort. On November 10, they asked for an additional 113,000 troops to shift from phase I of the fighting, in which U.S. forces had stopped "losing the war," to phase II, in which we would "start winning it." They also recommended intensified bombing, highlighted first by strikes against petroleum, oil, and lubricant facilities and electric power installations and then military targets in the Hanoi-Haiphong area.

Johnson didn't want any part of a policy that might provoke a wider war. He didn't think the Chiefs had a clue as to what they were proposing. He responded with an explosion of invective that stunned them. Johnson's response partly rested on messages from Peking that China would join the fighting if Washington supported a South Vietnamese invasion of the North.

At the same time, however, Johnson's intemperate response to the Chiefs demonstrated how anguished he remained about the conflict. In the spring and summer of 1965, Moyers and others had seen him agitated by the belief that Vietnam might destroy him. Similarly, in November he viewed the recommendations of the Chiefs as leading to an international and personal catastrophe.

Johnson hoped for a negotiated settlement rather than a military victory. But he saw peace only following a sustained, strong military effort. He saw no sensible alternative to expanding America's combat role. Despite Hanoi's strong response to American escalation, he still believed it necessary to show the Communists that America would not be intimidated by aggression, even if it meant fighting a limited war at considerable cost in lives and dollars. Johnson now considered whether "a frontal confrontation with Congress, laying all the cards face up, would be helpful." But, as in July 1965, the President concluded that such an open discussion of war needs would give the conflict a centrality in public affairs that would become a reason to starve and dismantle the Great Society. Consequently, Johnson again chose to be less than candid about what would be required to fight the war.

It was a tragic error. Instead of openly confronting the hard choices the country now faced in Vietnam and encouraging a national debate, he obscured the harsh realities—planning, for example, to expand troop commitments month by month without acknowledging that decisions had been made for a doubling of forces by the end of 1966. For the second time in six months he had a chance to rally a generally receptive public to fight a difficult limited conflict and make Vietnam America's war. Instead, he chose the path of indirection, which irrevocably made the struggle Lyndon Johnson's war and all that would mean for a President presiding over a potentially losing cause.

A national debate was no guarantee that the country wouldn't first support and then later want to abandon a costly limited war. But it would have given Johnson political protection from charges that he escalated without giving Congress and the public their democratic right to choose. Moreover, it would have given him greater political and psychological freedom to alter policy in response to developments at home and in Vietnam. It seems fair to say that Johnson's political instincts failed him or that his imperious self eclipsed his accommodating side in making war policy.

By the end of 1965 many congressmen, journalists, and ordinary citizens found it difficult to understand Johnson's policy in Vietnam and doubted the wisdom of a larger war. Jack Valenti drove home the point to him in January. "We have to, simply, logically and honestly, tell the people why we fight, and how enormous are the stakes in their future," Valenti wrote the President. "One reason for some unpopularity of the war is the queasy notion that we ought not be there since our vital interests are not really involved."

But Johnson couldn't understand the confusion over American goals. He thought the matter pretty straightforward. Communist North Vietnam was trying to destroy South Vietnamese independence and bring Saigon under its control. The Chinese supported Hanoi as part of a drive for a Communist Asia. America's national interest dictated the containment of Asian Communism as it had blocked Soviet expansion in Europe and the Middle East.

The antiwar opposition read Hanoi's actions differently. This was essentially a civil war, with North Vietnam sustaining a long-term anticolonial struggle to free all of Vietnam from Western control. As for China, it saw America's war in Vietnam aimed as much against Peking as Hanoi. The struggle in Vietnam was part of a larger American campaign not simply to contain Communism but to destabilize and defeat it everywhere.

Johnson began to think of his opponents as unwitting Communist dupes. He asked the FBI to keep a close watch on Communist diplomats in the United States to see if they were "making contacts" with U.S. citizens. He believed that "much of this protest concerning his foreign policy ... had been generated by" Communist officials.

But the quickest way to silence critics, he believed, was to win the war. Johnson now pressed the Joint Chiefs to tell him how long it would take to break the Communists' will. General Earle Wheeler thought "within the next two years we ought to get favorable results." But Max Taylor believed that Hanoi would keep going as long as they saw divisions in the United States that might force us out of the war. "Our enemy gets great encouragement from the opposition voices here. Is that right?" Johnson asked. "Yes. It's true," Taylor replied. Johnson then said: "I am not happy about Vietnam but we cannot run out."

Tensions over the war now made for adversarial conditions that discouraged reasoned discussion of an escape from the fighting. The traditional middle ground of American politics was giving way to ideological strains that left little room for maneuver between "hawks" and "doves." "You are either with us or against us" became the posture both sides adopted toward the war. After retired General James Gavin testified before the Senate Foreign Relations Committee against the war, Johnson, or so Gavin believed, arranged an IRS audit of his tax returns. When retired Ambassador George Kennan, who was also critical of the war, appeared before the committee, CBS President Frank Stanton, a friend of LBJ's, decided to show reruns of old television comedy series. News division head Fred Friendly resigned in protest.

In March 1966, Johnson told a group of state governors that "our country is constantly under threat . . . —Comm[unists] working every day to divide us, to destroy us. Make no mistake about the Comm[unists]" he said. "Don't kid yourself a moment. It is in the highest counsels of gov[ernment] —in our society. McCarthy's methods were wrong—but the threat is greater now than in his day."

Who was Johnson thinking of? Were his remarks just hyperbolic rhetoric meant to scare war critics into "getting on the team"? Or did he actually believe that congressmen, senators, and journalists were intent on overturning the country's traditional institutions? It is difficult to take his comments at face value. Whatever his propensity for suspicion —even paranoia —it is hard to imagine that he genuinely saw high government officials and prominent reporters as secretly promoting Communism at home or abroad.

At the same time, he could not accept the view that his opponents were expressing independent judgments. From his perspective, anyone in America who thought carefully about the war would see the need to resist a Communist advance. Johnson believed that some academic critics were "gullible" men mesmerized by romantic assumptions about the virtues of Communism in Vietnam. Their naïveté made them vulnerable to the Communists, who, he believed, skillfully encouraged and orchestrated their opposition to the war.

Johnson now saw no reason to discuss the war with critics. Advice that he talk to Gavin and Kennan about the conflict and that he reconcile differences with dissenting Senators, for example, fell on deaf ears. With diminishing prospects for some sensible consensus on what to do about Vietnam, each side waited on events to prove that their judgment on the war was right.

:: REALITY BITES

Johnson behaved as if the United States had no choice but to fight on. In March, he agreed to deploy another 65,000 men by August 15, bringing the total to 325,000.

At the same time, the White House expanded its campaign to unite Americans behind the war. Nothing was to be said about troop increases until the additional forces arrived in Vietnam. Nor were there to be any indication that we were taking more control of Saigon's domestic and administrative affairs; any hint of this seemed certain to provoke additional war protests in the United States.

Despite all our efforts, Johnson wondered whether we could prevent a Communist victory or hold American public opinion in line. During March he saw a steady erosion of support for himself and Vietnam policy. Poll results released early in the month showed Johnson's approval rating at 46 percent, its lowest level since he had taken office. The survey also registered a sharp jump in public disapproval to 34 percent. Pollsters agreed that the cause was frustration over Vietnam.

One pro-war congressman warned that the President was piling up a lot of trouble for himself by not being honest with Congress. At the White House briefing on February 24, the President had given "no indication whatsoever that any substantial troop increases were being contemplated for the immediate future. . . . Then just a very few days later the announcement came that 20,000 more U.S. troops were on their way. This . . . had created considerable disillusionment . . . and . . . raised the question of the credibility of the administration."

But in the spring of 1966 Johnson thought he could outlast the domestic opposition. He believed that U.S. military power was beginning to be decisive. Since 1961 the Viet Cong had allegedly suffered three times as many battlefield deaths as South Vietnamese and U.S. forces and four times as many wounded. Moreover, on April 8, Deputy Defense Secretary Cyrus Vance reported after a trip to Vietnam that "we are doing well militarily and are continuing to impose heavy losses on both the VC and North Vietnamese."

Maxwell Taylor also urged an expanded air war. "In the eyes of the Hanoi leaders, the ground war in South Viet-Nam must now appear to be going rather badly," Taylor told the President, "and it is important that they receive an equally discouraging impression from the air war. Not until they get a gloomy composite from both is there much hope of bringing them to negotiations."

And with these reports of better results in the fighting came news that the public was stiffening its resolve to stay the course. An opinion poll in New York reaching Johnson on April 11 showed a resurgent approval rating of 67 percent. Better yet, 78 percent of a Massachusetts poll said that the government's handling of Vietnam was "satisfactory." The President heard additional good news from Bill Moyers, who reported that prominent columnists "from Reston to Russ Wiggins to David Lawrence are quietly applauding the reserve and patience you are showing in the midst of so much flux in Vietnam."

During this time, Johnson received fresh news of military gains that heartened him. Robert Komer, Johnson's deputy on pacification, returned from Saigon in mid-April to report that "our splendid military effort is going quite well." On the 20th, an estimate of Communist casualties showed startling results: Where from November 1965 to February 1966 the enemy had suffered total loses of between 8,700 and 12,000, the numbers for March alone were between 11,000 and 15,700. In early May, Johnson received a report from the Rand Corporation "on the extensive damage done to the Viet Cong and North Vietnamese during the past three months." As Rostow told him, "It is distinctly encouraging, but does not indicate a decisive break in VC morale yet." Moreover, as one national security analyst cautioned, "you can make a case for a somewhat less optimistic view of VC casualties than . . . presented." Estimating total losses for March at between 6,600 and 7,500, this analyst thought "there might not be any erosion at all" in Communist strength. Since the VC/DRV buildup might be larger than estimated, the enemy might have ended the month with more troops in the South than assumed.

With so much uncertainty over Vietnam's political future, Johnson and his advisers decided to make some "basic" policy decisions. At a meeting on April 25, Johnson agreed "to continue roughly along present lines. . . . We shall stay on course and explore with Lodge a cautious Track B," meaning an attempt to draw the Viet Cong into talks, with an eye to causing divisions among them. The embassy was also to reiterate to the Saigon government "that our continued support is contingent upon adequate unity and effectiveness on the part of the Vietnamese."

But all the discussions in Washington and verbal pressure on Saigon couldn't shape affairs in Vietnam. The State Department believed that the election of a constitutional assembly was essential for domestic and international "support of our Vietnam policy." Ky, however, put this in jeopardy by announcing on May 6 that he would hold power until elections in 1967. Rusk wanted to threaten to leave Vietnam if Ky didn't give control to an assembly before then. Johnson rejected the suggestion: He told the National Security Council on May 10 that "we are committed and we will not be deterred." In other words, even if democracy were deferred in Vietnam, it was essential that we prevent a Communist takeover in Saigon.

American incapacity to shape events in Vietnam made itself clearer in mid-May, when Nugyen Cao Ky, South Vietnam's military strong man unilaterally decided to end a political crisis by forcibly repressing dissent. Rusk saw it as "intolerable" that Ky had acted "without consultation with us." The challenge now was "to pick up [the] pieces and prevent a major debacle."

Johnson was determined to carry on as before and try to persuade the Vietnamese to end their internal divisions before they lost their country to the Communists. Lodge, who was back in Washington for consultations, declared: "Damn the torpedoes! The hell with it. Even if we haven't got a government in Saigon, let's keep going." Johnson tried to put the best possible face on the difficulties. At a press conference on May 21, he defended the South Vietnamese, saying, "They are trying to build a nation. They have to do this in the teeth of Communist efforts to take the country over by force. . . . There is . . . no instant solution to any of the problems they face."

Though Ky succeeded during May and June in suppressing his political opponents, the crisis took a substantial toll on American public confidence. As Wheeler told Westmoreland, "even if we get some semblance of solidarity and common purpose among the contending factions, . . . we have lost irretrievably and for all time some of the support which until now we have received from the American people. In other words, regardless of what happens of a favorable nature, many people will never again believe that the effort and the sacrifices are worthwhile."

:: THE WAR AT HOME

The political crisis in Vietnam in the spring of 1966 intensified divisions in the United States over the war. Where about half the country believed it best to continue the current policy, 35 percent wanted to withdraw, a 15 percent increase over the previous year. The most striking feature of the polls in the midst of the political divisions in South Vietnam was American confusion and frustration. Our inability to force Hanoi to the peace table or into submission bewildered Americans. How could a country as powerful as the United States be unable to work its will on so weak and undeveloped a nation as North Vietnam?

The impulse was to blame LBJ. It seemed up to him to find a way out of the mess by either applying more power or relying on diplomacy to end the fighting. People didn't want to hear about the way in which a limited jungle war against a determined adversary operating under favorable circumstances blunted the effectiveness of U.S. power. Richard Russell reflected the national mood when he declared that it was time to "get it over or get out." By June 1966 only 41 percent of Americans approved of the job the President was doing in Vietnam, with 37 percent disapproving.

Public attitudes toward the war, in turn, bewildered Johnson. He had made sincere efforts to negotiate but the Communists would not talk. He believed it was going to take more troops, more bombs, and more enemy losses before they came to the peace table. But there was no shortcut to doing this. If he expanded the war too much—striking at targets indiscriminately in the North or invading with ground forces—it might lead to a wider war with China and/or Russia. The need was for patience and moderation. But U.S. losses in the fighting and pessimism about getting results from a policy of measured force heightened American impulses either to "declare victory and leave," as one senator counseled, or "bomb 'em back to the stone age," as an air force general advised.

The divisions and uncertainty frustrated no one in the United States more than Johnson. As he told a press conference on May 21, "the longer we are there [in Vietnam], the more sacrifices we make. The more we spend, the more discontent there will be. The more dissatisfaction there will be, the more wish and desire there will be to get out. Leading that parade is the President. If you want to feel that it troubles you 100 percent, just double that and make it 200 percent for the President."

Since Johnson believed it irresponsible to withdraw or escalate too much and since he had no magic bullet for ending the conflict quickly and in line with what he saw as U.S. interests, he renewed his efforts to educate the public and strengthen support for his policy of limited but unrelenting military pressure on Hanoi. "We are trying to provide the maximum deterrents that we can to Communist aggression with a minimum of cost," he told the press. He didn't think his "explanation will change anyone's mind," but he hoped it clarified what he was doing and what he intended to do "down the road."

Though he made light of changing anyone's mind, the President, in fact hoped that he could weaken opponents of his policy by fair means and foul. One side of him saw the need for a thoughtful, reasoned appeal to Americans to understand and support what he believed was in the best interest of the United States. Another side encouraged him to view opponents as Communists or at least sympathizers who had few qualms about undermining the well-being of the country and against whom he should pull out all stops.

In May, Johnson took his case to the country through speeches at Princeton University and at Democratic party dinners in Washington and Chicago. Speaking with "great feeling," he urged his audiences to understand that America's presence in Vietnam served no selfish gain. To the contrary, it involved the sacrifice of American lives to aid the cause of democracy and freedom. America's struggle in Vietnam was not an act of arrogance but an agony to deter aggression with limited means and for specific ends. He emphasized the need for American unity in this time of testing, for the only hope of success held by our adversaries rested on "a weakening of the fiber and the determination of the people of America."

Johnson couldn't understand how people saw him as a villain in the struggle. He sincerely believed that the war from the American side was a fight for people everywhere—not just in Vietnam—to enjoy freedom from political oppression and economic want. He was so convinced of the rectitude of fighting in Vietnam that he could only ascribe the worst motives to his antiwar opponents. On the plane to and from Princeton, for example, he spoke about "the concerted effort [in universities] to destroy the CIA." He "discussed FBI evidence of how the Communist sources stimulate propaganda lines on Vietnam."

If he had used the theme of Communist subversion in March as essentially a political weapon against antiwar opponents, by May he seemed to have convinced himself that the danger was real. The proliferation of student protests against the war, including marches, rallies, picketing, and sit-ins on university campuses, the decision of professors around the country to deny information on students to the Selective Service without the student's permission, the tactic of civil rights leaders in trying "to drive a wedge between the poor and the rest of the country" by arguing that Vietnam meant taking money from the ghettos, and a media he saw giving one-sided "nation-wide publicity" to war opponents persuaded Johnson that sinister forces were behind the push to abandon Vietnam.

Animated by his suspicions, Johnson publicly belittled and privately harassed war critics. Johnson was particularly keen on striking out against the media. Their occasional carelessness in inaccurately attributing to the "Johnson administration" a view or policy described by a junior official stirred him to complain privately. In April, when he caught the *New York Times* in such an error, he instructed Rostow to bring it to Tom Wicker's attention. Though Wicker assured him that "this was a professional error of judgment" and not an indication of "ill will on the part of the *Times*, or an effort to do a hatchet job on our administration," the President was not appeased.

He saw the television networks as even worse than the press. He believed they gladly showed pictures of atrocities by South Vietnamese or U.S. troops, but ignored a UPI story in May about the killing of twenty-seven women and children and the wounding of twenty-eight others by the Viet Cong. He pressed the networks to show pictures of this horror on the evening news, and asked the United States Information Service to distribute them in "this country." He also wanted to know why NBC undercut him by using a first-take of him speaking, in which his glasses glistened, rather than a third tape that made him look better.

Johnson was convinced that the press hated him and wanted to bring him down. Newspaper, magazine, and television reporters complained to Robert Kintner in April, as he began working at the White House, that the President was overly sensitive about what "is printed about him." The journalists believed that Johnson would "not be able to work most effectively as President because of this concern. A great many of the people talked about how they were cut off from White House offices if they disagreed with administration policy." The reporters also complained about the President's tendency to mislead them.

By early June, Moyers was reporting that "the White House Press Corps has come to believe that we antagonize them deliberately, keep them as uninformed as possible, make their personal lives as difficult as we can, play games with them, are unduly secretive, massage them when we need them and kick them when we don't and generally 'downgrade the profession.'"

If these complaints were suppose to cure Johnson of retaliatory impulses, they failed badly. In May, when he reviewed a White House guest list for a Presidential Scholars' ceremony, he approved everyone invited "except in category 17, newspapermen." He added the names of eleven journalists he considered friendly to him and deleted six he viewed as hostile. To Johnson, the war in Vietnam now had a parallel in his struggle against dissent at home.

:: THE ILLUSION OF OMNIPOTENCE

In 1952, D.W. Brogan, a British historian and commentator on American affairs, described U.S. foreign policy as suffering from the "illusion of American omnipotence": The belief "that any situation which distresses or endangers the United States can only exist because some Americans have been fools or knaves." In Vietnam, as the limits of American power in a jungle war against a determined enemy became clear, policymakers in Washington succumbed to false convictions that our real enemy was the "fools and knaves" at home who gave encouragement to Hanoi and sapped our will to fight.

Johnson, impelled by the same grandiosity and energy that encouraged him to think he could conquer poverty and build a Great Society, gave himself over to breaking the will of North Vietnam. He simply couldn't believe that they could sustain indefinitely American military punishment. Nevertheless, he also worried that further escalation might bring domestic riots, a draining war against China, and a dire confrontation with Moscow. Yet as he moved toward a greater emphasis on military actions in the air and on the ground, he worried whether he was doing the right thing. Was he now taking steps that would finally bring the war to a close or was he rushing headlong toward some disaster?

His first order of business in June was to decide on an escalation of the air war. He and his advisers had been talking about this since early in the year. Though there was no persuasive evidence to show that more bombing would compel Hanoi to negotiate, Johnson and his advisers convinced themselves that attacks on petroleum, oil, and lubrication (POL) facilities and transportation lines would disrupt North Vietnam's communications system and reduce its capacity to move men and supplies South.

Assurances from military chiefs in late June that he was on a proper course cinched his decision to expand the bombing. On the 21st, he received a report from Paris that Vietnamese Communists in France had begun to doubt the likelihood of a Viet Cong victory and would sue for peace after one last try at weakening U.S. morale. "Here is some more noise indicating a wobbling mood in Hanoi," Rostow wrote the President. "It also reinforces our instinct that they are waiting to assess our political strength, as well as the outcome of the rainy season operations." Four days later, Rostow told Johnson, "Mr. President, you can smell it all over: Hanoi's operation, backed by the Chi[nese] Com[munist]s, is no longer being regarded as the wave of the future out there. U.S. power is beginning to be felt. We're not in; but we're moving."

"Good," Johnson wrote on the bottom of the memo, "See me." On June 29 U.S. air forces began bombing POL targets. The day before Johnson had asked McNamara to accelerate the movement of U.S. ground troops to Vietnam "so that General Westmoreland can feel assured that he has all the men he needs as soon as possible."

The expanded bombing was partly aimed at Americans who hoped that it might force Hanoi to negotiate. On June 4, Johnson gave Rusk the bad news that "those approving my conduct of the presidency have fallen to 46%. Those who believe it was a mistake to send troops to fight in Vietnam have risen from 25% in March to 36%. Only 49% now believe it was not a mistake." The mounting criticism in the country that the administration was not "properly or comprehensively explaining our plans," especially for Vietnam, also troubled Johnson. "We may not agree with the criticism," he told the Cabinet in mid-June, "but it does exist." Moreover, by the end of the month, only 40 percent of the country approved of the President's "handling" of Vietnam, with 42 percent disapproving.

Johnson was now so apprehensive about facing hostile audiences during domestic appearances that he asked the FBI to "send 'an advance man' along with Secret Service to survey the situation" in Des Moines, Iowa, and Omaha, Nebraska, where he was slated to speak. He "wanted the FBI's opinion as to whether or not it would be safe for him to go."

The best answer Johnson saw to the growing opposition was not only to increase military pressure on Hanoi but also to lobby Americans to "get with the program" or back their President and the "boys" in the field.

During June, memos flew back and forth at the White House on how to orchestrate this latest campaign for the country's hearts and minds. Bob Kintner took the lead on how to make the President more appealing to the "people" and more persuasive on Vietnam. But most everyone on Johnson's staff got into the act. Kintner urged him to hold "informal" discussions with the press; Rostow suggested a speech at Notre Dame University on reconciliation. "It would be, in effect, your Gettysburg Address of the Cold War."

Johnson himself wanted to leak supporting data to a friendly columnist, and directed Califano to work with the National Security staff in preparing a brief defending the administration's "credibility" on Vietnam. Larry O'Brien suggested a meeting with nine House members with outstanding war records who, after visiting Vietnam, would give the President "a solid report in full support of you." Komer wanted Lodge to take "a more active role in 'guiding' the Saigon press corps on what's really going on out there. It's the Saigon datelines that cause most of the trouble," he told LBJ. Most of all, Johnson wanted critics to understand that dissent and division were hurting the war effort and needed to be curbed. After Kenneth Galbraith gave a critical commencement speech on Vietnam, LBJ answered him in a letter: "And did I misread your admonition to quit talking about Viet Nam and discuss the gains of the Great Society?" he asked. "Then why don't *we?*"

The expanded bombing produced expected results only in its impact on U.S. public opinion. During the first half of July, as Americans learned about the stepped-up air war, their hopes for a quick end to the fighting soared and their support of the President's Vietnam policy jumped 12 points from 42 percent to 54 percent. Eighty-six percent of the country believed the bombing would "get it over with" in Vietnam "fairly soon, either by military victory or by negotiations."

Hopes for an end to the conflict were quickly disappointed. Two months after the POL strikes began, military planners described the bombing as having no significant impact on Hanoi's economy, will to fight, or capacity to move men and supplies to the South. An analysis of the fighting by the U.S. mission in Saigon in mid-July painted a bleak picture: It concluded that a *"decisive military victory for either side is not likely."* On August 8, the *New York Times* reported that a Pentagon study predicted it would take eight years to win the war unless U.S. forces were increased to 750,000, and then it would take five.

Johnson refused to concede these realities. To be sure, he kept saying that no one should assume that the conflict will end soon, but he held to the conviction that American power was hurting Hanoi and that we were moving forward. On July 11, he met with fourteen congressmen who had come directly to the White House after a trip to Vietnam. Their report from the fighting front was everything Johnson wished to hear: We were winning, and it was the "Peaceniks" in the House and the Senate who "caused the Viet Cong to fight harder and gave them cause to hold out."

A week later, when he met with congressional leaders, Johnson reported that "Viet Cong morale had been lowered by U.S. successes. The Viet Cong are recruiting teenagers 12 to 16. There have been reductions in food rations in each unit. U.S. forces have broken their transportation system.

The Viet Cong have lost popular support. The Viet Cong exploit dissension in the United States." He had some hope that the war might be over by June 1967.

In public Johnson was as upbeat and optimistic. At a press conference on July 20 he pointed to an improved economy, steps toward an orderly democratic election, and ten-fold enemy losses compared with America's in South Vietnam. "We have ceased speculating a long time ago on how long this situation would endure," he declared. "But I have said to you and to the American people time and again, and I repeat it today, that we shall persist."

Johnson's pronouncements were more the product of wishful thinking than realistic assessments. By saying repeatedly that we were making progress in Vietnam and that we would not give in to aggression, it seemed to make it so. In July he instructed all Cabinet members to talk to congressmen and senators, to public groups, and to appear on television in behalf of our Vietnam policy. "We need this widespread explanation not only so that the public may be informed but so we may obtain a more united public support of our efforts."

The President seemed to think that if he and his aides spoke long enough and loud enough about Vietnam, he could bend the American public and the North Vietnamese to his will. Because so much of what he hoped for in the war was at variance with the realities of the conflict, his expressions of faith, which rested on sincere convictions about what the U.S. military could achieve in Vietnam, made him seem devious.

Time-Life journalist Robert Sherrod described Johnson's problems with the war in a memo of a confidential conversation with the President on August 1. Johnson gave Sherrod forty minutes. Seated in a rocker, the President "squirmed and scrunched as he talked, and wound up his legs and torso, corkscrew fashion." In reply to Sherrod's question about how the war was going, Johnson replied: "'It looks pretty good, improving all the time, but we've got a long way to go. We clean up these villages, we fill in the tunnels, we feed the people, we doctor them, we rebuild their houses and dig them wells. We start teaching them.' He leaned forward in his rocker, pulled up his pant leg, pulled down his sock and scratched his bare leg, and said, "But there are 14,000 of these villages and we've taken care of maybe a hundred of them. . . . A long way to go."

When Sherrod asked what the President thought of a prediction from "military sources" that it would take 700,000 men to win the war, Johnson bristled: "'Nobody mentioned that figure to me, I haven't heard it before.' He paused for a few minutes. 'Whether it takes 700,000 or a million, we are going to do the job. . . .' He said this with that unfortunate smirk that betrays him so badly on television—a sort of gloating smile that comes out as something he doesn't intend at all. Throughout the interview Johnson was almost belligerently defensive."

:: NEGOTIATIONS AND PACIFICATION

During the summer and fall, Johnson heard continuing predictions of Communist faltering and growing eagerness for peace. Lodge was confident that the war was now moving in the right direction and that Hanoi saw itself as unable to win. The Viet Cong were also showing "a progressive decline in morale and fighting capacity." There is "a smell of victory" in the air, Lodge cabled the President on August 10. "We are not losing; we cannot lose in the normal sense of the word; never have things been going so well."

Despite the good news, abundant evidence of a likely stalemate in Vietnam prodded Johnson to remain alert to any signs of Hanoi's interest in talks. Though nothing seemed in the offing, it allowed him to answer critics that he was eager to negotiate. He was under constant pressure to begin talking. Journalists, academics, members of Congress, protestors, and foreign leaders continually urged the White House to start discussions.

Johnson took pains to let the world know that the Communists, not the American government, blocked the path to a settlement. "I am ready to go anywhere, anytime," he told congressmen and senators. "Mr. Rusk will be there tomorrow morning to talk instead of fight, and to reason the thing out. We are willing to go . . . but it takes two to make a contract."

But trying to find an end to the war was not simply a case of public relations. Johnson was eager to throw off the burden of Vietnam as quickly as possible, though, of course, only on acceptable terms. "It's like a prizefight," he said in July 1965. "Our right is our military power, but our left must be our peace proposals. Every time you move troops forward, you move diplomats forward."

Johnson didn't want for peace initiatives. Not a month went by in 1966 without some new proposal for discussions. United Nations, African, and Asian leaders urged talks and offered to mediate differences.

But the gap between the two sides was unbridgeable. Hanoi insisted that the United States stop bombing, withdraw its forces, and include the Viet Cong in peace talks; Washington demanded that North Vietnam reciprocate a bombing halt with a cessation of infiltration. Despite the impasse, Johnson accepted the need for continuing efforts to begin negotiations. In the summer of 1966, the White House kept close track of every initiative and made "preparations for a 'cessation of hostilities.'"

Johnson was serious about finding some basis for negotiations. At the beginning of August, for example, when he heard that a South Vietnamese official had "talked to Lodge about possible contacts with VC," the President instructed Lodge "to encourage SVN to begin to see what contacts [they] can make covertly with VC." Johnson wanted Ky, who at a July 27 press conference had called for an invasion of North Vietnam, to quit sounding off about going North and instead "launch [a] peace campaign."

Johnson hoped that "pacification" in South Vietnam might be an alternative to peace talks. If programs of "revolutionary development" could improve living standards in the countryside and tie rural villages to Saigon, the Communists would lose their base of support and be compelled to fade away or reach a settlement with the South Vietnamese government.

But hopes for pacification generated at the various meetings were not being realized. In June the President pressed Westmoreland to get behind the effort. "I've put the best man on my own staff to work on getting the civil side rolling." After a trip to Vietnam in June, Komer told the President that our "other war" did not yet match our military effort. He was more candid with another official, whom he told that pacification was a "mess" and "farcical" compared with military actions.

The stumbling pacification efforts added to Johnson's frustration over Vietnam. It was clear to him that U.S. forces were not losing in Vietnam, but it was also evident that negotiations to end the fighting were nowhere in sight. He felt trapped and besieged by an increasingly unpopular war. Speeches in the U.N. attacking American policy, coordinated nationwide antiwar demonstrations, and threats to his personal safety during public appearances disturbed him. Yet however much he wished to throw off the burden, he believed it wrong to let go, back away, or abandon the cause: It would be a betrayal of America's national self-interest, of the fighting men who had lost their lives and the hundreds of thousands more now at risk.

:: THE SEARCH FOR A WINNING STRATEGY

But figuring out how to win the war seemed increasingly difficult. Should he increase the military pressure on Hanoi? Should he gamble that pacification or revolutionary development would overcome the Viet Cong? Should he try a bombing pause to stimulate negotiations? Everyone he spoke to had opinions on these issues, but who was right? "During the past ten days I have heard a hundred diagnoses of our problems and about as many prescriptions for solving them," Harry McPherson told LBJ in December. Johnson had limited confidence in the calculations put before him by the military chiefs or the CIA or his own National Security advisers.

His only certainty now was that he had to see the job through. In an emotional speech to U.S. servicemen in October during a visit to Vietnam, he had pledged to "never let you down, nor your fighting comrades, nor the 15 million people of Vietnam, nor the hundreds of millions of Asians who are counting on us to show here — here in Vietnam — that aggression doesn't pay, and that aggression can't succeed." He urged the troops, in an injunction that later subjected him to much ridicule, to "nail that coonskin to the wall." He said of his visit to the troops: "I have never been more moved by any group I have ever talked to, never in my life."

He was impatient to get on with the struggle. Johnson knew that the longer the war went on the more difficult it would become to sustain domestic support, whatever faith he or anyone else might have in the country's "will to persist." At the end of November, Missouri Senator Stuart Symington told Rostow that "you and I have been hawks since 1961. I am thinking of getting off the train soon. . . . We are getting in deeper and deeper with no end in sight. In 1968 Nixon will murder us. He will become the biggest dove of all times. There never has been a man in American public life that could turn so fast on a dime." The President replied: "I know at least one more fellow who can turn faster on a dime than Nixon. Guess who!"

A Gallup poll at the beginning of December illustrated the limits of Johnson's support. His overall approval rating had fallen back to 48 percent; on Vietnam, it was down again to 43 percent, with 40 percent disapproving. "It is going to be hard work in the months ahead to hold the Congress and the country together," LBJ told Rostow on December 9.

In mid-October, after returning from a trip to Vietnam, McNamara had put an eight-page memo before the President proposing a solution to his dilemma. He saw "no reasonable way to bring the war to an end soon." Despite some improvement in the military situation, the Communists were not about to crack. They had "adopted a strategy of keeping us busy and waiting us out (a strategy of attriting our national will)." Pacification was "a bad disappointment." So was the air campaign, which had neither "significantly affected infiltration [n]or cracked the morale of Hanoi."

McNamara recommended that we "continue to press the enemy militarily; . . . make demonstrable progress in pacification"; and "add a new ingredient forced on us by the facts." He urged a "military posture that we credibly would maintain indefinitely — a posture that makes trying to 'wait us out' less attractive." He suggested adding 70,000 troops in 1967 to the

400,000 already committed and holding at that level. It would be ample to "punish the enemy" and keep him "from interrupting pacification." It would remove "the specter of apparently endless escalation of U.S. deployments."

He also urged the construction of an infiltration barrier near the 17th parallel running from the South China Sea across the neck of Vietnam and the trails in Laos. He recommended stabilizing the air attacks with no increases in the level of bombing or changes in the areas or kinds of targets being struck. A vigorous pacification program principally involving the South Vietnamese was crucial to persuading the enemy "to negotiate or withdraw." Finally, we needed to make our negotiating efforts more credible by promising to withdraw from Vietnam at the end of the fighting, quietly trying another bombing pause, and developing a realistic plan for including the Viet Cong in the negotiations and a postwar government.

Military and civilian advisers disputed much of what McNamara recommended. They saw a need for between 530,000 and 750,000 troops, more bombing of old and new targets, and an expanded pacification effort under U.S. military control. Rostow urged the need "now to lean more heavily on the North." He had reviewed all the bombing reports and concluded that Hanoi and Moscow and the Eastern European countries as well were paying a significant military and economic cost for the air war. They didn't like it and "that increased burden may add to their interest in a negotiated settlement."

Likewise, a CIA report challenged McNamara's conclusions about bombing and pacification, arguing that attacks on Haiphong and rail lines to China could have an impact on Hanoi and that pacification was doing better than the Defense Secretary believed and seemed likely to do even better in the next two years.

The President agreed to most of what McNamara recommended. On November 11 he committed himself to stabilizing troop deployments to South Vietnam and bombing in the North. He endorsed McNamara's view that pacification was "critical to the success of our effort in South Vietnam," and he agreed to press the case for negotiations by appointing Nicholas Katzenbach, who had become Under Secretary of State, Komer, Rostow, Vance, and a "good military man" to a committee that was to "meet three times a week on Vietnam and all its dimensions."

But Johnson found it difficult to stick to McNamara's formula. He was especially ambivalent about inhibiting the use of air power. The reports from the Joint Chiefs and CIA saying that bombing was achieving more than McNamara believed and that it was a U.S. trump card in forcing Hanoi to the peace table made the President reluctant to veto more aggressive air action. On October 15, he had told McNamara and Wheeler that he would hold to the limitations in place on bombing around Hanoi and Haiphong, but would agree to striking new targets.

Johnson's willingness to broaden the air war reflected a larger conviction that there was some progress in the fighting and that 1967 could be a decisive year in compelling the Communists to begin peace talks. "By early 1967 most of my advisers and I felt confident that the tide of war was moving strongly in favor of the South Vietnamese and their allies and against the Communists," he later wrote in his memoirs. In December 1966, however, he was less certain than this. McNamara's assessment alone was enough to make him harbor substantial doubts about what the coming year would bring. But given his determination to stay the course, he welcomed every scintilla of good news and expression of optimism.

And most of his advisers who, like him, felt compelled to see the bright side, to believe that somehow or other American power had to prevail over so weak an enemy, gave him words of constant encouragement about the likely outcome in Vietnam. *"You* are still dead right on all the big issues & you still know more about how to make them come out right than any man in America," Mac Bundy told him in November. "For the first time since 1961 the U.S. military in Saigon and Washington estimate a net decline in VC/NVN forces in South Viet Nam," Rostow wrote him two days later.

Rostow and Komer sent him a series of papers in December laying out strategic guidelines for 1967. They brimmed with optimism. Despite "the immensity of the task," Komer was "convinced that if we can jack up our management in Washington and especially Saigon, and press the GVN a lot harder than we have, we'll be able to see daylight by the end of 1967." Besides, Komer asked, "Do we have a better option?" He knew his "recipe does not guarantee success but . . . does anyone have a better one?" Johnson thought not. When Rostow told him that Komer's 1967 plan for Vietnam made "a good start," the President replied: "I agree — it's good."

In the context of so much optimism, Johnson believed it essential to maintain pressure on Hanoi. In November, he agreed to attacks on new targets around Hanoi. Having largely committed himself to McNamara's strategy of restraint, he felt compelled to give military chiefs, who were pressing for more aggressive action, the freedom to step up the air war.

Secret talks in Saigon, Hanoi, and Warsaw, Poland, about negotiations gave Johnson little reason to inhibit his military. On November 11, a cable from Warsaw indicated that Hanoi would not bend on its demands for an unconditional halt to American bombing, a withdrawal of allied forces from South Vietnam, and a place for the National Liberation Front at the peace table. Six days later, Rostow told the President: "It is certain that the men in Hanoi have not yet decided that their best option is to negotiate." Rostow also thought it may "be important to communicate to them soon that we do not intend to let the war drag on; that we plan to up the ante; and our present offers to them may not hold indefinitely."

At the same time, the State Department sent word to Hanoi through a Polish diplomat that the United States would stop bombing unconditionally if North Vietnam would agree soon after to take mutual steps of deescalation. The diplomat reported that the North Vietnamese had now agreed to secret discussions in early December in Warsaw. On December 2, Rostow told Johnson that Rusk saw this message as "of importance," and Rostow himself believed that an emphasis on secrecy and speed voiced by Hanoi made the initiative, code named MARIGOLD, seem genuine.

The same day that word reached Washington of North Vietnamese interest in talks, American planes, under the President's authorization of additional bombing targets, struck military installations around Hanoi, the first attacks near the city since the POL raids in June. On December 4, U.S. planes hit the North Vietnamese capital again. More attacks were scheduled for mid-December, but McNamara, Katzenbach, and Lodge urged Johnson to hold off until they could see if MARIGOLD was leading anywhere.

But the President believed that Hanoi might see this as a sign of weakness. Besides, he was just then rejecting a Joint Chiefs demand for stronger air action, and scheduled attacks on Hanoi was a concession to military brass convinced that the White House was being too timid in fighting the war. "The President considered the problem of next steps in hitting targets in North Vietnam," Rostow summarized a meeting of December 9. "Broadly speaking, the decision was made to carry forward with what was necessary but at this particular moment not to expand our targeting." On December 13 and 14 U.S. planes staged even larger raids against Hanoi.

The attacks now seemed to kill off the talks. There is good reason to think that Hanoi was not serious about these discussions anyway. But currently there is no way of knowing exactly what the North Vietnamese intended. It is certain, though, that the Johnson administration took a public relations beating over the bombing. During the last week in December, Harrison E. Salisbury, assistant managing editor of the *New York Times*, began publishing a series of articles on the air raids, asserting, in contradiction of Pentagon assertions, that the attacks had killed civilians. The reports embarrassed the White House and further called into question the credibility of the American government.

As 1966 came to a close, Johnson's frustration with trying to defeat the Communists in Vietnam, hold the economy together, sustain Great Society programs, and position himself and the Democrats for another successful election campaign in 1968 became almost more than he could bear. He was livid at Salisbury and the press for challenging him over Vietnam. Moyers told James Reston that the President wouldn't allow him to raise any questions about the bombing. All the press wanted to talk about, Johnson complained, was "Veetnam, Veetnam, Veetnam, Veetnam." But it was constantly on his mind as well. Whenever he found himself with the President, Admiral Thomas Moorer, Chief of Naval operations, remembered, "you always discussed Vietnam, no matter where you were."

And one result was that Great Society programs were "falling far short of the contributions they could make. . . . This is a problem," one White House aide asserted, "that can be solved only by the more direct exercise of presidential authority, direction, and muscle."

Democratic governors meeting in West Virginia in December vented their anger at the President for neglecting them, administration programs, and domestic politics. It incensed Johnson, who in "heated" remarks to them during a meeting at his ranch "said that he resented very deeply the remarks by the governors, publicly at the Greenbrier, and personally to him at the Ranch." He described it as "unfair to say because of my image, my popularity — that this caused us to lose these [congressional seats]. I do not like to hear this.""A pall seemed to have settled over the nation as a result of Johnson's continued escalation of the war in Vietnam," a White House chronology of events noted for December 31, 1966. It was a prelude for worse to come.

11 :: A SEA OF TROUBLES

By the beginning of 1967, the dissent over Vietnam, urban riots, political reverses, and doubts about administration programs to elevate poor folks into the middle class and transform America into a Great Society made Johnson wonder why he had ever wanted to be President. In the winter of 1966–67, even before a host of new difficulties appeared, he found himself defending his administration from attacks by friends and foes alike. Governor Warren Hearnes of Missouri told Johnson that if he were running in his state now he would lose by 100,000 votes, despite a half-million margin in 1964.

However much the criticism hurt and agitated him, he refused to show his true feelings in public. He put the best possible face on everything. The economy was a case in point. During the first half of the 1960s an amazing 96 percent of Americans believed that their standard of living would improve. In January 1967, when Johnson told the country that wages were the highest in history, unemployment was at a thirteen-year low, and corporate profits and farm incomes were greater than ever, Americans nodded in agreement. True, a 4.5 percent jump in consumer prices over the previous eighteen months and an "excessive rise" in interest rates were disturbing elements in the national economic picture. But, the President reassured the country, "as 1966 ended, price stability was seemingly being restored," while interest rates were retreating from their earlier peaks.

Johnson knew, however, that his public rhetoric masked potential budget deficits. Additional defense outlays and cost-of-living increases might lead to a recession and political defeat in 1968. But no one in the administration was sure. Their watchwords on the economy in early 1967 were: "Where are we headed?"

Mixed advice and confusing statistics were the answers given Johnson. The economic reports between February and April gave mixed signals. Wholesale prices jumped 0.3 percent in January, the first increase in four months. But the Consumer Price Index told a different story, increasing only a scant 0.1 percent in February, marking four straight months in which it had shown little change. Further, the gross national product in the first quarter was surprisingly weak, its poorest performance since the 1960 recession.

The uncertainty frustrated and agitated Johnson. He complained that trying to manage fiscal policy in current circumstances was like driving a car with the gas pedal tied down.

But his greatest complaint was against Congress, which showed little sympathy for his dilemma and, worse, used the uncertainty to beat up on him. Republicans and Democrats alike seized upon the President's problems to score political points. Congressmen and governors lobbied against spending cuts affecting their constituents, but endorsed reductions and limited government in principle.

The uncertainties, when added to frustration over Vietnam, kept Johnson's approval ratings below 50 percent. A late January survey showed that "strong approval" of the President's leadership had fallen from 23 percent in September 1966 to 16 percent in January 1967. A February poll on a tax increase and spending cuts placed the public on the anti-Johnson side. Only 24 percent favored a surcharge, with 65 percent opposed. If something was needed to hold down inflation, 75 percent of the public preferred less spending. In March and April, 45 percent of Americans approved of Johnson's overall job rating and 42 percent disapproved. The results were decidedly worse on Vietnam, with only 37 percent approving and 49 percent disapproving—an all-time low.

Though Johnson was unhappy about the downturn in his political fortunes, he believed that he could make a quick comeback if he held to a consistent line about the economy and Vietnam. His strategy now was to go back to basics—to do what he saw as right for the country without focusing on the personal political results. Moreover, he refused to be anything but optimistic. The nation's economic growth had raised six million people above the poverty line, education was receiving $12 billion a year compared with $3 billion a few years ago, and his administration had produced a health care "revolution." If he was "so unpopular, why have I been so successful in winning so many elections?" he asked *Time*'s Hugh Sidey. And why did people accept him with open arms in so many places he went?

Johnson's bravado hid a self-serving conviction that his rhetoric would serve his public standing, as indeed it did. His greater consistency on the economy and declarations of selfless politics helped improve his poll numbers in the spring. A May survey showed a rise in his approval rating to 48 percent, with his disapproval index falling to 37 percent.

But the uptick was short-lived. Developments in the summer shook public confidence in the administration's ability to stabilize the economy. Ironically, it was not a business slowdown and growing joblessness that undermined Johnson's credibility as a promoter of prosperity. Quite the opposite: the economy boomed between June and October—a solid 2.5 percent increase in gross national product and a decline in unemployment to 3.9 percent in the second quarter became a "whopping" 4.5 percent GNP expansion and 3.8 percent joblessness in the July to October period.

The problem now was inflation and a potential runaway budget shortfall. Consumer prices jumped one point between June and August. At the same time, the federal budget deficit was threatening to reach $29 billion for the 1968 fiscal year that had begun on July 1, 1967. Higher spending and a drop in anticipated revenues accounted for the unwelcome budget run-up.

In August, Johnson felt compelled publicly to describe the current economic problem facing the country and the austerity measures needed to solve it. He promised restraints on federal spending wherever possible, but the costs of Vietnam and mandated civilian programs limited what he could do. The only remedy he saw were temporary surcharges on corporate and personal income taxes of 10 percent beginning July 1 and October 1, 1967, respectively. They would expire on June 30, 1969, "or continue for so long as the unusual expenditures associated with our efforts in Vietnam require higher revenues."

Congress and most people in the country were not persuaded. Wilbur Mills believed that a tax hike might precipitate rather than head off a recession, and he thought the Congress would reject Johnson's recommendation. Senator Russell Long also disputed the need for additional taxes, but was pleased to leave the issue to the House, where money bills had to originate. Businessmen and congressmen who showed some sympathy for Johnson's recommendation hedged their support with demands for "much larger" cuts in nondefense spending than LBJ wanted.

Despite a campaign of public education, the President made little headway in convincing either reluctant House members or the mass of Americans that he was right. By September, the dispute over taxes and the future of the economy had contributed to a renewed downturn in Johnson's standing that left him "brooding" and snappish. In August and September his approval ratings fell to new lows of 39 and 40 percent, with disapproval numbers reaching highs of 47 and 48 percent.

:: FAREWELL TO REFORM

It is a given of U.S. history that war kills reform. Populism could not out-
live the Spanish-American clash; progressivism largely succumbed to
World War I; "Dr. New Deal" gave way to "Dr. Win-the-War," in FDR's
memorable phrase; Korea overwhelmed Truman's Fair Deal; and Vietnam
largely stalled the War on Poverty and blocked Johnson's reach for the
Great Society. The country had never had the psychological and fiscal
wherewithal to back reform and war at the same time.

Johnson didn't need a war to limit his reform plans. As he understood,
there was plenty of hostility to his social engineering from conservatives
convinced that traditional laissez-faire—not government-sponsored
efforts—was the best means to national prosperity and wider distribution of
wealth. Even without Vietnam, LBJ and other reformers believed that their
hold on the popular imagination would be fleeting.

But whether ideologically or pragmatically inspired, attacks on administration reforms impressed Johnson as the predictable outgrowth of a public shift back to traditional verities about the limited role of government,
especially federal authority, in the country's life. Once the war took center
stage in his administration, however, he saw it as largely hopeless to expect
much domestic advance. To be sure, he spoke repeatedly of the country's
capacity to fight a war and change its domestic life, but this was essentially
"window dressing" or "brave words," Gardner Ackley says, that masked
Johnson's conviction that he had to cut reform programs to the bone.

As in 1966, Johnson had no intention of acknowledging that he saw distinct limits to what we could spend on domestic reform or how far they
could carry us toward a better world. To concede such limits would be to
accept Richard Nixon's description of the poverty war as a "cruel hoax."
Accepting this proposition, Johnson said, would have meant turning "the
American dream into a nightmare."

Johnson's strategy was to pump as hard as ever for antipoverty and Great
Society programs. He still believed that strong expressions of support would
have the advantage of holding at bay conservatives eager to scrap the whole
thing and primarily devote national resources to fighting in Vietnam. Pressing the case for domestic reforms would also have the advantage of keeping most liberals on his side, or at least enough in his camp to give him
some prospect of running successfully again in 1968.

But speaking out for domestic advance wasn't simply good politics. It
was also Johnson's way of keeping reformers engaged and social programs
going until the war ended and opened the way to a fresh surge of activism.

Johnson's rhetoric in 1966–67 far outran his substantive support of the great domestic changes he still envisioned. As a keen student of American government and public affairs, Johnson understood that rhetoric and gestures or symbols carried significant consequences. Hence, whatever the realities —and they were increasingly at odds with the words and deeds of his administration—Johnson wanted no letup in the call to fulfill the promise of American life.

In public and private, the year 1967 was as much a summons to domestic advance as the preceding three years. His January State of the Union address was a new call to action: Reciting the litany of achievements, he declared the moment ripe for renewed commitments to improving the quality of life and enlarging the meaning of justice for all. Specific recommendations followed Johnson's general appeal. In the course of the year he called for: A renewed attack on Appalachian poverty; a 20 percent increase in Social Security payments, wider availability of Medicare, and an end to age discrimination in hiring; expanded Head Start programs; a new national policy against housing discrimination; consumer protections against hidden lending costs, unsound investments, and unsafe products; more and better housing, especially for the poor; more effective community action, expanded legal services, and a wider attack on inner city blight, including a rat extermination program; and an air quality act.

Behind the scenes, Johnson was as aggressive as ever in pumping for his programs. At a Cabinet meeting in January, Johnson challenged his department chiefs to do their best for new antipoverty and Great Society measures. "It's all up to you—so get going, write your messages, make your contacts, explain your programs, and get the votes. There is nothing more important you have to do."

No one tracing Johnson's lobbying efforts would see them as anything but commitments to more reform laws and bigger programs. In May, LBJ told business leaders that antipoverty programs were "much misunderstood"; they were neither "handouts" nor "impractical giveaways" but essential measures for turning tax eaters into tax payers.

In August, he complained to news commentators about congressional foot-dragging on urban programs needed to prevent riots. In September, he told newspaper publishers that $6.8 billion in pending urban programs represented "the most comprehensive package on cities ever presented to Congress."

Much of what Johnson did in behalf of domestic advance, however, masked a less ambitious agenda—a commitment to reform programs that could fit into a war economy and would more or less stay in place until an end to the fighting freed resources for a renewed crusade against domestic evils.

Johnson was usually less direct about his intentions. In the summer of 1967, for example, the President's task force on education recommended stepped-up efforts to help poor urban and rural students. Johnson feared that the report might create pressures for greater spending. Normally, he wanted task force recommendations held in strict confidence until he decided their fate. Premature leaks would alert opponents to administration thinking and help them prepare the ground for effective counter action. On this occasion, however, Johnson instructed Califano to leak the report without any clue that the story had come from the White House. After the *New York Times* published a front-page article, Johnson gave Douglass Cater a tongue-lashing for the leak, which reduced him "almost to trembling."

Johnson's action mystified Cater, who learned of the leak from Califano. Johnson's deviousness served two purposes. The story allowed him to scrap the recommendations and blame the failed hopes for more education spending on Cater and liberals, or those who would complain most loudly about cutbacks in education programs. He was not proud of what he had done. When Califano showed the *Times* story to the President, asking if he had seen it, Johnson "grunted yes, and never mentioned it again to me, or Cater, or anyone else."

Johnson also reined in liberal impulses to respond aggressively to urban riots and the "crisis in the cities." In July, after Newark and Detroit exploded over rumors of police brutality against inner-city blacks, Johnson asked Humphrey to chair a Cabinet working group on the crisis.

He made clear to Humphrey that proposed remedies should not include new legislation or new funding. But Humphrey, who saw the riots as a demonstration of "widespread rejection of our social system," urged the President to announce his determination to avoid cuts in existing programs affecting the cities. Moreover, despite the President's admonitions, the Vice President asked the secretaries of labor and commerce to work on a major new job program that, Califano warned Johnson, would entail "significant spending." Califano recommended that the President follow Budget Director Schultze's suggestion that they "tactfully disband the Vice President's group." After Humphrey issued a final report on August 23, Johnson put his committee "on ice."

Johnson wished to mute the fact that current budgets neither matched past gains nor even kept funding abreast of inflation. But he couldn't hide the fact that Vietnam spending now made him an ally of domestic budget-cutters in Congress. In May, for example, when Henry H. Wilson, Jr., a principal White House congressional liaison, tried to inform Johnson that the House was reducing model cities money to $12 million for planning and was deleting all funds for rent supplements, the President wouldn't take his call. It was a far cry from Johnson's involvement of just two years before.

In August, as the reality of a potential $30 billion deficit and no tax increase became a distinct possibility, Johnson's budget office laid plans to cut "heavily into Space, HEW, Agriculture, HUD, and OEO." In November, when Johnson accepted the need for across-the-board cuts of 2 percent in personnel and 10 percent in controllable domestic programs, Califano warned that Cabinet officials "will take cuts of this nature . . . very hard." But with no tax increase and ever more spending on Vietnam on tap, Johnson saw no escape from "substantial cuts in Great Society programs."

:: CRIME AND POLITICS

Nothing signaled the waning of liberal influence and freedom to carry forward the reform agenda of 1964–65 more clearly than the emergence of crime as a major domestic issue in 1966. By March Johnson had felt compelled to send Congress a special message on the rise in murders, rapes, aggravated assaults, robberies, burglaries, and car thefts that had sparked an epidemic of fear in the nation and was costing the country some $27 billion a year. A law enforcement assistance act in 1965 had established a federal program to help local police agencies combat crime. But it was time now, Johnson said, for a coordinated campaign by local, state, and Federal authorities to reverse the trend and strike at the roots of the problem. Though Johnson's call to action produced four minor bills, they did little to satisfy the national desire for substantive and symbolic responses to the country's growing lawlessness.

Johnson's administration was seen as more the cause than the solution to the problem. Crime increased six times faster than population during the Kennedy-Johnson presidencies, Richard Nixon asserted in 1966. In the sixties, Supreme Court decisions widening the legal definition of obscenity, barring required prayer in schools, guaranteeing accused lawbreakers a right to an attorney, and compelling police to inform criminal suspects of their rights provoked complaints that liberal justices were more intent on protecting criminals than victims and were subverting the American way of life. "They've put the Negroes in the schools," an Alabama congressman complained, "and now they've driven God out." "Impeach Earl Warren" became a rallying cry of American conservatives.

Though the Court's decisions were not Johnson's responsibility, the country, especially after the Fortas appointment, identified the President with the Court's "bleeding heart" liberalism. Inner-city riots in 1965–66, which many saw as a result of indulgent policies toward blacks, added to the feeling that Johnson's liberal excesses had undermined traditional restraints and given license to criminal behavior.

By the beginning of 1967 Johnson felt compelled to identify himself with an anticrime crusade. Whatever its merits as social policy, it was essential politics. In January, Johnson asked Congress to pass a Safe Streets and Crime Control Act. Quoting Lincoln, Johnson asked that "'reverence for the law . . . become the political religion of the Nation.'"

Perhaps the most surprising part of Johnson's anticrime message was a recommendation that the Congress enact a Right of Privacy Act, which outlawed all public and private wiretapping. The only exceptions were to be for the sake of national security—"and then only under the strictest safe-guards."

The record of Johnson's presidency hardly suggests a man who was fastidious about constitutional guarantees of privacy or excessive government intrusion into private conversations and behavior. During his five-plus years in office Johnson secretly recorded over 10,000 conversations without the knowledge of other parties on the telephone or in his White House offices. Moreover, he had little hesitation about using the FBI to make secret recordings of actual and potential political opponents during the 1964 Democratic Convention; about planting bugs in embassies and private residences to monitor Nixon campaign activities in 1968; or about reading FBI and foreign intelligence reports obtained by electronic means.

Yet at the same time, his memos and private conversations on tapping and bugging bristle with indignation about such information-gathering. In February 1966, for example, when Califano asked Johnson's preference on wiretap legislation, he favored "a *complete ban* on all taps, even in national security cases." He also wanted a law banning "the use of non-telephone electronic 'bugging' devices." In May, when IRS Commissioner Sheldon Cohen justified his agency's use of eavesdropping and wiretapping, Johnson emphatically told him: "Sheldon—stop it all at once—and this is final—no microphones—taps or any other hidden devices, legal or illegal if you are going to work for me." Johnson disliked the idea of anyone having the kind of control over political leaders Hoover and the FBI obtained through secret listening devices. But he also saw this technology as a political reality to which he accommodated himself. He rationalized his tappings and FBI tappings and bugs as necessary evils in the political and national security wars that he assumed were an inescapable part of contemporary public life.

During 1967 anticrime declarations aimed more to advance the political fortunes of the White House and the Republicans than to offer realistic plans for reducing lawlessness. Despite much rhetoric from the White House and congressional leaders on both sides of the aisle, no significant legislation on crime control reached Johnson's desk. At the end of the year, Safe Streets, as the failed crime bill was called, and gun control topped Johnson's list of unfinished congressional business.

:: NEWARK AND DETROIT: A NATION DIVIDED AGAINST ITSELF

The lawlessness troubling the public and undermining confidence in the Johnson administration consisted of not only crimes against individuals but also inner-city riots that by 1967 had become an annual summer event. Johnson was convinced that inner-city poverty and despair were the principal ingredients behind the summer upheavals. In private and public, he made repeated references to the comparative deprivation afflicting African Americans. Where 7.8 percent of white families lived below the poverty line, 29.1 percent of black households were impoverished. Eighteen percent of white families occupied substandard housing, while almost 50 percent of nonwhites were trapped in such dwellings. Despite a drop in the number of Americans living in poverty from 38.9 million in 1959 to 32.7 million in 1965, the percentage of poor blacks had increased from 27.5 percent to 31 percent. Seven percent unemployment among blacks was more than twice the percentage of joblessness among whites; 23 percent black teenage unemployment compared with 10.8 percent for whites.

In the spring of 1967, the White House fretted over dangers to the national well-being and the administration from another round of urban riots. Johnson aides, anticipating that the coming violence would "have broad political as well as social effects," laid plans to minimize the white backlash against the administration and its legislative programs.

But the effort was too little and too late. In July, when rumors of police brutality against a black cab driver spread through Newark's ghetto, six days of rioting took twenty-six lives, injured 1,500, and burned out much of the inner city. It was the worst urban violence since Watts in 1964.

The riots threw Johnson into a mood of near despair. He did not want to send in federal troops and was eager for New Jersey's Governor Richard

Hughes to handle the problem without direct intervention from Washington. Johnson feared that federal help would be seen as a case of black rioters blackmailing the government into giving them more federal money.

Johnson could not understand why the ghettos were exploding now. No administration had ever been as attentive to the problems and needs of African Americans as the current one, and Johnson felt that they were paying him back with riots that embarrassed and undermined him. And the liberals as well, with their incessant attacks on the war and "unrealistic" demands for more money for domestic programs, impressed him as intent on destroying him and, as he judged it, the most progressive presidency in American history.

Johnson's frustration also stemmed from a sense of helplessness about how to ease poverty and prevent riots. He had no answers beyond what he had been doing, he told reporters. He had been trying to provide employment opportunities, better schools, better recreation areas, and better housing, but Congress, which was so intent on cutting programs, was now adding to the difficulty. His unspoken complaint was against a war in Vietnam that was eroding his freedom to mount a possibly more effective attack on poverty.

On July 23, Detroit erupted in the country's worst rioting since disturbances there in 1943. The civil disorders underscored Johnson's sense of immediate limits, but they also strengthened his resolve to do something for the long run about the problem. He announced the appointment of a bipartisan commission headed by Illinois's Democratic Governor Otto Kerner. The other members included Republican Mayor John Lindsay of New York as vice chairman, national and local government officials, business and labor leaders, and prominent blacks. The commission was to recommend means "to prevent or contain such disasters in the future."

But even before the commission reported, Johnson saw the need for "an attack—mounted at every level—upon the conditions that breed despair and violence." He chided those who decried the antipoverty programs, and declared resistance to current congressional proposals to overcome urban misery as misguided and inhumane.

Califano warned Johnson that setting up the Kerner commission would be seen as a delayed and weak means of dealing with an immediate and severe problem. In addition, Califano predicted that the liberals Johnson had selected as commission members would recommend massive additional spending, which the administration would be unable to fund. But Johnson saw a commission as an effective means to head off a congressional investigation, which would produce attacks on him from the right for indulging rioters and from the left for not doing enough for the poor. A commission also seemed useful in underscoring the need for Congress to fund the administration's programs, especially Model Cities and rent supplements, which he viewed as the best potential means for dealing with inner-city suffering.

But Johnson principally saw the commission as a way to buy time until he could shift money from Vietnam to the cities. In response, the *New York Times* urged Johnson not to use the commission as an excuse for delaying forceful leadership to initiate and enlarge programs that might ease urban ills. It was fine for the President to ask action on his urban proposals, the *Times* declared, but "the events of the past few weeks have demonstrated . . . that they [alone] are not adequate" to the immediate or long-term challenge. The $662 million proposed for Model Cities and the $2.06 billion for the War on Poverty impressed the *Times* as "a mere drop in the bucket against the needs of 193 cities and counties that have applied for urban renewal."

As the *Times* saw, Johnson's thinking on how to deal with black riots and urban blight was unrealistic, but with his presidency now in a steep decline—at the beginning of June only 34 percent of Americans gave him a vote of confidence—he indulged in some wishful thinking. Unable to find many bright spots abroad or at home, he boosted himself with any ray of hope he could find.

:: THE SIX DAYS WAR

Middle East problems added to Johnson's difficulties in 1967. For more than ten years since the Suez crisis of 1956, Israel and its Arab neighbors had fought a limited war. Attacks and counterattacks across the Israeli borders with Egypt, Jordan, Lebanon, and Syria had been commonplace. If this had been America's only problem in the Middle East, the Johnson administration would have been elated. The heavy dependence of Western Europe on Persian Gulf oil and aggressive Soviet efforts to expand Moscow's influence with radical Arab states led by Egypt, Syria, and Iraq gave Johnson constant concerns rivaling Vietnam. Though the struggle in Southeast Asia was at the center of Johnson's foreign problems, Middle East tensions, with the potential for a Soviet-American confrontation as dangerous as the Cuban missile crisis, was a constant concern.

During the first three years of his presidency Johnson had struggled to contain an Israeli nuclear program. Surrounded by well armed hostile neighbors with twenty times its population, Israel saw a nuclear capability as essential to its national survival. Fearful that Israel's acquisition of "the bomb" would encourage proliferation in the region and around the world, the Johnson administration discouraged Tel Aviv's nuclear plans with assurances about its security and military supplies. At the same time, the Johnson State Department cultivated relations with Jordan, Iran, and Saudi Arabia, "moderate" Arab states frightened by Soviet support of "radicals" committed to overturning their governments.

Despite the administration's efforts to stabilize the region, by the spring of 1967 another Arab-Israeli war seemed in the offing. Increased Soviet support of Baghdad, Cairo, and Damascus had encouraged Palestinian guerrilla attacks on Israel from Syria, Jordan, and Lebanon. In April, after a Syrian artillery barrage triggered by a Palestinian incursion in northern Israel, Israeli jets bombed terrorist bases in the Golan Heights and shot down six Syrian MIGs twenty miles from Damascus. In May, after Syria called on Cairo to discourage an Israeli military buildup on its borders, Nasser pressured Secretary-General U Thant into withdrawing U.N. observers in the Sinai and replaced them with Egyptian forces. On May 22, Nasser announced the closing of the Strait of Tiran and access to the Israeli port of Eilat from the Red Sea.

The Israeli government pressed Johnson for a public statement on the extent of America's commitment to Israel's security. In a private response, the President sympathized with Israel's predicament, asked for patience while mediation efforts went forward, and warned that without prior consultation on unilateral actions Tel Aviv should not expect any commitment of support from the United States.

On May 23, the President issued a pro-Israel statement deploring the U.N. withdrawal, denouncing the closing of the Gulf of Aqaba as "illegal" and a potential threat to peace, backing Thant's efforts to alter Egypt's action, and reaffirming America's commitment to political independence and territorial integrity for all nations in the Middle East.

Johnson's dilemma was how to prevent a war, or, if a war occurred, how to assure against a U.S. confrontation with the Soviet Union and heightened domestic opposition to Vietnam as a distraction from the "more important" Middle East conflict.

The Israelis were willing to give Johnson's diplomacy a chance. But on May 30, when Jordan and the United Arab Republic, as Egypt called itself, announced a mutual defense pact, Tel Aviv saw almost no hope of an Arab retreat on Aqaba. Israeli Prime Minister Levi Eshkol pressed Johnson anew for a commitment to join in forcing open the gulf, but Johnson refused to go beyond what he had said and counseled continued patience.

On June 5, the Israelis began a six-day war in which they defeated Egyptian, Jordanian, and Syrian forces, taking the Sinai, the West bank of the Jordan, east Jerusalem, and the Golan Heights. After the outbreak of hostilities, the White House immediately began trying to arrange a cease-fire and more extended agreements for a stable Middle East peace. But developments at home and in the region made it impossible for the United States to have a significant impact.

Johnson now found himself attacked by Arabs and Jews alike. With the Egyptians complaining that U.S. planes had supported initial Israeli ground actions, several Arab states broke relations with Washington. To appease Arab sentiment, the State Department issued a declaration of neutrality, but its principal result was to leave the Arab governments unconvinced while angering the Israelis and their American supporters. Johnson's diplomacy over the next several days repaired the political damage inflicted by the State Department. A significant element in the turnabout was the President's handling of the worst crisis in U.S.-Israeli relations since U.S. recognition of Israel in May 1948. On the afternoon of June 8, Israeli planes and torpedo boats attacked the USS *Liberty*, an electronic spy ship operating in international waters east-northeast of Port Said in the Mediterranean Sea. The assault killed thirty-four and wounded 171 American sailors.

Initially, the President thought Soviet forces had staged the attack, but a prompt signal from Tel Aviv that they had mistaken the *Liberty* for an Egyptian ship, which had allegedly been shelling the Israeli coast, identified the attacker as Israel.

The Israelis insisted that the attack had been a mistake. The presence of a U.S. ship in an area being used by Egypt for hostile action caused the error. The Israelis expressed "deep regret" and offered "to make amends for the tragic loss of life and material damage."

The White House disputed Tel Aviv's version of events. To be sure, the President's Foreign Intelligence Advisory Board (PFIAB) placed the *Liberty* closer to the coast than initially thought, acknowledged that the Israelis had not been informed of the ship's presence in a region of hostilities, and accepted that Israeli defense forces had misinformation about a coastal attack. The PFIAB also granted that Israeli forces had reason to think that the *Liberty* was an Egyptian supply ship.

More important, the board concluded that available information did not "reflect that the Israeli high command made a premeditated attack on a ship known to be American." Nor did evidence "support the theory that the highest echelons of the Israeli government were aware of the *Liberty*'s true identity or of the fact that an attack on her was taking place."

So much for the official version of events, which was calculated to avoid a crisis with Israel in the midst of an all-out war against Arab states with ties to Moscow. Behind the scenes, the highest officials of the U.S. government, including the President, believed it "inconceivable" that Israel's "skilled" defense forces could have committed such a gross error.

They assumed that the Israelis saw their attack on the *Liberty* as an act of self-defense. Fearful that the American ship was monitoring and transmitting information about Israeli military preparations against Syria, the Israelis felt compelled to silence the *Liberty*: If its intelligence inadvertently fell into the hands of the Arabs, they could use it to inflict significant casualties on Israeli forces, and U.S. government forewarnings of Israeli military plans might make it more difficult for Tel Aviv to secure its war aims.

By June 8, Israeli-American differences over acceptable cease-fire conditions had become a major concern. On the evening of June 6, after the U.S. government had persuaded the U.N. Security Council not to insist on a cease-fire with a pullback to previous borders, Johnson announced American support of "a simple cease-fire" as a necessary first step toward a "settled peace" in the Middle East. Only after Israel had seized all Jordanian territory west of the Jordan River, however, did Tel Aviv take heed of Washington's warning that King Hussein might lose power and agree to a cease-fire with Amman on June 7. Moreover, Israel and Egypt continued fighting until Israeli forces had reached the Suez Canal and surrounded Egyptian units in the Sinai on June 8.

The fighting with Syria went on until June 10, despite Syrian agreement to call a halt on June 9. Eager to take advantage of Syrian weakness by seizing the Golan Heights on its Syrian border and, if possible, topple the Ba'athist regime, Tel Aviv would not stop fighting on the 9th. Israel ignored a warning from Secretary Rusk that it faced a Security Council condemnation unless it ended hostilities.

A Soviet threat carried more weight. On June 10, Moscow, which in Johnson's estimate "had lost their shirts" in the conflict, told the White House that unless Washington "made its influence with Israel felt and weighed in to stop this war . . . the Soviet Union was going to have to take whatever actions it had within its capacities, including military actions." Unwilling to be bullied by Moscow, Johnson ordered the U.S. Sixth Fleet, "orbiting around Sicily," to head toward the eastern Mediterranean. Because Soviet naval forces were watching the Sixth Fleet "like a hawk," the message got "back to Moscow in a hurry." Nevertheless, the Soviet pressure disturbed Johnson, who "alarmed" Tel Aviv with a "'clear signal' of American anxieties." With the Golan Heights already occupied, Israel agreed to a cease-fire on all fronts.

The cease-fire concluded the immediate crisis, but left problems that could bring a renewed outbreak: Israel's occupation of Arab territories, militant Palestinian guerrillas threatening instability in Jordan, and Moscow's unprecedented opportunity to ally itself with anti-American Arab states were all predictable flashpoints. On June 16, the White House took note of Soviet arms shipments to the Middle East, which might lead to an Arab counterattack against Israel. On the 21st, Johnson privately described the region as "an explosive" area, where the United States had limited influence.

Johnson's frustrations and anxieties about the Middle East would last to the end of his term, despite U.N. Security Council Resolution 242 passed on November 22, 1967. Though the resolution struck a number of correct rhetorical chords about a "just and lasting peace," "secure and recognized boundaries," Israeli withdrawal "from territories occupied in the recent conflict," and the "sovereignty, territorial integrity and political independence of all states," the opposing sides refused to concede anything in practice that could advance the region toward a genuine peace. Though Johnson understood that "the basic problems have been there all the time," that "we can't solve the Middle East with two men in a room over a highball" and that people in the area would "have to talk to each other," the dilemma of the Middle East represented another of the intractable problems that besieged him during 1967.

:: U.S.–SOVIET RELATIONS: GLASSBORO

The Six Days War had at least one salutary effect: It forced Soviet-American differences to the forefront of concerns in Washington and Moscow, propelling them into discussions that had been inhibited by Vietnam. Every President since FDR had held summit meetings with their Soviet counterparts. But three and a half years into his presidency, LBJ had had only written and electronic communications with officials in Moscow. More important, the White House had been unable to make any significant progress in major arms control discussions on nuclear proliferation and antiballistic missile systems. Likewise, the tensions between the two over the Middle East added to the dangers of a Soviet-American clash similar to the 1962 Cuban crisis.

An opportunity presented itself when Soviet Premier Aleksei Kosygin attended a special session of the U.N. General Assembly convened at Moscow's request to demand Israel's withdrawal from Arab territories. Kosygin came to New York for two apparent purposes. The Arab defeat required a show of support, which the presence of the Soviet leadership at the U.N. in behalf of an unrealizable goal largely fulfilled.

Kosygin also wanted to meet with Johnson. The Soviet leadership feared a Sino-American accommodation over Vietnam, which might force a U.S.-Soviet confrontation. A meeting with the President might ease some tensions and deter the White House from any arrangement with Peking. "Kosygin had an obsession about China," LBJ told Senator George Aiken on the eve of Kosygin's visit, "he was scared to death."

Johnson's advisers urged him to allay Soviet suspicions about American intentions in the Middle East and Vietnam by meeting with the Premier. Zbigniew Brzezinski at the State Department's Policy Planning Council believed it "important that Kosygin emerge from any eventual meeting with the President disabused of the notion that the United States is out to humiliate the Soviet Union and is currently engaged in a broad political offensive directed against it. Some gesture may be in order." Fulbright thought there was a chance for genuine progress on the Middle East and Vietnam, and at the very least a meeting would advance the President's wish to build bridges that could lead to later progress.

Johnson foresaw no concrete agreements coming from a conference. And he worried that the only gains would go to the Soviets. "Kosygin had suffered a fiasco [in the Middle East] worse than the Bay of Pigs, and was struggling to recover," he told network bureau chiefs on June 19.

Nevertheless, Johnson felt compelled to meet the Kremlin's head man. He wanted to discuss the Middle East and Vietnam. He intended to emphasize that we had no foreknowledge of Israel's offensive, nor had we conspired with Israel or anyone to bring down the Egyptian and Syrian regimes. In addition, he hoped to persuade Kosygin that our only interest in Southeast Asia was the independence of South Vietnam, and he intended to sound him out about possible peace talks. He also had some hope that he could effectively advance the case for a nuclear nonproliferation treaty and an arms control agreement covering antiballistic missile systems.

Problems finding a mutually agreeable site to meet foretold the difficulties of reaching substantive agreements. Johnson proposed the White House as a first choice or Camp David, a presidential retreat in Maryland, where security would present no problem. But being an official guest of the

U.S. government would undermine Soviet relations with the Arabs and Hanoi and give Peking a propaganda advantage. Why not meet in New York? Kosygin asked. But a meeting in the city, and especially at the U.N., seemed certain to attract "a sea of pickets and protestors" from both sides of the political spectrum who would embarrass Johnson and Kosygin. The White House, which was now terribly apprehensive about any LBJ public appearance as a magnet to anti-Vietnam War opponents, suggested Maguire Air Force Base in New Jersey, where there could be no demonstrators. But Kosygin saw a military setting as an attempt to intimidate his government.

With the help of Governor Richard Hughes, the two sides settled on Glassboro, New Jersey, a small college town halfway between New York and Washington and easily accessible from the Philadelphia airport and the Jersey Turnpike. With the college out of session and the meeting convened overnight, the conference was insulated from hostile demonstrators.

Johnson and Kosygin agreed to meet for four hours on June 23 beginning at 11 a.m. Hollybush, the home of Thomas Robinson, the president of Glassboro State College, became the conference site. As the host, Johnson arrived half an hour ahead of Kosygin, and then greeted him with "an elaborate negotiated handshake" as he left his car. Johnson, leaving no doubt who was in charge, led the Premier by the elbow into the house, where he introduced him to the supporting cast, posed for pictures, offered his guest a glass of ice water, and escorted him into Robinson's small study furnished with a rocking chair for the President, a three-seat sofa for Kosygin, and two large upholstered easy chairs for the translators.

Kosygin impressed the President "as an extremely intelligent and competent person with a personal capacity for humor and human feeling." American accounts to the press of the meeting stressed the cordiality between the two sides. The Soviet press, by contrast, described the conference as initiated by Johnson and as an occasion for stern lectures to the Americans on "Israel, Vietnam, and other assorted American misdeeds."

Privately, Johnson did not discount the hard edge to the meeting. Afterward, he described Kosygin as "an extremely disciplined Communist leader" who presented "existing Soviet positions hard" and refused to make agreements.

The two days of meetings on June 23 and 25 were largely an exercise in "cordial disagreement." But the subtext was a wish for better relations that would take months and years to blossom. During the morning talks, both men outdid each other in professions of peaceful intentions. But, as Kosygin then put it, "However, . . . when we began to discuss specific problems and practical steps for their solution, then a great many difficulties and differences arose."

The Middle East was Kosygin's first case in point. They could not agree on which of them bore responsibility for the recent fighting; nor could they agree that Israel would have to withdraw from conquered territories before peace talks could begin. Kosygin predicted renewed hostilities unless Israel withdrew. Johnson emphasized Israel's insistence on security as a prelude to any restoration of boundaries. When Kosygin replied that a war might provoke a Soviet-American confrontation, Johnson "leaned forward and said very slowly . . . , let us understand one another. I hope there will be no war. If there is a war, I hope it will not be a big war. . . . I hope you and we will keep out of this matter because, if we do get into it, it will be a 'most serious' matter." Both sides denied that they were giving ultimatums and turned to other problems.

During an hour-and-a-half lunch session, the two sparred over antiballistic missile systems. Initial Soviet deployments of ABMS to counter America's advantage in offensive weapons stimulated a similar U.S. program and development of multiwarhead missiles.

Asked by Johnson to make the case against ABMS, McNamara described a vicious circle in which defensive missiles would beget offensive ones in ever larger numbers: An "insane" cycle of more weapons-building provoking a greater sense of insecurity and ever more defensive and offensive weapons. "It is our ability to destroy the attacker as a viable 20th-century nation that provides the deterrent," McNamara declared, "not the ability to limit damage to ourselves." Kosygin dismissed McNamara's argument for building only less expensive offensive missiles as "a commercial approach to a moral problem." McNamara denied Kosygin's assertion, but the Premier refused to see any merit in the secretary's argument.

The afternoon session focused on Vietnam, with no indication that Soviet overtures to Hanoi would lead to peace talks. Johnson saw Kosygin as under instructions not to budge one inch: "His position was rigid and familiar: we should stop the bombing and get out of Vietnam."

Only on nonproliferation of nuclear weapons was there any sign of movement. Though no commitments were made, the American delegation saw "definite headway" on the subject. "It is perfectly clear that they want a non-proliferation treaty if they can get one," a U.S. summary of the talks stated. Despite the want of substantive gains, Johnson and Kosygin agreed to meet again two days later on Sunday. Kosygin emphasized "that there were forces in the world [China's Communists] which were interested in causing a clash between the United States and the USSR. He assured the President that such forces did exist." He was ready to meet again in the service of U.S.-Soviet peace.

Johnson wanted discussions focused on reducing military budgets. Kosygin declared this an admirable but impractical idea as long as the United States spent $20 billion a year on fighting in Vietnam. Johnson countered that Soviet military supplies to Vietnam kept the war going. At the very least they should try for an agreement on limiting ABMS, Johnson said. But Kosygin saw no chance for disarmament gains without settlements in Vietnam and the Middle East. And the ensuing discussion of Middle East and Vietnam differences demonstrated that no agreements on these problems would emerge from the talks.

But Johnson was dogged about at least keeping the dialogue alive. Let us put aside a week every year to meet and talk, he proposed. Kosygin, who could not agree to anything without Kremlin approval, suggested that they stay in touch through the hot line, which, during the Middle East war, had allowed them to accomplish more in one day "than others could accomplish in three years."

Johnson left Glassboro disappointed at his inability to coax Kosygin into anything concrete. But he had genuine hopes that agreements on major issues were within reach. These were boosted when Cyrus Eaton, a wealthy Ohio industrialist with special ties to the Soviets, reported in July that Kosygin described himself as "glad to meet again with President Johnson" and that Eaton considered it a "propitious" time for "a long-term arrangement with the Soviets." In August, after Eaton agreed to a proposal from Dmitri Polyansky, a Deputy Soviet Premier, to meet in Canada, Eaton urged Johnson to "move swiftly for a permanent accommodation with the Soviets."

"You seem to be fairly sanguine about your relations with Russia," an English journalist told LBJ in a private conversation in October. Eager for both international and domestic purposes to put the best possible face on Soviet-American relations, Johnson said he didn't "know of any period in history when there have been more agreements between the U.S. and the USSR."

Possibly believing that the military collaboration in World War II had faded from American minds, Johnson rested his case on a recent Soviet decision to work toward a nuclear nonproliferation treaty. He also believed that a McNamara speech in September announcing American intentions to go forward with a limited ABM deployment designed to meet a Chinese nuclear attack would push Moscow into serious discussions about limits on ABMS. Though it would take until the summer of 1968 before a nonproliferation agreement was concluded and commitments to begin ABM talks were announced, Johnson could see the glimmerings of what would become known in the 1970s as Soviet-American Detente.

:: THURGOOD MARSHALL

At the same time Johnson saw the potential for better Soviet-American relations as one bright spot in an otherwise gloomy world, he viewed an appointment to the Supreme Court as his principal chance in 1967 to make a major advance in domestic affairs. In its 178-year history Supreme Court justices had all been white males. No president had ever proposed appointing a person of color or a woman to the Court. Johnson believed that, as with desegregation of all public institutions, the Court should now reflect the shift in social and political mood toward fulfilling constitutional mandates on equal treatment under the law. And what better place to promote equality and justice for all than in the institution most responsible for defining the law of the land?

In February, when Tom Clark announced that he would resign from the Court at the close of its current term to assure against conflicts of interest with his son Ramsey, LBJ's choice for Attorney General, Johnson had a second chance to appoint an associate justice. Having convinced Abe Fortas to replace Arthur Goldberg on the bench, Johnson now wanted another liberal who would legitimize his Great Society reforms. But he also wanted someone who would underscore his administration's commitment to the civil rights revolution of 1964–65. In a discussion with advisers, he mentioned several black jurists but declared that he was also considering appointing the first woman to the Court. Lady Bird encouraged Lyndon to do just that.

But Johnson concluded that a black had a prior claim on the position. Having made no major civil rights advances in almost two years and believing it impractical to expect any to pass Congress in the current or next session, Johnson saw a black appointment to the bench as a compelling alternative. Such a selection would have great symbolic as well as substantive significance. At a time when inner-city riots and black radicalism attached a stigma of lawlessness to black behavior, he wanted to reaffirm the commitment of blacks to American institutions and the rule of law.

No one promised to serve Johnson's purposes better than Thurgood Marshall. The fifty-eight-year-old Marshall was a seasoned jurist with a record of extraordinary accomplishment as an attorney and a judge. The son of a Pullman car steward and kindergarten teacher, Marshall grew up in Baltimore, as racially segregated as any Deep South city. "The only thing different between the South and Baltimore was trolley cars," Marshall said later. "They weren't segregated. Everything else was segregated." As a child and adolescent, Marshall had a comfortable existence with little impulse to rebel against the accepted social mores. During his years at Lincoln University in Pennsylvania, a black college with a white teaching staff, he was exposed to arguments about integrating the faculty that encouraged him to oppose separation of the races. Barred by the color line from attending the University of Maryland law school, he graduated first in his class from Washington, D.C.'s, Howard University with an LLB in 1933.

Under the tutelage of Charles H. Houston, the dean at Howard and later director of the NAACP's Legal Defense and Education Fund, Marshall launched a career as an advocate of black rights. Pressuring white store owners in Baltimore to hire blacks and the steel workers union to integrate, Marshall won a landmark case forcing the Maryland law school to accept a black applicant. Beginning in 1936, he joined the NAACP's legal office in New York, where he set legal precedents with cases ending restrictive covenants against selling homes to blacks, bars to black voting in Texas party primaries, and less pay to black school teachers for the same work done by whites. His successful advocacy in 1954 of school desegregation in *Brown v. Board of Education*, coupled with twenty-eight other winning pleas out of thirty-two made before the U.S. Supreme Court, secured Marshall's place as one of the greatest jurists in American history.

In 1961 President Kennedy appointed Marshall to a lifetime position as a judge of the U.S. Court of Appeals for the Second Circuit, which handles appeals for New York, Connecticut, and Vermont. His confirmation was held up for twelve months by Senate Judiciary Committee Chairman James O. Eastland of Mississippi.

In July 1965, Johnson nominated Marshall for appointment as Solicitor General, the U.S. government's top litigating lawyer. Marshall had understandable reservations. He had to give up a lifetime judgeship, take a pay cut, and risk losing his position should the President become dissatisfied with his performance or leave the presidency in 1969. Moreover, Johnson emphasized that the solicitor's job had "nothing to do with any Supreme Court appointment. I want that distinctly understood," he told Marshall.

Marshall saw compelling reasons to accept. As solicitor, he would have the power to influence what cases would come before the Supreme Court and how they would be framed; the job would assure him of "a powerful policy influence throughout the Executive Branch." In addition, as Johnson emphasized to him, he would become a standing example of what a black man could achieve—a powerful image for young people of all races that the "man up there with that swallow tail coat on arguing" before the Court was "a Negro" who had become Solicitor General of the United States.

Despite LBJ's injunctions about no "quid pro quo," Washington pundits predicted that the position was a way station for appointment to the Supreme Court. And Johnson himself said privately that if Marshall "proved himself outstanding as [solicitor] perhaps when a vacancy on the Supreme Court opened up, he might nominate him as a Justice — the first of his race." Johnson also said that Marshall's service as solicitor was a chance to assure that he wasn't "considered simply a one-issue lawyer concerned only with civil rights." When Johnson and Marshall walked into the White House press room to announce his appointment, "a murmur went around the press boys," Marshall recalled, "and I found out afterwards that the question they were asking was, 'Who has resigned from the Supreme Court?'"

Twenty-three months later, Johnson gave Marshall the prize. But until the moment he offered him the seat, Johnson refused to acknowledge his appointment as a given. During Marshall's service as solicitor, Johnson kept reminding him that an opening on the high court would not necessarily lead to his appointment. At the same time he told Louis Martin, a well-to-do black newspaper publisher and Johnson spokesman to African-American leaders, that Marshall "wasn't worth a damn as an administrator, because [Archibald] Cox, who had preceded him, was a very efficient operator." Johnson complained to Martin that Marshall didn't "'pay any attention to half the cases; he just gets those he likes.'"

But Johnson's critical comments were meant to create suspense about whom he would select as his second appointment to the bench. Even Marshall didn't know he was being appointed until the day the President announced it. On June 13, Ramsey Clark advised Marshall that "the boss wants to see you" at 10:45 a.m. Marshall was to enter the White House without being seen by reporters. To escape detection, he joined a tour group and then made his way through a corridor to the Oval Office. After some pleasantries, Johnson told him: "'You know something, Thurgood, I'm going to put you on the Supreme Court.' I said, 'Well thank you, sir.' We talked a little while. We went out to the press and he announced it."

Marshall's appointment generated some predictable opposition. His confirmation took two and a half months, which was an unusually long time for that era. Southern senators, led by Sam Ervin of North Carolina and John McClellan of Arkansas, were particularly outspoken. But the public opposition to Marshall was not overtly racial; by then, just three years after the 1964 civil rights bill condemned southern segregation, it was already impolitic to fight openly against someone of Marshall's exceptional competence on racial grounds. Instead, the southerners challenged his liberal views of the Constitution, particularly his reflection of the current impulse to assure alleged criminals their "constitutional rights." Richard Russell complained of Marshall's "extreme liberal views . . . and his apparent agreement with [Chief Justice] Warren that the Constitution is to be twisted to suit the views of the Court" as ample reason to vote against his selection.

But the outcry was relatively muted and ineffective. Although the opposition delayed the confirmation until August 30, the vote was a decisive 69 to 11. The Marshall appointment was the high-water mark for Johnson in an otherwise miserable political year.

12 :: STALEMATE

In February 1966 Chief Justice Earl Warren had told Drew Pearson that a seasoned politician like Lyndon Johnson would surely find his way through the maze of Vietnam. "This is going to last a long time, and the President will go through some rough sailing," Warren said. "But he's used to it. . . . He's working hard on Vietnam and has been for a long time, and he knows the answers for it. He will find some way out."

Warren's confidence in the President exceeded Johnson's capacity to set things right. Vietnam was a stalemate producing irreconcilable domestic divisions and a nightmare, to borrow from James Joyce, from which Johnson could not awake. More than ever in 1967 the war made him irrational and repressive toward opponents, provoking illusions about "winning" or negotiating our way out one moment and fears of losing the next. At a meeting with Senate leaders Mike Mansfield and Everett Dirksen in January, he "said he personally wished he had never heard of South Vietnam." The anguish was causing him indescribable grief.

With the likelihood that a continuation of the fighting into 1968 would be a political disaster for Johnson and the Democrats, he was almost desperate to end the war. But no one knew how to do it, at least on terms that Johnson believed acceptable. When Fulbright told him that "the President's first priority must be liquidation of the war—that the war poisons everything else—the President said he totally agreed."

Yet however great the pressure to end the fighting before American civil strife became intolerable, Johnson wouldn't agree to military steps that might precipitate a larger conflict with China and/or Russia. A suggestion from Texas Governor John Connally that Johnson use tactical nuclear bombs to end a war that otherwise would destroy his administration non-plused LBJ.

Nor would he give in to the doves: "We just have to save" South Vietnam, he told Nicholas Katzenbach. He believed it would be shattering to America's national security and international confidence in U.S. commitments if we cut and ran.

The best hope most Americans had in 1967 for an end to the conflict was a negotiated settlement that would preserve South Vietnamese independence and allow U.S. forces to go home. Every hint of Hanoi's willingness to talk became an occasion for inquiry and reiteration of American readiness to reach an agreement that promised the survival of Saigon's freedom from Communist control.

In December 1966, State Department analysts concluded that, since we could not possibly "win" the war by the summer of 1968, when the conflict would dominate electoral politics, the administration had no choice but to negotiate. And the only way to start peace talks was for the United States to convince Hanoi that we wanted discussions and that our only non-negotiable conditions were a "separate state in SVN, and a government which is not overtly Communist."

Johnson would have been happy to settle for such arrangements, but he saw little prospect of a positive response from the Communists. He wished to keep trying nevertheless, lest anyone say that he hadn't given peace every possible chance. Consequently, on December 19, Goldberg asked U Thant to initiate "discussions which could lead to a cease-fire." On the 23rd, the President temporarily suspended U.S. bombing of the North. The next day Johnson ordered a three-day Christmas truce and then repeated the suspension of hostilities for two days from December 30 to January 1 as additional demonstrations of U.S. goodwill.

In January, Harrison Salisbury reported that Hanoi's Foreign Minister had signaled an interest in opening discussions, but Johnson had little real hope that Hanoi was about to enter into meaningful discussions. It was no surprise to him, then, at the end of January, when Hanoi rejected talks unless the United States first stopped bombing and "all other acts of war" against North Vietnam.

However eager Johnson was to end the war, he refused to make concessions to Hanoi. On the contrary, he was increasingly optimistic that, as South Vietnam President Ky put it on February 1, "'We are getting stronger every day, and they are getting weaker every day — and they know it.' They are hurt by the bombing, and by the tremendous military 'meat-grinder' which devours the troops which they send into South Vietnam."

For the moment, Johnson saw peace efforts as sops to domestic and international opinion. At the beginning of February, when the British and Soviets offered to mediate, he reluctantly accepted. He saw nothing from North Vietnam that could be taken seriously, he told reporters. But he was "anxious for them [the Vietnamese] to make any proposal," which we will give "very prompt and serious consideration." Believing that the exchanges between the four capitals would become public knowledge, Johnson saw the discussions as an exercise in public relations.

:: THE WAR AT HOME CONTINUES

By the winter of 1966–67 public doubts about Johnson's war leadership had deepened and spread. Johnson's failure to be more candid about expanding the fighting was eroding his credibility. Harrison Salisbury published articles in the *New York Times* in December and January that reported civilian casualties from air raids and strengthened the feeling that the White House was hiding the truth about the war. A Defense Department spokesman saw Salisbury's revelations as a "national disaster."

But even if Johnson changed his "image" from a secretive manipulator, as his critics now described him, to a forthright educator, it could not eliminate or mute the problem that was diminishing his popularity. The country wanted him to end a war that was taking so many lives and costing so much money for a cause it didn't quite understand.

Johnson tried to rally the country to his standard with some straight talk. In his State of the Union address on January 10, 1967, he wondered "whether we have the staying power to fight a very costly war, when the objective is limited and the danger to us is seemingly remote." He saw the will of the American people being tested, and he predicted that it would take "a great deal of patience" before we could assure the independence of "all the small nations in Southeast Asia" as well as peace in the region and "perhaps the world." He wished he could report "that the conflict is almost over. This I cannot do. We face more cost, more loss, and more agony. For the end is not yet. I cannot promise you that it will come this year — or come next year." He only promised persistence, which would assure eventual success.

But Johnson's words changed nothing. The mass public now had grave doubts about the wisdom of being in Vietnam. An opinion poll at the end of January showed only 41 percent approval for Vietnam policy. A poll in Minnesota was more revealing. Seventy-two percent were dissatisfied with progress in the war, with only 22 percent satisfied.

As telling, the President's overall approval rating in February stood at 46 percent, with 37 percent negative about his performance. By March, Johnson's general job rating had slipped another point, while his numbers on Vietnam fell to an all-time low: 49 percent disapproved of his war leadership and only 37 percent approved.

Senators echoed public doubts. In the first quarter of 1967, moderates and conservatives joined doves in urging an end to the war. It was "costing too much," Symington told the President, and counseled a greater, less restricted use of American air power. Russell of Georgia and Lister Hill of Alabama proposed a win or get out policy. People couldn't understand a conflict in which we held back from beating an avowed enemy of our institutions and national survival, they said. Moderates like Edmund Muskie of Maine and Joseph Pastore of Rhode Island emphasized the need to end a struggle that was spreading consternation across America and threatening Johnson's political life.

Opposition from senators, academics, and business and religious leaders incensed Johnson. He complained that petitions, letters, op-ed articles, and public demonstrations were giving aid and comfort to the enemy. He was particularly enraged at young people, who made life miserable for administration figures trying to convince college and university students that we were fighting a just war with no ulterior motives. In November 1966, when McNamara spoke at Harvard, a crowd of unruly students shouting obscenities mobbed his car and threatened his person.

No one was more the object of the antiwar anger than Johnson himself. Animated by an unshakable conviction that they held the moral high ground, some war opponents engaged in unrestrained attacks on LBJ as unworthy of the deference normally shown a President. In the spring of 1967, UPI journalist Merriman Smith decried the shameful attacks on the President and his family. He objected to demonstrators carrying signs asking, "Lee Harvey Oswald, where are you now?"

Polls in the first quarter of 1967 showed Johnson how to fight back. The public strongly favored sustained bombing and intensified military pressure as the best way to end the conflict. A survey published on March 13, for example, cited a four-to-one margin against a halt in the bombing to test Hanoi's interest in peace talks. Between November 1966 and March 1967, the number of Americans favoring a "total military victory" rose from 31 percent to 43 percent.

The polls strengthened Johnson's determination to give military action priority over negotiations. In private, he belittled those who thought Hanoi's demands for an unconditional bombing halt would bring talks and an end to Communist aggression against Saigon. We can't have peace "crawling on our stomachs," he told congressmen on February 15. ". . . We can't have it begging."

:: THE MILITARY OPTION

During the first quarter of 1967, almost everyone in the administration and the great majority of Americans agreed on the need for more effective action in Vietnam. But the goal remained as elusive as ever; no one had a surefire means of getting there. The prognosis for 1967 "was not comforting."

The Joint Chiefs of Staff and the U.S. military command in Vietnam did not disagree. They would only say that "the war could be long and difficult, and the field commander should be granted the operational flexibility and resources he needed to do the job as he perceived it."

As far as anyone could tell, the war was now stalemated. American military power was a standing assurance against South Vietnam's collapse, but it guaranteed nothing about North Vietnamese and Viet Cong defeat. Moreover, there was limited reason to believe that a Saigon government and independent South Vietnam would survive a U.S. withdrawal. A CIA report in January stated that the "chances that the Communists would win South Vietnam by a military victory had vanished, but everything else about the "course of the struggle" was "inconclusive."

Despite difficulties assessing the impact of U.S. ground and air actions on opposing forces, Johnson and his advisers chose to put the best possible face on progress in the fighting. But rosy assessments were largely wishful thinking by advocates convinced they were pursuing a just cause. In fact, no one could speak with certainty about conditions in Vietnam. A captured V.C. notebook, for example, indicated that they had lost control over a million people during 1966, and the U.S. mission in Saigon was glad to get out this news. But the notebook also claimed that the Viet Cong still controlled 5 million people, and this differed sharply from U.S. estimates that only 20 percent of the population (3.3 million people) were under V.C. dominance.

Johnson seized on such reports to accentuate the positive. In February, he told NBC's president that he wasn't "sure that the North Vietnamese would not win, but thought it very unlikely. . . . He also could not be sure we'd win, but thought that quite likely. The President said he thought we could clean up Viet Nam, perhaps this year."

There was little basis for Johnson's prediction. In early March, the U.S. military command in Saigon revised its estimates of battalion and larger size enemy-initiated actions for the twelve months between February 1966 and February 1967: There were many more attacks than previously thought. The implications of this data, Wheeler cabled Westmoreland, "are major and serious." "If these figures should reach the public domain," Wheeler declared, "they would, literally, blow the lid off of Washington."

There had been no attempt to "cook" the numbers; the discrepancies were the product of genuine uncertainty over how to measure enemy actions. When Lodge reflected this confusion in a cable which described "an average of last year's 'reasonable assumptions' reflecting contemporary 'monthly variations,'" a White House aide told Rostow that, if such a "formula got to the press, it would reinforce the 'credibility gap' and play right into the hands of those critics who assert that all statistics on Vietnam are cooked."

Did Johnson know about these uncertainties? Though the records do not indicate exactly which assessments reached him on these various matters, it is clear that he had substantial doubts. On March 24, Rostow told the President that he had briefed ABC's Howard K. Smith on progress in Vietnam. Smith counseled against saying "that we do not see a way out of the problem of Viet Nam. We should not say that we do not have the answer."

The doubts over Communist strength "became well known" to the President, McNamara said later. He also denied that Westmoreland, as some claimed after the war, had tried to hide such information from Johnson, and even if he had, which McNamara emphatically says he didn't, "he could not have succeeded because of the alternative information channels available to us."

McNamara is surely right. No President who paid as close attention to Vietnam as Johnson would have been deceived for long about military conditions. McNamara himself assured that the President heard all estimates of what our military actions were achieving. On February 17, for example, when General Wheeler presented the case for increased bombing of the North, McNamara described the limits of what bombing had accomplished. He said that more attacks would not "affect the net flow of supplies into the South. The logistical capacity of the North was well beyond infiltration requirements." As for attacks on POL, which Johnson wanted evaluated, McNamara "said there was no obvious net reduction in consumption," and explained how Hanoi had managed to disperse their stocks and evade the loss of storage capacity.

Johnson's description of progress in the fighting and a possible end to the war in 1967 rested more on a determination to boost American morale rather than confront the reality of a stalemate. Because he saw little real military advance early in 1967 and had a sense of urgency about ending the war, he decided to increase American military pressure on the Communists.

On February 17, he asked for "all the alternatives . . . with respect to accelerating the effort in the North." He also wanted to hear "every possibility for accelerating action in the South . . . : more personnel, if necessary; more initiatives; more aggressiveness; additional efforts in Laos. Our Viet Nam policy was operating on borrowed time," he declared.

On February 22, Johnson agreed to expanded military actions in the North and the South and against infiltration routes in Laos. Fifty-four additional targets were to be struck in the North, while selective mining of inland waterways and estuaries, naval gunfire, and artillery attacks across the DMZ (demilitarized zone at the 17th parallel) were to complement the bombing. In the South, existing military actions were increased and new initiatives were set in motion. Wheeler advised Westmoreland that he believed the President would now be receptive to increasing U.S. ground forces from 470,000 to the 550,000 asked for in 1966.

In light of evidence that the war was stalemated, why did Johnson decide to expand military efforts rather than conclude that the time had come to cut losses and plan an early escape from a deepening morass? Johnson's motives are not easy to discern. No doubt he believed that the Communists had a breaking point, that if we could keep the military pressure on them long enough, they would give up the fight. But he also knew that they had great numbers of troops they could throw into the struggle, and he believed that they had few qualms about sacrificing lives for their ideological ends.

It is surprising that Johnson did not make some contingency plan for a U.S. withdrawal before the country had lost patience with a lengthening war and the conduct of the struggle became a debating point in the 1968 campaign. It is clear that he was not going to let electoral politics stop a war he believed America needed to win or at least end with a peace that preserved South Vietnam. Still, he knew there was more at stake here than his reelection. The war was alienating the administration from many of the country's most thoughtful leaders; it was crippling Johnson's freedom to go forward with the Great Society and threatening to destroy programs that were already in place; it was casting a shadow over Johnson's presidency and changing the way in which history might judge him and his administration.

For a politician as resourceful as LBJ it was not beyond his capacity, as Senator Aiken had advised, to declare victory and leave. The South Vietnamese had been given ample opportunity to take up their own defense. After one more round of U.S. military escalation and a national election in the South in September 1967, Johnson could have declared South Vietnam reasonably safe and begun the withdrawal of American forces. He could have stifled possible Saigon objections with threats to cut off the U.S. aid needed to survive. And even if they lasted only a few more years and fell under North Vietnamese control, how many Americans would be ready to complain about how Vietnam was lost? Some would, of course; but, given U.S. sacrifices in the conflict and the growing mood of war weariness, most Americans were unlikely to oppose political leaders who saw the wisdom of ending a miserable drain on the country's blood and treasure.

But for Johnson most of this was muted or lost from view. The war had become a personal test of his judgment, of his wisdom in expanding the conflict in the first place. True, there was all the talk about avoiding a larger war by fighting a smaller one, and the fear that retreat would undermine international confidence in America's willingness to preserve its national interest in the face of a painful challenge. To leave Vietnam was tantamount to running up the white flag, as Johnson described it.

But so much of this was rhetoric. Who really believed that retreat from Vietnam would convince a divided China roiled by the cultural revolution or a cautious Soviet Union, ever concerned to avoid another massive conflict like World War II, to seize upon America's withdrawal from Vietnam as a reason to expand and risk a nuclear war?

The real issue now was Johnson's unrealistic optimism that we could still work our will in Vietnam and his stubborn unwillingness to admit that Vietnam was a "mistake." Having invested so much of his presidency in the conflict, having allowed the war to become the centerpiece of his four-year term, he would not acknowledge that his principal foreign policy initiative had largely failed.

:: BETWEEN HOPE AND ILLUSION

Throughout the spring of 1967 public feeling about Vietnam could have convinced Johnson that it was time to prepare a U.S. withdrawal. Polling data indicated that the war was weakening support for Great Society programs. Where 72 percent of the country opposed cuts in domestic programs in 1966, the number had fallen to 54 percent by April 1967, and seemed certain to drop more as the cost of financing the war became more apparent.

Surveys on Johnson's public standing and reelection prospects were also disquieting. In an April straw poll pairing him with George Romney, the Governor of Michigan, the President commanded only 43 percent of the vote against Romney's 48 to 52 percent.

Vietnam was central to Johnson's decline: 45 percent of Americans gave him a negative rating on the war, while 65 percent complained that he was not fully informing the country about it. In May, Gallup found that the 26 percent of Americans who saw the war as immoral "could be a major obstacle to [Johnson's] reelection." Thirty-seven percent considered the involvement of U.S. troops a mistake, up from 32 percent in February.

In June, a decisive 66 percent of the country said they had lost confidence in the President's leadership. Half the country had no clear idea what the war was about; only 25 percent believed that South Vietnam could survive a U.S. withdrawal. A planned trip to Los Angeles by the President in late June promised to provoke the largest antiwar demonstration in the city's history.

In May, Taylor told the President that he sensed "a new wave of pessimism regarding Viet-Nam pervading official circles in Washington, apparently arising from renewed doubts about the bombing of the North and increased concern over future troop requirements to carry on the war in the South."

Was there a way to surmount existing obstacles and bring the war to an end soon? McNamara saw none. He told the President in May that he saw "no attractive course of action. The probabilities are that Hanoi has decided not to negotiate until the American electorate has been heard in November 1968. Continuation of our present moderate policy . . . will not change Hanoi's mind."

U.S. military Chiefs also saw no light at the end of the tunnel unless we resorted to greater force. The present "bombing campaign in the North," Wheeler said, "has not and cannot succeed in coercing the North Vietnamese into a settlement or reduce the flow of men and matériel to the South to the extent that victory is possible. The main-force war in the South is stalemated."

Prospects for negotiation were no better. In June, Senator Claiborne Pell of Rhode Island, an outspoken advocate of deescalation without withdrawal, went to Paris at the invitation of a senior North Vietnamese diplomat. The envoy reiterated Hanoi's insistence on an unconditional U.S. bombing halt as a prelude to talks.

When Kosygin passed along the same suggestion from Hanoi at the Glassboro meeting, Johnson replied that a bombing halt would enable the North Vietnamese to send five additional divisions south, where they could inflict a "great many casualties among our boys," and he "would be crucified in this country."

If Johnson wanted a way out of the war, McNamara offered him a plan on May 19. The administration would declare that its objective in the war — South Vietnam's self-determination — was being achieved. We had "already either denied or offset the North Vietnamese intervention." Moreover, September elections in the South would provide the chance for a coalition government, including the V.C. If this government collapsed under the weight of continuing Communist attacks, we could encourage the creation of a non-Communist regime, which would bear responsibility for maintaining internal stability. For this government to go Communist, it would take three to five years, and whether this "would appear to be a 'defeat' for the U.S. in, say, 1970 would depend on many factors not now foreseeable."

But Johnson remained as reluctant as ever to cut losses and accept a fig leaf for American defeat. Moreover, in the spring of 1967, he had enough good news to keep hope alive that all might turn out well yet. Though there was more illusion than sensible judgment in what Johnson now did, he had some reason to think that he was acting on developments that could change the course of the war.

Between April and July, a steady stream of optimistic reports more than matched negative assessments about the conflict. They stressed that Hanoi's greatest hope for victory lay in U.S. "war weariness" and desertions from the South Vietnamese Army.

At the end of April, during briefings in Washington, Westmoreland declared himself "very optimistic" about progress in the war. If the American public backed our troops, he assured everyone that "our struggle will succeed."

In May, the CIA described success in attracting non-Communist members of the National Liberation Front into a coalition government that would come out of the September elections. Max Taylor urged Johnson to sustain the bombing as a way to move toward peace. "We must pass this test of persistence. . . . If we yield on the bombing issue, we can be quite sure of no future 'give' by Hanoi on any important point."

Whatever doubts Johnson had about the war and Saigon's readiness for self-government gave additional ground in June to fresh "evidence" of advances in the fighting. Viet Cong and North Vietnamese casualties seemed to be mounting. Where the Communists in the five years from 1961 to 1966 suffered about 100,000 battlefield deaths, the number had doubled in 1966 and was running at a similar level through the first half of 1967. Likewise, according to latest estimates, the bombing was beginning to inflict serious losses on the North Vietnamese.

By the end of June, the White House was convinced that it was only a matter of time before Hanoi agreed to talk. "Hanoi is moving towards negotiations," Rostow told the President on June 28. "Just as we never had to conduct the great offensive of 1919 or actually invade Japan in 1945," so we might be able to end this war without further escalation. The Communists cannot win in South Vietnam, Johnson told Virginia Senator Harry F. Byrd, Jr., the next day. "That is, they cannot if we stand firm and if our Vietnamese allies continue to move forward on their urgent internal political and economic and social tasks."

Johnson was convinced that winning the struggle at home against antiwar opponents was now as crucial as the continuing "progress" in Vietnam. Administration leaders told him that as Hanoi paid a heavier price for the war, it invested more hope in American unwillingness to sustain the costs of the struggle.

By the spring of 1967 the antiwar movement in America was at fever pitch. Students, faculty, clergymen, professional and business leaders, and numerous mainstream politicians were convinced that the war was a great mistake and must be ended as soon as possible.

In response, the administration gave increasing attention to combating antiwar opponents. Johnson saw their agitation sapping the will of ordinary Americans to sustain the war effort and giving the Communists emotional strength to continue the struggle.

Though Johnson saw the antiwar movement eroding his freedom to fight a long war, he couldn't come to terms with its appeal—the growing skepticism that the price of fighting in Vietnam was worth paying. Johnson preferred to believe that antiwar critics were mainly radical intellectuals and misfits incapable of shaping majority sentiment.

Yet however much Johnson and others saw war opponents as extremists with limited appeal, they felt compelled to counter the effects they saw from unanswered criticism and demonstrations. Bill Moyers wanted the President to get out from behind a teleprompter and the setting of a press conference to talk things over with the country in more informal settings. Jim Rowe also urged a counterattack against dissenters. "It is elementary that this is an unpopular war," he wrote Johnson on May 17. The bulk of the country supported LBJ's policies, but it was "restless" in the face of the opposition. These "opinion makers" may eventually "convert the people, particularly if unopposed."

Johnson didn't wish to get out front in this campaign, believing that he was already something of a redundancy in arguing the case for Vietnam.

He was comfortable speaking to journalists off the record, but he was eager for "prompt counter attack[s]" from administration leaders "against widely exaggerated media criticism" and for "plenty of backgrounders" from embassy and military staff in Vietnam.

During the spring, Johnson convinced himself that he was winning both wars—at home as well as in Vietnam. According to the polls, the majority of Americans wanted no halt to the bombing; in May, based on promises of more effective military action, public approval of Vietnam policy exceeded disapproval for the first time in five months; Robert Kennedy's dissent on Vietnam made him less popular than LBJ; while straw votes on Johnson against Romney and Nixon gave him reason to think he could be reelected.

At the same time Johnson assessed his standing at home, he was trying to decide on additional air and ground actions. Westmoreland and the Joint Chiefs recommended a "relentless application of force." They urged expanded strikes against North Vietnam to eliminate military and industrial facilities in the Hanoi-Haiphong area, destroy crops by hitting dams and dikes, and disrupt freedom of movement by bombing ports and rail lines to China. They also wanted a U.S. reserve call-up, which would give Westmoreland 200,000 more troops to attack North Vietnamese main units in the South, support pacification, and expand the war to Cambodia, Laos, and southern North Vietnam, just above the 17th parallel, to counter infiltration.

McNamara and civilian aides in the Defense Department opposed the JCS proposals as likely to provoke China and Russia and increase domestic divisions over the war. They suggested instead that the President "limit force increases to no more than 30,000; avoid extending the ground conflict beyond the borders of South Vietnam; and concentrate the bombing on the infiltration routes south of 20 degrees."

Johnson was reluctant to do anything that might provoke the Soviets and Chinese. As always, Johnson's impulse was to find some middle ground between competing recommendations. Above all, he didn't wish to rush into anything. Before he decided on future military actions, he wanted another close appraisal of existing conditions. At the beginning of July he sent McNamara, Wheeler, and other Defense, State, and White House officials to reach an agreement with Westmoreland on how to proceed. The only certainty in the picture as the mission went forward was that the war would go on.

:: "THERE IS NO STALEMATE"

By early July the word most often used to describe the war was "stalemate." The war was deadlocked—American ground forces in South Vietnam made it impossible for the Communists to win, but Viet Cong–North Vietnamese tactics and greater manpower made it unlikely that they would lose.

The suggestion that the United States was on a treadmill in Vietnam frustrated and angered Johnson. Americans were growing impatient with a war costing so much blood and showing few signs of a discernible end. By the middle of 1967, nearly 70,000 Americans had been killed or wounded. But, to give up now—to declare victory and leave—was unacceptable. To declare war on Hanoi and risk a larger conflict with China and Russia was also out of the question. Keep going, muddle through, and hope that Hanoi would cave in before we did seemed the only alternative. But to reach this goal required a steady commitment from the American people. By the summer of 1967, holding the country on course seemed as uncertain as knowing when Hanoi might give up the fight.

If his military gave him assurances that American firepower was working—that the ground war in the South and the air war in the North were grinding down the enemy—Johnson would keep the country on course at home. When McNamara returned from Vietnam on July 11, the President asked: "Are we going to be able to win this goddamned war?"

Johnson wanted to hear only one answer: It may take additional time and more men and more bombing, but *we will win*. Everyone high in the administration and military chiefs in Vietnam knew what the President wanted them to say. And like Johnson they had invested their reputations in the war. They could not tell him that the war was a lost cause or an open-ended struggle that could go on for years. Like the President they wanted to believe that they had acted wisely—that their decisions had been sound and the lives lost were in the service of a realizable goal.

Consequently, Johnson's principal aides told themselves and him what they all wanted to believe: We are going to "win." During McNamara's visit to Vietnam, Westmoreland said, "The situation is not a stalemate. We are winning slowly but steadily, and the pace can accelerate if we reinforce our successes."

Johnson's aides were echoing his hopes. And he reinforced them with public expressions of optimism. At a news conference he put the best possible face on the war. The objective was simply to give U.S. military power more time to work. Johnson declared himself happier than ever with U.S. military and civilian leadership in Vietnam. He was "generally pleased with the progress we have made militarily. We are very sure that we are on the right track."

Johnson's greatest worry was the U.S. press corps in Saigon; its reporting could sap American domestic morale and force an unsatisfactory end to the war. USIA Director Leonard Marks returned from Vietnam in early July with a discouraging report about the journalists. They were more pessimistic and critical than at any time in the past two years. They doubted our ability to defeat the Communists, saw the South Vietnamese government as hopelessly corrupt, and refused to believe that the September election would be anything but a mockery of democratic procedures.

Johnson asked McNamara, Wheeler, Westmoreland, and press secretary George Christian what they thought of censoring U.S. correspondents in Vietnam. All agreed that the price of censorship would be "too great." Christian said it would create a "morass. We cannot do it." Instead, Johnson and his advisers tried to muzzle press critics as best they could. Despite brave talk about no stalemate and winning, they feared that the journalists might be accurately describing conditions in Vietnam.

The unacknowledged doubts about U.S. effectiveness in Vietnam moved Johnson and his aides to mislead the press and the public. They didn't want the country to know, for example, that Westmoreland wanted another 200,000 troops above the 470,000 already committed to the fighting. Since a force of 670,000 would require a reserve call-up and provoke additional domestic divisions, Johnson wanted nothing said about so large an increase. In fact, he would give Westmoreland only another 55,000 troops for a total of 525,000. And Westmoreland was expected to describe the increase as entirely sufficient.

Faced with so many questions about progress in the fighting, the administration saw every negative Vietnam story as a blow to America's war morale. Dean Rusk told the Cabinet that "there is no evidence of a stalemate in Vietnam." The assumption was the product of a press corps, that "are more antagonistic now than they ever have been." We had stopped all "major enemy offensives," and "roads have been opened where they were not before." The President cited a confidential report showing increased effectiveness in bombing the North; there was "no question about progress."

All the positive talk, however, couldn't dispel increasing doubts. At a meeting of Senate leaders with the President on July 25, Fulbright frankly declared the war "a hopeless venture." He thought it was "ruining our domestic and our foreign policy. I will not support it any longer," he said. Johnson told him he had "a blind spot" on Vietnam, and challenged the senators to repeal the Gulf of Tonkin Resolution. "You can tell the troops to come home. You can tell General Westmoreland that he doesn't know what he is doing."

The administration simply lacked compelling information to convince most Americans that the war was going well. A Gallup poll at the end of July showed 52 percent of the country disapproving the President's handling of the war, his highest negative rating to date. Only 34 percent thought we were making progress in the fighting. Westmoreland and Wheeler responded with a stepped-up effort to convince newsmen and the American public that "nothing could be farther from the truth" than descriptions of the war as either a stalemate or a struggle in which we had lost the initiative.

But military and civilian proponents of the war had lost public trust. The journalists in Vietnam seemed more reliable. Despite what Johnson and others in the administration might think, the press's critical view of the war seemed to come not from youthful inexperience or personal ambition or any lack of patriotism, as Johnson believed, but from information and detached analysis showing the war at a standstill and unlikely to change.

It was not the journalists who were frustrating Johnson's efforts in Vietnam but battlefield realities and pressure on the U.S. military to provide false reports. Company commanders pressed for body counts gave what *New York Times* reporter Johnnie Apple describes as "WAGs—wild-ass guesses." Apple remembers spending a night with an American provincial adviser. When he showed him a printout of secure provincial hamlets he had obtained in Saigon and asked to visit one, the adviser exclaimed: "You can't go there. We'll get killed if we try to go there." The adviser explained that he had reported those hamlets as "insecure," but "when it got up to corps level or to country level, they had to make a quota; they felt they had to show those hamlets secure."

Johnson's real quarrel should have been with himself and advisers whose errors of judgment had drawn the United States into a quagmire from which they could not extricate themselves. His quarrel should have been with a mindset that insisted on hopeful assessments—with an outlook demanding that the military give "the old man good news." Acknowledging a failed policy that had cost so many lives was more than someone with so fragile an ego as Johnson's could manage. Losing was never a word in Lyndon Johnson's vocabulary.

:: THE SEARCH FOR A MAGIC BULLET

In the summer of 1967 Johnson hoped that a combination of heavier bombing and the election of a popular government in Saigon would prod Hanoi into peace talks. He saw these two conditions as making it so difficult for the Communists to seize power that they would negotiate a settlement. "The problem is how to get free and honest elections and not have a coup," Johnson told Peter Lisagor in August. "When they have that election, that's when South Vietnam stops crawling and begins to walk—when they get a democratic government."

In July and August U.S. military chiefs urged the President to believe that American bombing against the North was beginning to have the desired effects. Johnson didn't need convincing. He was eager to believe their reports. Johnson wanted to give the military more latitude. On July 15, he asked Rostow: "How could our bombing of the North Vietnamese transport system be intensified without excessive public clamor here and abroad?" Johnson ordered "a limited extension of previous targets." It was not as much as the military wanted, but it demonstrated that the President would not reduce bombing. He told Fulbright: "General Westmoreland told me . . . that the bombing is our offensive weapon. And it will be just like tieing his right hand behind him if we were to stop it."

During the first week of August Johnson received fresh indications that the bombing had reduced infiltration by forcing between 500,000 and 700,000 North Vietnamese into repair work. Clark Clifford and Maxwell Taylor urged him to expand the target list and move the "margins" closer to China. They predicted that unless we increased the bombing to reduce the flow of men and supplies south, we would find ourselves no further along toward winning the war a year from now. Clifford and Taylor were only reflecting what Johnson had already stated to them as his preference. He wanted to expand the target list and make Hanoi pay a greater price for its aggression. "We have got to do something to win. We aren't doing much now," he told advisers. (It was as close as Johnson came to acknowledging that the war was stalemated and that we could not end the fighting without some additional use of force.) "Our strategy," he said, ". . . is that we destroy all we can without involving China and Russia between now and September 1," two days before elections in South Vietnam. The American people "will not stay with us if we do not get destroyed all we can. . . . Let us find the least dangerous and the most productive targets."

Johnson knew that the air war was insufficient to break Hanoi's will to fight. As long as the North Vietnamese believed that American resolve was likely to collapse before theirs and that South Vietnam lacked the political stability to remain a viable country without U.S. power, they saw every reason to fight on. If he could convince them, however, that America would not relent in its military campaign and that South Vietnam was evolving into a durable national state, he saw hope for some kind of settlement. Moreover, withdrawal from Vietnam in 1967 or 1968, especially when so many of his principal advisers foresaw eventual success in the fighting, was unacceptable to him.

An election establishing a legitimate constitutional government in the South was an essential counterpart to increased bombing. With Ky agreeing to accept the vice presidency in a newly elected government, a Thieu-Ky conflict for political control largely ended and, in LBJ's view, opened the way to fair and honest elections on September 3. Twenty-two U.S. observers Johnson sent to oversee the elections reported that they were "clean" and a demonstration of democracy in action.

Yet whatever the political realities in Saigon, Johnson took the elections as a reason to hope that Hanoi might now be more receptive to talks. The elections were a reason "now to probe in every way to find some way to get Ho Chi Minh to talk, even as they continue to fight if necessary." Current U.S. opinion polls gave Johnson added reason to seize any possible initiative for peace talks. Fifty-six percent of Americans did not think the Vietnamese elections would lead to a stable government in Saigon; 54 percent were skeptical that the voting would reflect "the true wishes of the South Vietnamese people." A Harris poll at the end of August gave Johnson a new sense of urgency about ending the war. Sixty-seven percent of Americans disapproved of the President's handling of Vietnam; 61 percent opposed sending more troops; while 71 percent favored a negotiated peace "as quickly as possible."

Shaky domestic support and Johnson's doubts about military progress made him eager for a prompt settlement. Consequently, at the end of July, when Ho Chi Minh and North Vietnamese Premier Pham Van Dong agreed to see two Frenchmen proposing to mediate the conflict, the White House saw new hope for negotiations.

On August 11, the White House gave Harvard political scientist Henry Kissinger, who was the U.S. contact with the French messengers, a statement for delivery to Pham Van Dong. "The United States is willing to stop the aerial and naval bombardment of North Vietnam if this will lead promptly to productive discussions. . . . We would assume that, while discussions proceed . . . , the DRV would not take advantage of the bombing cessation or limitation." When Kissinger presented the statement to the

Frenchmen for transmittal to Hanoi, they urged a reduction in bombing during their next visit as a signal of U.S. intentions. During a White House discussion of bombing targets on August 18, Johnson agreed to a temporary cessation of bombing inside a ten-mile zone around Hanoi. Both Rusk and McNamara saw greatly improved chances of "secret contacts" resulting from this initiative. Johnson remained skeptical. On September 5, he told a group of American correspondents that "the new South Vietnamese government would seek peace . . . and that we would encourage them. We would stop bombing tomorrow if that could lead to productive talks, . . . but he said North Vietnam would offer no assurances that they won't use a pause to their military advantage." On September 11, when Hanoi responded to Johnson's August 11 statement, it complained about continuing heavy raids against North Vietnam, despite reduced attacks on Hanoi, and restated its refusal to talk until there was an unconditional halt to all acts of war. A message to the North Vietnamese on September 13 declared that the U.S. "proposal contained neither conditions nor threats and should not be rejected on these grounds." The U.S. government assumed that the DRV "would be willing promptly to engage in productive discussions leading to peace when there was a cessation of aerial and naval bombardment."

No meaningful response from Hanoi during the next two weeks made Johnson furious. At a meeting with advisers on September 26, Johnson complained that the North Vietnamese "are playing us for suckers. They have no more intention of talking than we have of surrendering." He now wanted the bombing to continue until it forced Hanoi into talks.

To win the public relations war in this latest round of abortive exchanges, Johnson gave a speech on September 29 in San Antonio, Texas. He emphasized his readiness "to send a trusted representative of America to any spot on this earth to talk in public or private with a spokesman of Hanoi. . . . The United States is willing to stop all aerial and naval bombardment of North Vietnam when this will lead promptly to productive discussions," he said.

Despite an unqualified rejection of his latest call for discussions, Johnson spent most of October ruminating over how to start talks. This impulse to see ongoing hints of interest in discussions had become a form of rationalization for continued bombing. If Hanoi seemed unreceptive to negotiations, it suggested that the bombing was having no effect. If the North Vietnamese showed some inclination to negotiate, or, more to the point, if the administration could see them as having such an inclination, it legitimized the bombing and even encouraged discussions of heavier bombing.

Though he had little or no reason to be optimistic about talks, Johnson continued to make negotiations a regular topic of his discussions about Vietnam. At a White House meeting on October 3, he asked about the status of the Paris talks, code-named "Pennsylvania," an initiative by the Shah of Iran to start peace talks, and Soviet Foreign Secretary Andrei Gromyko's views on Hanoi's response to a bombing halt. Johnson also asked his advisers to say what effect a decision by him not to run again for President might have on the war. Rusk urged him not to stand down, saying it "would have a very serious effect on the country. . . . Hanoi would think they have got it made." Johnson replied: "Our people will not hold out for four more years. I want to get rid of every major target. Between now and election, I am going to work my guts out. I would be 61 when I came back in, and I just don't know if I want four more years of this. . . . But I am afraid it would be interpreted as walking out on our men." He described congressional opinion as convinced "we will lose the election if we do not do something about Vietnam quick."

:: THE YEAR-END STRATEGY: WORDS AND BULLETS

Johnson had no intention of giving up on negotiations, but with nothing concrete to go on in late October he felt compelled to focus once again on combating the antiwar movement by convincing Americans that we were making progress and would eventually get a settlement. In a discussion with McNamara, Rusk, and Wheeler on the 23rd, he declared: "We are back to where we started. We've tried all your suggestions. We've almost lost the war in the last two months in the court of public opinion. These demonstrators and others are trying to show that we need somebody else to take over this country. . . . The hawks are throwing in the towel. . . . We've got to do something about public opinion."

Mounting expressions of opposition to the war in the second half of 1967 deepened Johnson's frustration with public opinion and Hanoi. Growing dissent in the Congress from hawks, doves, and moderates eager for an end to the fighting particularly troubled him. In early October, he complained that 95 percent of the Congress believed that U.S. public opinion was turning against the war.

Johnson wanted time to combat the downturn in public support. The polling data in October added to his sense of urgency about boosting national sentiment. A Gallup survey released on the 4th showed a decided advantage for a Rockefeller-Reagan ticket in 1968. The source of Johnson's decline was frustration over Vietnam. At the start of October only 28 percent approved of his "handling of the war," with 57 percent disapproving. When Gallup asked whether it was a mistake to have become involved in Vietnam, 46 percent said, "yes."

On October 19, Johnson told Robert Manning of *The Atlantic* that he had "never thought there shouldn't have been intervention or bombing. If history indicts us for Vietnam," Johnson said, "it will be for fighting a war without trying to stir up patriotism." Nothing could have been further from the truth. From day one of the escalation in 1965 Johnson had doubted the wisdom of a wider war. Moreover, a two-pronged strategy for combating public demoralization gave the lie to his assertion about shaping opinion: On one hand, he approved a campaign to discredit antiwar demonstrators, and on the other, he tried to convince the country that the war was being won.

Johnson agreed to have every government intelligence agency investigate, monitor, and undermine antiwar activists. Under its antisubversion or Communist Infiltration and Counterintelligence programs, the FBI assigned thousands of agents to these tasks. In response to urban riots and antiwar rallies, the army set up an Intelligence Command unit that infiltrated and reported on the work of peace and civil rights groups. Despite bars on domestic spying, the CIA created a Special Operations Group to look for connections between American dissenters and foreign operatives. The Justice Department and the National Security Agency also joined in the surveillance of radicals who were seen as disrupting domestic tranquility and undermining the war effort.

For Johnson, the question at the end of 1967 was not whether U.S. war protests were Communist-inspired but how to convince Americans that the war was going well and would be won if only they continued to back the boys in the field. At a late September meeting with college and university educators "troubled about Vietnam," Johnson declared that "many people are being used in this country and are hurting the country perhaps without even knowing it." He urged the educators to understand that North Vietnamese "losses have been very heavy. We are trying to hold them there. . . . We believe the time will come when their power to make war will no longer be there. The price will be enough to make them talk."

Johnson's statements to the educators reflected the concerted effort he now thought necessary "to sell our product to the American people. I want to counter these arguments" in the press, he told McNamara, Rusk, Rostow, and Christian on October 4, "about the South Vietnamese not fighting, about the value of an enclave theory, [which he saw as a prelude to getting out] and about the pay-off to stopping the bombing."

Johnson knew that it wasn't enough to fight back; there also had to be a convincing argument made by persuasive people. Finding Vietnam advocates was no problem. Johnson himself made the case to journalists, congressmen, interest groups, and the mass public. "Do you think that you, personally, can help to alleviate some of the uncertainty in the country over Vietnam?" a journalist asked him at a November 1 press conference. "I am doing my best to do that every day," he replied.

In private conversations with reporters, he described "phenomenal progress in the last two years in building a democratic government in South Vietnam and in the conduct of the war." He said that "North Vietnam hasn't won a single victory" during this time. "We are making steady progress," he advised one journalist. Saigon was "in a constitutional process." Your speech to the international labor group was "great," a congressman told him in late October. "You put Viet Nam in just the proper perspective."

But Johnson found it difficult to sustain his rationality in dealing with war critics. During a private conversation with some reporter who pressed him to explain why we were in Vietnam, Johnson lost his patience. According to Arthur Goldberg, "LBJ unzipped his fly, drew out his substantial organ, and declared, 'This is why!'"

Johnson took special pains to keep Congress behind the war. In a briefing of House members on November 2, he emphasized that the rapport between him and military advisers had never been better. They were in full agreement on all the "basic decisions." Their policies had assured against a war with Russia or China by convincing them that Ho was not going to win, that the United States would not abandon the struggle, that we had no designs on North Vietnam or China, and that we would leave South Vietnam when the violence stopped. The air war was the product of the shared judgments of himself and air commanders, and, where there was some disagreement on targets, hitting them would reduce Communist supply shipments by only 1 percent. Most important, the Communists were now "suffering terribly": they were losing 1,500 men a day to our 15.

Two weeks later, Johnson asked Westmoreland to give a congressional briefing. The general couldn't have been more upbeat. "We have got our opponent almost on the ropes," he declared. "We are confident that we are winning this war. . . . We are grinding this enemy down. And at the same time, we are building up the South Vietnamese to the point where they will be able to progressively take over the greater part of the load."

Johnson wanted all the help he could get in making the case for Vietnam. On November 1, he told Rostow, "I can't clean up all the mess the *New York Times* leaves behind while these old pros and intellectuals [at

Radio Free Europe] sit silent." At a White House meeting with Acheson and other "wise men" on November 2, he pressed the case for "far more vigorous action to stabilize public support for our policy in Vietnam." Everyone from Supreme Court Justice Abe Fortas to old political friend Jim Rowe, columnist Joe Alsop, former President Eisenhower, former conservative Congressman Walter Judd, a White House-inspired National Citizens Committee for Peace with Freedom in Vietnam, the American Legion, the Veterans of Foreign Wars, Senators Paul Douglas of Illinois and Gale McGee of Wyoming, and the U.S. Embassy staff in Vietnam were enlisted in the effort.

But Johnson knew that statements about progress in the war needed to have the ring of truth. Harry McPherson brilliantly made the point in a letter to him on October 27. The air war, he said, "has just about become *the war* in the eyes of the press and the minds of the public." And with so many middle-road Democratic supporters growing "edgy about the bombing program," it was time to make clear "what we hope to gain from it." More important, the President needed to describe progress in the South, where the war was going to be won or lost. He needed to show "whether the [Saigon] government works, whether ARVN improves, whether substantial areas are and will remain pacified, whether corruption and inefficiency are reduced, whether people start to trust their leaders, whether the VC is losing support, whether we are licking them on the ground in all four Corps areas."

Johnson had anticipated McPherson's suggestion. On October 25, Walt Rostow told McNamara, Rusk, and Helms that "the President has an urgent need for reliable, usable data on Vietnam and ways of measuring the evolution of the conflict." Rostow asked "that a special interagency task force be established to develop further ways of measuring the progress of the war in all its facets." The "process" was to "be started immediately so that reporting" on this more convincing basis could begin on January 1, 1968.

When David Halberstam revisited Vietnam in December 1967, he rediscovered a world of illusions. Light at the end of the tunnel, corners being turned, victory in a matter of months were some of the upbeat descriptions on the lips of U.S. officials. But Halberstam came away doubting "our capacity to win." It was not that U.S. military power lacked victories. They were real, but ephemeral. American military successes had done little, if anything, to help the South Vietnamese to help themselves. Their society was "rotten, tired, and numb" after twenty-one years of war. The government of South Vietnam was "largely meaningless to its citizens," and U.S. programs and wishes could not change that.

"I do not think we are winning in any true sense," Halberstam concluded, "nor do I see any signs we are about to win. . . . I do not think our Vietnamese can win their half of the war, nor do I think we can win it for them." Even if we stayed for another five years, we could achieve no more than a settlement the Vietnamese would have to make themselves. The best we could hope for in an unwinnable war was the stalemate that had taken hold in 1967 and seemed all too likely to continue for the foreseeable future. No amount of number juggling or posturing about significant gains could change the harsh realities of Vietnam.

13 :: LAST HURRAHS

In the fall of 1967, more than anything, Johnson wanted to end the uncertainty over Vietnam. The "most important decision" we now have, the President told Rostow in October, was a "strategy for the next 12 months on Vietnam — military, political, negotiating." There had been "too much vague talk," Johnson complained.

It was clear to Johnson that the North Vietnamese "simply are not yet ready to quit," and a fresh look at the war was now in order. He asked the "Wise Men" — Dean Acheson, General Omar Bradley, George Ball, Mac Bundy, Arthur Dean, Douglas Dillon, Abe Fortas, Averell Harriman, Henry Cabot Lodge, Robert Murphy, and Max Taylor — to meet with him on November 2. As a prelude, the President asked McNamara, Wheeler, and George Carver, the CIA's expert on Vietnam, to brief them.

At lunch with the "Wise Men" on October 31, McNamara gave vent to his growing doubts about the war. "Perhaps everything I and Dean Rusk have tried to do since 1961 has been a failure," McNamara said. He also declared that "continuation of our present course of action in Southeast Asia would be dangerous, costly in lives, and unsatisfactory to the American people."

McNamara's anguish over the war found fuller expression in a memo he gave the President on November 1. Because he was proposing a change of course on Vietnam, which might be "incompatible with" LBJ's view, McNamara withheld the paper from other administration officials. He foresaw our present course as leading to U.S. troop increases in 1968 and a doubling of casualties, which would further erode popular support. Instead, McNamara urged Johnson to announce "a policy of stabilization": a cap on U.S. ground forces at 525,000; a unilateral and indefinite halt to bombing the North, which was gaining us little, if anything; and a transfer of greater responsibility for ground operations to the South Vietnamese, which would reduce U.S. casualties.

McNamara's recommendations agitated Johnson. The Secretary, who had been so committed to escalating the war, was now all but conceding defeat. McNamara's change of view left Johnson feeling abandoned and angry. Johnson now described McNamara to several people as in a state of near collapse. He worried that McNamara might "pull a Forrestal," meaning he might take his own life as the former Defense Secretary had in 1949. McNamara, in fact, manifested considerable strain. His haggard appearance—glazed eyes and jowly face—was accompanied by erratic behavior. He would speak with "terrible emotion" about the war, with tears "in his eyes and in his voice." At one meeting he went on for a full five minutes "in rage and grief and almost disorientation." During conversations in his office, he would turn away from his visitors and cry into the curtain.

McNamara denies that he was "near emotional and physical collapse. I was not. I was indeed feeling stress. I was at loggerheads with the President of the United States; I was not getting answers to my questions; and I was tense as hell. But I was not under medical care, not taking drugs except for an occasional sleeping pill, and never contemplated suicide."

Nevertheless, given McNamara's characteristically contained, even stoic, behavior, it is understandable that Johnson now saw him as near collapse, and so Johnson now decided to get him out of the administration by making him the president of the World Bank.

By dropping McNamara, Johnson was signaling that he would not follow his lead; at least, not now. To Johnson's satisfaction, his advisers uniformly argued for continued firmness in the war. After briefings describing "a good chance of success," they all agreed that there was "great improvement and progress" in Vietnam, and that the administration should "press forward" with its program.

However strong Johnson's resistance to McNamara's change of course, it heightened his sense of urgency about bringing America's military involvement in South Vietnam to a speedy and successful conclusion. At a Tuesday lunch meeting on November 4, Johnson wondered "how we are going to do a better job of winning the war in the South. We've been on dead center for the last year," he said, acknowledging a stalemate in the fighting he had been denying so vehemently in public. Two days later, he asked for a military plan bringing faster results.

At every meeting on Vietnam during the rest of November, Johnson pressed the case for quick results. "What about pushing up the arrival time of more units?" he asked advisers. He also ordered the military chiefs to get the number of bombing targets "down to the absolute minimum," and to get the additional "troops out there as rapidly as possible." Johnson's priority was clear to anyone attentive to his comments. He wanted to find ways in which the South Vietnamese could take over the fighting from American forces. He also wanted to hit all remaining targets in the North on the Pentagon's list.

Westmoreland had no doubt what Johnson wanted. During a visit to Washington in November, he began discussing his "withdrawal strategy." In congressional testimony and in meetings with LBJ, McNamara, and the Joint Chiefs, he foresaw a larger role for South Vietnamese forces in the fighting during the next two years and the beginnings of a phased withdrawal by U.S. forces.

Johnson was never more mindful of how much Americans wanted to end the war. To win time for the "withdrawal strategy," he launched a fresh campaign to rekindle public hope that an honorable peace was within reach. In December, partly in response to the "withdrawal strategy," which the public favored by a 66 to 15 percent count, Johnson's approval ratings on his handling of Vietnam increased from an August low of 33 percent to 40 percent. Lou Harris reported that the public now heavily favored "escalation over deescalation" as a prelude to withdrawal, and supported "the administration position that the war is preventing further Communist aggression in Southeast Asia." Harris believed that the upturn in public support resulted from assurances that we were doing better in the war and had a better plan to end it than antiwar protestors.

Johnson had no illusions about the upturn in public support. As long as Americans saw him moving toward an honorable withdrawal from Vietnam, the public would remain more supportive of his leadership. Should it begin to see him again as stubbornly committed to an inconclusive struggle, his approval ratings were certain to tumble. As much as anyone, he wanted to end America's involvement in the war. But he refused to go without believing that a non-Communist South Vietnam would survive American departure. When the journalist David Brinkley asked him why he simply didn't give up on Vietnam and save American lives that Brinkley thought were being needlessly lost, Johnson replied: "I'm not going to be the first American President to lose a war."

Johnson didn't know how long it would take to secure his goal, but he hoped, given all the talk of progress, that we might get there in 1968 or 1969.

In the meantime, he intended to facilitate American military advance in Vietnam while he encouraged domestic opinion to believe that we would stop fighting before too long.

Johnson had no illusion that peace was at hand. There was an almost universal feeling, he told New Hampshire's Senator Tom McIntyre on December 28, "that Hanoi will not negotiate until they see the outcome of the election of November 1968 here." In the meantime, though, Johnson promised to use every resource at his command to advance the goal of peace, especially through efforts in South Vietnam rather than against the North. Whether it would be sufficient to end the war in 1968 was a prediction Johnson refused to make.

:: VIETNAM: TET

At the beginning of 1968 Johnson genuinely hoped that a settlement in Vietnam was within reach. However difficult to describe with precision, he believed that slow, steady progress in the fighting and toward a stable South Vietnamese government were forcing the NLF and Hanoi toward an inevitable settlement. His upbeat mood, which polling data in December indicated had impressed itself on the public, found fresh expression in his State of the Union address on January 17. Acknowledging that the country was still being challenged in Vietnam and that the enemy was not yet ready to make peace, he nevertheless saw an America having "the will to meet the trials that these times impose."

A belief that a Communist "general counteroffensive and general uprising" would occur in January or February fueled Johnson's optimism. Recent defeats and hopes that it could spark the military and political collapse of South Vietnam's army and government moved Hanoi to plan a widespread assault. Johnson was confident that American military power would prevail in this coming clash and would force the Communists to negotiate.

Yet U.S. analysts did not anticipate the time or locale of the attack. Because Tet, the Vietnamese New Year holiday, was seen as a kind of inviolable period, an annual event "cherished by every religious group and social class," neither South Vietnam's leaders nor America's military and civilian officials foresaw the timing of the attack. When the Viet Cong and North Vietnamese struck on January 30–31, GVN and American forces were surprised; and not simply by the timing, but also the extent and ferocity of the offensive.

The Communists assaulted thirty-six of South Vietnam's provincial capitals, five of its six largest cities, and almost one-third of the country's district centers. In Saigon itself, they struck the U.S. Embassy compound, Tan San Nhut Air Base, the Presidential Palace, South Vietnam's Joint General Staff headquarters, and other government installations. Effective resistance blunted their attacks in Saigon, but most of Hue, the country's ancient capital and site of the symbolically important Imperial Citadel, fell under Communist control. Except for Hue, where the enemy held out for twenty-six days against a massive counterattack, the fighting slowed after two weeks.

Much would be made later of Westmoreland's alleged willingness to deceive the President about Communist strength as a reason for Johnson's failure to foresee what was coming. But the problem was not with Johnson's knowledge of enemy strength. Rather, it resulted from a kind of auto-intoxication or self-deception as to allied progress in the fighting and limited enemy capacity. After three years of bombing that had unleashed more tonnage on Vietnam than in all of World War II, and after so many ground actions in which Viet Cong and North Vietnamese forces had supposedly suffered demoralizing losses, it was difficult, if not impossible, for Johnson and most of his advisers to imagine the sort of offensive mounted during Tet.

Tet was a major military defeat for the Viet Cong and North Vietnamese. Estimates of Communist losses range between 33,000 and 58,000, with thousands more wounded and captured. Many of the Viet Cong's and Hanoi's best troops were lost in the fighting. By contrast, between 1,100 and 4,000 U.S. troops were killed, depending on whether one counts losses for two weeks or two months. During February and March about 5,000 South Vietnamese soldiers died in action. The Communists achieved neither of their immediate objectives: to cripple the South Vietnamese military or topple the government in Saigon. Nevertheless, the Tet attacks succeeded in forcing the American government to retreat from an expansion and even continuation of the war as it had been fought.

The principal casualty of the Tet offensive was U.S. public opinion. Johnson had been saying for months that the Communists hoped to win the war not on the battlefields in Vietnam but by sapping the American will to fight. His first response to the expanded fighting was to assure the public that the offensive was not what it appeared to be—a demonstration of Communist capacity to sustain the conflict despite the alleged losses described in recent months by the U.S. government.

Johnson mounted a public relations campaign to counter any advantage Hanoi would try to gain from Tet. On January 31, he sent word to Westmoreland and Bunker that he wanted them to give daily press briefings that would "convey to the American public your confidence in our capability to blunt these enemy moves, and to reassure the public here that you have the situation under control."

Initially, Johnson took heart from polling data showing an upsurge of public support in response to Tet. On January 31, he received "evidence that the people's commitment to the Vietnam war is 'real and abiding.'" By a 64 to 24 percent vote the public said that, despite the war, the Johnson domestic program does not have to be reduced. But if a choice had to be made between guns and butter, the public gave priority to the war by 52 percent to 30 percent. Moreover, in mid-February, Gallup and Harris found a surge in "hawk" opinion, with 61 percent, a five-point increase from January, saying they favored stronger military measures to end the conflict.

Tet produced a "rally" effect, with 70 percent of Americans — up from 63 percent in December — saying they wanted the United States to continue the bombing of North Vietnam, and 53 percent favoring either a gradual broadening and intensifying of military operations or "an all-out crash effort in the hope of winning the war quickly even at the risk of China or Russia entering the war."

The increased support was temporary. By March the public impulse to back the troops and sustain U.S. involvement until the North Vietnamese made peace fell victim to doubts about the war. News stories on American television were particularly instrumental in strengthening public reluctance to "stay the course" in Vietnam. When newsmen reported that a U.S. major had said it was necessary to destroy a village to save it from the Viet Cong, and when television broadcast images of South Vietnam's national police chief executing a bound V.C. prisoner, it intensified feelings that neither we nor the Vietnamese were winning anything in a conflict that seemed principally to produce brutal actions and endless casualties.

The polling numbers showed a "new wave of pessimism on Vietnam." In early March, 49 percent of Americans thought it was a mistake to have sent troops to fight. Forty-one percent believed it was right. Only 35 percent of the country saw the conflict ending in less than two years. Sixty-nine percent of Americans approved of a "phase-out plan" to replace U.S. troops with South Vietnamese.

The President's job ratings now reached new lows: 26 percent approved of his handling of Vietnam; 63 percent disapproved. Thirty-six percent gave him overall approval, but 52 percent were negative. Despite a growing "cut and run" attitude, Johnson assumed that most Americans still preferred to hold out against defeat. Since he initially feared additional Communist attacks, which might destroy the South Vietnamese Army and compel a coalition government asking U.S. withdrawal, the President sent word to Westmoreland on February 8 that "the United States government is not prepared to accept a defeat in South Vietnam. In summary, if you need more troops, ask for them." Westmoreland responded, "I would welcome reinforcements at any time they can be made available."

Johnson agreed to send an additional 10,500 troops. He also discussed the possibility of taking stronger action. The Joint Chiefs saw the President's worries as an opportunity to press for a large call-up of reserves. When Clark Clifford, who was about to replace McNamara, questioned the sudden sense of urgency about getting all these additional forces, Westmoreland and the Chiefs described the request as a chance to seize the initiative and decisively defeat the enemy.

The Chiefs now asked for a reserve call-up of 206,000 troops, half to go to Vietnam and the rest to form a backstop for possible use in other hot spots around the globe. Wheeler gave a gloomy report about conditions in South Vietnam, describing the Tet offensive as "a very near thing" and the additional troops as allowing the United States "to counter the enemy offensive."

The size of the Chiefs' request, Clifford says, "astonished Washington, and triggered the first fundamental debate over the course of the war since the decisions of 1965." Recognizing that he was faced with a major decision that contained "military, diplomatic, economic, congressional, and public opinion problems," the President asked Rusk and Clifford to consider every alternative in recommending what should be done. A commitment of this size would mean a further Americanization of the war, a substantial new strain on the budget, and a challenge to U.S. public opinion, which would want assurances that such an increased commitment would bring a quick end to the war.

Because an increase in U.S. force levels proposed by the Chiefs seemed likely to produce a fiscal-economic crisis and a renewed assault on his credibility, which would further weaken his political hold on the country, Johnson decided against the request. Instead, with the Tet fighting largely over and the diminished likelihood of a defeat, which Johnson had feared at the start of the offensive, he reverted to his end-of-year strategy for a reduced American role in the war coinciding with increased South Vietnamese action.

By March 1968 Johnson was desperately eager for an honorable way out of the conflict. He would not commit himself to a straightforward plan for ending U.S. involvement lest it look too much like an acknowledgment of defeat. Nor would he say anything in public that suggested he was giving up on the possibility of an American victory. But his shift to a slow with-drawal strategy came from a recognition of the reality that the war was stale-mated and unwinnable without an escalation that would risk a domestic and international crisis unwarranted by the country's national security.

In a nationally televised speech on March 31, Johnson described "Steps to Limit the War in Vietnam." The address began: "Tonight I want to speak to you of peace in Vietnam and Southeast Asia." He then reminded Americans that for years representatives of the U.S. government had unsuccess-fully traveled the world seeking a basis for talks. He announced an imme-diate unilateral halt to the bombing of North Vietnam, except in the area north of the DMZ, where a continuing buildup threatened "allied forward positions." He named Averell Harriman as his personal representative who would go anywhere, any time to talk peace. Reviewing the growing effec-tiveness of the South Vietnamese in their own defense and the need for a tax increase in the United States to meet expenditures in the war and at home, Johnson expressed the "fervent hope" that North Vietnam would cease its efforts to achieve a military victory and agree to join us at the peace table.

:: THE UNHAPPY STATE OF THE UNION

On January 17, 1968, Johnson gave his fifth State of the Union address. It was the least hopeful and most constrained of his messages. Gone were the optimistic forecasts of 1964 and 1965 about conquering poverty and building a Great Society; gone were the emphases on advances toward a Brave New World in the 1966 and 1967 speeches. The tone in 1968 was defensive—the acceptance implicitly, if not explicitly, that America was "challenged, at home and abroad."

The most striking feature of Johnson's address was his sense of constraint: the implicit message that Vietnam had put limits on what the country could now do at home and abroad. He never believed that this was a permanent state of affairs, but only a consequence of his depleted political influence, which an end to the war could replenish. And given his evangelism—his undiminished passion for grand designs, for history-making deeds—he faced 1968 with half a mind to reach for large goals anyway. But economic and political realities dictated otherwise. Indeed, Johnson later said that he expe-rienced so much "frustration and genuine anguish" during that year, he "sometimes felt" as if he were "living in a continuous nightmare."

Johnson's economic problems at the start of 1968 were one source of anguish. The costs of Vietnam and the Great Society were producing an estimated 1968 budget deficit of $19.8 billion. The Republicans predicted that the deficit would run between $25 and $30 billion. Johnson himself, trying unsuccessfully to frighten the Congress into passing his tax surcharge, had warned the previous November that the deficit might reach $35 billion. Without additional taxes, the administration saw an $8 billion deficit for fiscal 1969 growing to $20 billion. Though Johnson's January budget message pegged the 1968 imbalance at slightly under $20 billion, his remarks had contributed to international fears that the U.S. economy now faced runaway inflation and a recession, if not a depression.

A widening imbalance in America's international trade accounts, a run on the country's gold supplies, and continuing poor prospects for a tax increase gave financial markets everywhere a case of New Year's jitters. For seventeen of the previous eighteen years the United States had run trade deficits. A 1967 imbalance of between $3.5 and $4 billion, almost three times the amount in the previous year, coupled with a drop in U.S. gold reserves to $12.4 billion, the lowest since 1937, excited concerns about the value of the dollar. When opinion surveys indicated that 79 percent of Americans opposed a tax increase, financial analysts began talking about the dangers of an economic collapse.

Johnson renewed calls for the 10 percent tax surcharge and announced steps to reduce the balance of payments and federal deficits and curb inflation. Once again, he felt compelled to inhibit domestic spending. Though reducing poverty and raising living standards remained abiding aims, he refused to consider launching new domestic programs.

The one area where Johnson felt he could make a domestic advance without spending federal monies was a 1968 civil rights law guaranteeing open housing to all Americans. He worried about the fact that one out of three nonwhite families still lived below the poverty line; that the infant mortality rate for nonwhite children was nearly double that of whites; that the percentage of black high school graduates remained well below that of whites; and that minority unemployment was still twice the rate of whites. But he offered no major legislative initiative to address these issues, because doing so would have required substantial financial commitments.

Instead, he focused on discrimination in housing. If America was ever to become a truly integrated society, he said, it would have to eliminate racial apartheid in neighborhoods. It was time to remedy the problem through a federal law prohibiting discrimination in the sale and rental of all housing in the United States.

The unspoken side of Johnson's message was that fair housing would be a major advance in civil rights at little financial cost. In a time of great federal stringency, Johnson saw fair housing as an ideal program. "He was relentless," Califano says. "I mean there was no give. We were pushing, pushing, pushing. This was going to be done."

Job training for minorities and low-income housing were other initiatives Johnson thought he could pursue without significant impact on the federal budget. His idea was to create a partnership between the federal government and private sector in developing jobs and building homes. In a conversation with television journalists in December 1967, Johnson said there are half a million "hard-core unemployed in our principal cities and we've just got to go find jobs for them." He declared his intention to call in the businessmen of America and press them to help develop jobs for the chronically unemployed. The alternative would be an expensive government program. Likewise, he saw a compelling need to rescue people living in "filth and dilapidated houses" through a public-private program.

Many liberals were not happy with Johnson's refusal to commit himself to new or expanded programs for social advance. HEW Secretary John Gardner resigned partly in protest against domestic budget cuts. And Bobby Kennedy "will sharply attack the administration's new housing program" as inadequate to the task, an aide warned Johnson. But LBJ had no patience with such complaints. He might not be able to focus the attention and resources on domestic difficulties as earlier in his term, but he believed that his administration had "*presided over the most remarkable period of economic and social progress in the Nation's history.*" Besides, he took pride in the fresh ways he saw to continue the good fight. The principal question before him at the start of 1968 was whether he should seek another term in which he could implement his evolving plans for domestic change.

:: "I SHALL NOT SEEK, AND I WILL NOT ACCEPT . . ."

By January 1968 Johnson had been struggling for more than a year with a decision about running again. After the Democratic losses in 1966, he began giving continuous thought to the question. In and of itself there was nothing surprising about incumbent party losses in a mid-term election, but other influences were at work that made Johnson think he might not win again. The inner-city riots had produced a backlash against his support of minority programs that seemed unlikely to soften in the next two years. Having assumed that the South would shift toward the Republicans in response to the civil rights and voting rights acts, Johnson now saw northern blue-collar whites also turning against him and the Democrats.

In deciding whether to run, Johnson also considered the possibility that Robert Kennedy might take the nomination from him. In July 1966, Bill Moyers privately reported from New York that Bobby's Senate staff was promoting the tale that Johnson would settle the Vietnam War by 1968 and then retire for health reasons. They were urging people "to get on the Kennedy bandwagon . . . now." In November, Marvin Watson told LBJ of reports that Kennedy was discouraging party donors from giving money to LBJ and suggested instead that donations go to the New York State Democratic committee.

The more Johnson thought about running, the more hesitant he became. True, by the beginning of May his approval rating was up to 48 percent, and he beat Kennedy in a trial heat by 49 percent to 37 percent. But only 43 percent approved of his handling of Vietnam, and a straw poll against Romney in June showed him trailing by three points.

More important, health concerns made him reluctant to serve another four years. In January 1965, he had been rushed to the hospital with chest pains, which turned out to be a serious respiratory infection causing a temperature of 104.4 degrees. In October, he had surgery to remove his gall bladder and a kidney stone. Given his medical history, the surgery raised concerns about a cardiac episode. There were also fears that he might have pancreatic cancer. Though neither of these problems occurred, his recovery from the surgery was more painful and slower than anticipated. In addition, when attempts to defuse rumors that he had had a heart attack by showing his surgical scar to reporters provoked attacks on his crudeness, he became depressed and discussed resigning. In late December, he returned to the hospital for throat surgery on a benign polyp and a repair on his gall bladder incision, which had never fully healed.

In 1967 he had a secret actuarial study prepared on his life expectancy. He wished an assessment of his own belief that his family history made it unlikely that he'd survive a second term. "The American people had enough of Presidents dying in office," he said.

If health worries weren't enough to drive Johnson out of the race, additional bad news in the summer of 1967 brought him closer to such a decision. Senator Daniel Inouye of Hawaii told an LBJ aide that if the Republicans had a chief of staff with "the power and the authority to dream up and impose upon the President the most burdensome problems the mind of man is capable of conceiving, the President would not have any more problems cast upon him than he now has." Poll numbers were depressing: Seven out of ten Republicans thought their chances in 1968 were good and four out of ten Democrats agreed. Johnson's job rating was down to 39 percent favorable, the lowest since he had taken office.

The war had become an unshakable burden. September polls showed Johnson's approval and disapproval ratings holding steady at 40 percent and 48 percent, respectively. The numbers on Vietnam were worse, with only 28 percent positive and 57 percent negative.

In September, Johnson reached a tentative decision not to run again. During an eight-hour conversation at his ranch on September 8 with Texas Governor John Connally, Congressman Jake Pickle, and Lady Bird, LBJ reviewed his options. Connally told him he didn't think he could get reelected. Johnson himself saw withdrawal as an opportunity to make peace without abandoning Vietnam. Pickle agreed with the President's reasoning, but worried that Johnson's retirement would make it difficult for Democrats to hold their congressional seats. Lady Bird expressed fears that bad health might overtake him in another term: something not incapacitating but enough to put a distinct limit on his capacity "to be the sort of a President he wanted to be . . . a physical or mental incapacitation would be unbearably painful for him to recognize, and for me to watch," she believed.

Johnson considered announcing his retirement at a Democratic party dinner in October or at a political function in December. Connally advised an early declaration, which would leave Johnson free to work exclusively on national problems, including Vietnam, and give other potential candidates a chance to prepare their campaigns. But Johnson did nothing in October, and though he asked George Christian and Connally to write a withdrawal statement for December, he still held back from acting.

At the same time he made plans to retire, he encouraged discussions about a 1968 campaign. In the fall of 1967, he gave Larry O'Brien, John Roche, Jim Rowe, and Marvin Watson reason to think he would run again. At the end of September, O'Brien completed a forty-four-page campaign strategy paper describing how to return LBJ to the presidency. When Rowe responded to O'Brien's paper by asking Johnson whether he would devote one or two evenings a week to campaign issues with "a number of people in whom he has confidence," Johnson checked the "yes" box.

In January 1968 Johnson again considered withdrawing. In December, after *U.S. News & World Report* had predicted that Johnson would win only twelve states with 110 electoral votes, he had told aides that he would step aside, and asked Busby to draft a withdrawal statement for his State of the

Union address. At the last minute Johnson decided against using it. He handed the text to Mrs. Johnson before leaving for the Capitol and did not have it with him during his speech. He said later that a withdrawal now would make him a lame duck and cripple chances of passing his legislative program. He kept delaying an announcement, Lady Bird recalls, because he thought another few months or even weeks could make a difference in getting "three or four cliff hangers" approved.

But more was at work here than Johnson's concern with bending Congress to his will. He was ambivalent about leaving the presidency while the war continued. Mrs. Johnson remembers how much he worried about the impact of his decision on the troops in Vietnam. Besides, in December and January, as impressions grew that he was heading toward a settlement in Vietnam, his political fortunes turned up. His approval-disapproval ratings reversed themselves. In December, he had a 46 percent to 41 percent positive margin, which improved in January to 48 percent to 39 percent.

However great his reluctance to bear the demands of another national campaign, he also relished the thought of beating liberal opponents, especially Kennedy, and winning vindication from voters. But the only candidate liberals seemed able to run against LBJ was Senator Eugene McCarthy of Minnesota, whose emergence as the point man in a "dump Johnson" movement at the end of November indicated that Johnson could be renominated. Johnson's supporters saw McCarthy as "more of a diversion than a serious threat." He was a one-issue candidate — Vietnam — with little public visibility. Polls in early December showed that only four out of ten Americans had heard of him, and these voters favored LBJ over McCarthy by a two-to-one margin. Among rank-and-file Democrats, Johnson led by three to one.

Though Johnson's "vulnerability" was widely discussed, in December and January he also heard much that encouraged him. Democratic party officials began organizing against McCarthy, while straw polls pitting the President against Nixon, Romney, and Rockefeller gave Johnson hope of winning again.

The upturn in Johnson's political fortunes was short-lived. The Tet offensive sent his approval ratings into a tailspin. In February, his positive standing with the public fell back to 41 percent, with 47 percent negative. On Vietnam, public confidence in his policy stood at only 35 percent, with 50 percent expressing disapproval; Lou Harris said the negative rating was at 62 percent.

The polling numbers were not decisive in reviving Johnson's impulse to step down. He understood that public mood shifted all the time and could

as easily turn in his favor over the next nine months as become more negative. More important, the demands of the office and especially of managing the war were wearing him down. The previous October, Dr. Willis
Hurst, the President's physician, had confided concern to Lady Bird about
Johnson's physical and emotional condition. "He did not see the bounce,
the laughter, the teasing quality in Lyndon that he has watched over these
twelve years. He thought he was running on marginal energy—that he was
bone tired."

Tet drained Johnson's resources beyond endurance. Senator John Stennis of Mississippi told Richard Russell that "The President is really under
a great strain." Stennis knew only half of it. During the week after Tet
began, Johnson got almost no sleep. He spent his nights distracting himself
from the anxieties of the war by shuffling between the Situation Room, the
Oval Office, and his living quarters, where he played dominoes with his
brother Sam Houston and old Texas friends. Sam remembers him as "very
tired and deeply worried." He was "tormented" by Vietnam. Sam watched
him in bathrobe and slippers shuffle "down the hall toward the elevator on
his way to the Situation Room in the basement to get the 3 o'clock report
from Saigon. He looked tired and lonely as he pushed the down button."
When Russell met with him alone at the White House, Johnson cried
uncontrollably.

As the Tet offensive became a military defeat for the Communists, Johnson's thoughts of staying in the race revived. A March 4 poll showed him
winning almost two-thirds of Democratic votes in New Hampshire against
McCarthy's 11 percent. The fact that all the President's votes would be
write-in ballots made it particularly impressive. The following day a *U.S.
News & World Report* reporter predicted that Nixon would win the Republican nomination and lose to Johnson in a close race.

Johnson's thoughts of running received a fresh blow on March 12 when
McCarthy shocked the country by winning 42 percent of the primary vote
in New Hampshire. Though Johnson received 49 percent, it was well
below the two-thirds predicted for him and suggested that his candidacy
faced greater difficulties than most analysts had anticipated. Some of
McCarthy's votes were from hawks fed up with Johnson's failure to win the
war. Johnson supporters had underestimated the extent to which voters saw
Tet as an American defeat, and overestimated gains to be made from
describing a vote for McCarthy as a vote for Ho Chi Minh.

For almost another three weeks, Johnson refused to give up the conviction that he could still be renominated and reelected. Political roundups
from nineteen states suggested that he could win enough delegates to

regain the nomination. And despite Bobby Kennedy's announcement on March 16 that he would enter the race, Johnson continued to promote his own candidacy.

But all the activity and positive speculation on his chances could not withstand the reality of Johnson's fall from political grace. The polling numbers in March told the story: 36 percent approval and 52 percent disapproval for his overall performance, and a meager 26 percent approval and a decisive 63 percent disapproval on Vietnam. Journalists and political insiders predicted that Johnson would lose in Wisconsin and then the nomination. But even if he managed to survive that test, Johnson would be an easy mark for a Republican nominee promising a change in current policies.

During the last days of March, Johnson decided not to run. Pessimistic assessments of his chances and sheer exhaustion strongly influenced his decision. He feared a stroke or some other debilitating disease that would incapacitate him. But as much as anything, Vietnam shaped his judgment to leave office. He saw the war as "a blot on his administration he wanted to remove." If he were running for reelection, he "might miss or postpone an opportunity to achieve peace." The issue now, as he saw it, was the historical reputation of his five-year administration.

Even with all the many reasons he saw for stepping aside, he clung to thoughts that he should run again. Only on the afternoon of March 31 did he convince himself to quit. And even then, aides were not sure he would follow through on his decision until he announced his withdrawal in his speech that night. At the close of his address on peace in Vietnam, he declared that he did not want "the presidency to become involved in the partisan divisions that are developing in this political year. . . . With our hopes and the world's hopes for peace in the balance every day, I do not believe that I should devote an hour or a day of my time to any personal partisan causes or to any duties other than the awesome duties of this office. . . . Accordingly, I shall not seek, and I will not accept, the nomination of my party for another term as your President." After his speech, one aide remembers that he "bounded from his chair in the Oval Office to join his family in watching the television reviews. His shoulders temporarily lost their stoop. His air was that of a prisoner let free," Mrs. Johnson recalls.

:: THE STATESMAN

The response to Johnson's announcement was the most positive expression of national support since his landslide election in 1964. Democrats and Republicans alike described his decision as an act of selfless patriotism.

Some of his most vocal critics, like William Fulbright, said this was "an act of a very great patriot." A number of Democrats thought Johnson's action would lead to a draft at the party's convention, and they hoped he would accept. Johnson himself declared that "I never was any surer of any decision I ever made in my life, and I never made any more unselfish one. I have 525,000 men whose very lives depend on what I do, and I can't worry about the primaries."

He even found common ground with Kennedy in the tide of good feeling that followed his announcement. Kennedy described his decision not to run as "truly magnanimous," and asked for an opportunity to see him as soon as possible "to discuss how we might work together in the interest of national unity during the coming months."

They met for an hour and a half in the White House Cabinet room on the morning of April 3. Johnson began by discussing Vietnam, the bombing halt, and his hopes for peace. Kennedy remarked on how helpful such a briefing was and hoped there would be others. Johnson promised to make Cabinet officers available in the future and to invite McCarthy and Nixon to speak with them as well. Kennedy turned the discussion to politics. "Where do I stand in the campaign?" he asked Johnson. "Are you opposed to my effort and will you marshal forces against me?" Johnson declared his intention to stand aside and keep the presidency out of the campaign.

Later that day Johnson discussed his decision and the presidential campaign with Humphrey. He repeated what he had told Kennedy about shunning involvement in the contest. But his partiality to Hubert over Kennedy kept poking through. However cordial the discussion with Kennedy that morning, it wasn't enough to wash away Johnson's animus toward him. Johnson said that he would be happy to see Humphrey as President, and that "some of the President's friends would probably be willing to help the Vice President.

Johnson's advice to Humphrey was a lapse in his self-denying proposition about involvement in the campaign. His focus during the three months after his withdrawal was largely on making final gains at home and abroad. As long as he remained in office, he intended to do what he could to ease national difficulties.

A fair housing bill remained high on his agenda. In January, he had told Congress that, despite local and state laws barring racial discrimination in housing, residential segregation was increasing in some cities, adding to national tensions over race relations. In February and March, he successfully pressured the Senate into passing a bill.

The House was more of a problem. The results of the 1966 elections had produced a twenty-two-vote loss in representatives favorable to a fair housing law. As Johnson aide "Barefoot" Sanders told him in February, "In order to command a House majority we must get a number of the new Republicans and try to change some of the Democrats who opposed us in 1966." Sanders was not optimistic. On March 19, the House Rules Committee voted 8 to 7 to delay floor action until April 9. Supporters of the measure feared that the start of a Poor People's Campaign in April would arouse opposition to the bill and that the delay was aimed at killing an open housing law.

But on April 4 Martin Luther King, Jr., was assassinated by a sniper, James Earl Ray, who escaped and would not be apprehended until June. King's death both demoralized and energized the President. "Everything we've gained in the last few days we're going to lose tonight," he said on hearing about King's murder. Though he accurately foresaw that the country's inner cities would explode again in rioting, he seized the occasion to press the case for the fair housing bill.

In response, on April 10, the House passed the bill. Johnson signed it the following day with an appeal for an end to violence and support for legal processes like the enactment of open housing and other social justice measures that were the work of democracy.

Johnson also wanted House action on his tax surcharge. He believed it vital to the national well-being. He needed it for spending on Vietnam. To cut war funds would reduce pressure on Hanoi to negotiate. He also saw a crisis in the cities, which the latest rioting made essential to address with federal monies. In addition, domestic budget and international balance-of-payment deficits threatened a crisis that a tax increase could partly relieve. Yet Mills would not agree to one without domestic cuts Johnson considered dangerous to national stability. In meeting after meeting during April he searched for ways to resolve the tax-budget stalemate with Mills and the Congress.

Johnson now brought all possible pressure to bear on Mills and Congress. At a May 3 press conference, he emphasized the need to fund the war and meet the "very serious problems in the cities" and of the poor. He described his $186 billion budget as "very lean." But if we were to avoid large deficits, stem inflation, win the confidence of world financial leaders, and "best serve our own people," there would have to be a tax increase. If Congress didn't like his budget, then they should "stand up like men and answer the roll call and cut what they think ought to be cut." It was time "to pass a tax bill without any 'ands,' 'buts,' or 'ors.'"

Even if congressmen and senators discounted Johnson's warnings about the state of national affairs as political arm-twisting, they didn't wish to risk an economic collapse. When the House finally acted at the end of June, it tied the bill to a $6 billion cut in domestic spending. Johnson reluctantly accepted the cuts, but in the belief that Congress would reduce outlays "by considerably less than $6 billion."

He was right about the need for the tax rise and Congress's inability to cut more than half the slated reductions. Getting the tax bill through Congress was a triumph of economic sense and political astuteness by a lame-duck President.

:: THE PEACEMAKER

But could he talk the Vietnamese into making peace? It was a formidable challenge. And he attacked it with the same determination and manipulativeness that had produced his greatest legislative successes. Clark Clifford later said that, "despite his overwhelming personality and unique understanding of political power, Lyndon Johnson during this period often acted more like a legislative leader, seeking a consensus among people who were often irreconcilably opposed to each other, rather than a decisive Commander in Chief giving his subordinates orders." Clifford doubts that Johnson had a clear idea of his objective in Vietnam after his March 31 speech. He sees Johnson as "torn between an honorable exit and his desire not to be the first President to lose a foreign war."

To Johnson, these were not mutually exclusive goals. Indeed, the key to his peacemaking was to arrange a settlement that both preserved South Vietnam as an independent state and sped America's exit from a war the country no longer wished to fight. Contrary to Clifford's belief, Johnson knew what he wanted. His problem was finding the means to get there, including the means to satisfy competing domestic factions urging different strategies for ending the war and the means to reach a settlement with Hanoi and an accommodation with Saigon.

During April and May, he struggled to begin negotiations with Hanoi. Despite suggestions that a wider bombing halt would facilitate talks, Johnson refused to alter the conditions described in his March 31 speech. He was more flexible about a site and an agenda for the negotiations. On April 3, the North Vietnamese announced an interest in "contact with U.S. representatives to decide . . . the unconditional cessation of bombing and all other war acts against the DRV so that talks can begin." Johnson responded with a public statement repeating his willingness to send representatives "to any forum, at any time."

Despite the rhetoric, Johnson bargained over the forum. He wanted a neutral site, where both sides would have "good communications," which would allow them to send and receive messages promptly. When Hanoi suggested Phnom Penh, Cambodia's capital, and then Warsaw, Poland, Johnson refused. Instead, he proposed Vientiane, Laos; Rangoon, Burma; Djakarta, Indonesia; and New Delhi—believing an Asian capital the best site for talks. If Hanoi preferred a European setting, Johnson was ready to accept Berne, Copenhagen, Helsinki, or Vatican City. When Hanoi rejected these proposals, Johnson added six Asian and two European capitals to the list. The meeting site now became a preliminary, month-long tug-of-war in the struggle over advantages in the negotiations.

By April 18, Hanoi's resistance to Johnson's choices moved him to announce, "It is time for a serious and responsive answer." Johnson was so eager to find a way through the deadlock that he accepted the possibility of going to Bucharest, the capital of a dissident Communist country. But Rusk thought Paris would be a better venue. The President was reluctant, believing that DeGaulle, who had removed France from NATO and been hostile to U.S. actions in Vietnam, would be friendly to Hanoi during the talks. But Johnson's determination to gain something from his March 31 initiative persuaded him to accept Paris as an alternative. On May 3, when Hanoi offered to meet in Paris the following week, Johnson announced American agreement.

The struggle over a meeting place was relatively minor compared with the debate over defining an agenda. During April, while discussion of a site proceeded, hawks and doves battled over what to offer the North Vietnamese. Rusk, Rostow, Bunker, Max Taylor, Fortas, and the military chiefs favored a tough declaration of terms: a cessation of bombing on condition that Hanoi did not then improve its military position, the onset of substantive talks within a week of reaching agreement, a willingness to discuss everything relevant to peace, and a place for South Vietnam at the peace table.

The doves—Clifford, Harriman, Cyrus Vance, Katzenbach, and Goldberg—wanted the American delegation to enter negotiations with the freedom to respond flexibly to the North Vietnamese. The hawks, by contrast, wanted to hold U.S. negotiators to a strict agenda dictated from Washington. Because they feared that Harriman would follow his own lead, they proposed reining him in with a deputy sympathetic to the hawks. But Johnson chose Deputy Defense Secretary Cyrus Vance, who favored Harriman's flexible approach.

Though estimates that Hanoi had sent between 80,000 and 100,000 men into South Vietnam in the previous four months greatly troubled him, Johnson remained determined to advance toward peace. Consequently, he agreed to an initial statement by the U.S. delegation that opened the way to a compromise formula on bombing. Instead of insisting on a North Vietnamese promise not to take advantage of a bombing halt, Harriman was to propose "prompt and serious substantive talks looking toward peace in Vietnam, in the course of which an understanding may be reached on a cessation of bombing in the North under circumstances which would not be militarily disadvantageous."

The talks beginning on May 13 proved to be as difficult as everyone had imagined. "The opening statement by the chief North Vietnamese delegate could have been an editorial in Hanoi's Communist party newspaper," Johnson said. "Their solution was for us to stop the bombing and pull all our forces out. . . . As these denunciations and demands were repeated, meeting after meeting, week after week, our hopes for a fair compromise and an early settlement grew dimmer." Adding to the problem was a series of attacks across South Vietnam and the aggressive use of the talks as a forum for public appeals to the American antiwar movement.

But Johnson refused to be discouraged or break off contact. Instead, he accepted Senator Mike Mansfield's suggestion that we continue "the negotiations in Paris in a low, patient, and determined key; we have tried to end this war by military means for about three years, at great cost and without success," he told LBJ on May 16, "and the negotiators have been at it for not much more than three sessions." As weeks passed with no discernible movement on Hanoi's part and the hawks pressed for military actions, which might force the Communists into substantive discussions, Johnson accepted the need for more patience. On May 21, Clifford told LBJ that there was no military solution to the war by either side and that something would eventually come out of the negotiations. "Our hopes must go with Paris," he said.

Johnson was skeptical. He saw "no evidence that the North Vietnamese will negotiate seriously. They will do no more than remain in Paris to talk rather than negotiate until the next administration takes over." Yet Johnson's interest in advancing the talks was as keen as ever. On June 14, he swore George Ball in to replace Arthur Goldberg as U.N. Ambassador. The appointment of someone so consistently opposed to the war was both a sym-

bolic and a substantive expression of the President's commitment to ending the conflict.

Johnson and his advisers believed that the best way now to advance the
negotiations was through private discussions. On June 12, Harriman and
Vance broached the subject with the North Vietnamese. Though saying
that they doubted whether anything could be achieved when our differences were so great, they agreed to take the suggestion under consideration. In fact, the North Vietnamese were fully receptive to the idea. That
day, one of their lower-level delegates agreed to have dinner with his U.S.
counterpart soon.

Two weeks later, the first private meeting between Vance and Hanoi's
second-ranking delegate occurred in a suburban Paris "safe house."
Though the exchange of comments was familiar and gave no indication of
a change in position on either side, Harriman was hopeful that private talks
would shield the North Vietnamese from having to acknowledge that they
had agreed to any conditions for a U.S. bombing halt. Nevertheless, Harriman anticipated no "miracles. We need patience above all." The coming
months testified to the wisdom of his advice.

:: POLITICS: THE NONPARTISAN AS PARTISAN

Johnson's withdrawal from the presidential race, coupled with a declaration of noninvolvement in "any personal partisan causes" during the rest of
his term, did not mean he would stay clear of politics. Whatever his public pronouncements, he could not abruptly end lifelong habits. As he freely
admitted, he was a political animal who loved the machinations, the give
and take, the brokering and deal-making that had always energized him.

Did he really intend to retire from the presidency? Some of the old pols
like House Speaker John McCormack refused to take Johnson at his word.
In mid-April he called Marvin Watson to say that "people at home . . . are
behind the President. . . . The country is really behind the President and
they are not confused by the few intellectuals who make all the news. . . . I
haven't given up hope on the President," McCormack concluded. "I
believe he will still be my candidate."

In the weeks after his announcement, Johnson had no intention of running again. This did not preclude a continuing interest in the emerging
campaign or, more to the point, in trying to shape its outcome. In April,
Johnson maintained a strong private interest in both the Democratic and
Republican nomination fights. On balance, he favored Humphrey among

the Democrats. His cordial meeting with Kennedy did little to soften Johnson's antagonism. He did not think McCarthy had a chance to win.

As for Humphrey, Johnson was ambivalent about his fitness for the presidency. He liked Hubert and believed he would be a staunch advocate of the domestic programs they favored. But he also considered him too soft or too much of a bleeding-heart liberal who would have trouble making tough decisions. He was a nonstop talker who wore his heart on his sleeve. "Maybe he doesn't have enough reserve because he feels very deeply about human problems," Johnson privately told a reporter in May. "I have noticed that people from Minnesota have a propensity for talking." After a meeting in which Goldberg and Humphrey did most of the talking, Johnson said to an aide, "Goldberg and Humphrey, my two silent partners."

Johnson was especially suspicious of Hubert's resolve to forge a proper peace in Vietnam. After McCarthy declared that Humphrey did not believe in his public position on Vietnam, Hubert told Johnson that McCarthy admits never hearing "me say anything on Vietnam privately that he had not heard me say publicly." Johnson had his doubts.

Johnson's choice as his successor was New York's Republican Governor Nelson Rockefeller. The two men had a high regard for each other. Johnson saw Rockefeller as a sensible moderate who, in Lady Bird's words, "was a good human being, a person who was for the disadvantaged, who was a man of compassion, with a capable and effective mind." He also believed that Rockefeller was the one man who could beat Bobby Kennedy, no small asset in Johnson's mind.

Rockefeller reciprocated Johnson's feelings. He saw the President as "a great statesman and a great American patriot." Rockefeller said later: "He was a tremendous guy." They and their wives enjoyed a warm personal relationship. Nelson recalled how frank his wife Happy could be with Lyndon, telling him at the ranch not to drive so fast or drink so much. "She was successful in getting him to slow down, which I don't think most people were."

Rockefeller also felt that they shared common political ground. "No President that I have known showed greater awareness, sensitivity to, or respect for the role of governors than he did," Rockefeller said. "Whenever there was a major problem he'd call us down and consult with us about it." Rockefeller sympathized with "the problems that he had in the Vietnam situation. So I felt badly for this man, I really did, because he was a tremendous patriot."

Toward the end of April, Johnson invited the Rockefellers to the White House for dinner, where he urged the governor to declare for the Republican nomination. "He was very friendly about '68, and very supportive of me for '68," Rockefeller said. Johnson also told him that he would never campaign against him. "You've been a long time friend." Happy Rockefeller remembered how during that evening Johnson urged Rockefeller to run. "He did want Nelson to be President," she said. Johnson encouraged others to back Rockefeller as well.

Rockefeller didn't need much prodding. On April 10, following a brief conversation with Johnson at New York's St. Patrick's Cathedral, where they attended Archbishop Terence Cooke's installation, Rockefeller announced his "availability" for the Republican nomination. On April 30, after the White House evening, Rockefeller declared himself a candidate for the presidency.

Partly to help Rockefeller and partly to keep focused on advancing peace talks and making domestic gains, Johnson insisted on political neutrality by everyone in his administration. It was very difficult. Cabinet secretaries and White House aides were eager to line up behind preferred candidates. When Humphrey decided to announce his candidacy at a luncheon on April 27, several Cabinet members, eager to demonstrate their support, planned to attend. Johnson ordered Califano to stop them: "I can't have the government torn apart by Cabinet officers and presidential appointees fighting among themselves about Kennedy, McCarthy, and Humphrey," Johnson said. Califano was to tell everyone in the Cabinet "to stay out of the race or get out of the government."

Yet it was difficult for Johnson to punish aides for favoring a candidate when he himself was partisan. At the same time he encouraged Rockefeller's candidacy, Johnson made clear that he preferred Humphrey over Kennedy and McCarthy. During a conversation with UAW President Walter Reuther, both men danced around the nomination question. Before they met, Califano reported that Reuther implied his support for Humphrey, but seemed likely to endorse the President's insistence on neutrality. Though Johnson refused openly to back Humphrey and Reuther avoided pressing the point during their talk, Johnson said: "Do whatever you are going to do and put it on the line. I don't have the slightest doubt where your best interest lies," implying that labor would want to back Humphrey.

Johnson couldn't keep his partisanship entirely hidden. On May 16, syndicated columnist Victor Riesel published an "almost verbatim report" of an off-the-record White House meeting with the AFL-CIO Executive Council. He described LBJ as understanding "that George Meany was right when . . . [he] warned that a cut in welfare and new era monies would be used by his political enemies to attack the President and his 'friends.' The political enemies are Bob Kennedy and Gene McCarthy. The friends mostly are Hubert Humphrey."

Despite his desire quietly to shape political developments, Johnson was without significant impact on either the Democratic or Republican campaigns. When Robert Kennedy won the California primary on June 5, he became the odds-on favorite to win the nomination. By then, it was also clear that Rockefeller had little chance of defeating Nixon's bid to be the Republican nominee.

Robert Kennedy's assassination by Sirhan B. Sirhan at the victory celebration in Los Angeles on the night of June 5 stunned Johnson. It was "too horrible for words," the President said on being awakened to hear the news. "Since he was well aware of his own psychological baggage," Califano says, "in no situation did Lyndon Johnson try harder to do the right thing—for the country, the Kennedy family, and himself—than in the hours and days following the shooting." Appreciating how antagonistic many of those closest to Kennedy would feel toward him, he tried not to intrude on their grief. He took a low profile at St. Patrick's Cathedral, where there was a funeral mass on June 8, and again at the funeral itself at Arlington National Cemetery, where Kennedy was laid to rest 100 feet from his brother's grave.

Kennedy's death revived Johnson's interest in a possible reelection campaign. One former national security adviser sent word to the President that he should consider running. "Many young people throughout the Washington area . . . are convinced that the President is the only man who can keep the country on the move after January." He didn't think Humphrey could beat Nixon, but he believed LBJ could.

Yet Johnson doubted that the nomination would be worth much in what seemed to be shaping up as a Republican season. Johnson told congressional Democrats that he saw "dissatisfaction with the 'ins' and thus the climate favors the Republicans." *New York Times* columnist Tom Wicker believed that "the thread" running "through the primary elections this year . . . is the rejection of the Johnson administration and its policies."

Still, Johnson could not quite let go of the thought that he might yet rescue the country from itself. Polls at the end of June showed Humphrey and McCarthy in a virtual deadlock with Nixon. But if Massachusetts Senator Edward Kennedy was the vice-presidential nominee, it decisively tipped the scale to the Democratic candidate. According to one Washington columnist, Kennedy was considering the possibility of running with

Humphrey. Johnson had a good relationship with Ted Kennedy. Nothing was said or done even to hint at a Johnson-Kennedy ticket. But, as events in the summer would make clear, Johnson had not yet definitively abandoned thoughts of another term.

14 :: UNFINISHED
:: BUSINESS

Johnson knew that exercising power in the waning months of a presidential term defied the laws of political gravity. But he had no intention of letting his time in office simply run out. As long as he held power, he was determined to use it. His diminishing capacity to make things happen stimulated not acceptance of the inevitable but vigorous efforts to dramatize the unfinished business he saw in domestic and foreign affairs.

He asked his staff for fresh proposals on what they should do in the last six months of his term. But not because he was short on ideas; he knew what he wanted to accomplish. He hoped staff initiatives might generate renewed enthusiasm among aides focused on post–White House careers. It was typical Johnson. Not a major problem would remain unaddressed, even if he saw little likelihood of getting much done. By describing the country's ongoing difficulties, he hoped to prod his successor, Congress, and the public into keeping the focus on its greatest challenges. In May, for example, when the House appropriation for HUD fell "far short" of what LBJ had asked for "programs so essential to ease the crisis in our cities," he publicly urged the Senate to restore the funds "so that we can move forward with the urgent task of rebuilding the American city."

At the end of June, after Califano told him that he had made his mark in the fields of education, health, jobs, poverty, and housing but needed, despite food stamps, to launch "a major food program" to assist America's hungry, LBJ proposed a "meeting to see where and how this should be developed." Toward the end of the year he publicly described "hunger and malnutrition as intolerable," and urged a 140 percent increase in food assistance programs between 1968 and 1970. In the second half of 1968 he was like a whirling dervish in behalf of domestic advance. Early in the summer, he pressed Congress for natural gas pipeline safety, the eighteen-year-old vote, an end to discrimination in hiring, more effective urban mass transit, a tenfold increase in low- and middle-income public housing, family planning and population control, stronger air pollution controls, more aggressive conservation of natural resources, expanded protections for security holders, a fresh attack on juvenile delinquency, and additional support for black economic progress.

At the end of July, he told the national governors' conference that he saw fifty major bills in Congress that he considered "essential to the well-being of all of the American people." He counted among these teenage protection from dangerous drugs, keeping guns from criminals, job security and safety, decent universal housing, and preservation of forests, scenic trails, and rivers.

As his presidency moved toward a close, his efforts for domestic advance quickened. On August 1, he hailed the passage of the HUD Act of 1968 as "the Magna Carta to liberate our cities." The law created "new means to win new rights . . . the fundamental and very precious American right to a roof over your head—a decent home." However hyperbolic, however unlikely that the law would assure his goal, he saw the occasion as a chance to challenge the country.

During the next four weeks, he celebrated laws eliminating barriers to the handicapped in public buildings and protecting Americans from flammable, toxic, and corrosive gases. On August 14, in a speech to the annual convention of the National Medical Association, a group of black physicians, he pled the case for assuring that "every boy and girl born into this land has a chance to start life with good health. . . . Medicare is a triumph of rightness," he said. "Now we must seek new ways to improve and to expand medical care." It was not only health but a chance at jobs, education, and homes that he declared the birthright of every American citizen.

On August 17, he announced the establishment of a National Eye Institute to prevent blindness, which afflicted 400,000 Americans, and the enactment of a Health Manpower Act to aid medical, dental, public health, and nursing schools to train health professionals, who were in short supply. Two days later, he signed the Wholesale Poultry Products Act, reminding the country of the poem: "Mary had a little lamb, and when she saw it sicken, she shipped it off to packing town, and now it's labeled chicken."

In the midst of the presidential campaign, he believed it essential that the country remember its "unfinished business," and that somehow the campaign might "lift the national spirit; . . . [and] make our people eager to get on with the business of the next four years." At a press conference on September 6, he reminded Congress that "we are paid on a year-round basis, and even while the campaign is on, we have business to do." He saw thirty or forty bills that needed action before the end of the year.

And where he could act on his own, he did. On September 9, he announced the creation of the National Housing Partnership and the appointment of industrialist Edgar F. Kaiser to head it. It was to begin a cooperative effort of government and the private sector to build 600,000 low- and middle-income housing units Johnson saw putting roofs over the heads of disadvantaged and middle-class Americans. On the 11th, he asked Congress to pass a coal mine health and safety act before adjournment. On the 12th, he publicly instructed HEW Secretary Wilbur Cohen to consider Social Security benefits "for not only next year, but for the decade ahead." On the 16th, he reported to Congress on adult basic education, calling attention to "the challenges ahead." On the 24th, he commended the President's Committee on Mental Retardation for its impressive achievement and urged no letdown in its efforts.

During the next ten days, he preached the virtues of conservation to Congress and the country, and took special pleasure in signing a Handicapped Children's Early Education Assistance Act. On September 26, he asked Wilbur Cohen to brief White House aides on future social challenges and the reforms needed to meet them. Between October 2 and election day, November 5, he signed bills extending the food stamp program and the Food and Agriculture Act of 1965, which had contributed to a resurgence of farm prosperity. He also approved the amended Merchant Marine Act of 1936, "a temporary palliative" toward revitalizing U.S. maritime capacities, and Public Health Service amendments, which increased the likelihood of better health for all Americans. Three education bills, affecting higher and vocational education and extending veterans benefits, a radiation control act, the 20th consumer protection measure of his presidency, a conservation statute making Florida's Biscayne National Monument into a national park, and a bill creating a Woodrow Wilson International Center for Scholars at the Smithsonian Institution concluded this burst of pre-election reform activism.

Liberals were not uniformly happy with Johnson's performance. So much of what he supported was more symbolic than substantive. Still concerned to hold down federal spending, he did not suggest immediate increases in domestic outlays. His proposals and declarations were aimed more at future administrations than his own.

Because he was so cautious about spending he was able to predict that at the beginning of 1969, for the first time since the 1950s, the country could expect to have a federal budget surplus. Though only $2.4 billion in fiscal 1969, he believed it would increase to $3.4 billion in 1970. More important, he thought it would facilitate "some necessary increases" in domestic programs. He would now be able to leave town on January 20 "a happy man and a thankful man."

Some of his satisfaction came from having carried forward international advances as well in the last eight months of his term. In July Johnson signed an agreement banning the spread of nuclear weapons. With fifty-six countries agreeing to the limitation, he declared it "a very reassuring and hopeful moment in the relations among nations." The provisions of the treaty committed the non-nuclear signatories to forego the production of such weapons, to receive "the full peaceful benefits of the atom," and committed the nuclear powers to work toward arms control and disarmament.

:: COURTPACKING: "THE FORTAS FIASCO"

In the closing months of his term, Lyndon Johnson thought not only about setting an agenda for future advances at home and abroad but also about how to assure that a next, possibly more conservative administration would not overturn or reduce the accomplishments of the last five years. He was particularly concerned that a Republican President not use appointments to the Supreme Court to promote judicial review of Great Society reforms.

The opportunity to counter such a development emerged in June 1968 when Chief Justice Warren advised Johnson that he wished to resign. Warren was in good health and seemed capable of continuing on the Court. But at seventy-seven he feared this might change at any time. Moreover, he was concerned that 1968 would bring a Republican victory and possibly a Richard Nixon presidency. Seeing Nixon as unethical, Warren couldn't stand the thought of Nixon choosing his successor. Warren said "he wanted President Johnson to appoint his successor, someone who felt as Justice Warren did. Johnson conferred with Clark Clifford about Warren's replacement. The President explained that he wanted to elevate Abe Fortas to the Chief Justiceship and replace him with a Texas jurist and old friend Homer Thornberry. Though a progressive Democrat, Thornberry was a southerner who had served in the House, been a federal circuit judge, and was currently on the federal court of appeals. Johnson believed that Russell and other southern senators would be enthusiastic enough about

Thornberry to accept Fortas, whose liberal opinions and Jewish identity seemed certain to arouse opposition.

Clifford was not convinced and predicted that Johnson would never get the appointments approved. The Republicans, expecting to win the presidency in 1968, would resist, and would win enough Senate support by complaining that Thornberry was a Johnson crony. Clifford suggested that Johnson name a moderate nonpolitical Republican instead of Thornberry as a way to win GOP support. But Johnson refused to listen.

There were warnings signs that Johnson's nomination of Thornberry would not stop southern opposition to Fortas. On June 25, Mike Manatos, Johnson's Senate liaison, reported that Robert Byrd of West Virginia "would do 'everything in [his] power' to oppose Abe Fortas, to whom he refers as that 'leftist' member of the Court . . . Russell Long classifies Fortas as 'one of the dirty five' who sides with the criminal against the victims of crime. He believes that . . . Fortas-Thornberry package would be real trouble."

Mississippi Senator James Eastland, the Judiciary Committee chairman, warned that Fortas could not be confirmed and that there would be a filibuster. Eastland also reported that he "had never seen so much feeling against a man as against Fortas."

Yet Johnson had some reason for optimism. After he announced the nominations on June 26, Manatos reported that they were "generally well received. The only soft areas are among certain Southern Democrats, and a small Republican group." Johnson's impulse to go ahead rested partly on his belief that he would win enough Republican support through Everett Dirksen's backing and enough southern votes through Russell's enthusiasm for Thornberry.

But even with Dirksen and Russell supporting Johnson's recommendations, LBJ knew that the outcome was too close to call. But he decided to go ahead anyway. He saw the potential gain as considerable and the possible loss as minimal. If he couldn't get Fortas and Thornberry approved, it would have little impact on the last months of his presidency. But if he could make Fortas Chief Justice and Thornberry an Associate Justice, it would strengthen the likelihood that the Court would sustain Great Society programs for the foreseeable future.

But Johnson could not overcome unforeseeable problems with Fortas's nomination. Allegations of breeching the tradition of separation of powers by secretly counseling Johnson on policy matters after joining the Court and of taking money for a course he taught at American University from former clients with business before the Court sunk his nomination. It was a grievous blow to Johnson's hopes for controlling the Court's actions during a period when Republicans might control the White House.

:: LBJ'S LAST CAMPAIGN

After Robert Kennedy died, Johnson began thinking about whether he should reverse course and run again. Part of his decision to step down rested on the conviction that Kennedy would either take the nomination from him or would so badly damage him in an intraparty fight that he would lose the fall election. As Humphrey put it, Johnson had decided against running because "he knew he couldn't make it." Vietnam had been central to these developments, and so even with Kennedy's death, another LBJ bid for the presidency would still face public tensions over the war. If, of course, he managed to end the fighting before November or if it was sufficiently clear that peace was in the offing, a Johnson reelection was not farfetched. In fact, a Johnson candidacy might convince Hanoi to move sooner on negotiations rather than wait to see who the Democratic or Republican alternative would be.

An initial spur to another Johnson bid came from the spring and early summer polling numbers. In April, 49 percent approved and only 40 percent now disapproved of Johnson's presidential performance. A 64 percent majority endorsed his March 31 decision to cut back on the bombing. In May, for the first time in five months, Johnson's job rating on Vietnam showed more Americans approving than disapproving—43 percent to 42 percent. Moreover, 59 percent of the country now saw the war as "morally justified."

Though presidential trial heats in June showed Humphrey with a small edge over Nixon, by July and August Nixon had taken a substantial lead. An August 21 poll put Nixon ahead of Humphrey by 16 points. Johnson, by contrast, beat Nixon by six points in a mid-July straw poll. If the Democrats were to hold on to the White House and sustain administration policies, Johnson seemed more likely than Humphrey to achieve this.

During July, Johnson acted as if he might run. He was concerned that the White House plan his public announcements more carefully and that the press office put out "two good news stories daily." Johnson wanted to structure his "weekly schedule for maximum press advantage."

Johnson was always eager to get the best possible publicity for himself, but this surge of pressure on his aides to burnish his image was partly a response to his doubts about Humphrey's candidacy. Newspaper columnists and Humphrey supporters were urging him to break with the President over the war, if he were to have any hope of being elected. It enraged Johnson. He also thought Hubert was being too soft in his bid for the nomination. To offset charges that he was steamrolling the convention, Humphrey agreed to concede some delegates to Gene McCarthy.

Humphrey wanted to give a speech in which he put some daylight between himself and Johnson on Vietnam. He hoped to convince "the large number of antiwar voters that he would somehow be more ready to compromise on Vietnam than the President." Humphrey hinted at the possibility that he would include the NLF in peace talks, a policy publicly opposed by the White House and the Saigon government.

Humphrey's proposed speech angered Johnson. In a conversation with the Vice President on July 25, after Hubert showed him a draft, Johnson said he "would be jeopardizing the lives of his sons-in-law and endangering the chances of peace. If I announced this, he'd destroy me for the presidency," Humphrey told an aide.

On July 24, Johnson told Clifford, Rusk, and Rostow that he wanted to discuss world affairs with Nixon. "When he gets the nomination he may prove to be more responsible than the Democrats. He says he is for our position in Vietnam. . . . The GOP may be of more help to us than the Democrats in the next few months," Johnson said.

Johnson's discomfort with Humphrey on Vietnam strengthened his impulse to run again. Humphrey tried to blunt Johnson's antagonism with assurances that he was solid on Vietnam. But Johnson didn't trust him, and laid plans to become the nominee. In August, he gave serious thought to attending the Democratic Convention. The ostensible reason was to be honored by his fellow Democrats on his sixtieth birthday, August 27. Numerous party leaders all urged him to attend. It was to be a triumphant moment, but some believed it would be more than that. They foresaw a draft nomination if the President would just give the word.

Johnson found the possibility compelling. He sent White House aides Harry McPherson and Larry Levinson to Hollywood to help script a film about his presidency, and he insisted that a movie about Bobby Kennedy be shown on August 29, the day after the nominations, when Senator Ted Kennedy, who was giving indications of running, couldn't stampede the convention. Several of Johnson's principal aides—George Christian, Harry Middleton, and Larry Temple—acknowledge that he was interested in being drafted. Califano says that as the convention began, it was "apparent to Temple at the ranch and me back at the West Wing of the White House that LBJ hoped, and probably anticipated, that the convention delegates in Chicago would offer to draft him to be their party's candidate, a draft," Califano believes, "he intended to turn down but one that validated his presidency in the eyes of fellow Democrats."

John Connally was Johnson's point man in Chicago. "What will throw a new wrinkle into history," Connally said in 1990, "is that I could make a very strong case that, notwithstanding his statement of withdrawal, he very much hoped he would be drafted by the convention in 1968." Connally said that Johnson sent Marvin Watson to Chicago to "assess the possibility of that convention drafting LBJ. . . . I want to get it on the record," Connally said, "that even though there had been a withdrawal, Marvin Watson was up there for the specific purpose of talking to delegates at Mr. Johnson's [direction]."

"I personally was asked to go to meet with the governors of the southern delegations to see if they would support President Johnson in a draft movement in 1968," Connally added. "Whether or not he really intended there to be a draft, who knows? Maybe it was a ploy to force Hubert Humphrey to support his Vietnam policy. But I believed it strongly enough that I went before all those southern governors and asked them if they would support Johnson in a draft, and they said, 'No way.'"

Events in Chicago destroyed all hopes of a draft. On August 23, three days before the convention began, an advance guard of "Yippie" protestors convened at the Chicago civic center to nominate their candidate, a pig named "Pigasus." The next day, the Women's Strike for Peace picketed at the Hilton Hotel, Democratic party headquarters, without incident. That night a hippie bonfire demonstration in Lincoln Park provoked a clash with police. A larger gathering in the park the next day produced more violence punctuated by verbal abuse, stone throwing, and police charges with batons. On convention eve, the 25th, the violence escalated, with protestors hurling rocks and bottles at police cars and the cops indiscriminately attacking demonstrators. By the 28th and 29th, the third and fourth days of the convention, melees between police and demonstrators stretched from Grant Park to the Amphitheater, where the Democrats were meeting. The worst violence occurred at the Hilton, when enraged police beat protestors in front of and then inside the hotel. Though the public generally blamed the violence on radicals, later assessments described a police riot sanctioned by Mayor Daley's refusal to grant demonstration permits and instructions to police to protect the convention from "extremists."

The riots foreclosed a presidential visit, which seemed certain to provoke more violence and might jeopardize Johnson's safety. Until the evening of the 27th, George Christian says, Johnson "fantasiz[ed] that the convention would be such a mess that he would go in on a flying carpet and be acclaimed as the nominee." When he met with the press at 5:45 p.m. on the 27th, he described himself as undecided about going to Chicago. By later that evening, however, he had given up hope of attending and being drafted. Instead, he sent a message to the delegates, which Carl Albert read on the 28th, asking that his "name not be considered by the convention."

Although he gave up on the nomination, Johnson did not concede control of the convention to Humphrey, who became the party's candidate. Against Humphrey's wishes, Johnson insisted on a convention vote endorsing his Vietnam policy. Johnson or his spokesmen at the convention won this fight, but at considerable cost to Humphrey. "At a moment when he should have been pulling the party back together to prepare for the battle against Nixon, Humphrey had been bludgeoned into a position that had further split the party and given more evidence of his own weakness," Clifford said later. It was the prelude to a fall campaign that would produce as much skulduggery and hidden actions as any in American history.

:: THE FALL CAMPAIGN: WHO WAS LBJ'S CANDIDATE?

As the fall campaign began, Johnson privately declared his backing for Humphrey. "I would like to see Humphrey elected and a Democratic Congress elected," he told Peter Lisagor on September 5. "'Not all the Democrats have been supporters of mine, but it has been my experience that Democratic Congresses are better than Republican Congresses.' 'Any politicking?'" Lisagor asked. "'Of course, I want to see Humphrey elected,'" Johnson replied. "'I frankly don't know whether I would do him good or harm—that is his judgment.

On September 12, after Humphrey had announced his intention to start bringing troops home in 1969, Johnson complained to his foreign policy advisers about Hubert's independence. When Clifford tried "to calm him down," Johnson declared: "'Look, I *want* the Vice President to win.' . . . I want the Democratic party to win. They are better for the country.'"

Johnson was much more antagonistic to Humphrey than his remarks to Clifford indicated. He understood that Humphrey was under great pressure to break with him. To keep close tabs on the inner workings of Hubert's campaign, Johnson had the FBI tap Humphrey's phones. If Humphrey were going to come out against the war, Johnson wanted advance notice and a chance to dissuade him.

Johnson was of two minds about Humphrey and Nixon. He understood that if Humphrey lost, it would largely be blamed on him and historians would interpret it as a repudiation of his presidency. He pressed administration officials to defend his achievements during the campaign, as a way to make a record for historians. Johnson saw the up side of a Nixon victory as a Vietnam policy that would save him from the historical complaint that he was the only President to have lost a war. Developments during the rest of September deepened Johnson's ambivalence about both candidates. The election contest revolved around the war and who would be able to end American involvement. Johnson wanted Humphrey and Nixon to follow his lead. He saw any dissent from his position, especially on the bombing, as an inducement to Hanoi to concede nothing in the negotiations.

To discourage Humphrey from siding with anti-bombing proponents, Johnson gave an uncompromising defense of his Vietnam policy on September 10 before the annual American Legion convention in New Orleans. Harry McPherson told him that everyone he spoke to took his remarks "as a 'real blast at Humphrey.'" It was what Johnson wanted. He told Clifford on September 24 that he doubted Humphrey's ability to be President. He lacked the guts for the job. He would have respected him more if he "showed he had some balls."

Nixon's public stance on the war also troubled Johnson. In a series of sixty-second television spots, he did "a brilliant job," using "war footage in the best antiwar new-wave style. Despite his clever attack on Johnson's war policy, Nixon took pains to neutralize him in the campaign. In August, after getting the nomination, he made informal remarks to a group of reporters, which got back to Johnson. He "hoped he shared with everybody in the room the view that the President and Vice President of the United States should have the respect of all citizens and he would do nothing to destroy that respect. He said anyone speaking on public policy in this country must be aware that he is being heard in Hanoi, and that voices heard in Hanoi are of major importance to our country. He said he thought the first priority of the Vietnam War now was not to stop the bombing, as some had suggested, but to stop the killing of American boys."

On September 15, the Reverend Billy Graham carried word to LBJ from Nixon that he would "1. . . . never embarrass him (President Johnson) after the election. I respect him as a man and as the President. He is the hardest working and most dedicated President in 140 years. 2. I want a working relationship with him. . . . And will seek his advice continually. 3. Want you (President Johnson) to go on special assignments after the election, perhaps to foreign countries. 4. I must point out some of the weaknesses and failures of the administration. But will never reflect on Mr. Johnson personally. 5. When Vietnam is settled he (Nixon) will give you (President John-son) a major share of credit—because you . . . deserve it. 6. Will do every-thing to make you . . . a place in history because you deserve it."

Graham went over Nixon's comments point by point. Johnson "was not only appreciative but I sensed that he was touched by this gesture on Mr. Nixon's part. . . . The President asked me to read him these points twice. Then he took the paper from my hand and studied it for a moment but I could see he was having difficulty reading my writing. He then said, 'Let me give you answers point by point.' The substance of his answers were warm appreciation.

Nixon's initiative influenced Johnson's view of him. During an NSC meeting on September 25, when an argument erupted between Clifford and Rusk over bombing and Rusk said, "if we stop the bombing with no conditions, many Democrats would vote for Nixon," Johnson sharply replied: "Mr. Nixon shouldn't enter into this in any way. The North Viet-namese feel the same about all of us." The problem, Johnson implied, was not with Nixon, who, like him, didn't want to give in to Hanoi, but with the doves, who were too ready to make unreciprocated concessions.

A Humphrey decision to separate himself further from the President in a September 30 speech strengthened Johnson's reluctance to help him. With the polls showing Humphrey trailing Nixon by between eight and fif-teen points, Hubert publicly declared on September 20 and 21, "I'm going to seek peace in every way possible, but only the President can do it now. Come January, it's a new ball game. Then I will make peace." Humphrey's qualifying phrases did not appease Johnson. When Hubert had called to tell him he was giving the speech, Johnson had said: "I gather you're not asking my advice." Humphrey had said that was true, but explained that the speech would neither embarrass Johnson nor jeopardize the peace talks. Johnson had replied "tartly and finally, 'Well, you're going to give the speech anyway. Thanks for calling, Hubert.'"

Publicly, Johnson avoided indications of tensions between himself and Humphrey. But a conciliatory public posture belied Johnson's antagonism to Humphrey, whom he refused to help by taking advantage of an oppor-tunity to hurt Nixon in the campaign.

At this time, Elias P. Demetracopoulos, a Greek journalist, who had fled Athens in 1967 after a colonels' coup, provided the President with a chance to damage, if not sink, Nixon's campaign. Demetracopoulos had informa-tion that Greece's military dictators had funneled more than half a million dollars into the Nixon-Agnew campaign. He gave this information to Larry O'Brien, who had been head of the DNC and had become Humphrey's campaign manager. Demetracopoulos urged O'Brien to put this before Johnson and to tell him that CIA Director Richard Helms could confirm its accuracy. O'Brien took the story to the President, but Johnson, according to what O'Brien told Demetracopoulos, refused to act upon it. He would neither ask Helms to investigate the report nor consider leaking it to the press, should it prove to be true.

Johnson had not developed a sudden fastidiousness about leaking stories that could not be traced to the White House. Rather, Johnson was reluctant to do anything that might help Humphrey win. Nixon's approach to him through Graham had, at least for the moment, neutralized LBJ in the campaign. In addition, Humphrey's speech had so irritated Johnson that he refused to talk to him. When Jim Rowe asked the President to campaign in October for Humphrey in New Jersey, Texas, and key border states, Johnson refused. "You know that Nixon is following my policies more closely than Humphrey," he told Rowe.

In addition to his reservations about helping Humphrey win, Johnson did not want to take time away from consideration of the Paris peace talks. Though the negotiations remained deadlocked at the beginning of October, every day brought additional developments, and he had some hope of a breakthrough before the election on November 5.

On October 9, the White House received indications of a major shift by Hanoi. That afternoon, the North Vietnamese delegates said they were ready to discuss the presence of the GVN at the talks in a private conversation later that week. When they met on the 11th, the North Vietnamese wanted to know whether we would quit bombing in return for including Saigon at the peace table. The North Vietnamese are "hurting and thwarted as never before and might be ready for real give-and-take peace negotiations," Rostow told the President. Johnson and his advisers seized upon the chance to advance the talks.

But he also worried that a bombing halt would bring charges of trying "to influence the election. Nixon will be disappointed," he said. "Many people will call it a cheap political trick." Johnson quoted Senator George Smathers, who "said the word is out that we are making an effort to throw the election to Humphrey. He said Nixon had been told of it."

Johnson didn't yet know the half of it. Bryce Harlow, a former member of Eisenhower's White House staff and a Nixon campaign adviser, had, in his words, "a double agent working in the White House. I knew about every meeting they held," Harlow said. "I knew who attended the meetings. I knew what their next move was going to be. I kept Nixon informed."

When White House discussions about a bombing halt began in October, Harlow warned Nixon, Johnson's "going to dump on you." If it happened, Nixon asked what Harlow thought they should do. Harlow had no good response. He could only warn that "it could be disaster, total. But at any rate, be prepared," he urged Nixon.

On October 16, Johnson used a conference call to inform Humphrey, Nixon, and Wallace of the developments in Paris. Johnson emphasized to Nixon that he was not being political—that he was ready to stop bombing because the North Vietnamese were agreeing to the conditions he had described to Nixon in earlier briefings. "Nixon," Bill Bundy says, "reaffirmed his support for a deal on that basis, and Mr. Johnson took him at his word." Yet the same day, as a demonstration of how little Nixon trusted Johnson, Dirksen declared in a speech that the "President will play politics with peace before [the] election."

In response to Johnson's maneuver, Nixon had begun a secret campaign to sidetrack the negotiations by discouraging South Vietnamese participation. Most everyone in the Johnson administration agreed that Saigon's presence was essential for any progress in the talks. If Nixon could convince Thieu that a Nixon peace arrangement would be better for South Vietnam than one made by Johnson, Saigon would undoubtedly wait until January 1969 before coming to the peace table.

Johnson got wind of this development on October 17. Leaks out of Saigon about the prospective bombing halt began, in Johnson's words, to "generate in the United States enormous confusion and pressure. They [the South Vietnamese] may very well interfere with the possibility of carrying forward a successful negotiation at a critical stage."

During the next ten days, Washington received growing evidence of Saigon's resistance to prompt involvement in the peace talks. But it was not until the end of October that Nixon's interference in the negotiations registered fully on Johnson. That morning, Rostow told him about a conversation his brother Eugene Rostow had with Alexander Sachs, a New York banker. Someone "very close to Nixon" had told Sachs that Nixon would block the negotiations by inciting "Saigon to be difficult." The Rostows considered the information "explosive . . . on how certain Republicans may have inflamed the South Vietnamese to behave as they have been behaving." Walt Rostow, however, saw "no hard evidence that Mr. Nixon himself is involved."

Johnson ordered that the greatest possible pressure be applied to Thieu, but stated his determination to go ahead with the bombing halt regardless of Thieu's response. "We can't walk out, quit, split," the President said. "We have got to hold together. We must tell them [the South Vietnamese] we won't stand for them vetoing this."

Because it was unclear how explicit the Republicans were being in their advice to Saigon, Johnson instructed the FBI to use wiretaps and other surveillance means to ascertain the facts. Since this was a national security matter involving possible violations of the Neutrality Act and Foreign Agents Registration Act, no questions of illegal bugging arose. Johnson asked that Anna Chennault, the widow of General Claire Chennault, a member of the China Lobby, and a co-chair of Republican Women for Nixon, be put under surveillance. She was carrying messages to the South Vietnamese, and Johnson wanted her watched and a tap put on her telephone.

Johnson was convinced that Nixon knew and had even ordered the initiative to discourage Saigon from coming to the peace talks. He had good reason for his suspicions. In July 1968, John Mitchell, Nixon's campaign manager, and Anna Chennault had discussed Vietnam with Nixon in his New York apartment. Nixon had asked Chennault to be "his channel to Mr. Thieu." On October 27, Chennault conveyed "apparently authoritative Republican messages urging Mr. Thieu to abort or cripple the [Paris] deal by refusing to participate." Johnson learned about these messages on the 29th when U.S. intelligence passed intercepted South Vietnamese Embassy cables to the White House.

Although Johnson could not convince Thieu to sign on to a bombing halt and participation in the Paris talks, LBJ went ahead anyway. In a national address on the evening of October 31, Johnson gave no hint of any political problem. He reaffirmed his nonpartisanship in taking this step and said that throughout the campaign "generally speaking . . . we have been able to present a united voice supporting our government and supporting our men in Vietnam."

Johnson, however, now had ample proof from taps, intercepted messages, and FBI observations of Chennault's movements that the Nixon campaign had discouraged Saigon from immediate participation in the talks. Moreover, it was clear from Thieu's actions in Saigon that he wished to do everything possible to help Nixon win.

The issue for Johnson in the second half of October was how far he should go to help Humphrey in the campaign and, more specifically, whether he should publicize Nixon's interference in the negotiations.

For all his irritation with Humphrey and doubts about his likely strength as a Chief Executive, Johnson was now even more antagonistic to Nixon. He was in fact furious at Nixon for undermining the peace talks and prospects for a settlement before he ended his term in January. He told aides that Nixon was guilty of "treason." American boys were dying in the service of Nixon's political ambition. The fact that he would have to leave office with the war unsettled also greatly frustrated him.

Johnson's anger toward Nixon drew him back into the campaign. Moreover, because a Humphrey victory would refute talk about a repudiation of Johnson, he warmed to the idea of helping beat Nixon. And so with Humphrey gaining ground in the last days of the campaign, Johnson thought a push for him might make a difference. With his approval rating up to 45 percent and the prospect of helping Humphrey, Johnson now agreed to do some campaigning. On the two Sundays before the election he gave radio and television talks. He also campaigned in Kentucky and West Virginia on October 26. The following day he attended a DNC luncheon in New York, where he gave what columnist Jimmy Breslin described as "probably the best speech anybody in the room can remember him making. He waved his fist, his voice thundered and he said he did not like Richard Nixon and he really did not like George Wallace. . . . He had the audience standing and cheering a couple of times."

On November 3, he joined Humphrey at a rally in the Houston Astrodome and broadcast a taped television talk from the White House. His Astrodome speech was a valedictory on his own career. He described the stakes in the election as nothing less than the fundamental way the country goes about doing its public business and how Humphrey would continue in the tradition of the New Deal and other, subsequent reforms.

Johnson also considered revealing Nixon's part in discouraging Saigon's involvement in the peace talks. But on November 3, after Nixon called Johnson directly and said: "There was absolutely no truth in it," Johnson backed away.

Yet Johnson saw other reasons to shield the story from public view. Should Nixon win the election, accusations that he had manipulated foreign negotiations as a private citizen would have opened him to possible indictment and prosecution. Such charges against a President-elect would have precipitated an unprecedented constitutional crisis. A Nixon presidency would have begun under a terrible cloud and made it unlikely that he could function effectively in office. And even if he were exonerated, it would have left him as a weakened Chief with diminished capacity to end the Vietnam War and make foreign policy.

On November 1, Johnson instructed Bill Bundy to brief Humphrey on the Nixon-Chennault pressure on Thieu. Since there was no direct evidence of Nixon's involvement, Humphrey also believed it unwise to leak the story or take it directly to the press. Besides, Humphrey told his aides, it would be "difficult to explain how we knew about what she had done." Some aides now pressed Humphrey to publicize the story as a way to gain an edge on Nixon in the last hours of an evenly divided campaign. Others warned that such a last-minute revelation would be seen as cynical politics and would produce a backlash that could cost Humphrey the election. With still no firm evidence to link Nixon to Chennault's actions, Humphrey decided against provoking a national crisis for the sake of an electoral gain.

On Election Day Humphrey fell short of Nixon by less than .01 percent of the popular vote, though he lost the electoral college by 301 to 191. As he himself said later, his defeat was not the result of any specific action but the loss of "some of my personal identity and personal forcefulness. . . . It would have been better that I stood my ground and remembered that I was fighting for the highest office in the land. I ought not to have let a man who was going to be a former President dictate my future." It was a sound assessment. The defeat belonged as much to Lyndon Johnson as it did to Hubert Humphrey.

:: FINAL DAYS

On November 22, UPI journalist Helen Thomas interviewed the President about his achievements, remaining days in office, and post-presidential plans. He spoke enthusiastically about the domestic and international accomplishments of his administration but spent more time describing his frustrations and regrets—particularly having had to fight in Vietnam, not having been able to do as much as he would have liked for the cities and the poor, and the terrible problems he had had with the media, newspapers, and television. He thought he might have "made a mistake of trying to go too far too fast, trying to do too much too soon, trying to correct the evils that have grown up over a century and to remake America overnight."

Characteristically, his response to feeling frustrated was to work harder to succeed—to try in the last weeks of his term to make some striking gains. He saw a key to this in good relations with Nixon's new administration. He intended to do all he could to help his successor, he told Thomas.

Johnson meant what he said. A White House meeting with Nixon on November 11 had been entirely cordial. Rusk, Clifford, and Wheeler briefed the President-elect on Vietnam and the Nuclear Nonproliferation Treaty (NPT). Nixon said he would do nothing on Vietnam unless "the President and Secretary of State thought it would be helpful. . . . We must be a united

front," Nixon declared. "There must be a conviction there will be a continuation of policy after January 20 in both Saigon and Hanoi." When Rusk
urged Senate action on NPT, Nixon declared himself "for the treaty, and
willing to support it if Johnson called a special congressional session."

Clifford remembers the contrasting styles of the two men. Nixon was
cautious, polite, deferential, measuring every phrase, calculating every sentence. "Where Johnson liked to obscure his strategy with a stream of Texas
stories and rhetoric, Nixon was self-controlled, and conveyed the impression of a man weighing every word. But one could easily overlook Nixon's
skill with words, because he left such a strong impression of physical awk-
wardness."

Johnson and Nixon spoke and met again before the transition on January 20. And though relations between the staffs remained correct, and even
cordial between the President and the President-elect, Nixon proved much
less forthcoming than Johnson hoped he would be. On November 11, for
example, after their private meeting, Nixon told the press that current
administration policies toward Vietnam, the Middle East, and the Soviet
Union would "be carried forward by the next administration." But Nixon
soon had second thoughts and announced that there would have to be
"prior consultation and prior agreement" if there were to be continuity in
policy.

Though Nixon had promised in their November 11 conversation to help
Johnson with the NPT, he reneged at the end of the month. Informed that
Republican senators were unenthusiastic about ratifying the treaty, Nixon
refused to endorse a special congressional session. Johnson saw Nixon's
refusal to commit himself to NPT approval as a blow to making some last-
minute gains in Soviet-American relations. In September, after the aborted
announcement of a U.S.-Soviet summit, the two sides had begun talking
about a presidential visit to Moscow before the end of 1968. Johnson and
Kosygin were both eager to discuss a strategic arms limitation agreement.
In mid-November, during a lunch Dobrynin initiated with Rostow, he said,
"Moscow is clearly ready to go—and eager—if you can work it out."

At the end of November, Johnson still wanted a meeting but worried
that strategic arms talks would stall without ratification of the NPT. At the
beginning of December, ABC news reported that Johnson would be the
first President to confer in the Kremlin. The report was premature. On
December 9, a back-channel message from the President to the U.S.
Embassy in Moscow described "the whole government" as in favor of missile talks. The failure to meet could mean a loss of "time, momentum, and
unity" toward an arms control agreement.

The meeting never occurred. "Everything we learned," Johnson later said, "indicated that they [the Soviets] were not" ready to meet. "I believed the Soviet leaders had been persuaded that it made more sense for them to deal with the incoming administration. I had a strong feeling that they were encouraged in that view by people who were very close to the Nixon camp." Clifford says that "near the end of December, President Johnson learned, rather bitterly, that Nixon had secretly told the Russians he was opposed to a Johnson-Kosygin meeting." Johnson believed that the failure to meet delayed the onset of strategic arms talks by a year.

Vietnam, above all, consumed the energies of Johnson during the final days. It was the focus of his November 11 discussions with Nixon and was at the center of most other post-election meetings. The goal was to get Saigon to the Paris talks. The South Vietnamese were warned that Americans opposed a delay in negotiations. But Johnson believed that without pressure from Nixon the South Vietnamese would stay on the sidelines until January.

By the middle of November, there were signs that Thieu would soon send a delegation to Paris. But as late as November 19, LBJ described Thieu as "intransigent" and told him that "he was dealing with a more friendly President now than he would be in the future." Clifford complained the following day that "we are getting a run-around in Saigon. . . . We cannot agree to what they are insisting on. We have a perfect right to go on with the talks." Only on November 26, after Nixon sent what LBJ privately called "a strong word" to Saigon, did they publicly agree to go to Paris. But even then, Thieu delayed sending representatives until December 8, and, when they got there, they argued about procedural questions, which delayed the start of substantive discussions until Nixon took office.

Despite the disappointments over Vietnam and the outcome in the November election, Johnson had no intention of leaving office with any sign of defeat. Though he had considered making his last State of the Union address only a written document, he decided instead to adhere to recent custom and deliver it in person as a farewell address. The speech was a celebration of not simply his administration with its landmark domestic reforms and eight years of economic growth but a paean to the compassion and decency of a great nation devoted to eliminating poverty and assuring equal justice and opportunity for all.

He freely admitted that his decision to come in person before Congress was partly sentimental, partly a chance to bid farewell to people and an institution he loved. The representatives and senators reciprocated the feeling with five minutes of applause as he entered the House Chamber and shouts, handshakes, tears, and a rendering of "Auld Lang Syne" as he left.

"Now, it is time to leave," Lyndon Johnson ended his address. "I hope it may be said a hundred years from now, that by working together we helped to make our country more just, more just for all of its people, as well as to insure and guarantee the blessings of liberty for all of our posterity. "That is what I hope. But I believe that at least it will be said that we tried."

15 :: AFTER THE FALL

It is no exaggeration to say that the return to Texas and a bucolic life on the banks of the Pedernales appealed to and troubled Johnson. For thirty-two years he had primarily lived in Washington, D.C., where he had observed and exercised political power every day of his life. His identity, his very being was bound up with his work. "My daddy committed political suicide for that war in Vietnam," younger daughter Luci told me. "And since politics was his life, it was like committing actual suicide."

Despite his love affair with politics and power, by 1969 one side of Johnson was ready to go home. He was exhausted and looked forward to escaping the hurly-burly of the presidency—the endless pressures over Vietnam, managing domestic and international crises, meeting deadlines, balancing budgets, stroking supporters, combating opponents, working sixteen- and eighteen-hour days in behalf of policies and programs that misfired as often as they succeeded. He was dead tired by the time he turned over the government to Nixon and boarded Air Force One for the trip back to Texas.

He no longer planned to worry about his relations with the press and all those people a politician, and especially a President, has to suffer for reasons of state and politics. He told his staff to keep reporters away from him. He wanted no more of their inquisitions, their probes and innuendos. "I've served my time with that bunch," he said, "and I give up on them. There's no objectivity left anymore. The new style is advocacy reporting—send some snotty-nosed reporter down here to act like a district attorney and ask me where I was on the night of the twenty-third. I'm always guilty unless I can prove otherwise. So to hell with it."

He was tired of indulging people he didn't care about, of going through the motions of politeness and social formalities expected of a public figure.

When Texas Governor Preston Smith asked to visit him at the ranch, Johnson felt compelled to invite him. He called aide Harry Middleton in Austin to find out what Smith wanted. Middleton had no idea. The next day Middleton called back to ask about the visit. "Well, he came down here, brought his wife and momma and sat around my living room for three hours," LBJ said. "The son of a bitch never said what he wanted. Maybe he wanted me to kiss his ass. If so, he should have just said so. After all that's the business I've been in for the last forty years."

Nothing signaled Johnson's post-presidential sense of freedom as clearly as his personal appearance. "His craggy face was kind and mellow in those days," Warren Woodward recalls. "His hair was long; it swept back and curled on the ends like that of an elder statesman in the Andy Jackson vein. The lines in his face were deep, but in all, Lyndon Johnson appeared less strange than in those horrendous days at the end of his term. Outside the gaze of the public eye, he aged gracefully."

The most startling demonstration of his liberation from White House formalities was his long silver hair. Like the rebellious students who had done so much to bring him down, Johnson now defied convention by refusing to have his hair cut. For someone who had spent a lifetime upbraiding aides and secretaries for the smallest departure from proper, formal dress, Johnson now announced his retirement from Washington's sartorial rules by sporting shoulder-length curls. His appearance formed a striking contrast with Nixon's White House staff, whose crew-cuts set them off from "long-hair" radicals.

But the return to the Hill Country wasn't strictly pleasurable. Mood swings were a common occurrence. "He was probably the most moody person I've ever known," Jewell Malechek, the wife of ranch manager Dale Malechek, says. "I guess working for him, that was one of the hardest things to adjust to. Some days you had to be quiet, and some days you could talk." He was his "normal manic-depressive self," Bob Hardesty says. Along with the sense of liberation and good times came feelings of diminished stature, of grief at losing his place of centrality in the country and the world.

In July 1969, he attended the launching of Apollo XI, which was to fulfill the goal of landing a man on the moon. He described the occasion to Doris Kearns as a misery he should not have exposed himself to. He remembered being one of thousands of people in the bleachers under a glaring sun, which left his clothes soaked and his stomach upset. The spotlight was on Vice President Spiro Agnew, who stood in for Nixon at the ceremony. The whole experience was a metaphor for Johnson's lost standing. As an ex-President he even had to take a back seat to a sitting Vice President.

:: PRODUCTIVE WORK

As he moved toward the end of his presidency, Johnson had mapped out a plan for keeping himself busy. For all his talk of relaxing, sleeping late, taking things easy, he also aimed to use his post-presidential time for productive ends. "He approached his life in retirement much as he had approached life in the White House," Tom Johnson says. "There was an urgency to everything he undertook."

He had five major projects he aimed to complete in the next few years: Write his memoirs, set up his presidential library in Austin, establish a Lyndon B. Johnson School of Public Affairs at the University of Texas, complete seven one-hour television interviews with CBS's Walter Cronkite, and put his ranch and business affairs in order against the day he died and Lady Bird would have to live off their estate.

Writing the book was an ordeal for Johnson and the several ghost writers who helped him. Though the final product was accurate, truthful, and significant enough as a history of the Johnson administration, Bob Hardesty, one of the authors, objected to its muted description of LBJ, the book's leading man. It was a shadow portrait that gave readers little sense of the real Lyndon Johnson. Because he wanted his memoirs to be statesmanlike rather than a full portrait of himself, Johnson pressured his collaborators into making it a bland exercise in self-congratulation that received negative reviews and reached only a small audience.

Johnson's hope that establishing the LBJ Library and Public Affairs School would be satisfying alternatives to sitting in the White House also fell short of expectations. Successful fund-raising for both institutions and an LBJ Foundation was gratifying. The $1.2 million he and Lady Bird received in advances for his memoirs and a White House diary she published, as well as lecture fees and $300,000 for the CBS interviews, were given to the library, the school, and the foundation. Johnson also enjoyed reviewing the architectural details of the library and consulting about the recruitment of a library staff and a faculty for the school.

The library's dedication on May 22, 1971, was a moment of reflected glory that he greatly enjoyed. Much of the Washington establishment showed up, including Nixon, Barry Goldwater, Humphrey, Muskie, most of the Johnson Cabinet, and congressmen and senators.

Yet the library and the LBJ School produced their share of frustrations. Johnson was unhappy with the library's first director. Chester Newland "was almost too much of a librarian and a professional," Tom Johnson says, "and there just wasn't the personal connection between the two men."

They "just never hit it off personally at all." The problem was settled when Harry Middleton, who "had the magic touch with President and Mrs. Johnson" and enjoyed the respect and confidence of the Johnson associates, replaced Newland. Nevertheless, the transfer of power, in Tom Johnson's words, "was not a pleasant undertaking."

The LBJ School also became a disappointing project for Johnson. He was keenly interested in its development and took much satisfaction from the appointment of John Gronouski as its first dean. Gronouski combined the academic and practical political credentials LBJ thought should be the distinguishing feature of the school's faculty. But he worried that the school would neglect the hands-on side of public affairs for the theoretical. Nevertheless, he knew and accepted the reality that his influence on building the faculty and choosing students would be distinctly limited by university rules of self-governance. Whatever his investment in the institution, it was not something he considered a major part of his daily post-presidential activities.

The Cronkite interviews produced more frustration. Hoping they would become largely a televised record of his administration's achievements, Johnson put great energy into preparing himself to discuss the seven prearranged topics — JFK's assassination and the transition, civil rights, space, Vietnam, the major decisions of 1968, Harry Truman, and politics. But instead of a pro-LBJ showcase, the documentary became a recounting of successes and failures. With CBS deciding what it would use from the interviews, Johnson, or more precisely his aides and lawyers, fell into a sharp struggle with the network over how it "cut and spliced" them. Compromises were reached, but only after much acrimony that left both sides partly discontented about the final product.

More satisfying to Johnson were business dealings by which he consolidated his holdings and turned much of his estate into cash. By 1969, he and Lady Bird had multimillion-dollar investments in radio-television properties, land holdings, and bank stocks. He had been very careful not to violate any conflict-of-interest laws as President. His assets had been put in a blind trust by Abe Fortas and were managed by Donald S. Thomas, an Austin attorney and business associate, and Jesse Kellam, the executive director of the Johnsons' broadcasting stations.

It is difficult to believe, despite the blind trust, that Johnson did not keep tabs on his financial holdings while President. Nevertheless, there is nothing to refute the Thomas and Tom Johnson assertions about his fastidiousness toward personal business affairs during his presidency.

But this says nothing about Johnson's pre-presidential behavior when he accumulated much of his wealth. The story of the radio and television assets is a tale of using influence at the FCC to assure the financial success of his broadcast stations. His land and bank holdings were the products partly of shrewd calculation and partly of his Texas connections to cut favorable deals.

By the time he had become Vice President the radio and television properties were generating considerable returns—about $1 million a year in net profits. "Don, what in hell are we going to do with this money?" he asked Thomas after being elected Vice President. Thomas urged him to invest in ranch and farm land, which would be owned and operated in partnership with Thomas and A.W. Moursund, another old Texas friend and associate, and folded into a Thomas-owned company in Austin, Brazos Tenth Street. Johnson found the advice irresistible and reaped considerable profits from the venture.

After Johnson left the White House he was free to resume control of his holdings. In 1972, an FCC ruling against owning a television station and a cable company in the same market compelled Johnson to sell one of these properties. He chose to sell the station to the Times-Mirror corporation for $9 million. It was an act of great shrewdness. "Who do you know that would have sold his television station and kept a half interest in a cable system that was just a source of . . . losses rather than profits?" Don Thomas wondered. "Who could have seen over the hill that way?" When the cable property was sold in 1979, it netted $23 million in cash and another $23 million in tax write-offs from debts owed by the company. "He was an extremely smart man in business," Thomas adds. "If he hadn't been President, I don't know how rich he would have gotten."

Lyndon Johnson saw the sale of family holdings as a way to provide for Mrs. Johnson and his daughters after he died. He told Tom Johnson several times: "You know, you can divide up stock or you can divide up cash between your children, but you can't very well divide up companies. You can't decide who gets the photo processing plant and who gets the radio plant and this kind of thing." To assure that much of the profits from his land and television deals did not go to the IRS, he balanced his capital gains with donations to the National Park Service of his ranch home and surrounding property on the condition that he and Lady Bird would have the use of them for the rest of their lives.

Nothing engaged LBJ more in his post-presidential years than the management of his ranch. While he had lived in Washington and was in office, the Stonewall ranch was a satisfying diversion or hobby. But beginning in 1969, it became a full-time avocation. Eighty percent of his time was spent on ranch business. "He went to work on the ranch," Tom Johnson says. "He started running that ranch the way he had the presidency—involved in every piece of it." And, Tom Johnson adds: "In a sense, rather than running the government he was running another little set of responsibilities." A friend who visited LBJ at the ranch complained: "He's become a goddamn farmer. I want to talk Democratic politics, he only talks hog prices."

The ranch became a cloistered world in which he controlled everything or tried to assure a kind of order and predictability he never found in the White House. Quickly, after coming to Stonewall, he fell into a comfortable routine, which made life on the Pedernales seem preferable to the strains of his tumultuous presidency. Up and out by six most mornings, he dogged the steps of ranch manager Dale Malechek and the several ranch hands who worked under him. He installed two-way radios in all the ranch vehicles and the rooms of his residence, so that he could reach them at any time during the work day. The only one who regretted Johnson's return to Stonewall was manager Malechek. He said: "I never worked for a harder man in my life." Malechek hoped Johnson would run again for the presidency.

:: POLITICS

Although he shunned reporters and largely closed himself off from national and international affairs, Johnson could not entirely escape domestic politics. In March 1969, he refused to support public attacks by Clark Clifford on Nixon's Vietnam policy. That spring, he gave indirect support to Congressman George Bush, who had declared himself a Republican candidate for Ralph Yarborough's U.S. Senate seat. In February 1970, he had Tom Johnson inform Haldeman that he had refused to discuss the Anna Chennault issue with a newspaper reporter and that "all our people in Austin had been directed not to say anything on the matter." Haldeman "was most appreciative" and "seemed genuinely pleased and surprised."

In May 1970, when domestic demonstrations resulting in deaths on the Kent State and Jackson State University campuses followed a U.S. ground attack on North Vietnamese supply routes in Cambodia, Johnson refused to criticize Nixon. Instead, in a Democratic party unity speech in Chicago, he blamed Hanoi for the continuing problems in Southeast Asia and urged all Americans to lend their backing to "our President."

Johnson also largely stayed out of the 1972 presidential campaign. The Democratic convention in Miami in July depressed him. The party leaders did not invite him, and, except for Ted Kennedy, party officials made no mention of him, even omitting his photograph from the customary picture display of former Democratic Presidents. After Maine Senator Ed Muskie, LBJ's choice, lost the nomination to South Dakota Senator George McGovern, a vocal Johnson critic, Johnson refused to issue a statement of support.

In August, when he announced his backing for McGovern and agreed to receive him at the ranch, it was about as low-key an endorsement as Johnson could give. He described their differences on foreign affairs and made clear that he was acting more out of loyalty to the Democratic party than out of any enthusiasm for McGovern.

Behind the scenes he did what he could to promote Nixon's reelection. He declared McGovern "the most inept politician, inept presidential candidate . . . in all of history. . . . I didn't know they *made* presidential candidates that dumb," he said privately. In July, before he went on record in support of McGovern, he told Nixon in a phone conversation that he would "encourage his people to support us behind the scenes. Although he will not come out himself, of course." Texas Democrats for Nixon, led by John Connally, George Christian, and Larry Temple, was the principal result of Johnson's promise.

For his troubles, Johnson got a symbolic slap in the face from Nixon. In October, Nixon told the press that he had no intention of making "the wrong kind of settlement [in Vietnam] before the election. We were around that track in 1968 when well-intentioned men made a very, very great mistake in stopping the bombing without adequate agreements from the other side."

More important, in January 1973, after Nixon had won a landslide victory and the Democratic-controlled Senate threatened an investigation of the Republican break-in of Democratic headquarters at the Watergate, Nixon tried to intimidate Johnson into having the inquiry called off. On January 9, Nixon asked that Attorney General John Mitchell talk to the FBI's Deke "DeLoach to see what he can get out of him on the LBJ thing, because if he can get that cranked up," Haldeman recorded in his diary, "LBJ could turn off the whole congressional investigation." Nixon hoped that the threat of a press leak about FBI bugs ordered by LBJ on his and Agnew's 1968 campaign planes would persuade Johnson to pressure congressional Democrats into dropping a Watergate probe.

When Johnson got wind of what Nixon was proposing, he called De-Loach "and said to him that if the Nixon people are going to play with this, that he would release (deleted material—national security)," Haldeman's published diary reads, "saying that our side was asking that certain things be done. By our side, I assume he means the [1968] Nixon campaign organization," Haldeman said. "DeLoach took this as a direct threat from Johnson. . . . As he recalls it, bugging was requested on the [Nixon-Agnew campaign] planes [in 1968] but was turned down, and all they did was check the phone calls, and put a tap on the Dragon Lady (Mrs. Anna Chennault)."

The deleted material from Haldeman's diary was Johnson's threat that if the Nixon White House released information about LBJ's alleged bugging of their campaign in 1968, he would retaliate with material from National Security Administration files demonstrating that Nixon's campaign had illegally interfered with the Paris peace talks by convincing Saigon to stay away until after Nixon came to office. Johnson may also have considered releasing material about the secret Greek money funneled into the Nixon campaign in 1968, but this was probably a backup piece of information that Johnson would use only if the Chennault material was not enough to blunt Nixon's threat, which, of course, it did.

:: LAST DAYS

Johnson's concern that he might not live out another presidential term was well-grounded. In March 1970, fourteen months after leaving office, he was hospitalized at Brooke Army Medical Center in San Antonio because of severe chest pains. Since his serious heart attack in 1955, he had had a number of medical problems, but there had been no other significant cardiological episode. The problem now, doctors told him, was not a heart attack but angina, a hardening of the arteries supplying blood to the heart. Heart specialists in Atlanta and Houston concluded that he was not a good candidate for bypass surgery. They recommended nitroglycerin to control the pain, weight loss, and a regimen of nonsmoking and less tension.

Though he relied on the nitroglycerine tablets for pain control and made some effort to change his diet, he resigned himself to the inevitable. In April, he came back to Washington, where he met with editors and reporters from the *Washington Post*. Richard Harwood remembers him "looking less tall, less bulky. . . . His hair was almost completely white, and was growing long in the back." LBJ said that he was on a daily 850-calorie diet and that he had suffered quite a bit of pain before being hospitalized.

Harwood recalls that as he spoke, he took on "another appearance: The pallor and signs of sickness went away and all of a sudden you were sitting with a vigorous, commanding, strong man whose mind was so clear, so well organized, so quick that you suddenly became aware of the power of that personality, of the ability to dominate and persuade and overwhelm." Harwood adds, "There were some bitter-end Johnson critics around that table," but they kept their peace. "They sat there, drinking it all in, and when it was over some had tears in their eyes and they all stood up and gave him their applause."

In June 1972, while visiting his older daughter Lynda and her husband, Charles Robb, in Charlottesville, Virginia, he suffered a severe heart attack. Believing that he was now dying and determined to be home when he did, he insisted on being flown to San Antonio. He survived the journey, and, after a two-week hospital stay, he recovered sufficiently to return to the ranch. There he moved and spoke more slowly, climbed no stairs, almost never drove, and vacillated between hope and resignation. His mornings were pretty good, he told friends, but by the afternoon he was drained of energy, suffered a lot of pain, had to lie down, and took oxygen from a portable tank next to his bed.

Yet he was not ready to see himself as an invalid passively waiting for the end. His fall schedule was full of activities, mainly at the ranch, with lots of interesting guests coming to visit. In December, he called Horace Busby to say that he wanted "'to get really active this year.'" He planned to "'speak up a little more . . . go more places and see more people again.'"

His attendance at a civil rights conference at the LBJ Library earlier in the month had stimulated his interest in once more influencing public issues. On December 11 and 12, all the notable civil rights activists of the fifties and sixties gathered in Austin: Associate Justice Thurgood Marshall, Roy Wilkins, Clarence Mitchell, Whitney Young, Hubert Humphrey, Chief Justice Earl Warren, and Burke Marshall. Younger, newer activists, who were less well known to LBJ came, too: Barbara Jordan, Julian Bond, Vernon E. Jordan, Jr., Reynaldo G. Garza, and Henry Gonzalez. And an anti-Nixon contingent led by the Reverend Kendall Smith of the Council of Churches in New York and Roy Innes, chairman of CORE, attended with the intention of denouncing the indifference of the current administration to advancing equal rights.

Johnson looked forward to the symposium with pleasure; it was a chance to remember the greatest moments of his presidency. But he was awfully sick by then, and his doctors urged him not to attend, and especially not to exert himself by giving a scheduled talk. He put aside their objections to drive the seventy miles from his ranch through an ice storm. The only concession to his pain and weakness was to watch the proceedings from a back room with a television monitor. But he was still in charge. When conference organizers wanted to deny Smith and Innes a chance to speak against Nixon, LBJ vetoed their decision and promised to give them some time.

It was evident to everyone who watched Johnson come to the podium for his talk that he was not well. He walked slowly and spoke in a low but steady voice. His message was inspiring: "Of all the records that are housed in this Library—31,000,000 papers accumulated over a forty-year period of public life—" he said, "it is the record of this work which has brought us here that holds the most of myself within it and holds for me the most intimate meanings. . . . I do not want to say that I've always seen this matter, in terms of the special plight of the black man, as clearly as I came to see it in the course of my life and experience and responsibility." But he had come to understand the urgency of equal rights in America, and he briefly cataloged the advances of the last ten years.

His concern now, he declared, was not to have this symposium "spend two days talking about what we have done. The progress has been much too small; we haven't done nearly enough. I am sort of ashamed of myself, that I had six years and couldn't do more than I did. . . . So let no one delude themselves that our work is done. By unconcern, by neglect, by complacent beliefs that our labors in the fields of human rights are completed, we of today can seed our future with storms that would rage over the lives of our children and our children's children. . . . The black problem today, as it was yesterday, is not a problem of region or states or cities or neighborhoods. It is a problem, a concern and responsibility of this whole nation. . . . To be black in a white society is not to stand on level and equal ground. While the races may stand side by side, whites stand on history's mountain and blacks stand in history's hollow. Until we overcome unequal history, we cannot overcome unequal opportunity."

"While I can't provide much go-go at this period of my life," he said in subsequent remarks, "I can provide a lot of hope and dream and encouragement and I'll sell a few wormy cows now and then and contribute."

But the time left to him was brief. After his trip to Austin for the symposium in December, he spent two days in bed recovering. During the next six weeks, he continued to feel poorly. He had a lot of pain and could relieve it only by lying in bed taking oxygen. Tom Johnson remembers thinking that "he was really getting close to his time."

On the morning of January 22, he discussed plans to go to Acapulco in February and went over a list of "action" items on the phone with Tom Johnson. He wanted to know about a visit of Israeli Premier Golda Meir to Austin and about a *Los Angeles Times* investigation of a state park being set up at his boyhood home in Johnson City. He urged Tom to encourage Pat Nugent, LBJ's son-in-law, to rejoin the Johnson radio company. With Tom planning to become editor of the *Dallas Times Herald* and Jesse Kellam past seventy-three, LBJ was eager to have Nugent become the station's chief executive. He discussed a visit to the ranch that afternoon of J.B. Fuqua, a Georgia industrialist. It evoked comments from him about distinguished Georgians, including Walter George, Richard Russell, and Carl Vinson. "Well, Tom, anything else?" he concluded their discussion.

Phone calls from and to his physicians, business associates, secretaries, and a staff aide dealing with matters at the library and LBJ School filled the rest of his morning. At 11:20 a.m., Jewell Malechek drove him around the ranch to check on some deer fencing. After a light lunch, he lay down for a nap.

At 3:49 p.m. LBJ called Secret Service agent Mike Howard, who was out of his ranch office. Johnson said, "Well send over whatever agent is on duty." Two other agents, alarmed by the President's tone, ran to his bedroom with a small oxygen tank. They found LBJ lying unconscious on the floor and began administering CPR. They called the President's physician in San Antonio, but it was apparent to them that Johnson was dead. A physician from Johnson City arrived as the agents were carrying the President on his plane to fly him to San Antonio. The eighteen-minute flight brought them to San Antonio at 4:35. But it was already too late. The physician on board pronounced him dead before removing his body from the plane. Mrs. Johnson, who had been in Austin, had been flown to San Antonio by helicopter. She arrived at 5:54 and was told by Agent Howard, "This time we didn't make it." She said, "Well, we expected it."

When Lady Bird called Tom Johnson to ask him to coordinate funeral arrangements, Tom remembered thinking: "Well, that rascal. He left on this trip just like he would have wished, without any advance notice to the press. He never wanted to go anywhere on a trip and let us tell the press about it beforehand. . . . He didn't do it like Harry Truman; lie around several days and have the press gather outside."

Johnson's body lay in state in his Austin library from the afternoon of January 23 until 9 a.m. the following morning. According to the library's count, 32,000 people paid their respects. When Library Director Harry Middleton assigned an assistant to keep track of how many people viewed the President's remains, an associate asked Middleton why he wanted that information. "Because," Middleton replied, "I know that somewhere, sometime, President Johnson's going to ask me."

From the 24th to the 25th, Johnson's remains lay in state at the Capitol Rotunda in Washington. One observer of the mourners paying their respects guessed that 60 percent were African Americans. He overheard one black woman say to her little girl: "'People don't know it, but he did more for us than anybody, any President, ever did.'. . . ."

"That was his epitaph as far as I was concerned," this observer said. After Leonard Marks reported Lady Bird's comment "that the thing Lyndon hated most was to be by himself," a group of Johnson's friends decided to keep watch at the casket all night.

On the morning of the 25th the casket was moved to the National City Christian Church. Leontyne Price sang "Onward Christian Soldiers," and Marvin Watson delivered the eulogy: "He was ours," Watson declared, "and we loved him beyond all telling of it." That afternoon the President's body was flown back to Texas, where it was carried to the family cemetery at the Stonewall ranch. Anita Bryant sang the "Battle Hymn of the Republic." General Westmoreland placed a wreath sent by President Nixon at the foot of the coffin. John Connally spoke the last words: "Along this stream and under these trees he loved he will now rest. He first saw light here. He last felt life here. May he now find peace here."

"But John," one can imagine him replying, "there's still so much more to be done."

:: AFTERMATH

It may be, as Russell Baker said, that Johnson was "a human puzzle so complicated that nobody could ever understand it." But I hope this short volume can bring us closer to some explanation of what drove this outsized man. Like the climber who ascends the mountain because it is there, knowing Johnson better can simply satisfy our curiosity. But his substantial impact on all our lives has made searching out his motives all the more compelling.

It may be that future biographers will have superior methods for deciphering a man of such uncommon ambition, capacity, and energy. But whether they do or not, it is difficult to believe that they will ever fully agree on how to assess this larger-than-life figure. There were enough surprises in what he did to rule out uncontested explanations of his actions. Johnson was one of those great success stories posing the question: Did he reach such great heights and ultimately fall so far because of or despite his inner demons?

More in order are a final few words about Johnson's antipoverty crusade, Great Society, and war in Vietnam. Thirty-five years after LBJ's great assault on domestic problems, it is possible to make assessments of the many programs he put in place to change race relations, ease the suffering of under-privileged Americans, and improve the national quality of life. As the text of this book makes clear, Johnson had his hits and misses. Civil rights and voting rights corrected long-standing wrongs and opened the way to the rise of a larger, more affluent black middle class. Likewise, Medicare, Medic-aid, urban renewal, aid to education, immigration reform, and safety and consumer regulations have indisputably bettered the country.

Debates about the sort of social engineering Johnson sponsored are a fixed part of the American experience. Nevertheless, there is at least one side of Johnson's reformism that the great majority of Americans have embraced and seem unlikely to abandon. There is a striking analogy here between Johnson and FDR. Roosevelt's New Deal never brought full recovery from the Depression. But it put in place a series of measures that humanized the American industrial system. Social Security, unemploy-ment insurance, public power, and regulatory protections for consumers command the allegiance of most citizens, many of whom may have no idea or even interest in knowing the origins of laws that seem essential in a civ-ilized democratic society.

Similarly, some of the laws spawned by Lyndon Johnson's war on poverty and Great Society have either fallen into disrepute or command limited support from many Americans. But the spirit and much of the substance behind Johnson's reform programs maintain a hold on the public imagi-nation that endures. Who among us would agree to return to the segregated world of the 1950s and early 1960s? How many in America are prepared to dispense with Medicare and Medicaid? Few are willing to abandon federal aid to education or environmental protections, even if the details of those programs seem imperfect. For all the recent recrimination over more con-troversial initiatives from the sixties like national public broadcasting, legal services, the national endowments for the arts and the humanities, conser-vatives have found it impossible to repeal them. Like FDR's New Deal, Johnson's poverty war and reach for a Great Society may seem less dazzling than when they were enacted, but the humanizing force behind them abides and gives both men historical standing as visionaries who helped advance the national well-being and fulfill the promise of American life.

Johnson's most far reaching contribution to national change was his part in bringing the South into the mainstream of the country's economic and political life. Beginning in the 1930s he saw New Deal federal programs as a means to raise the southern standard of living. As a senator in the fifties and then as president, he understood that civil rights would do more than assure equal treatment for African Americans. It would also help make the

South a more equal member of American society. Johnson recognized that segregation not only separated the races in the South, it also set the region apart from the rest of America. An end to southern apartheid meant the reintegration of the South into the nation. The prosperity enjoyed by the region since the 1960s and four southerners in the White House — Jimmy Carter, George W. H. Bush, Bill Clinton, and George W. Bush — out of the last seven presidents demonstrate the point.

Johnson's domestic record is ultimately a study in paradox. His strength as a President partly rested on his affinity for doing big things: taking on the largest problems others have been either too timid or too politically opposed to federal activism to address. But in doing so, he overreached himself. His grandiosity led him to promise more than he could ever possibly deliver: an end to poverty, a Great Society of contented citizens largely free of racial tensions were exaggerated hopes that did more to spawn national cynicism than turn America into a perfect Union.

Vietnam was a larger mistake. It was the worst foreign policy disaster in the country's history. Aside from the sacrifice of the many brave men and women who lost their lives or suffered because of the conflict, there seems nothing heroic about the struggle. Where World Wars I and II and even Korea had set-piece battles that seemed to lead somewhere, where high level meetings engaged thoughtful civilian and military chiefs in difficult decisions that demonstrated the general wisdom of the country's leaders, Vietnam was a morass. The battlefield clashes and constant discussions in Washington and Saigon about the war were a confusion leading nowhere. For all the determination and dedication to duty of the decision makers, the planning for Vietnam led to unproductive commitments in what came to seem like an open-ended conflict.

Defenders of the war believe that America's ten-year presence in Vietnam spared Southeast Asia from Communism, giving the region time to develop and resist subversion from socialist neighbors. The assertion is impossible to prove. Moreover, it leaves out of the equation the likelihood that a Communist takeover in Vietnam would have spurred a U.S. effort in Thailand, a more congenial place to make a stand against falling dominoes.

The principal products of administration discussions about the fighting were false hopes, self-generated illusions, and paranoid fears of domestic opponents, who were not the Communist dupes Johnson believed them to be but men and women as devoted to the national security and well-being as anyone in the government and military.

Johnson knew from the first that he might be pursuing a losing cause in Vietnam. Why then didn't he cut his losses in 1967 or 1968 by declaring victory and getting out? Domestic sentiment coupled with developments in Vietnam made this possible beginning in September 1967. Richard Nixon's later fig leaf for ending a fruitless commitment, Vietnamization, was available to Johnson. But he chose to continue and escalate U.S. involvement until the Tet offensive clearly demonstrated that Americans had lost patience with a costly struggle leading only to more losses.

Johnson's reasons for "staying the course," as he described it, were a combination of noble and ignoble motives that little serve his historical reputation. To the end of his presidency, LBJ believed his own rhetoric about dominoes and Munich and right-wing domestic control compelling him to fight the war. Though Johnson, in the words of his younger daughter, may have committed political suicide or courageously fallen on his own sword for Vietnam, it still does not speak especially well of his judgment. None of Johnson's fears have come to pass despite U.S. defeat in Vietnam. The dominoes in Southeast Asia never toppled; Russia and China took no greater risks in the Cold War, which could have heightened the likelihood of an East-West confrontation; conservative critics made no direct political gains from the outcome in Vietnam; and Communist victory in the war did nothing to prop up socialism in Russia, Eastern Europe, or even China.

Even less flattering to LBJ is the reality that he also pursued the war for selfish motives. To admit failure on so big an issue as Vietnam would have been too jarring to Johnson's self-image as a can-do leader. Moreover, realizing by 1966–67 that defeat in Vietnam would blight his reputation as the only President in American history to have lost a war and intent on proving his critics wrong, especially Robert Kennedy, whose emergence as a political opponent revolved around differences over Vietnam, Johnson refused to acknowledge that he had led the country into a stalemate, which would require large additional commitments to break.

Plaguing Johnson as well was an irrational conviction that his domestic opponents were subversives or the dupes of subversives intent on undermining national institutions. Johnson's paranoia raises questions about his judgment and capacity to make rational life and death decisions. I do not raise this matter casually. It is a frighteningly difficult issue, which the country has never seriously addressed. And for good reason. It is one thing if a President is seriously incapacitated by some physical malady that bars him from performing his duties. And even then, as in the case of Woodrow Wilson, few, if any, were ready to demand that the Vice President assume the responsibilities of office.

Determining psychological incapacity may be impossible. We have never had a President who was so demonstrably depressed or unstable that he had to temporarily or permanently give up governing. Richard Nixon's decision to resign was a rational response to legal and political circumstances beyond his control.

Who then is to say when a President has passed the bounds of rational good sense? Certainly in Johnson's case, for all the cranky nonsense he espoused about his enemies, he remained largely in control of his faculties and more than capable of functioning as President. Still, no one should make light of how much his suspicions and anger toward his domestic critics distorted his judgments in dealing with Vietnam. It may be that he would have pursued the war as avidly even without his personal antagonisms. But it is clear that his personal quirks in dealing with war opponents contributed nothing constructive to the national dialogue on a failing war.

How then to sum up Johnson's nearly four decades in politics? He stands in the front ranks of those who served as congressional aides, NYA directors, congressmen, and senators. His vice presidency was no more nor less than what others had suffered through in that office.

His presidency was a story of great achievement and painful failure, of lasting gains and unforgettable losses. Whatever impulse future historians may have to pigeonhole Johnson as a near great, average, or failed President, I am confident that a close review of his time in office will leave them reluctant to put any single stamp on his term. Some people loved the man and some despised him. Some remember him for great works and others for a legacy of excessive governance at home and defeat abroad. In a not so distant future, when coming generations have no direct experience of the man and the passions of the sixties are muted, Johnson will probably be remembered as a President who faithfully reflected the country's greatness and limitations—a man notable for his successes and failures, for his triumphs and tragedy.

Only one thing seems certain: Lyndon Johnson will not join the many obscure—almost nameless, faceless—Presidents whose terms of office register on most Americans as blank slates. He will not be forgotten.

Suggestions for Further Reading

As I stated in the Preface, this volume is an abridgment of *Lone Star Rising: Lyndon Johnson and His Times, 1908–1960* (New York: Oxford University Press, 1991) and *Flawed Giant: Lyndon Johnson and His Times, 1961–1973* (New York: Oxford University Press, 1998). These studies rest on fourteen years of research and writing. The *Sources* section of each volume lists the vast array of manuscripts and oral histories underpinning it. Most of these materials are in the Lyndon B. Johnson Library in Austin, Texas, but a number of other archives contain important materials relating to Johnson's life and political career.

For additional biographies and monographs on specific subjects relating to Johnson's political actions, see Craig H. Roell et al., *Lyndon B. Johnson: A Bibliography* (2 vols.: 1984 and 1988). A good general starting point for the study of Lyndon B. Johnson's personality and public life is Doris Kearns, *Lyndon Johnson and the American Dream* (1976); other general studies are Paul K. Conkin, *Big Daddy from the Pedernales: Lyndon Baines Johnson* (1986), and Bruce J. Schulman, *Lyndon B. Johnson and American Liberalism* (1995).

PRE-PRESIDENTIAL YEARS

Chapter 1: Origins. See Part One (chapters 1–5) of *Lone Star Rising*. Also see Robert Caro, *The Path to Power: The Years of Lyndon Johnson, Vol. 1* (1982).

Chapter 2: The Congressman. See Part Two (chapters 6–10) of *Lone Star Rising*. Also see Robert Caro, *Means of Ascent: The Years of Lyndon Johnson, Vol. 2* (1990); both Caro volumes include discussions of Johnson's controversial 1948 election to the United States Senate.

Chapter 3: The Senator. See Part Three (chapters 11–15) of *Lone Star Rising* and Caro's *Master of the Senate: The Years of Lyndon Johnson, Vol. 3* (2002). An older but still valuable book on the Senate years is Rowland Evans and Robert Novak, *Lyndon B. Johnson: The Exercise of Power* (1968).

Chapter 4: The Vice President. See *Lone Star Rising*, chapter 16, on the nomination, and *Flawed Giant*, chapter 1, on the vice presidency.

THE PRESIDENCY

For good overviews of Johnson's presidency, see the essays in the three volumes edited by Robert A. Divine: *Exploring the Johnson Years* (1981); *The Johnson Years: Vietnam, the Environment, and Science* (1987); and *The Johnson Years: LBJ at Home and Abroad* (1994). Vaughn Davis Bornet's *The Presidency of Lyndon Johnson* (1983) is another good study.

The domestic side of Johnson's presidency is covered in Joseph Califano, *The Triumph and Tragedy of Lyndon Johnson* (1991), and Irving Bernstein, *Guns or Butter: The Presidency of Lyndon Johnson* (1994). Also see Hugh Davis Graham, *The Civil Rights Era: Origins and Development of National Policy, 1960–1972* (1990), and Gareth Davies, *From Opportunity to Entitlement: The Transformation and Decline of Great Society Liberalism* (1996).

On foreign affairs in general, see Warren Cohen and Nancy Tucker, eds., *Lyndon Johnson Confronts the World* (1994), and H. W. Brands, *The Wages of Globalism: Lyndon Johnson and the Limits of American Power* (1995).

On Vietnam, see two volumes by Larry Berman: *Planning a Tragedy: The Americanization of the War in Vietnam* (1982) and *Lyndon Johnson's War: The Road to Stalemate in Vietnam* (1989). A three-volume official history by William C. Gibbons is based on a vast Defense Department, State Department, and congressional documentary record: *The U.S. Government and the Vietnam War: Part 2, 1961–1964; Part 3, January–July 1965; Part 4, July 1965–January 1968* (1986–1994). Also see Bruce Palmer, Jr., *The 25-Year War: America's Military Role in Vietnam* (1984); Ronald Spector, *After Tet: The Bloodiest Year of the Vietnam War* (1985); George C. Herring, *America's Longest War: The United States and Vietnam, 1950–1975* (1986); Brian VanDeMark, *Into the Quagmire: Lyndon Johnson and the Escalation of the Vietnam War* (1991); Lloyd C. Gardner, *Pay Any Price: Lyndon Johnson and the Wars for Vietnam* (1995); Robert S. McNamara, *In Retrospect: The Tragedy and Lessons of Vietnam* (1995); and Tom Wells, *The War Within: America's Battle Over Vietnam* (1996).

For Johnson's taped White House conversations about domestic and foreign affairs during the first twenty-one months of his presidency, see Michael Beschloss, ed., *Taking Charge: The Johnson White House Tapes, 1963–1964* (1997) and *Reaching for Glory: Lyndon Johnson's Secret White House Tapes, 1964–1965* (2001). The Beschloss books contain selections from the roughly two-thirds of the tapes that have been declassified. The remaining tapes will be opened probably in the next five years, and W. W. Norton will publish a complete multi-volume edition of the tapes. The Miller Center at the University of Virginia will edit them as well as the bulk of the John F. Kennedy and Richard Nixon recordings.

Lyndon Johnson's presidency is covered in chapters 5–15 of this volume. These chapters are abridgments of chapters 2–12 of *Flawed Giant*, which remains the most detailed reconstruction of Johnson's five years and two months as president.

:: *Index*

NOTE: References to Lyndon Johnson are abbreviated as "LBJ."

Acheson, Dean, 103, 108, 218, 316, 318
Ackley, Gardner, 275
Act of Dominican Reconciliation, 216
Adams, Horatio H., 25
Adams, John, 121, 122
Adenauer, Konrad, 130
AFL-CIO, 238
African Americans, 137, 206–7, 280–82, 291–94, 370, 372–73. *See also* desegregation; racial issues
Agnew, Spiro, 363
Agriculture Adjustment Act, 23
Agriculture Committee, 23
Ahmad, Bashire, 129
Aid to Families with Dependent Children (AFDC), 245–46
Aiken, George, 103, 287, 301
air and bombing campaigns (Vietnam): assessments of, 304, 308, 310, 315; diplomatic efforts and, 268–69, 312, 337; disagreements over, 353; elections and, 352; expansion of, 256, 261–62, 306; failures of, 267; halted, 354–55; Joint Chiefs on, 252; LBJ's commitment to, 219; public opinion on, 263, 316; "Rolling Thunder" campaign, 209–11
Air Force, 59
Albert, Carl, 351
alcohol use, 7
Alger, Bruce, 120
Allred, Jimmy, 31, 36, 70
Alsop, Joe, 92, 115, 138, 232, 316
Alsop, Stewart, 89
Ambrose, Stephen, 92, 102
American Federation of Labor, 238
American Medical Association, 199–200
American Trucking Association, 235

Anderson, Clint, 98, 103, 104
antiwar movement. *See under* protests and demonstrations
Apple, Johnnie, 309
approval ratings. *See* public opinion
Armed Services Committee, 58, 59
arms control, 185, 286, 289, 296, 346, 359–60. *See also* nuclear weapons
Army Corps of Engineers, 236
assassinations, 143, 145, 163, 334, 341
The Atlantic, 314
Attorney General's office, 240–41. *See also* specific office holders
Austin Statesman, 31
Autry, Gene, 75

Baines, Rebekah, 2–3, 4
Baker, Bobby: civil rights efforts, 107, 141; on corruption charges, 142; on LBJ's candidacy, 114, 116; on LBJ's work ethic, 73; legislative efforts, 89–90
Baker, Russell, 373
Baldwin, Hanson, 217
Ball, George: on Tonkin Gulf incident, 177, 179; UN Ambassador post, 337–38; Vietnam War and, 210, 218, 221–22, 318
Bardwell, Malcolm, 26
Barkley, Alben, 82, 83
Bay of Pigs incident, 130, 132
Belaguer, Joaquin, 216–17
Belden, Joe, 60
Bennett, William Tapley, 214–15
Bentsen, Lloyd, 119
Berlin, Germany, 131
bipartisanship, 81, 97
Birdwell, Sherman, 29
Biscayne National Monument, 345

Black, Hugo, 68–69
Black Star, 14–15
Blanco News, 3
"Bloody Sunday," 203
Bluebonnet, 18
Boatner, Charles, 134
Boggs, Hale, 143
bombing campaign. *See* air and bombing campaigns (Vietnam)
Bond, Julian, 370
Bosch, Juan, 214, 216–17
Bowles, Chester, 108
Bradlee, Benjamin, 87
Bradley, Omar, 318
Braun, Werner von, 133
Brazos Tenth Street Company, 366
Breslin, Jimmy, 357
Bridges, Styles, 109, 110
Brinkley, David, 320
Brogan, D. W., 261
Brown, George, 39–40, 42, 44, 63–64, 70
Brown, H. "Rap," 242
Brown, Herman, 39–40, 44, 63–64, 70
Brown & Root, 39–40, 46, 51–53, 54
Brown v. Board of Education, 292
Bryant, Anita, 373
Brzezinski, Zbigniew, 287
Buchanan, James B. "Buck," 31, 37
budgetary issues. *See* economic and budgetary issues
Bunche, Ralph, 106
Bundy, Bill, 355, 357–58
Bundy, McGeorge: on air campaign, 211; foreign policy and, 158–60; as National Security Advisor, 230; on Tonkin Gulf incident, 177, 178; Vietnam policy and, 209, 269, 318
Bunker, Ellsworth, 322–23, 336
Bureau of Public Roads, 236
Burns, James MacGregor, 41
Busby, Horace, 150, 329–30, 370
Bush, George H. W., 367, 375
Bush, George W., 375
Byrd, Harry F., Jr., 79, 305
Byrd, Robert, 347

Cabral, Donald Reid, 214
Califano, Joseph: civil rights issues, 240–41; Democratic Convention, 349–50; domestic affairs, 228–32; food program, 343–44; on housing issues, 327; on Kerner Commission, 281; legislative efforts, 237–38; on transportation negotiations, 235; Vietnam speeches, 262–63; on Walter Reuther,

340–41; White House leaks, 277; on wiretapping, 279
California, 8
Cambodia, 162
campaigns. *See* elections
Capitol Parade, 232
Carmichael, Stokely, 242
Carter, Amon, 63, 119
Carter, Cliff, 247
Carter, Jimmy, 375
Carver, George, 318
Cater, Douglass, 231, 277
caucuses, 173. *See also* Democratic Party
censorship, 308
Central High School, Little Rock, Arkansas, 107
Central Intelligence Agency (CIA), 259, 267–68, 299, 304, 314
Chancellor, John, 219–20
Chavez, Dennis, 78
Chennault, Anna, 356, 367
Chicago Daily News, 139
China: Cold War, 376; Communist expansion, 253; Soviet Union and, 287; Vietnam War and, 252, 258, 289–90, 302, 306, 307, 310, 315
Christian, George, 308, 314, 329, 349, 350–51, 368
Christian Church, 7
Church, Frank, 102, 104
Citizens' League, 24
Civil Aeronautics Board (CAB), 236
civil rights issues. *See also* racial issues: censorship, 308; compromise on, 165; conference, 370–71; counterintelligence and, 314; desegregation, 97, 103, 135, 137–38, 165–66, 195, 201, 204, 239, 292; economic issues and, 164, 326; "Freedom Summer," 202; housing discrimination, 240–41, 326–27, 332–34, 344; Humphrey's support of, 91; integration, 97, 103, 239; John F. Kennedy and, 136–38; LBJ's efforts on, 74, 97–108, 125–26, 147–48, 162–70, 370; legislation, 97–108, 141, 148–51, 167–69, 193; opposition to, 77; political considerations, 134, 172; Robert Kennedy and, 139; speeches on, 205–6; Texas electorate and, 56–57; Thurgood Marshall and, 292; Vietnam War and, 239–42; voting rights, 102–3, 138, 201–7, 374; welfare rights, 245; white primaries, 54; wiretapping, 279, 356, 368–69
Civilian Conservation Corps, 27
Clark, Jim, 202

Clark, Ramsey, 69, 291, 293

Clark, Tom, 63, 68–69, 291

Clifford, Clark: administration turnover, 358; bombing campaign and, 310, 353; campaign efforts, 188; on civil rights issues, 100; criticism of Nixon administration, 367; on Democratic convention, 351; diplomatic efforts, 336, 360; on LBJ's leadership style, 335; on LBJ's nomination, 116; on Supreme Court nominations, 346; Vietnam policy and, 218, 324, 337, 349

Clinton, Bill, 375

cloture, 168

Coast Guard, 236

Cohen, Ben, 103, 104, 106

Cohen, Sheldon, 279

Cohen, Wilbur, 198, 199, 245, 345

Cold War, 58–59, 161, 192–93, 376

College Star, 15

Collins, LeRoy, 117

Colorado River projects, 39–40

Commerce Department, 236

Commission on Heart Disease, Cancer and Strokes (HDCS), 197

Committee on Equal Employment Opportunity (CEEO), 125–26, 133–36, 140–41

Communism: counterintelligence and, 314; Dominican Republic crisis, 214–17; LBJ's concern about, 127–31, 158, 183, 254–55, 376; national security issues and, 220–21; presidential race and, 114; subversion threat, 259; Vietnam War and, 161, 225

Community Action Program (CAP), 154, 155, 243, 244

Congress. *See also* House of Representatives; Senate: committee appointments, 83; Congressional Campaign Committee, 41; divisions within, 22; Hoover presidency and, 20; LBJ's frustration with, 273; LBJ's offices, 124; presidency and, 191; Republican control, 56; Vietnam War and, 162, 212, 221, 224, 313–14, 315

Congress of Industrial Organizations, 238

Congressional Record, 86, 102–3, 247

Conkin, Paul, 86

Connally, John: campaign efforts, 41, 61, 63, 119; Democratic Convention and, 350; LBJ's candidacy decision and, 329; at LBJ's funeral, 373; Texas Democrats for Nixon, 368; Vietnam policy and, 295–96

Connally, Tom, 27

Connor, Eugene (Bull), 138

conservatism, 24, 374

conspiracy theories, 143, 144

Consumer Price Index, 273

consumer safety, 238, 374

Cook, Donald, 58

Cooke, Terence, 340

Coolidge, Calvin, 13

Cooper, John Sherman, 143

Corcoran, Thomas G.: campaign efforts, 248; Democratic Convention, 96; on election fraud, 47; on LBJ as Congressman, 39; as LBJ's assistant, 37; on LBJ's majority leadership, 117; on LBJ's Senate election, 69; lobbying efforts, 75–76; oil industry, 64; on presidential elections, 94

corruption, 142, 187

Cotulla, Texas, 15

Council of Economic Advisors, 154

court packing attempts, 32, 346–48

Cox, Archibald, 293

Cox, Ava Johnson, 9

credibility problems of LBJ, 225, 228, 250, 260, 264

Crider, Ben, 8

crime, 240, 278–80

Cronkite, Walter, 364, 365

Cuba, 131, 215

"Daisy" advertisement, 185–86

Daley, Richard, 115, 350

Dallas Morning News, 70

Dallas News, 64

Dallas Times Herald, 371–72

Dallas Veterans for Johnson, 61, 63

dams, 32, 39. *See also* rural electrification

Darden, William, 89

Davidson, T. Whitfield, 68

DE SOTO patrols, 176–77

Dean, Arthur, 318

Defense Department, 297

DeGaulle, Charles, 336

DeLoach, Deke, 229–30, 368–69

Demetracopoulos, Elias P., 353–54

Democratic Party: civil rights and, 99, 164; declining influence, 246; Democratic conventions, 95–96, 112, 113–17, 174, 180, 349–50, 351, 367; Democratic Leaders, 82; Democratic National Committee (DNC), 41, 184, 229, 246, 248, 249; Democratic Policy Committee, 81, 84; Democratic Steering Committee, 83–84; Depression and, 22; Hoover presidency and, 20; internal conflicts, 79–80; LBJ's

frustrations with, 273; LBJ's withdrawal and, 327–32; National Youth Administration and, 28; space race, 108–11; Texas Democrats, 20, 368
Denny, Charles, 76
Department of Education, 196
Department of Housing and Urban Development (HUD), 236, 343, 344
Department of Justice, 314
Department of Transportation, 233, 234–39
Depression, 19–20, 32, 38–39
desegregation: compromise on, 165–66; in education, 292; in employment, 135; Kennedy administration and, 137–38; LBJ and George Wallace meeting, 204; LBJ's support for, 97–108, 195; political limits on, 239; voting rights and, 103, 201
Detroit, Michigan, 281
Diem. *See* Ngo Dinh Diem
Dies, Martin, 27, 45, 47
Dillon, Douglas, 318
Dirksen, Everett: civil rights issues and, 167, 168, 240, 241–42; criticism of LBJ, 355; Jack Valenti and, 151; judicial nominations and, 347; Vietnam policy, 295
DiSapio, Carmine, 115
discrimination, 118, 240–41, 326–27, 332–34, 344. *See also* civil rights issues; racial issues
Dobie, J. Frank, 65
Dobrynin, Anatoli, 359
domestic affairs and reforms, 81, 147. *See also* Great Society
domestic spying, 314
Dominican Republic, 214–17
Douglas, Paul, 79, 84–85, 101, 103, 106, 316
Douglas, William O., 46, 69
Doyle Dane Bernbach (ad agency), 185
drug coverage, 201
Dugger, Ronnie, 13
Duke, Angier Biddle, 124
Dulles, Allen, 143
Duong Van Minh, 161

Eastland, James O., 101, 107, 292, 347
Eaton, Cyrus, 290
economic and budgetary issues: budget deficits, 274, 277–78, 326; civil rights and, 164, 326; defense spending, 58; Depression, 19–20, 32, 38–39; domestic legislation and, 91–92; economic indicators, 272–74; inflation, 274; New Deal and, 23; pork-barrel spending, 133; poverty, 152–53;

racial tensions and, 99, 100; spending cuts, 327, 335; Texas poverty, 28; unemployment, 20, 27, 327; Vietnam War and, 277–78, 326
Economic Opportunity Act (EOA), 154
Edmund Pettus Bridge, 203
education policy: Cater's focus on, 231; college education subsidies, 196; educational reform, 156; Elementary and Secondary Education Act (ESEA), 194; LBJ's presidency and, 374; task force on, 277; work study programs, 154, 192–94, 196
Egypt, 283–84
Eisenhower, Dwight: Central High School crisis, 107; civil rights issues, 101–2; Democratic Party conflicts and, 79–81; electoral defeat, 122; health issues, 93; LBJ's leadership position and, 116; missile program, 109–10; presidential elections, 95; presidential style, 114; public opinion, 251; space race, 108; on vice presidency, 124; Vietnam policy and, 316
elections: campaign finance, 41–46, 51–53, 249, 353–54; Democratic conventions, 95–96, 112, 113–17, 174, 180, 349–50, 351, 367; Eisenhower election, 94–97; election fraud, 47; FDR elections, 41–43, 181; Goldwater and, 77, 173–74, 181–89; Great Society programs and, 189, 190–92; gubernatorial campaigns, 246, 248, 250; JFK election, 111, 117–21; Kleberg campaign, 23–24; LBJ vs. Goldwater, 173–74, 181–89; LBJ's congressional campaigns, 31–35, 61–62; LBJ's father, 6; LBJ's presidential election, 171–72, 173–74, 181–89; LBJ's Senate races, 43–48, 61–71; midterm elections, 246–50; Nixon election, 351–58; pre-election polls, 348; primary elections, 54, 61, 66–67, 173–75, 341; Rayburn's electoral challenges, 54; Republican losses, 20; Rockefeller-Reagan ticket, 313–14; Senate Democratic Campaign Committee, 86; social programs and, 344–45; in South Vietnam, 310–11; straw polls, 330–31; Texas electorate, 56–57; vice president selection, 180–81; Vietnam War and, 189, 247, 301, 321, 348; white primaries, 54
electrification, rural, 39, 129
Elementary and Secondary Education Act (ESEA), 194–95
Elk Hills Naval Petroleum Reserve, 58
Ellzey, Russell, 30

employment issues: employment discrimination, 133–36, 135; employment policies, 133–36; Fair Employment Practices Commission (FEPC), 54; unemployment, 20, 27, 327

Emporia Gazette (Kansas), 187

Engle, Clair, 169

Ensley, Grover, 85

environmental issues, 156, 374

Erhard, Ludwig, 176

Ervin, Sam, 101–2, 293

Eshkol, Levi, 284

Estes, Billie Sol, 141

Evans, Rowland, 87, 89

Everson v. Ewing Township, 193

Executive Office Building (EOB), 124

Fair Deal, 275

Fair Employment Practices Commission (FEPC), 54

fair housing legislation, 333–34

Fair Packaging and Labeling Act, 238

Farley, Jim, 184

Farm Security Administration, 39, 53

Farmer, James, 137, 242

Faubus, Orval, 107, 108

Federal Aviation Agency (FAA), 236

Federal Bureau of Investigation (FBI), 229, 253, 259, 262, 279, 314, 351, 356

Federal Communications Commission (FCC), 52–53, 75–77, 366

Federal Emergency Relief Act, 23, 27

Feldman, Myer, 117

Ferguson, "Ma," 9

filibusters, 91, 105–6, 137, 168, 206, 241

Fleeson, Doris, 89, 111

Food and Agriculture Act, 345

food stamp program, 345

Ford, Gerald, 143

Fore, Sam, 31

Foreign Agents Registration Act, 356

foreign policy. *See also* Cold War; Vietnam War: bipartisanship and, 97; Communism and, 183; Diem regime and, 130; Eisenhower administration, 80; "illusion of omnipotence," 261; LBJ's focus on, 157–59; LBJ's staff on, 230

Foreign Relations Committee, 85

Forrestal, James Vincent, 319

Fortas, Abe: campaign efforts, 63, 188; civil rights issues, 104; Johnson's Senate election, 68; LBJ's finances, 365; LBJ's intellect, 73; LBJ's Senate election, 68–69; peace talks, 336; support for Vietnam policy, 316; Supreme Court appointment, 219–20, 279, 291, 346–48; Vietnam war briefings, 318

Francis, Charles, 64

"Freedom Summer," 202

Friendly, Fred, 254

Fulbright, J. William: antiwar sentiment, 224; bombing program, 310; committee appointments, 85–86; dissent of Vietnam, 308–9; Glassboro conference, 287; LBJ's withdrawal, 333; on "The Treatment," 88; on Tonkin Gulf incident, 177; Vietnam policy, 295

fundraising, 41–46, 249. *See also* elections

Fuqua, J. B., 372

Galbraith, John Kenneth, 128, 263

Gallup, George, 172

Gallup polls. *See* public opinion

Gardner, John, 327

Garner, John Nance, 19, 38, 116, 124

Garza, Reynaldo G., 370

Gavin, James, 254

George, Walter, 82, 83, 372

Georgetown University, 25

G.I. Bill, 192

Gillespie County, 2–3

Glassboro, New Jersey meetings, 288–91, 303

Gliddon, Stella, 5–6

Golan Heights, 285, 286

Goldberg, Arthur, 291, 296, 315, 336–38, 339

Goldman, Eric, 155–56, 180, 194, 212

Goldwater, Barry: electoral defeats, 188–89; electoral victories, 77; at LBJ Library opening, 364; LBJ's opinion of, 182–85; potential candidacy, 172–74; on Tonkin Gulf incident, 179; on Vietnam War, 176

Gonzalez, Henry, 370

The Good Society (Lippmann), 156

Goodwin, Richard, 155–56

Gore, Albert, Sr., 96, 123

Graham, Billy, 352–53

Graham, Phil, 115

Great Society: assessment of, 373–74; civil rights and, 239–42; Department of Transportation and, 234–39; elections and, 246–50; LBJ's election and, 189, 190–92; LBJ's staff efforts, 227–32; State of the Union address, 232–34; Supreme Court and, 347; term coined, 155–57; Vietnam War and, 221, 252, 263, 271, 275–76, 301, 326; War on Poverty and, 242–46

Green, Theodore Francis, 78, 117

Greer, Walter, 51

Gromyko, Andrei, 313
Gronouski, John, 365
gubernatorial campaigns, 246, 248, 250
guerrilla warfare, 220
gun control, 280

Hagerty, James, 93
Halberstam, David, 316–17
Haldeman, Henry Robbins, 367–69
Haley, J. Evetts, 187
Halleck, Charlie, 166
handicapped access, 344–45
Handicapped Children's Early Education
    Assistance Act, 345
Hardesty, Bob, 363, 364
Harding, Warren, 181
Harlow, Bryce, 50, 59, 72, 82–83, 118, 354, 355
Harriman, Averell: Democratic convention,
    112; diplomatic efforts, 325, 337, 338; nom-
    ination ballot, 96; peace talks, 336; on
    Robert Kennedy, 138; on Vietnam policy,
    224; war briefings, 318
Harrington, Michael, 147, 154
Harris, Lou, 173, 225, 320, 330
Harris-Blair Literary Society, 14
Harte, Houston, 63
Harwood, Richard, 369–70
Hatch Act, 42
Hayden, Carl, 169
Hayes, Wayne, 151
health care policy: Cater's focus on, 231; drug
    coverage, 201; Health Manpower Act,
    344; Medicaid, 199, 201, 374; Medicare,
    185, 196–201, 344, 374
Health Manpower Act, 344
Hearnes, Warren, 272
helicopter campaigning, 61–62
Heller, Walter, 147, 243
Helms, Richard, 316, 354
Higher Education Act (HEA), 196
Highway Department (Texas), 8–9
Highway Safety Act, 238
Hill, Lister, 69, 298
Hill-Burton law, 196
Hill Country of Texas, 2–3
Ho Chi Minh, 212, 213–14, 311
Holding Company Act, 53
Hoover, J. Edgar, 20, 22, 163, 279
Hopkins, Harry, 28, 37
House of Representatives: election results,
    250; House Naval Affairs Committee, 37;
    LBJ as Congressman, 36–71; LBJ's com-
    mittee work, 38; LBJ's majority leader-
    ship, 81–92, 116–17, 124; Republican con-

trol, 56; Rules Committee, 334; Ways and
    Means Committee, 197, 199
housing discrimination, 240–41, 326–27,
    332–33, 344
Houston, Andrew Jackson, 45
Houston, Charles H., 292
Howard, Mike, 372
Hue, Vietnam, 322
Hughes, Howard, 63
Hughes, Richard, 281, 288
Hughes Aircraft, 63
Humphrey, Hubert: candidacy, 174–75,
    180–81, 333, 351; civil rights efforts, 91,
    165, 168–70, 370; committee appoint-
    ments, 83; Democratic convention, 96,
    112, 349; education policy, 192; on
    Kennedy nomination, 114; at LBJ Library
    opening, 364; LBJ on, 349, 351–52; on
    LBJ's candidacy, 348; on LBJ's party
    work, 246; on LBJ's rivalry with Kennedy,
    121; LBJ's support for, 338–39, 340, 351,
    356–57; on LBJ's work ethic, 72–73, 190;
    on Nixon/Chennault incident, 357–58;
    party conflicts, 80; relationship with LBJ,
    341, 354; on "The Treatment," 87; on
    urban riots, 277; on Vietnam policy, 211,
    224, 353
Hurst, Willis, 331

Ickes, Harold, 37
immigration reform, 374
India, 128
inflation, 274
Innes, Roy, 370
Inouye, Daniel, 328
integration, 97, 103, 239
Intelligence Command unit, 314
Inter-American Peace Force, 216
intercontinental ballistic missiles (ICBMs),
    108–11. *See also* nuclear weapons; space
    program
Internal Revenue Service (IRS), 46, 51–52, 53
Interstate Commerce Commission, 137, 236
Iran, 283
isolationism, 80
Israel, 282–86

Jackson, Henry, 88, 238
Jackson, Robert, 21
Jackson State University, 367
Jacobson, Jake, 228
Janeway, Eliot, 37, 116–17
Jenkins, Walter, 93, 119, 150, 188
Jester, Beauford, 60, 70

Job Corps, 154
John Birch Society, 187
Johnson, Boody, 15
Johnson, Claudia Alta (Lady Bird): campaign efforts, 34, 120; childbirth, 59; on election results, 47, 66; estate, 52–53, 75–77, 364, 365–66, 370; introduction to LBJ, 24–25; KTBC radio station, 52–53, 75; LBJ's candidacy, 172, 329, 330; at LBJ's funeral, 373; LBJ's health and, 93, 331; on Nelson Rockefeller, 339; on Supreme Court nominations, 291; on Vietnam, 210
Johnson, George, 17
Johnson, Louis, 70
Johnson, Lucy (Luci) Baines, 59, 362
Johnson, Lyndon Baines: NOTE: As LBJ is the subject of the work, readers can find more specific information throughout the index.; alcohol use, 7; ambition, 1, 2, 4–5, 10, 36; ancestry, 1–2; appearance, 363; assertiveness, 12; birth, 4; charity, 16–17; childhood, 1, 4–9; children, 54, 362, 370; confidence, 1; credibility problems, 225, 228, 250, 260, 264; deference for authority, 14; education, 1, 5, 7–8, 9–18, 25; end-of-term efforts, 343–46; estate, 52–53, 75–77, 364, 365–66, 370; farewell address, 360–61; grandiosity, 375; health issues, 92–94, 328, 369, 370–71; ideology, 24; intellect, 4, 73; language skills, 146; leadership qualities, 82–83; legacy, 373–74, 377; memoirs, 364; military service, 50–51; Navy service, 48–51; paranoia, 376, 377; parents, 2–6; partisanship, 338–42; persuasive powers, 86, 88, 204; physical stature, 11–12; rebelliousness, 8–9; religion, 7; retirement from office, 358–61, 362, 364, 367; secretary position, 18, 21, 25; siblings, 5; sympathetic nature, 16; teaching job, 15–16, 17–18; temper, 119; work ethic, 21, 29, 62, 72, 88, 92, 151, 190, 229
Johnson, Sam Ealy, Jr., 2, 4, 6, 26, 45, 97
Johnson, Sam Houston, 331
Johnson, Thomas, 364–67, 371–72
Johnson City, Texas, 5
Joint Chiefs of Staff: air campaign, 210, 252, 270, 303; peace talks, 336; troop deployments, 324; on Vietnam stalemate, 299; Vietnam strategies, 320; war assessments, 254, 268, 306
Joint Committee on Atomic Energy, 58
Jones, Luther E., 21–22, 25
Jordan, 283, 284

Jordan, Barbara, 370
Jordan, Vernon E., Jr., 370
Judiciary Committee (Senate), 101, 241, 347
juries, 101, 103–5, 239–40
Justice Department, 314

Kaiser, Edgar F., 345
Karnack, Texas, 24
Katzenbach, Nicholas: on bombing campaign, 270; on civil rights issues, 241–42; peace talks, 336; Vietnam policy and, 268, 296; on voting rights, 201–2
Kearns, Doris: on Apollo XI launch, 363; on civil rights efforts, 99, 164; on LBJ's Senate ambitions, 60; on LBJ's sense of purpose, 148; on LBJ's work ethic, 88; on legislative tactics, 84; on rural Texas, 13; on "The Treatment," 87
Kefauver, Estes, 79, 84, 95
Kellam, Jesse, 29, 31, 365, 371–72
Kennan, George, 254
Kennedy, Edward (Ted), 341–42, 349, 367
Kennedy, John F.: assassination, 143, 163; campaign efforts, 120–21; civil rights movement, 137; committee appointments, 84; Democratic convention, 96, 112; elections, 111, 114; father's influence, 95; foreign policy, 160; judicial appointments, 292; on LBJ's candidacy, 113; on LBJ's diplomacy, 129–30; LBJ's vice presidency and, 122–23; legacy of, 163; space race, 132–33; support for LBJ, 78, 125
Kennedy, Joseph P., 94–95, 121–22, 139
Kennedy, Robert: assassination, 341; candidacy, 180, 244, 328, 330, 333; civil rights movement and, 137, 139, 165; Democratic Convention and, 349; dissent on Vietnam, 306; LBJ compared to, 140; primary contests, 174–75; public opinion of, 251; tensions with LBJ, 94, 113, 117, 138–42, 327, 339, 376
Kent State University, 367
Keppel, Francis, 193–94
Kerner, Otto, 281
Kerner Commission, 281–82
Kheel, Theodore, 136
Khrushchev, Nikita, 109, 188
King, Martin Luther, Jr.: assassination, 334; civil rights efforts, 125, 137–38; divisions within movement, 242; on LBJ's speech, 206; praised by *Time*, 97; Selma march, 202–3
Kintner, Robert, 232, 248, 260, 262
Kissinger, Henry, 311

Kleberg, Alice King, 20
Kleberg, Richard, 18–27, 30, 237
Kleberg, Robert, 20
Knowland, William Fife, 98, 101, 105
Koeniger, John, 8
Komer, Robert, 256, 263, 266, 268, 269
Korean War, 222
Kosygin, Aleksei, 209, 286–90, 303, 359
Krock, Arthur, 115, 125
KTBC (television station), 52, 75, 76, 151
Ku Klux Klan, 137, 163, 186
Ky. *See* Nguyen Cao Ky

labor. *See* organized labor
Lady Bird Johnson. *See* Johnson, Claudia
    Alta (Lady Bird)
Landrum, Lynn, 70
Lanham Act (1940), 192, 193
Laos, 130, 162
Latimer, Gene, 21–22
Lawrence, David, 115
LBJ Company, 76–77
LBJ Victory Special, 119
Lebanon, 283
legislative process: civil rights and, 166–69;
    Department of Transportation, 237; LBJ
    staff and, 84–85, 89–90, 166, 237–38;
    LBJ's skill at, 86–87, 90–92, 126, 148–51,
    152–55, 166–67, 190–92, 220–21; poverty
    and, 152–55; tactics, 84–85; Vietnam pol-
    icy and, 217–18
Lehman, Herbert, 91
Leuchtenburg, William E., 13
Levinson, Larry, 349
Lewis, Anthony, 144
Lewis, John L., 104
Life, 76, 187
Lincoln, Evelyn, 142
Lindbergh, Charles, 46
Lindig, Otto, 4
Lindsay, John, 281
Lippmann, Walter, 153, 156, 209
Lisagor, Peter, 139, 310, 351
Lloyd, Ed, 67
lobbyists, 2, 18, 25
Lockheed Aircraft Corporation, 135
Lodge, Henry Cabot: on battlefield esti-
    mates, 265, 300; on bombing campaign,
    270; diplomatic efforts, 257, 266; media
    and, 263; potential candidacy, 172; Viet-
    nam policy and, 160, 251–52; war brief-
    ings, 318
Long, Russell, 102, 274
Looney, Katie Deadrich, 194

Los Angles Times, 371
Lower Colorado River Authority, 32
Lucas, Scott W., 77, 82
Lyndon B. Johnson School of Public Affairs,
    364–65

MacArthur, Douglas, 50, 51
Macdonald, Dwight, 147
Magnuson, Warren, 101
Maguire Air Force Base, 288
Malechek, Dale, 367, 372
Malechek, Jewell, 363
Manatos, Mike, 347
Mann, Gerald C., 45, 46–47
Mann, Thomas, 214
Manning, Robert, 314
Mansfield, Mike: civil rights issues and, 98,
    101, 167; diplomatic efforts, 337; on
    implementing legislation, 232–33; sup-
    port for LBJ, 123; on Vietnam War,
    208–9, 295
marches and protests. *See* protests and
    demonstrations
MARIGOLD, 270
Maritime Administration, 236, 237, 238
Marks, Leonard, 308, 373
Marsh, Charles, 44, 46, 47
Marshall, Burke, 140, 370
Marshall, George C., 50
Marshall, Thomas R., 122
Marshall, Thurgood, 137, 291–94, 370
Marshall Plan, 58–59, 65
Martin, Joe, 105
Martin, Louis, 293
Martin, Tom, 8
Matusow, Allen J., 195
Maverick, Maury, 27, 40
McCarthy, Eugene, 175, 330, 341, 349
McCarthy, Joseph, 80–81, 209, 254, 331–32,
    339, 341
McClellan, John, 236–37, 293
McCloy, John J., 143
McCone, John, 160, 179
McCormack, John W., 38, 110, 115, 117, 191,
    199
McDougall, Walter A., 110
McElroy, Neil, 109
McFarland, Ernest, 77, 78, 82
McFarlane, W. D., 40
McGee, Gale, 316
McGovern, George, 368
McGrory, Mary, 89
McIntyre, Tom, 321
McKinley, William, 145

McKissick, Floyd, 242

McNamara, Robert: on air campaign, 211, 270; battlefield estimates, 300, 316; on censorship in Vietnam, 308; diplomatic efforts, 312; foreign policy and, 157–61; Glassboro conference, 289–90; as Kennedy appointment, 227; potential candidacy, 175; public opinion efforts, 313–14; student protests and, 298; on Tonkin Gulf incident, 177, 178; Vietnam policy, 209, 267–69, 303–4, 306, 307, 319–20; war briefings, 318

McPherson, Harry: civil rights issues, 99, 100; Democratic Convention and, 349; on implementing legislation, 232–33; as LBJ staff member, 231–32; on LBJ's criticism of Humphrey, 352; on LBJ's intellect, 73; on public opinion of air campaign, 316; Vietnam policy, 267; on War on Poverty, 242–43

Means, Marianne, 248–49

Meany, George, 104, 238, 340–41

media and journalism. *See also specific publications*: LBJ's campaigns and, 33; LBJ's dealings with, 89; LBJ's tensions with, 260–61, 362; press conferences, 218–19, 264; press support, 194; retrospective of LBJ's presidency, 358; on Vietnam War, 224, 254, 256, 259, 260, 308

Medicaid, 199, 201, 374

Medical Tribune, 184

Medicare, 185, 196–201, 344, 374

Meir, Golda, 371

Merchant Marine Act, 345

Meredith, James, 137

Mexican-Americans, 16, 30

Meyner, Robert, 114

Middle East, 282–90

Middleton, Harry, 349, 363, 365, 372

Military Affairs Committee, 44

military policy, 58–59, 110, 209–10, 261, 263. *See also* foreign policy; nuclear weapons; Vietnam War

Miller, Roy, 18, 23, 25

Miller, Tom, 31, 47

Mills, Wilbur, 197–98, 274, 334

Mink Coat Mob, 120

Minow, Newton, 132

missile program, 108–11. *See also* nuclear weapons

Mississippi, 206

Mitchell, Clarence, 166, 167, 170, 370

Mitchell, John, 356, 368

Montgomery, Robert, 27

Moody, Dan, 9

Moorer, Thomas, 271

Morgenthau, Hans, 230

Morgenthau, Henry, Jr., 25

Morrow, Wright, 70

Morse, Wayne, 84, 101

Moursund, A. W., 366

Moyers, Bill: on antiwar movement, 305; on approval ratings, 247; campaign efforts, 185–86; civil rights efforts, 167–68, 170; on Goldwater, 173; on Great Society programs, 157; as LBJ staff member, 150–51, 227–28; on LBJ's campaign, 120; on LBJ's work ethic, 190; on Medicare, 200; on Press Corps, 260; resignation, 228; on Robert Kennedy's nomination, 328; on Vietnam War, 160, 176, 211, 213, 223, 251, 256, 271; on War on Poverty, 244

Mundt, Karl, 86

Murchison, Clint W., 42

Murphy, Robert, 66, 318

Murray, Jim, 101

Muskie, Edmund, 298, 364, 368

Nasser, Gamal Abdel al, 283

National Aeronautics and Space Administration (NASA), 108–11, 125, 126

National Association for the Advancement of Colored People (NAACP), 135

national defense. *See* military policy; nuclear weapons; Vietnam War

National Defense Education Act, 192–93

National Education Association (NEA), 194

National Eye Institute, 344

National Guard, 107

National Housing Partnership, 345

National Industrial Recovery Act, 23

National Institute of Education, 195

National Liberation Front, 269–70, 304

National Medical Association, 344

National Park Service, 366

National Resources Planning Board, 53

National School Lunch Act (1946), 192

National Science Foundation, 192–93

National Security Administration, 369

National Security Agency, 314

National Security Council, 157, 257, 262–63, 267

National Traffic and Motor Vehicle Safety Act, 238

National Transportation Safety Board, 236

National Youth Administration (NYA), 26, 27–31, 53

Naval Affairs Committee, 37, 58

naval power, 37. *See also* Tonkin Gulf Resolution
Navy Under Secretary's office, 48
Nehru, Jawaharlal, 128
Neutrality Act, 356
New Deal: agencies, 153; effect of war on, 275; LBJ's support for, 23, 32, 36–40, 53, 55, 73, 127, 147, 235; legacy of, 374; National Youth Administration, 27–31
New Leader, 104
The New Republic, 92
New York Times: on bombing campaign, 270; on casualty assessments, 309; on civil rights issues, 102–3, 136, 141; on Kennedy assassination, 144; on Kerner Commission, 282; LBJ's frustrations with, 260; on LBJ's Senate election, 69; on LBJ's vice presidency, 125; on presidential primaries, 341; on Vietnam War, 210, 217, 263, 297, 315–16; White House leaks to, 277
The New Yorker, 147
Newland, Chester, 364
news conferences, 218–19, 264
Newsday, 227
newspapers. *See* media and journalism; *specific publications*
Newsweek, 92
Ngo Dinh Diem, 128, 130–31, 160
Nguyen Cao Ky, 218, 257, 266, 296, 311
Nguyen Khanh, 161
Nguyen Van Thieu, 218, 355–56, 360
Nixon, Richard: administration turnover, 358–59; bombing campaign and, 355; candidacy, 172, 332; on civil rights legislation, 98, 105; criticism of Johnson administration, 278–79; Democratic support for, 368; Earl Warren on, 346; at LBJ Library opening, 364; LBJ on, 351–52; peace talks, 355–57; pre-election polls, 348; primary contests, 341; public opinion, 306; resignation, 377; Vietnam policy, 349, 352, 376; on War on Poverty, 275
Novak, Robert, 87, 89
nuclear weapons: Glassboro conference, 289; Goldwater campaign and, 185; intercontinental ballistic missiles (ICBMs), 108–11; nonproliferation efforts, 286, 289, 290–91, 346, 359–60; nuclear program, 283; Vietnam War and, 295–96
Nugent, Pat, 371–72

Oberholtzer, E. E., 17
O'Brien, Lawrence F.: campaign efforts, 187, 353–54; corruption charges, 142; as Kennedy appointment, 227; as LBJ staff member, 149; LBJ's candidacy and, 329; LBJ's difficulties with, 159; legislative efforts, 166; on Medicare, 197; on Vietnam policy, 263
O'Daniel, W. Lee, 44–47, 60, 64
O'Donnell, Kenneth, 124, 125, 167, 174, 185
Office of Economic Opportunity (OEO), 155, 243, 244–45
oil industry, 42–43, 46, 57, 282
Old Age Assistance Special Fund, 65
O'Mahoney, Joe, 83, 85–86, 98
O'Neill, Tip, 115–16
Operation 34-A, 176, 179
Organization of American States (OAS), 216
organized labor, 56, 104, 163, 246, 340–41
Oswald, Lee Harvey, 143
The Other America (Harrington), 147
"Our Invisible Poor" (Macdonald), 147

pacification, 266–68, 313
Parr, Archer, 67
Parr, George, 67
partisanship, 246, 248–49, 338–42
Pastore, John, 105
Pastore, Joseph, 298
Patillo, Minnie Lee, 24
patriotism, 57–58
peace talks, 213, 296–97, 311–13, 336–38, 354–57, 360, 369
"Peaceniks," 263
Pearl Harbor, 48
Pearson, Drew, 295
Pedagog, 15
Peddy, George, 65
Pell, Claiborne, 303
Pentagon, 263
Persons, Jerry, 93
Pham Van Dong, 311
Pickle, Jake, 166, 329
"Plans for Progress," 135–36, 140
Policy Planning Council, 223
politics. *See also* elections: bipartisan politics, 78–81, 97; LBJ's interest in, 14, 22; machine politics, 67; political favors, 86; pork-barrel spending, 133; postwar politics, 56–60; Sam Johnson's influence on, 6; state Senate campaign, 17
"Politics and Victory in Vietnam" (Rostow), 223
poll taxes, 137. *See also* civil rights issues; voting rights
polling. *See* public opinion
Polyansky, Dmitri, 290

Poor People's Campaign, 334
populism, 2, 275
pork-barrel spending, 133
Porter, Jack, 69, 70
Porter, Paul, 63
poverty. *See also* economic and budgetary
    issues: Depression, 19–20; domestic
    reforms and, 147; education and, 195;
    food stamp program, 345; in Houston,
    Texas, 17; LBJ's childhood, 1, 3; legislative
    process and, 152–55; National Youth
    Administration and, 28; Poor People's
    Campaign, 334; in rural Texas, 16; unem-
    ployment, 20, 27, 327; urban riots and,
    280–82; Vietnam War and, 275–76; War
    on Poverty, 148–49, 152–55, 157, 172, 189,
    239, 242–46, 275, 373–74
presidential library, 364
President's Club, 249
President's Committee on Mental Retarda-
    tion, 345
President's Foreign Intelligence Advisory
    Board (PFIAB), 284
press conferences, 218–19, 264
Press Corps, 241, 260, 308
Price, Leontyne, 373
primary elections, 54, 61, 66–67, 173–75,
    341
progressivism, 275
Prohibition, 7
protests and demonstrations: antiwar senti-
    ment, 222–24, 253, 259–60, 298, 303, 305,
    314, 337; campus protests, 298, 367;
    Democratic convention, 350; Selma
    march, 201–7; urban riots, 277, 280–82,
    350
Prouty, Winston, 194
public education. *See* education policy
Public Health Service, 345
public opinion. *See also* protests and demon-
    strations: civil rights, 164; economic mat-
    ters, 272–74, 326; election polls, 181–83,
    186–87; Great Society programs, 302–3;
    JFK assassination, 146–47; LBJ's approval
    ratings, 172, 247–48, 255, 256, 267, 348;
    LBJ's candidacy, 175, 328–32; Tonkin
    Gulf Resolution, 180; Vietnam War, 162,
    209, 211, 212, 214, 219, 222–26, 230, 251, 258,
    262, 263, 297–98, 306, 309, 313–15, 320–21,
    322–23, 348; War on Poverty, 157
Pusey, Nathan, 230

Qui Nhon military base, 209
quotas, 135

racial issues. *See also* civil rights issues: dis-
    crimination, 118, 133–36, 241; housing dis-
    crimination, 240–41, 326–27, 332–33, 344;
    Kennedy administration and, 140; presi-
    dential race and, 113; quotas, 135; race
    crimes, 240; race war, 239; racial tension
    in the South, 99; Selma march, 201–7
radio, 52–53, 63, 70, 75
railroads, 5, 18–19, 118–19
Rand Corporation, 256
Randolph, A. Phillip, 106, 242
"Range Conservation" program, 39
Rather, Mary, 31
Rauh, Joe, 69, 103, 106
Ray, James Earl, 334
Rayburn, Sam: bipartisanship, 79; civil
    rights, 99; on Coke Stevenson, 65; com-
    mittee appointments, 83–84; Democratic
    convention, 96, 112; elections, 41, 54;
    LBJ's Senate election, 68; LBJ's vice pres-
    idency, 115–16, 122–23; party leadership,
    97; relationship with LBJ, 26, 38, 93
Reagan, Ronald, 199, 200
recession, 272
Reedy, George: on Bill Moyers, 228; civil
    rights and, 98, 100, 106–9; on Eisen-
    hower, 81; as LBJ staff member, 150; on
    LBJ's candidacy, 113; on LBJ's intellect,
    73; on LBJ's nomination, 116; on legisla-
    tive efforts, 90; on press response to LBJ,
    146
reform bills and legislation, 23, 234–35,
    275–78. *See also* Great Society; *specific
    topics of reform*
religion, 7, 118
Republican Party: civil rights and, 98, 242,
    328; Congressional seats, 51, 56; Depres-
    sion and, 22; fundraising efforts, 42;
    gubernatorial gains, 246; health care leg-
    islation, 199; Hoover presidency and, 20;
    internal conflicts, 172–74; isolationism,
    80; LBJ's frustrations with, 273; LBJ's
    withdrawal and, 332; negative attacks,
    186–88; nonproliferation efforts and, 359;
    Old Guard, 80–81; peace talks, 356;
    space race, 108–11; Supreme Court nomi-
    nations and, 347
Resor, Stanley, 219
Reston, James, 210, 271
Reuther, Walter, 104, 340
Richardson, Sid, 42, 63
Riesel, Victor, 340
Right of Privacy Act, 279
Robb, Charles, 370

Robb, Lynda, 370
Robinson, Joseph T., 78, 82
Robinson, Thomas, 288
Roche, John P., 173, 329
Rockefeller, Happy, 339–40
Rockefeller, Nelson, 172, 339–40
Rogers, Will, 79, 106
"Rolling Thunder," 209–10, 212, 223. *See also* air and bombing campaigns (Vietnam)
Romney, George, 248, 302, 306, 328
Roosevelt, Eleanor, 28, 30, 104, 106
Roosevelt, Elliott, 34, 52
Roosevelt, Franklin Delano: death, 55; electoral victories, 41–43, 181; Johnson and FDR compared, 374; LBJ's appointments, 27; LBJ's first meeting with, 29; LBJ's support for, 23, 32, 34, 48, 54; LBJ's travels with, 36–37; LBJ's war service and, 49; presidential style, 114, 171; regard for Johnson, 37–38; Texas visit, 30–31; third term, 40
Roosevelt, Theodore, 145
Roosevelt administration, 30
Rostow, Eugene, 355
Rostow, Walt W.: on air campaign, 261–62, 310; battlefield estimates, 269, 300, 316; diplomatic efforts, 336, 354; media problems, 260; National Security Advisor, 230, 231; Nixon's interference with peace talks, 355; nuclear weapon negotiations, 359; public opinion efforts, 314; Vietnam policy, 223, 256, 267–68, 269–70, 305, 349; war briefings, 318
Rovere, Richard, 182
Rowe, Jim: on antiwar movement, 305; campaign efforts, 44; civil rights and, 98, 103, 107, 108; Democratic convention, 96, 112; election results, 43; on Johnson/Kennedy rivalry, 121; on LBJ's campaign efforts, 119; LBJ's candidacy and, 329; tensions with LBJ, 354; Vietnam policy and, 316
Ruby, Jack, 143
Rules Committee, 85
rural electrification, 39, 129
Rusk, Dean: administration turnover, 358, 359; appointment by Kennedy, 227; battlefield estimates, 316; bombing campaign, 353; diplomatic efforts, 265, 270, 312, 336; foreign policy, 157, 158; on LBJ's candidacy, 313; on LBJ's vice presidency, 125; public opinion efforts, 313–14; Six Days War and, 285; on troop increases, 324; Vietnam policy and, 160, 211, 217, 257, 262, 308, 349

Russell, Richard: campaign efforts, 120; civil rights issues and, 98, 100–102, 104, 106–7, 162–63, 165, 167–68, 170; committee assignments and, 83; Democratic convention, 96; Democratic Party conflicts, 79; Fortas nomination and, 346–47; on LBJ's candidacy, 172; LBJ's relationship with, 73–74, 372; LBJ's Senate leadership, 77, 82; on missile program, 109; on public opinion, 258; on Thurgood Marshall, 294; Vietnam policy and, 298; Warren Commission, 143
Russia. *See* Soviet Union
Rustin, Bayard, 106

Sachs, Alexander, 355
Safe Streets and Crime Control Act, 279–80
Saigon, Vietnam, 128
Salinger, Pierre, 150
Salisbury, Harrison E., 270, 296, 297
Sam Houston High School, 17–18
San Antonio, Texas, 6–7
San Marcos, Texas, 5, 11, 13, 17
Sanders, "Barefoot," 334
Sanford, Terry, 142
Saudi Arabia, 283
Schlesinger, Arthur, Jr., 98, 116, 139
Schoolmaster's Club, 14
Schultze, Charlie, 237, 244, 277
Scranton, Bill, 179
Secret Service, 262
Securities and Exchange Commission (SEC), 53
segregation, 16, 99, 164, 292, 332–33, 374–75
Selective Service, 259–60
Selma, Alabama, 201
Senate. *See also specific senators*: Democratic Campaign Committee, 86; Democratic cloakroom, 90; Democratic Policy Committee, 79; Democratic Steering Committee, 79–80; elections, 43–48, 61–71, 250; filibusters, 91, 105–6, 137, 168, 206, 241; Foreign Relations Committee, 254; funding for housing measures, 343; Judiciary Committee, 101, 241, 347; Marshall appointment, 293–94; Republican control, 56; rules, 79–80, 83, 90–91; Vietnam, 298
Sevareid, Eric, 155
Seward, William, 123
Shakespeare Literary Society, 15
Shapley, Deborah, 177
Shelton, Emmett, 34
Shepard, Alan, 132

Sheppard, Morris, 19, 44
Sherley, Swager, 42
Sherrod, Robert, 264
Shoreham, 22
Shriver, Sargent, 153–54, 174–75, 245
Sidey, Hugh, 222, 273
Siegel, Gerry, 103, 107
Sirhan, Sirhan B., 341
Six Days War, 282–86
Skouras, George, 63
Smathers, George, 83, 92, 102, 126–27, 354
Smith, Howard, 166, 193, 300
Smith, Jean, 127–28
Smith, Kendall, 370
Smith, Margaret Chase, 86
Smith, Merriman, 298
Smith, Preston, 363
Smith, Stephen, 127–28
Smithsonian Institution, 345
social issues and programs, 23, 220, 343–46,
    374. *See also* Great Society
Social Security, 23, 186, 197, 199, 345
socialized medicine, 198. *See also* Medicaid;
    Medicare
Solicitor General, 292–93
Sorensen, Theodore, 115, 116, 138, 141
Southern Christian Leadership Conference,
    125, 202
southern states, 55, 99, 164, 374–75
Southwest Texas State Teachers College, 8,
    9–11, 26
Soviet Union. *See also* Cold War; Commu-
    nism: China and, 287; national security
    issues and, 58; nuclear weapons negotia-
    tions, 359–60; Six Days War and, 282–86;
    space race, 108–11, 132; U.S. relations
    with, 286–91; Vietnam War and, 258, 287,
    289, 302, 306, 307, 310, 315, 376
Space Council, 110
space program, 110, 126, 132–33, 363
Sparkman, John, 74, 85
Special Committee on Space and Astronau-
    tics, 110
Special Operations Group, 314
speeches. *See also* State of the Union
    addresses: campaign speeches, 33–34;
    civil rights, 205–6, 371; "Great Society"
    speech, 156; on Humphrey candidacy,
    357; national addresses, 146; security
    measures, 262; speech writers, 231–32; on
    Vietnam War, 213, 259, 262–63, 267, 312,
    325; withdrawal speech, 332
Sputnik I, 108
staff of LBJ, 84–85, 89–90, 149–51, 166,

227–30, 230–32, 237–38. *See also* Joint
    Chiefs of Staff; *specific individuals*
*The Stages of Economic Growth: A Non-
    Communist Manifesto* (Rostow), 230
Stalin, Joseph, 109
Standard Oil, 58
Stanton, Frank, 254
State Democratic Executive Committee, 68
State Department, 236, 257, 270, 283, 296
State of the Union addresses: farewell
    address, 360–61; focus on domestic
    issues, 232–34, 276; Great Society pro-
    gram, 191–92; on Social Security, 198; on
    Vietnam's impact, 325–27; War on
    Poverty and, 148; withdrawal statement
    drafted for, 329–30
Steele, John, 91
Stennis, John, 84, 163, 218, 331
Stevenson, Adlai, 79–80, 92–95, 112–14, 175
Stevenson, Coke, 44, 60–61, 63–65, 70, 96
Stewart, Maco, 63
strikes, 56
Suez Canal, 285
Summy, Otho, 8
Supreme Court: *Brown v. Board of Educa-
    tion*, 292; civil rights issues and, 97,
    99–100, 170, 278; court packing attempts,
    32, 346–48; *Everson v. Ewing Township*,
    193; Thurgood Marshall appointment,
    291–94
Symington, Stuart: committee appointments,
    83; Democratic convention, 96, 112, 114;
    friendship with LBJ, 58; on LBJ's legisla-
    tive efforts, 85; on presidential elections,
    111; Vietnam policy, 267, 298
Syria, 283, 284, 285

Taft, Robert, 78
Taft-Hartley bill, 56
taxes: budget deficits, 326; campaign contri-
    butions, 41–42; tax bills, 149; tax cuts, 147,
    148–49, 152–55, 172; tax increases, 274,
    325, 334–35
Taylor, Claudia Alta. *See* Johnson, Claudia
    Alta (Lady Bird)
Taylor, Hobart, Jr., 136
Taylor, Hobart, Sr., 63
Taylor, Maxwell: on air campaign, 176, 304,
    310; on antiwar sentiment, 303; diplo-
    matic efforts and, 176, 336; on Vietnam
    policy, 223, 254, 256; war briefings, 318
Taylor, Thomas Jefferson, 24
television, 75–77
Temple, Larry, 349, 368

Tennessee Valley Authority, 23
Tenth District, 31
Tet offensive, 321–25, 330, 331, 376
A Texan Looks at Lyndon (Haley), 187
Texas: civil rights and, 56–57; Cotulla, 15;
    Democratic Party, 20, 368; Highway
    Department, 8–9; Hill Country, 2–3;
    Houston, 17–18; Johnson City, 5; Karnack,
    24; National Youth Administration in, 27;
    poverty, 16, 17, 28; Roosevelt's visit to,
    30–31; rural Texas, 13; San Antonio, 6–7;
    San Marcos, 5, 11, 13, 17; Texas Election
    Bureau, 66; Texas legislature, 6
Texas A&I University, 25
Texas Broadcasting Corporation, 75, 76
Texas Eastern Transmission Company, 64
Texas Election Bureau, 66
Texas legislature, 6
Thant, U, 283, 296
Thomas, Donald S., 365
Thomas, Helen, 358
Thompson, Llewellyn, 210
Thornberry, Homer, 346
Thurmond, Strom, 105–6
Time, 97, 273
Time-Life, 264
To Secure These Rights (report), 56
Tonkin Gulf Resolution, 175–80, 208, 230,
    309
Tower, John, 120
Traffic Safety Act, 236
trains, 5, 18–19, 118–19
transportation policy, 234–39
Troutman, Robert, 135, 140
Trujillo, Rafael, 214
Truman, Harry: campaign efforts, 118; death,
    372; Korean War and, 222; LBJ on, 145;
    LBJ's Senate election and, 68; LBJ's sup-
    port of Truman Doctrine, 58–59; presi-
    dential style, 114; on vice presidency, 124
Tully, Grace, 94, 104
Twenty-fourth Amendment, 137

U.N. Security Council, 285, 286
Underwood, Oscar, 82
unemployment, 20, 27, 327
United Arab Republic. *See* Egypt
United Mine Workers, 42
United States Information Service, 260
urban renewal, 374
urban riots, 277, 279, 280–82, 350
U.S. Marines, 212, 215
U.S. Naval Reserve, 48
U.S. News & World Report, 329, 331

U.S. Press Corps, 260, 308
U.S. Sixth Fleet, 285–86
USS *Liberty*, 284–85
USS *Maddox*, 176–78

Valenti, Jack: on antiwar sentiment, 222;
    campaign efforts, 183, 186; civil rights
    efforts, 163, 166; as LBJ staff member, 151,
    227; resignation, 228; staff duties, 230;
    Vietnam policy, 253
Van Buren, Martin, 122
Vance, Cyrus, 256, 268, 336–37, 338
Vandenberg, Arthur, 168
vice-presidency, 115–18, 121–26, 142, 180–81
Viet Cong: casualties, 256, 304, 322; popular
    support for, 264; population controlled
    by, 299; Tet offensive, 321–25
Vietnam War: battlefield estimates, 300;
    casualties, 256, 304, 322; changing policy
    on, 220–22; DE SOTO patrols, 176–77;
    declining military position, 208–10;
    Democratic convention and, 351; Diem
    regime and, 128, 160; diplomatic efforts,
    213, 265–66, 269, 290, 296–97, 311–13,
    335–38, 354–57, 360, 369; dissent on, 272;
    Earl Warren on, 295; economics of,
    277–78; elections and, 189, 247, 348; exit
    strategies, 301, 320, 324–25; LBJ adminis-
    tration and, 130–31, 160–62, 255, 360,
    373–74, 375–76; legacy of, 375–76; legisla-
    tion supporting, 217–20; media, 308;
    military policy, 217, 252; pacification
    efforts, 265–66, 266–68, 313; physicians,
    200; priority status, 249; public opinion,
    212–14, 222–26; Robert Kennedy on, 306;
    Soviet Union and, 287, 289; stalemate,
    299–302, 307; State of the Union address,
    233–34; Tet offensive, 321–25, 330, 331,
    376; Tonkin Gulf Resolution, 175–80,
    208, 230, 309; troop deployments, 223,
    252–53, 255, 264–65, 267–68, 301, 306,
    308, 319, 320, 324
Vinson, Carl, 372
Volunteers in Service to America (VISTA),
    154
voting rights, 102–3, 138, 201–7, 374

Wall Street Journal, 187
Wallace, George, 138, 203, 204–5, 355
War on Poverty. *See* poverty
Warren, Earl, 81, 143, 278, 294, 295, 346, 370
Warren Commission, 143–44
Washington Post, 87, 92, 115, 214, 224, 234,
    369

Washington Star, 187, 188
Watergate, 368
Watson, Marvin, 229, 328–29, 338, 350, 373
Watts riots, 207, 239
Ways and Means Committee, 197, 199
Webb, James, 133
Weedin, Harfield, 46
Weisl, Edwin, 37, 63
Welhausen Elementary School, 16
West, Wesley, 63
West Bank, 285
Westmoreland, William, 320; air campaign, 310; on censorship in Vietnam, 308; diplomatic efforts, 266; at LBJ's funeral, 373; public opinion efforts, 309; Tet offensive, 322–23; troop deployments, 301, 324; Vietnam policy, 218, 262, 306, 307; war assessments, 300, 304, 315
Wheeler, Earle: administration turnover, 358; assessment of war effort, 300; on censorship in Vietnam, 308; public opinion and, 309, 313–14; troop deployments, 301; Vietnam policy, 254, 257, 269, 306; war briefings, 318
White, Lee, 169
White, Theodore, 183
White, Walter, 91
White, William S., 89
White House Press Corps, 241, 260
white primaries, 54. *See also* elections

Wholesale Poultry Products Act, 344
Why Not Victory? (Goldwater), 183
Wicker, Tom, 260, 341
Wild, Claude, 31, 34, 63
Wilkins, Roy, 153, 164, 167–68, 242, 370
Williams, Aubrey, 26–28, 30–31
Willkie, Wendell Lewis, 43
Wilson, Henry H., 278
Wilson, Woodrow, 129, 158, 376
wiretapping, 279, 356, 368–69
Wirtz, Alvin J., 31, 39, 44–45, 53
Wirtz, Willard, 140
Women's Strike for Peace, 350
Woods, Wilton, 14
Woodward, C. Vann, 107
Woodward, Warren, 363
Works Progress Administration (WPA), 28, 39
World Bank, 319
World War II, 41
Wortham, Gus, 63
Wright, Zephyr, 163
Wurzbach, Harry M., 18

Yalta agreements, 80
Yarborough, Ralph, 367
"Yippies," 350
Young, Andrew, 165
Young, D. G., 44
Young, Harold, 44
Young, Whitney, 242, 370

CPSIA information can be obtained at www.ICGtesting.com
Printed in the USA
BVOW041549240512
290821BV00007B/1/A

Unicorn Riding Camp

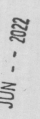

For Pip & Jess, xx
—SARAH KILBRIDE

To Agnieszka
—SOPHIE TILLEY

ALADDIN
An imprint of Simon & Schuster Children's Publishing Division
1230 Avenue of the Americas, New York, New York 10020
First Aladdin paperback edition June 2021
Text copyright © 2014 by Sarah KilBride
Cover illustration copyright © 2021 by Paula Franco
Interior illustrations based on artwork originated by Sophie Tilley copyright © 2014
Originally published in Great Britain in 2014 by Simon & Schuster UK Ltd.
Also available in an Aladdin hardcover edition.
All rights reserved, including the right of reproduction in whole or in part in any form.
ALADDIN and related logo are registered trademarks of Simon & Schuster, Inc.
For information about special discounts for bulk purchases, please contact
Simon & Schuster Special Sales at 1-866-506-1949 or business@simonandschuster.com.
The Simon & Schuster Speakers Bureau can bring authors to your live event. For more
information or to book an event contact the Simon & Schuster Speakers Bureau
at 1-866-248-3049 or visit our website at www.simonspeakers.com.
Cover designed by Tiara Iandiorio
The text of this book was set in Sabon LT Std.
Manufactured in the United States of America 0421 OFF
2 4 6 8 10 9 7 5 3 1
Library of Congress Cataloging-in-Publication Data
Names: KilBride, Sarah, author. | Tilley, Sophie, illustrator.
Title: Unicorn riding camp / Sarah KilBride ; interior illustrations by Sophie Tilley.
Description: New York : Aladdin, 2021. | Series: Princess Evie ; 2 | Audience: Ages 6 to 9. |
Summary: Princess Evie's magical pony Diamond transforms into a unicorn during
Unicorn Riding Camp in Cloud Kingdom where they help a runaway unicorn and her
cloud sprite rider find their way back home.
Identifiers: LCCN 2020051867 (print) | LCCN 2020051868 (ebook) |
ISBN 9781534476318 (hardcover) | ISBN 9781534476301 (paperback) |
ISBN 9781534476325 (ebook)
Subjects: CYAC: Princesses—Fiction. | Horsemanship—Fiction. |
Unicorns—Fiction. | Fairies—Fiction.
Classification: LCC PZ7.1.K5464 Un 2021 (print) | LCC PZ7.1.K5464 (ebook) |
DDC [Fic]—dc23
LC record available at https://lccn.loc.gov/2020051867
LC ebook record available at https://lccn.loc.gov/2020051868

Princess EVIE

By Sarah KilBride

Interior illustrations by
Sophie Tilley

Unicorn Riding Camp

ALADDIN
NEW YORK LONDON TORONTO SYDNEY NEW DELHI

CHAPTER 1
A Sunny Start

CHAPTER 2
Away to Unicorn Stables

CHAPTER 3
Unicorn Camp Chaos

CHAPTER 4
Raphaela's Magic

CHAPTER 5
The Rescue Party

CHAPTER 6
Home and Dry

CHAPTER 7
Team Cloud Sprite

CHAPTER 1

A Sunny Start

"What a perfect day, Diamond!" said Princess Evie as she trotted through the gates of Starlight Stables.

Even though it was early, the sun was scorching. It was much hotter in the stable yard than on the top of the Golden Mountain, where they had enjoyed a lovely, cool breeze. The bright morning sun made Evie's Connemara pony's coat gleam.

"I think your friends are pleased to see you, Diamond!"

Evie was right. All her lovely ponies
were trotting to the gate, neighing,
squealing, and welcoming Diamond back.

It wasn't only Evie's ponies that were
glad to see them. Evie's little kitten,
Sparkles, skipped over to the tie post
and rubbed against Evie's ankle.

"We've just had the most amazing ride," Evie said with a smile. "The Golden Mountain is ever so high. At first we were surrounded by mountain clouds, but they soon cleared and then we could see for miles."

Diamond was the perfect pony for mountain rides. She had great stamina and was very strong. Of course, Evie loved riding all her ponies, especially on summer days like these. But Evie's ponies weren't any old ponies—they were magic ponies. Whenever Evie rode them through the tunnel of trees, they took her on magical adventures in faraway lands.

Evie's ponies were transformed the moment they came out of the tunnel. For instance, when Neptune galloped out onto a beach, her coat became the color of the sparkling ocean. And that wasn't the only magic that happened— Evie's clothes changed too! She loved the beautiful new outfits she wore on their adventures. When she went to the North Pole with the snow fairies, she wore a gorgeous fluffy pink cloak and warm boots. Evie looked up at the cloudless sky—it was hard to imagine snow today!

Evie checked to see if Diamond had cooled down, especially where the saddle had been and under Diamond's elbows and hind legs. Because Diamond's breathing had slowed down to normal, Evie could now give her some fresh water and brush out her shining coat.

"You've worked hard this morning,
Diamond, climbing up that steep
mountain and galloping along the
ridge."

Evie went into the tack room to get
her grooming kit and Sparkles padded
in after her. It wasn't just Diamond
who was hot. Evie had been out in
the sun for quite some time, and the
tack room felt lovely and cool. The

walls were lined with saddles, bridles, and, of course, rosettes. Evie walked toward the metal trunk where she kept her grooming kit. As her eyes adjusted to the shadows of the tack room, she noticed something.

"Have we had visitors this morning, Sparkles?"

Sparkles meowed. Of course he couldn't talk—he was only a cat, but Evie was positive that he could understand every word she said.

"I think someone's been here while I was out on the mountain. Look!"

Evie pointed to the metal trunk and Sparkles hopped up for a closer inspection.

There, leaning against a bottle of hoof oil, was a golden envelope.

"Who's it from?" asked Evie.

Sparkles sniffed the envelope and then looked at Evie, blinking patiently.

"You're right—there's only one way to find out!"

Evie picked the envelope up and took out the letter. As she read it, she smiled.

"Come on, Sparkles, I have to read this to Diamond!" And they raced out to the sunny yard with the letter.

To
Princess
Evie

Dear Evie,

How are things at Starlight Stables? I hope you're enjoying this lovely summer with all your gorgeous ponies—fantastic riding weather, isn't it?

I'm writing to you because I wondered if you and Diamond would like to come to the Cloud Kingdom and join our Unicorn Riding Camp. It starts today and should be great fun. There'll be lots of cloud sprites there, and there'll be lots of lessons and activities to help us learn all about our unicorns. Just leave your kit in the stable yard and I'll send a cloud to pick it up. I'll be waiting for you on the clouds when you come out of the tunnel of trees.

Really hope you can make it—it would be wonderful to see you and Diamond again.

Lots of love,

Skye xxxxxx

PS: PLEASE bring Sparkles too xxxxxxx

PPS: Please give all your ponies a hug from me.

PPPS: PLEASE give Sparkles an extra-special hug too!!!!

Diamond neighed. She loved taking Evie away on adventures, and Unicorn Riding Camp certainly sounded very exciting. Diamond and Evie had shared an amazing adventure the last time they'd visited the Cloud Kingdom. They had competed in the Unicorn Games and had even won first prize in the obstacle race!

There was no time to lose. Evie raced into the tack room to pack. She found the special riding gloves that Skye had given her, embroidered with little gold unicorns. Then she checked her grooming kit, making sure that everything was clean and in good condition.

"How thrilling—we're going to see Skye and her magic unicorn, Jewel, again," said Evie as she took her backpack of useful things down from its peg. "I can't wait!"

She carried her kit out into the yard.

"Skye said to leave our kit here," said Evie. "I wonder if that's the cloud that's going to take it to the Cloud Kingdom?"

The blue sky had been clear a moment ago, but now there was a large white cloud floating over the Golden Mountain. As it came toward Starlight Castle, it floated lower and lower, drifting past the turrets and over the gardens. By the time it arrived at Starlight Stables, it was skimming along the ground.

Sparkles jumped up into Evie's arms—he'd never seen anything quite like this before! The cloud came toward them and for a few seconds they couldn't see a thing, then it floated back up into the sky.

"Look at that!" said Evie.

There was just an empty space where her kit box had been.

"Hop up, Sparkles. It's time to go to the Cloud Kingdom!" said Evie as she put on her backpack of useful things. "I think our luggage will be there before us!"

Evie and Sparkles mounted Diamond, and soon they were galloping toward the tunnel of trees. Evie closed her eyes and took a deep breath.

CHAPTER 2

Away to Unicorn Stables

When Evie opened her eyes, the Cloud Kingdom stretched out around them for miles. The sunshine made the clouds glitter with pretty pastel colors. Diamond's coat shimmered with the same soft colors and she now had a magnificent golden unicorn's horn that sparkled in the sunshine. Evie looked down and saw that she was wearing a stylish riding jacket embroidered with fine gold thread, a pair of jodhpurs, and gleaming riding boots.

"I think we're ready for Unicorn
Camp," she whispered as they trotted
out onto the soft, fluffy clouds.

"You certainly are!" called a friendly voice.

It was Skye. The cloud sprite appeared from the shimmering mist on her beautiful unicorn, Jewel. Her pretty vest was edged with daisies and her pale pink jodhpurs were decorated with silver thread.

"Skye!" Evie said with a laugh. "How lovely to see you."

Jewel whinnied, and Diamond and Jewel touched noses and said their unicorn hellos.

"I'm so pleased you could make it, Evie," said Skye.

"We wouldn't have missed Unicorn Riding Camp for the world!" said Evie.

"Are you ready for a gallop, Diamond?" asked Skye.

Diamond neighed and tossed her sparkling mane.

"Follow me, Evie! We'll be there in no time," said Skye.

Skye turned her unicorn around and broke into a fast trot, a canter, and then a gallop. Diamond didn't need

any encouragement to follow and soon
they were racing along the clouds. Evie
could feel her cheeks glow as the wind
whistled past.

They sped through puffy white clouds
that splashed the girls with rainbow
drops. They sailed over great powdery
plains and jumped across small pink

clouds that patterned the sky like
stepping stones.

Normally when Diamond galloped,
Evie could hear her pony's hooves on
the ground, but Diamond was galloping
along silently with her glittering mane
flying. Evie remembered that a unicorn's
hooves never make a sound—it was one

of the magical things about them.

Skye was right; it wasn't long before they were at the gate of the riding school in the clouds.

"This is where they train the Unicorn Olympic Team," said Skye excitedly. "I've always dreamed about riding here."

The friends dismounted, landing softly. Evie thought that walking on clouds felt a little like walking on snow. Her feet gently sank, leaving little prints. Skye opened the beautiful golden gate.

"We'll take our unicorns to the stables first and get them settled in," she said. "Then it'll be time to go to the Great Hall to meet the instructors."

As they led their unicorns into the yard they spotted a map pinned on to a post. A little cloud sprite was looking at it. She

turned and called over to the friends.

"What are your unicorns' names?"

"My unicorn is called Diamond," replied Evie. "And this is Jewel."

"You're in stables eleven and twelve and we're in stable thirteen." She smiled at her unicorn. "Unlucky for some!"

She turned to take her unicorn to

the stable block when two other cloud sprites arrived and trotted silently across the yard on their unicorns, almost knocking her down.

"Watch where you're going!" shouted one rider, who had a long golden braid.

The little cloud sprite was too stunned to say anything. The riders smirked at her as she stood with her mouth open.

"You'll catch flies if you stay like that!" said the rider with the long braid. She checked the map and the other rider giggled.

"Come on, let's go and make ourselves at home," said the first rider. "We're in stables fourteen and fifteen."

They trotted off to find their stables.

"They're going to be our neighbors,"

the little sprite said to her unicorn.
"I told you thirteen was unlucky for
some."

"Are you all right?" asked Evie.

Tears had begun to well up in the
little sprite's eyes.

"I'm fine."

"I'm sorry—we should have stuck up
for you," said Evie.

"It's a good thing you didn't," said
the sprite, looking down at her scuffed
riding boots. "They're the Sunshine
Girls, and you don't want to get on the

wrong side of them. I met them at last year's camp. It's best to keep out of their way."

The little cloud sprite turned and led her unicorn away.

"What's your name?" Skye called after her, but she had already disappeared around the corner, taking her unicorn to her stable.

"Let's have a look at the list," said Evie as she scanned the map. "Here we are. She's called Wanda and her unicorn is Zephyr. I wonder if she has any friends at the camp."

"Well, I think we should be her friends. That's what camp is all about," said Skye. "Let's keep an eye on her and make sure that the Sunshine Girls don't try picking on her again."

Evie and Skye led Diamond and Jewel to their stables, where their grooming kits were waiting for them.

"I told you they'd be here before us, Diamond!" said Evie.

"We're across from Wanda," Skye said with a smile.

"And the Sunshine Girls," added Evie.

The riders who had just been so rude to Wanda were now busily settling their unicorns in. They were making quite a lot of noise about it—singing and shouting, shrieking with laughter and chasing each other around.

"They look like they're having fun," said Evie as she gently put her hand on Diamond's muzzle.

She could feel her unicorn getting

twitchy and knew that Diamond didn't
like all this noise.

"Let's get our unicorns settled," said
Skye. "We need to be in the Great Hall
for the introduction to camp in half an
hour. If we team up with Wanda, we'll
get it done quickly."

So Evie and Skye went to Wanda's

stable and introduced themselves. Soon they were busy helping one another.

Wanda collected some golden apples from the barrel in the yard while Skye filled three buckets with fresh water. Evie and Sparkles went to the barn to collect some straw for their unicorns' bedding. They needed a whole bale, but the bales were too heavy for Evie to pick up on her own.

"Do you need a hand?" asked a kind voice.

Evie turned around. Standing behind her was the most beautiful cloud sprite she had ever seen. Light seemed to shine from her sky-blue eyes and soft curls floated around her face. She wore a pair of pale blue jodhpurs and her silk shirt had tiny pearl buttons.

"Come on," she said with a smile.
"Let's go and find a wheelbarrow."

As they lifted the bale into an old
wheelbarrow, Evie found out that
the beautiful cloud sprite's name was
Raphaela Plume and she was one of the
camp's instructors.

"I used to come to Unicorn Camp when I was younger," said Raphaela. "I hope you have as much fun as I did!"

Evie smiled—then she remembered the Sunshine Girls. She hoped they weren't going to spoil things.

The wheelbarrow wobbled all over the place, and by the time they got back to the stable, Raphaela and Evie were giggling.

Evie introduced her new friend to Skye and Wanda, but the cloud sprites didn't say hello or even smile. They just went red!

"See you at the meeting!" said Raphaela.

She waved and headed off toward the Great Hall. Wanda and Skye stared after her, speechless. Even the Sunshine

Girls had stopped messing around and were staring at the lovely sprite as she disappeared around the corner.

"I don't believe it!" gasped Skye. "Raphaela Plume—the most famous Olympic gold medalist in the Cloud Kingdom."

"She was chatting and laughing with you, Evie, like a normal sprite!" said Wanda.

"Well, she is normal," said Evie. "Not like you two—staring at her and not saying a word!"

"You don't understand, Evie," said Wanda. "She is the most fabulous unicorn rider in the entire Cloud Kingdom!"

"I hope she's going to teach us some of her riding secrets," said Skye. "Oh, this is going to be such an amazing camp!"

She did an excited little jump into the air.

"Come on, you two, before you get

any giddier!" said Evie as she picked
Sparkles up. "We've got five minutes
to get to the Great Hall for our
meeting."

CHAPTER 3

Unicorn Camp Chaos

The Great Hall was on an enormous cloud. Sparkles led the way along the path that followed the soft curves of the cloud. As they climbed the steps, the hall's magnificent door magically opened.

"Look at that!" Evie gasped.

She pointed to the domed ceiling. It was painted with a beautiful skyscape of shimmering clouds. On one side of the dome, the morning sunrise was painted in warm colors. The evening

sky was on the opposite side. It was a
deep blue that looked as if it went on
forever, scattered with constellations of
gold stars. The arched windows were
open and pale blue curtains floated
gently in the breeze.

A little crowd of sprites was already waiting, and the air was full of chattering and laughter. Clouds the size of plates floated from sprite to sprite, carrying tasty marshmallows, pink cotton candy on cocktail sticks, and tiny fairy cakes that were so fluffy they almost floated away! Whenever a plate began to look empty, it magically filled up with more treats.

Skye and Wanda met a few sprites they knew, and Evie recognized Rosy from when she, Diamond, and Sparkles had taken part in the Unicorn Games. Rosy smiled and waved as she came over to say hello. Then the huge wooden doors at the end of the hall opened and in walked three important-looking cloud sprites.

"The instructors," whispered Skye.
"Look! There's Raphaela."

"I hope we don't get Professor
Nimbus first," said Wanda. "She's the
one on the left. She trains riders for the
Olympic team."

Evie could feel poor Sparkles jump when the professor began to speak.

"Welcome to this year's Unicorn Riding Camp," said Professor Nimbus. "I hope all your unicorns have settled in. This afternoon I will be teaching the training session on riding technique."

"I am Madam Mariposa," said the older, shorter sprite, who was standing beside the professor. She had a warm smile and fluffy white hair that had a silver lining like a halo. "I will be helping you learn about unicorn well-being and stable management."

"And I'm going to be helping you bond with your unicorns," said Raphaela. "And together, we will develop your unicorn empathy skills."

There was a ripple of excitement among the cloud sprites.

"There will be a list of the groups on the noticeboard after lunch," said Professor Nimbus.

Evie spotted Professor Nimbus winking at the girl with the long blond braid before turning to leave.

"That's Professor Nimbus's niece," Rosy whispered in her ear. "Her name's Storm."

All the cloud sprites filed out of the Great Hall and followed the long corridor to the dining room.

The dining room was hung with paintings of unicorns and each of the round tables was lit with a golden candelabra. Everyone was hungry; it

had been a long morning and the room
buzzed with anticipation. Wanda, Skye,
and Evie shared a table and enjoyed
the fluffy bread and hot soup. Dessert
was the most delicious cake Evie had
ever tasted—layers of light sponge with
heavenly mousse in between.

"Imagine learning how to
communicate with your unicorn like
Raphaela does!" said Wanda when they

had all finished their lunch. Everyone
was starting to leave the dining room
to have a look at the list that had been
pinned on to the noticeboard.

"Nonsense!" snorted Storm as she
and her friend pushed past Wanda's
chair. "My aunt says the only way to
communicate with a unicorn is to show
it who's the boss."

"Let's hope we're not in Storm's

group," said Wanda, and all the friends nodded.

"There's only one way to find out," said Evie. "Come on, let's go and have a look at the lists."

"Oh, this is so exciting," said Skye. "I hope we're all in the same group."

But they weren't. Skye had been put in Rosy's group.

"What a shame I'm not with you," said Skye.

PRINCESS EVIE
& DIAMOND

WANDA
& ZEPHYR

STORM
& MISTY

JUNO
& CHERUB

"It might have been a lucky escape, Skye," said Evie. "Look who's in our group."

Princess Evie & Diamond
Wanda & Zephyr
Storm & Misty
Juno & Cherub

"The Sunshine Girls," said Wanda.

"Never mind," said Skye. "They're probably lovely once you get to know them."

"Well, there's one good thing," said Evie, seeing that Wanda was looking a little worried. "Our first lesson is with Raphaela in the arena."

"Lucky you," said Skye. "I'm with Professor Nimbus."

The friends went off to saddle up their unicorns for the first lesson. But when they reached the stable yard, they were met with complete chaos. Cloud sprites were running about and shouting, trying to catch a unicorn that had escaped from her stable. She was rearing like a wild animal. When the unicorn was finally cornered by the sprites, the friends saw it was Zephyr—Wanda's unicorn.

"Zephyr!" shouted Wanda.

As soon as Zephyr heard Wanda's voice, she neighed, looking wildly around the yard for her owner.

"That animal is out of control!" said Storm, just as the instructors appeared. "Look at this mess."

"What's made Zephie do this?" asked Wanda, completely baffled by the scene of devastation.

The barrel of apples had been kicked over, straw was strewn across the yard,

water buckets had been knocked over, and some tack and a grooming kit lay in the big puddles.

"This is not acceptable," said Professor Nimbus, looking around the yard. "You will not join in any activities, Wanda, until you have cleaned this up. Is that clear?"

As the professor was talking,

Raphaela walked carefully toward Zephyr, murmuring quietly to the frightened unicorn. She helped Wanda put a halter on Zephyr and tied the unicorn up.

"Come along, everyone. Tack up, time for your first lesson," continued the professor.

As the other sprites tacked up, Wanda, Evie, and Skye looked at one another.

"There's no way you can be late for Professor Nimbus's lesson, Skye; she'll be annoyed," said Evie. "I'll help Wanda clear this up."

"I don't understand," said Wanda, looking at the stable door hanging off its hinges. "Zephyr has never done anything like this before. Why would she kick her door down?"

Evie and Wanda set about sweeping and cleaning the yard. Sparkles tried to cheer Wanda up by chasing after apples and catching straw that was blowing in the breeze, but the little sprite found it hard to smile.

"I just can't understand what got into Zephyr," she said.

CHAPTER 4

Raphaela's Magic

Wanda and Evie worked together to clear all the mess and were only ten minutes late for the start of their lesson. Storm and Juno were standing by their unicorns listening to Raphaela, who was resting her hand gently on her magnificent unicorn, Galaxy.

"Hey, sprites! I'm just giving a quick history of unicorns," said Raphaela. "The important thing to remember is, if you want your unicorn's trust, you must make them feel safe. When they

feel safe with you, they can relax and will let you lead—and that's when the magic begins!

"Our first exercise will help you get in tune with your unicorn. Every neigh, whinny, and squeal has a meaning, and the more you listen, the more you'll begin to understand. It all starts with the breath. Listen to your unicorn and copy her breathing."

The sprites and Evie stood closely by their unicorns. In a few moments, Evie and Diamond were almost touching noses and Wanda and Zephyr were leaning shoulder to shoulder. Juno and her unicorn were nodding heads in unison, with Juno giggling and Cherub whickering.

"It's great to see you share the same sense of humor, Juno!" said Raphaela.

"Ow!" yelped Storm. "Stop that now!"

Misty had been resting her head over Storm's shoulder and had started to nibble her fashionable riding jacket.

"Hold on, Storm."

Raphaela and Galaxy raced over to them. "She was telling you that she's your friend."

"Ruining my jacket is more like it," said Storm. "That's disgusting, Misty!"

Misty whinnied and shook her mane.

"Careful, Storm—that's not the way to speak to your unicorn," said Raphaela. "She's grooming you like a mother does to comfort her foal."

"I don't need to be comforted," snapped Storm.

"Well," replied Raphaela, "it seems your unicorn believes that you do."

Storm looked angry and turned away.

The next part of the lesson was what everyone had been looking forward to—developing unicorn empathy skills.

"Practice this on your unicorn, and one day you'll be able to calm and ride any unicorn in the Cloud Kingdom," Raphaela said.

"Stand close to your unicorn's midpoint. The midpoint is just by the withers, in front of your saddles. Stand quietly and try to feel your unicorn's beat. It's a cross between a pulse and a heartbeat," said Raphaela. "Let them feel your beat too."

Evie could feel Diamond's beat pulsing quietly and steadily. Diamond was standing so still and alert, Evie was sure that her unicorn was listening to hers. Next, Raphaela told the sprites to rest their arms over their unicorn's withers.

"Apply pressure so your unicorn

understands what's going to happen next," she said. "Once they steady themselves, it's time to hop up."

Everyone copied Raphaela as she demonstrated on her unicorn, Galaxy, and soon they were all up in the saddle. Everyone, that is, apart from Storm. Misty was still shifting her weight and hadn't yet settled, but instead of steadying her with the weight of her arm, Storm was pulling hard on her reins. This was making Misty raise her head and try to move away.

Raphaela rode over to Storm and let Galaxy gently breathe onto Misty's muzzle. The little unicorn relaxed and Storm was able to get up into the saddle.

The next task was to ride with
loose reins. "I want you to practice
going from a halt to a walk to a trot,"
said Raphaela. "Direct your unicorn
by visualizing what you want her to
do and where you want to go, and
remember to talk to her."

The unicorns and their riders moved
around the space. Soon, Wanda and

Zephyr were weaving in and out of some rainbow cones. Juno giggled as Cherub began to trot after a little cloud that had floated into the arena.

"Excellent, Juno; Cherub can sense that you like to play," said Raphaela.

Evie was amazed at how Diamond seemed to be able to read her mind. All she had to do was look in the direction she wanted to go, visualize turning, and Diamond would take the turn.

"This is such fun!" said Wanda, laughing as Zephyr jumped over a row of little sunbeams.

"How much longer?" asked Storm. "I can't wait till our next lesson so we can start learning useful stuff."

Her unicorn was standing by a rainbow jump and wouldn't budge.

"Try not to get angry," said Raphaela as Storm started to use her heels to try to make her unicorn move. "Perhaps it's time for a break—we've all been working hard."

Raphaela was giving Storm the chance to dismount and calm down, but Storm took no notice.

"Come on!" Storm shouted. "Move it!"

She smacked Misty's hindquarters and everyone gasped. Misty reared

up high on her hind legs and let out
a piercing neigh that made the other
unicorns jump. Her nostrils flared and
the whites of her eyes flashed wildly.
Before anyone could take hold of
Misty, she bolted over the arena's high
fence and disappeared into a cloud.

Everyone watched in amazement and
the air filled with squeals of panic from
the unicorns.

The unicorns and their riders all
knew the danger Storm was in as
Misty, angry and frightened, took her
into the Cloud Kingdom. "What on
earth is going on here?" demanded
Professor Nimbus, bursting into the
arena.

Evie and the sprites looked at
Raphaela. No one wanted to be the

one to tell the angry professor what had happened to her niece. Raphaela looked uncomfortable, but she managed to explain.

"My niece is in terrible danger," said the professor. "The clouds are beginning to separate and a storm is brewing. How on earth could you have let this happen? That unicorn of hers doesn't need empathy; it needs discipline."

"Now isn't the time to discuss our differences," said Raphaela. "Our unicorns have a connection with Misty. I'll lead the group to find their friend and bring Storm back to safety."

"The Cloud Kingdom is a dangerous place. If we hear nothing from you within the hour, then I'll have no choice but to contact the Rainbow Rescue Team and tell them you have lost my niece."

The unicorns moved close together,

their noses almost touching. The
riders waited, feeling the beats of their
unicorns racing. Then the unicorns
began to whicker—little noises that
shivered out on their breath.

"They're talking," whispered Wanda.

"They're going to call to Misty," said Raphaela. "I hope that she can hear her friends."

Diamond raised her head, her unicorn horn glittering in the sun. She let out a neigh that Evie had never heard before. Evie could feel it travel through Diamond's body, starting at the top of her range. As it spiraled down, all the other unicorns in the circle joined in.

The unicorns' call seemed to go on for minutes, and as it went down to the lowest notes, all the unicorns at the camp had joined in. When it ended, everyone listened.

After a minute, out of the blue, came the sound everyone had been waiting

for. It was Misty's reply, but it was
coming from far, far away.

The unicorns pawed the ground,
their ears forward, their horns
glittering, and their eyes searching the
horizon of clouds. Together, with their
riders holding on tightly, they galloped
out of the arena, through the yard
and the golden gate, and onto the vast
blanket of clouds.

"Slow down, everyone. The clouds are beginning to thin," said Raphaela.

She was right: little gaps were beginning to appear as some of the clouds began to float away. Evie could see glimpses of what lay beneath and felt Sparkles snuggling up close to her to be safe. If any of the unicorns lost their footing, it would be a long way down!

CHAPTER 5

The Rescue Party

Raphaela led them carefully in single file, scanning the clouds and making sure they rode a safe path. They kept their distance from any thinning clouds, and when they heard Misty neigh again, it was a little closer.

"Hooray!" said Juno. "We're on the right track."

"I hope Storm has managed to stay on," said Evie.

"She doesn't seem to get along very well with her unicorn," said Wanda.

"Storm has never been happy with Misty," said Juno. "She always thinks other sprites' rides are better than hers." Juno turned and looked apologetically at Wanda. "She wanted Zephyr and thought that if she made your unicorn look wild, you might want to get rid of her."

Everyone looked shocked. They all knew that pairing with a unicorn was for life.

"Get rid of Zephyr!" gasped Wanda.

"Was it Storm that broke Zephyr's door?" asked Raphaela.

"Yes," said Juno in a small voice.

"I knew Zephyr couldn't have done it." Wanda placed her hand on her unicorn's neck and pressed gently. "I never doubted you, Zephyr. I knew it wasn't you."

"You were with Storm when she
turned this unicorn out of her stable
and made that mess," said Raphaela.
"Why would you stand by when she
was being so cruel?"

"She's my friend," Juno said. "I
know she was doing the wrong thing,
but I feel sorry for her. She's been
having a tough time."

"Feeling sorry for a friend who doesn't

know any better isn't enough," said Raphaela. "You need to be strong and help Storm do the right thing, even if that means risking losing her as a friend."

The procession fell silent. The clouds were darkening and a mist was beginning to form on them.

"Will the unicorns know their way back?" asked Juno.

"Only when the mist and the storm have cleared," said Raphaela.

"That might take longer than an hour," said Wanda, remembering Professor Nimbus was going to call the Rainbow Rescue Team.

Everyone knew that if they weren't back within an hour, Raphaela would be in a lot of trouble.

"We don't want to get caught in the storm," said Juno.

"Let me see if I've got anything that might help," said Evie. "I'm sure there's a compass in here."

She opened her backpack of useful things and, while she was looking, pulled out a pencil and a ball of red string. The instant Sparkles saw the string, he started to unravel it with his paws.

"You're brilliant, Sparkles!" said Evie. "We'll leave a trail of string and follow it on our way back."

Everyone felt better knowing they would be able to get back safely. They had traveled a long way from the Unicorn Riding Camp, and no one wanted to get caught in a cloud storm.

"What's that?" whispered Raphaela.

Everyone stopped and listened.

"Help!"

It was Storm shouting.

The search party hurried through the mist, following her calls. And there they were, Storm and Misty, stranded on an island of cloud. Evie could see the gap between their cloud and Storm's was widening. Storm was looking pale and Evie could see that Misty was trembling; they were both petrified.

"Help!" shouted Storm. "Help me!"

"The only one who can help you is

your unicorn," called over Raphaela.
"Stay calm and try to remember what
you learned this morning."

The only way Storm was going to
be able to get off the cloud was if her
unicorn could jump over the gap.

"Misty is a good jumper, Storm,"
called Juno. "Remember when she won
the rainbow jumping at the Unicorn

Games? She can jump that gap easily."

Storm and Misty's cloud was floating farther away. If Misty was going to jump, she would have to do it quickly.

"Calm your unicorn with your breathing and soothe her with your words," Raphaela shouted across to Storm. "She has to trust you and feel safe."

Storm walked steadily to her unicorn's midpoint.

"Good girl, we'll be all right, just you see," Storm said, breathing slowly.

The unicorns, Evie, Sparkles, and all the sprites watched as Storm tried to calm her unicorn. Their little cloud island drifted away a bit more and Evie could see the huge drop below. It made her feel dizzy. Evie knew she'd be terrified if she had to make this jump.

Storm mounted Misty, and Evie was amazed to see that, for the first time, they looked like a riding pair.

"Well done, Storm," called Raphaela. "Now take your time and try to visualize Misty soaring through the air and landing safely, just like we did in the arena."

The pair stood still, and Storm closed

her eyes. When she opened them, Misty began to paw at the ground as if she couldn't wait, her eyes sparkling and her golden horn gleaming. The little unicorn reared up proudly and then began a fierce gallop toward the edge of the cloud.

They only had a short run-up before jumping. No one dared to breathe as the little unicorn flew into the air. She

sailed over the gap and landed silently not far from Evie, Sparkles, and Diamond.

Everyone cheered and whooped and neighed; the sound echoed through the clouds for miles around. "Thank you for saving us," said Storm as she leaned over to Raphaela and hugged her.

"It was you and your brave unicorn that did all the hard work," said

Raphaela. "I'm very proud of you."

"I'm very proud of Misty," said Storm, giving her unicorn a gentle hug. "I've been so hard on her. No wonder she wanted to run away from me!"

"I think she's seen another side of you," said Evie. "We all have."

Storm's face changed and her smile disappeared.

"There's something that I need to tell you, Wanda," she said, "about what happened in the yard after lunch."

"You can talk while we make our way back," said Raphaela. "We have to follow the red string and find the stables quickly."

"Before the storm starts," said Evie, looking at the dark clouds that had begun to hiss and spit.

Poor Sparkles hid under Evie's jacket! He hated thunder and could feel in his whiskers that the storm was about to start.

CHAPTER 6

Home and Dry

The unicorns followed the trail of red string, walking nose to tail through the crackling fog and storm clouds. Underneath their silent hooves the dark clouds rumbled. The cloudscape was changing fast. When they came to the end of the red string, Evie searched the horizon but the Unicorn Stables were nowhere to be seen.

After a few seconds, the sound of neighing filled the air.

"It's the other unicorns," said

Raphaela. "They're calling us back."

The unicorns pricked up their ears
and neighed back to their friends
joyfully. Before Evie and Sparkles knew
it, Diamond and the other unicorns
were racing over the snarling black

clouds back to the stables. Soon they were in view.

"We've made it!" cheered Wanda.

Raphaela led Evie, Juno, Wanda, and Storm into the stable yard just as the first flash of lightning lit up the clouds beneath them, making the clouds shudder. All the other unicorns and riders welcomed the rescue party back, relieved and happy to be together again. Professor Nimbus and Madam Mariposa were standing at the front. As soon as the riders dismounted, Professor Nimbus rushed up to Storm.

"I'm so glad you're safe," she said, giving her niece a big hug. "I've been so worried."

"I'm all right," replied Storm, "thanks to Misty. You should have seen her jump. She was amazing!"

"Well, maybe you'll make the Olympic team after all!" said Professor Nimbus, stroking Misty's mane.

Storm told her aunt all about how she and Misty had been stranded on the cloud island. While she listened to

her niece, Professor Nimbus glared at Raphaela.

"Please don't be angry with Raphaela," said Storm as Raphaela led Galaxy to her stable. "I wouldn't have been able to get off that cloud without her help."

"Don't you worry yourself," said Professor Nimbus. "Just settle your unicorn and then come to the Great Hall. I'm sure you and your friends need some cake after all that excitement."

All the other cloud sprites had fed and groomed their unicorns, so Professor Nimbus took them to the Great Hall for tea. Juno, Wanda, Storm, and Evie took off their unicorns' tack, brushed out their coats, and helped them to recover from their

adventure with a gentle massage. The
unicorns settled quickly and enjoyed
the fresh water and hay that Skye and
Madam Mariposa brought them.

"Well done for today," said Evie to
Storm. "I never could have jumped
over that gap. You and Misty are an
amazing team."

"She's the best unicorn ever," said Storm, giving Misty a gentle hug.

"Your aunt seemed very proud of the way you rode today," said Madam Mariposa as she helped Storm brush out Misty's mane.

"I never thought my riding would be good enough for her," said Storm.

"Is that why you wanted a different unicorn?" asked Evie.

Storm looked embarrassed.

"I'm sorry, Misty," she said. "I thought you weren't as good as the other unicorns, but today I realized that it was me that was stopping us from being a team. I wouldn't bond with you, so you couldn't trust me."

"Trust is the key," said Madam Mariposa. "You learned that just in time, and it saved you and your unicorn from being lost in the sky."

"I'll never forget it," promised Storm. "It's not about being the boss like my aunt said—it's about getting to know each other, listening to each other, and being the best team you can be."

"That sounds like good advice," said Skye. "Not just for riders and their unicorns, but for friends too."

Storm smiled at them all and then took Wanda's hand.

"I know it won't make up for what I did," she said, "but I'm so sorry about the way I've treated you and Zephyr. I won't ever make the same mistake again."

"I'm so glad you're bonding with Misty," said Wanda. "You make a great team."

"I think we all make a great team," said Evie. And everyone cheered.

CHAPTER 7

Team Cloud Sprite

When all the unicorns were settled, Sparkles led Evie, Juno, Wanda, Skye, Storm, and Madam Mariposa to the dining room. As they followed the path, Madam Mariposa told them something about Raphaela and Professor Nimbus.

"Storm, your aunt used to love coming to Unicorn Riding Camp years ago," she said. "It was here that she met Raphaela and they became best friends. But after a few years they had to compete for a place on the Olympic team. Raphaela beat your aunt by a whisker in the finals, and Professor Nimbus never got over it or forgave her old friend."

"That's so sad. I wonder if they'll ever be able to be friends again," said Storm as they walked into the dining room. "I hope so. After all, Raphaela helped me bond with Misty!"

"It looks like they might have started," said Wanda.

She was right; Professor Nimbus and Raphaela were sharing a pot of tea. They had a lot of catching up to do.

The friends sat down at their table, which was full of the most divine-looking cakes.

"All this adventure has given me the most enormous appetite!" said Juno with a laugh as they all tucked in.

Evie's favorites were the cloudberry puffs. They were sprinkled with tiny rain crystals that exploded in her mouth!

"Well, Evie," said Skye. "I know I said that Unicorn Riding Camp would be fun, but I didn't think for a minute that it would be quite so exciting!"

"I don't think any of us will be awake for the midnight feast tonight," said Wanda. "I'm exhausted."

"Can you stay, Evie?" asked Storm.

"I'd love to," said Evie, "but we really have to get back so that I can settle all my ponies for the night."

"You must come for the next Riding Camp now that you're part of our team," said Wanda.

The friends all agreed that Evie, Diamond and, of course, Sparkles would always be welcome. Then they got up to help Evie prepare for the ride home. Professor Nimbus and Raphaela came over to say goodbye.

"Thank you for coming to our camp," said Raphaela. "You've been a great team player."

"Who knows," added Professor Nimbus, "if you keep training at Unicorn Riding Camp, you may be selected for the Olympic team one day!"

When they got to the stables, Evie could see that her unicorn was tired from the day's adventures.

"Don't worry, Diamond," said Evie. "We'll soon be home. But first we have to say goodbye to all our friends."

The unicorns whickered and touched noses, saying their unicorn goodbyes.

"We'll see you all next time!" said Evie as she mounted Diamond using the technique Raphaela had taught them. "Hope you all have fun at camp tomorrow!"

"We will!" Wanda said with a smile.

The thunderstorm was over and the sunset clouds had begun to glow with warm pinks. As soon as Diamond trotted out through the golden gate, Evie and Sparkles spotted the tunnel of trees.

When they arrived at Starlight Stables, the sun was setting behind the Golden Mountain and the clouds burned with pinks, reds, and magentas. There, waiting beside Diamond's stable door, was Diamond's kit. A riding jacket was folded neatly on top of the brushes.

"It's a unicorn rider's jacket for the Olympic team," said Evie as she tried it on.

It didn't fit her at all; it was
far too big. Evie tried to hide
her disappointment and Sparkles
comforted her with a purr.

"Of course, Sparkles," Evie said
with a smile. "This isn't for me to
wear now. It's for when I'm ready for
the team—when I'm older and I've
perfected all the skills an Olympic
rider needs."

Evie hugged her beautiful new riding
jacket.

"Thank you, cloud sprites," she said,
"and thank you, Diamond. What a very
special unicorn!"

"Meow!" said Sparkles as he chased
a tiny pink cloudlet that floated across
the yard.

Pony Facts
&
Activities

Evie

LIVES AT:
Starlight Castle

FAVORITE FOOD:
Apple-blossom ice cream

FAVORITE PASTIME:
Going on adventures
with magic ponies

FAVORITE FLOWER:
Violets

FANTASY JOB:
Training unicorns
for the Olympics

Diamond

BREED:
Connemara pony

FEATURES:
Very strong and very good jumper

HEIGHT:
Up to fourteen hands

COLOR:
Gray is the most popular color but they can be black, bay, brown, dun, roan, and chestnut.

Step-by-Step

Evie goes to riding camp to learn how to be an even better rider. Can you put these steps to riding a pony in the right order? Once you've done this, put the other pony facts in order.

A.

Getting your horse ready to ride

Check that the saddle is on securely.

Put the bridle on.

Check that your pony is calm and has no injuries.

Mount your pony.

Put the saddle on.

Put your foot in the stirrup.

Make sure your riding hat is on securely.

B.

After a ride

Take off the saddle.

Loosen the saddle slightly.

Take off the bridle.

Walk the horse around until it is cool.

Comb where the saddle was.

Put your pony back in its stable or pasture.

C.

The speeds of a horse

Gallop

Trot

Halt

Walk

Canter

ANSWERS: A) 3, 5, 2, 1, 7, 6, 4 / B) 2, 4, 3, 1, 5, 6 / C) 3, 4, 2, 5, 1

Unicorn Facts

Unicorns have appeared in many stories throughout history. The descriptions of them have varied—some are described as ponylike, white with golden horns, while others are more goatlike! The word "unicorn" means "single horn," and all unicorns in history have had this in common. Unicorns are supposed to have great powers but are very hard to catch.

Their tears and blood are supposed
to have healing powers. For this reason
there have always been people trying
to catch them. Unicorns are mentioned
in many historical texts, but a lot
of these authors could actually be
confusing them with rhinoceroses,
white deer, and narwhals.

Scrambles

Can you unscramble these pony words?
Check your answers at the bottom of the page.

1. aerm

2. olaf

3. adleds

4. irens

5. fhoo

6. stpareu

7. bletsa

8. phrsdujo

9. nypo

10. ital

Fantasy Job

Evie had such fun at Unicorn Riding Camp that
she'd love to compete in the Unicorn Olympics
one day. What would be your fantasy job?

....
....
....
....
....
....
....
....
....
....
....
....
....
....
....
....

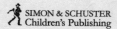

READ & LEARN
with *simon kids*

Keep your child reading, learning, and having fun with Simon Kids!

A one-stop shop where you can **find downloadable resources, watch interactive author videos, browse books by reading level, and more!**

Visit us at SimonandSchusterPublishing.com/ReadandLearn/

And follow us @SimonKids

SIMON & SCHUSTER
Children's Publishing